Tamil History:
The Spread of the Publishing Industry and Technology 1578 to 1873

Tamil History:
The Spread of the Publishing Industry and Technology 1578 to 1873

S. Jeyaseela Stephen

KALPAZ

First Published, 2020

Published by

Kalpaz Publications
C-30, Satyawati Nagar,
Delhi – 110052
Ph.: 011-47034999, 9811692060
www.kalpazpublications.com
E-mail: kalpaz@hotmail.com

Printed at: G. Print Process, Delhi

Cataloging in Publication Data—DK
Courtesy: D.K. Agencies (P) Ltd. <docinfo@dkagencies.com>

Stephen, S. Jeyaseela, author.
Tamil history: The spread of the publishing industry and technology 1578 to 1873 / by S. Jeyaseela Stephen.
pages cm
Includes bibliographical references.
ISBN 9789353240875

1. Printing—India—Tamil Nadu—History. 2. Publishers and publishing—India—Tamil Nadu—History. 3. Tamil imprints—History. I. Title.

LCC Z186.I4S74 2019 | DDC 686.2095482 23

Contents

Preface

Indian development planning methodology endeavoured for various approaches and instruments for progression and redistributive justice. Despite of heavy budget programs, there is a meagre improvement in status of marginalized. It is vital to analyse the applicability of development models in varied regions of India. India represents regional diversity, so region's need based plans and models are required for its development. Confluence of State, Market and Civil Society is considered the best model for development. After the devastation of top-down approach, bottom up approach sets dynamicity in social change. In some regions these bottom line marginalized groups delineate their empowerment process in an exclusive manner. The uniqueness lies in the fact that these models embroil the marginalized groups as negotiators of their own development. This book is focusing on one such type of tripartite model of development. This model is adopted by state of Himachal Pradesh. One of the partners of development model is group of marginalized hilly women of district Kangra. And the other two are the State of Himachal Pradesh and its vivacious civil society. This book discusses the execution of multipartite model of development in the state of Himachal Pradesh. An attempt is made to interpret the influence of this model as a result of experience in observation. Simultaneously, this exclusive trio model adds to the prospects of descriptive research on women empowerment, voluntary action and social change.

This book also predominantly focuses on the interventions of civil society organisations i.e. NGOs in bringing up change in the lives of marginalised hilly women. For concentrated and detailed study, district Kangra of Himachal Pradesh has been selected. The study, thus, looks at the experiences of participation and perceptions of two hundred and fifty women about the interventions of their respective NGOs. This book also discloses the NGOs ' methodologies to empower women. The study was conducted in different sub-divisions of district Kangra (Kangra, Palampur, Dharamshala, Nurpur, Dehra Gopipur, Baijnath. Jwali and Jaisinghpur) in Northern India. The study is based on descriptive research design. Both qualitative and quantitative methods were used for the study. The methods employed for the study comprise of case studies, focused group discussions, individual interviews, and observation of different activities of NGOs and women's participatory levels. One fourth of women were Tibetan Buddhists. Tibetan women confront problem of cultural adjustments. They are not proficient in regional or official language such as English. Some Tibetan women living in exile in Mc. Leodganj region of district Kangra resort to prostitution. Their delineation of empowerment completely differs from regional women. The model of composite relationship of state. vivacious civil society and its active women agency may set guidelines for neighbouring states like Punjab, Haryana in India too, where the situation of women is also not so upright. It cannot be claimed that women's development is at peak in one of the regions in Northern India But the subsistence struggle to bring change both by hilly women and NGOs is phenomenal.

Acknowledgements

Printing industry and technology in Tamil fascinated me to launch a project separately while working on the history of sciences in the age of European encounter. I collected a vast amount of primary data from libraries and archives and it took years to examine and analyze. The chapters have been written and rewritten for long because of the pouring in of a lot of new data having added from time to time. The study offers an exploration into printing books, pamphlets, journals, periodicals, calendars, newspapers and advertisements in Tamil, which hold a hitherto untapped wealth of valuable information helping us to understand better the ins and outs of the early modern publishing and finally trade. I owe a substantial debt to the Comissão Nacional Para as Comemoraçoes dos Descobrimentos Portugueses, Government of Portugal, and the Société des missions étrangères de Paris, for funding and extending invaluable help to me in assisting to conduct research. Therefore, I express my profound gratitude.

I extend sincere and warm thanks to the authorities of the Biblioteca Nacional de Lisboã, Portugal; Archivum Romanum Societatis Iesu, Roma, Biblioteca Apostolica Vaticana, Città del Vaticano, Archiv der Franckeschen Stiftungen and Bibliothek der Franckesche Stiftungen, Halle, Bibliothek der Evangelisch-Lutherisches Missionsanstalt, Leipzig, Bayerische Staatsbibliothek, Munich, Universitats bibliotheek, Gottingen; Bibliothèque Nationale de France, Centre des Archives d'Outre–Mer, Aix–en–Provence, Bibliothèque Asiatique des missions étrangères de Paris, Archives de la Société des missions étrangères de Paris, Archives Françaises de la Compagnie de Jésus, Vanves; Koninklijke Bbiliotheek, Den Haag, Universiteits Bibliotheek, Leiden, Universiteits Bibliotheek, Amsterdam, Universiteits Bibliotheek, Utrecht, Hendrik Kramer Instituut, Oegstgeest; Det Kongelige Bibliotek, Kobenhavn; British Library, London, School of Oriental and African Studies Library, British and Foreign Bible Society's Library, Cambridge; New York Public Library, American Bible Society Library; Colombo Museum, National Library of Sri Lanka; Tamilnadu State Archives, Chennai, State Central Library, Goa, Madurai Province Jesuit Archives, Shenbaganur, Archives of the Gurukul Lutheran Theological College and Research Institute, Chennai, Sarawathi Mahal Library,

Thanjavur, Rojah Muthaiah Library, Chennai and Maraimalaiadigal Library for providing facilities and help. Last but no means least, I thank Shri. Amit Garg, Gyan Books for printing. It is hoped that the study will inspire new generation of book historians.

LISBON

Illustrations

Abbreviations

AAPC	:	Archives of the Arch-diocese of Pondicherry and Cuddalore.
ABSL	:	American Bible Society Library, New York.
AFCJ	:	Archives Françaises de la Compagnie de Jésus, Vanves
AFSt	:	Archiv der Franckeschen Stiftungen, Halle
AGLTC	:	Archives of the Gurukul Lutheran Theological College and Research Institute, Chennai
AMEP	:	Archives de la Société des missions étrangères de Paris
ARSI	:	Archivum Romanum Societatis Iesu, Roma
BAMEP	:	Bibliothèque Asiatique des missions étrangères de Paris
BAV	:	Biblioteca Apostolica Vaticana, Città del Vaticano
BELM	:	Bibliothek der Evangelisch-Lutherisches Missionsan-stalt, Leipzig
BFBSL	:	British and Foreign Bible Society's Library, Cambridge
BFSt	:	Bibliothek der Franckesche Stiftungen, Halle
BL	:	British Library, London
BNF	:	Bibliothèque Nationale de France
BNL	:	Biblioteca Nacional de Lisboã
CAOM	:	Centre des Archives d'Outre–Mer, Aix–en–Provence
DI	:	Documenta Indica
HB	:	Hallesche Berichte
HKI	:	Hendrik Kramer Instituut, Oegstgeest
KB	:	Det Kongelige Bibliotek, Kobenhavn
KBDH	:	Koninklijke Bbiliotheek, Den Haag
MPC	:	Madras Public Consultations
MPJA	:	Madurai Province Jesuit Archives, Shenbaganur
NHB	:	Neue Hallesche Berichte, Neuere Geschichte der Evangelischen
NYPL	:	New York Public Library

OIOC	:	Oriental and India Office Collection
SCL	:	State Central Library, Goa
SOASL	:	School of Oriental and African Studies Library, London
TDR	:	Tanjore District Records
TNSA	:	Tamilnadu State Archives, Chennai
UBA	:	Universiteits Bibliotheek, Amsterdam
UBL	:	Universiteits Bibliotheek, Leiden
UBU	:	Universiteits Bibliotheek, Utrecht

1

Introduction

The advent of the printing press in the early modern age led to innumerable changes in Tamil society and history. The spread of Christianity is very much closely associated with print in Tamil and the missionaries published numerous books and pamphlets. The printing industry and technology greatly got extended and added to publishing calendars, journals, newspapers, periodicals and advertisements in Tamil under the patronage of the East India Companies and European missionaries. The varieties of printing industrial functions and publications fascinated and caught the attention of some scholars. As a result we find some interesting works on the subject. Ma. Su. Sambandham wrote extensively on the general history printing and publishing in Tamil and focused largely on the British colonial age. His works did not expose the nature, course and the multiple directions of Tamil printing that developed.[1]

Stuart H. Blackburn identified two distinct Tamil formulations of folklore and the nation and he contributed to the beginnings of the printing press in Tamil country and gave a history of Tamil books. However, the technological advances made in printing and the socio-cultural changes occurred had not been well documented. He opined that printing should be examined alongside a set of literary practices that were largely set in train by the encounter with Europeans. He described the polemical writings and print rivalry developed between the Lutherans and Jesuits in addition to the publishing carried out at the College of Fort St George press in Madras, the local responses of the pundits who set up their own printing presses that campaigned against missionary activity by producing books of folklore.[2] In contrast, the publications of classical Tamil literature printed in the colonial Tamil region were examined by Sascha Ebeling and V. Rajesh.[3] A.R. Venkatachalapathy also wrote in the same direction but referred to the reading practices and the readers.[4] The study of P. Uma Maheswari highlights the role of printing in the city of Madras under the English. She outlines the progress of transport and communication like the postal department, telephones, tram and the artefacts of print culture besides the rise of various libraries of the printed specimens between 1820 and 1900.[5] Based on the survey of historiography, it must be stated at the outset, that the existing writings largely have highlighted and contributed to the understanding of the relationship between print, publishing and the making of modern Tamil literary history canon between 1800 and 1947. The arrival of the press and printing in Tamil since 1578 had been largely ignored till 1800 in addition to the activities of the French in printing Tamil books in Pondicherry.

A.R. Venkatachalapthy in his introduction covered the long period from 1556 to 1800 by limiting to three pages. He committed many factual errors. He mentioned the year 1577 as the publication of the first Tamil book *Thambiraan Vanakkam*. In fact it was printed on 6 November 1578 as found recorded in the book. All the more, he wrongly assigned to printing the *Doctrina Christam* (in Portuguese) in Goa in 1577 while it actually got printed twenty years before (i.e., in 1557). Further, he added a clumsy mistake and said that a new edition of *Thambiraan Vanakkam* was published in 1578 in Quilon. The book was not an edition as in Portuguese Language but it was the translation into Tamil which appeared. Anrique Anriquez the co-author (with Fr. Manuel de Sao Pedro) in his letter dated 20 February 1578 expressed that he had translated the *Doctrina Christam* into Tamil. Venkatchalapathy had further committed a blunder by admitting Fr. Xavier Thaninayagam (1913-1980) into the Religious order of the Society of Jesus. Thaninayagam was not a Jesuit but a diocesan priest and he was with the diocese of Trivandrum since 1934 and served later in the diocese of Tuticorin since 1940.

The fashioning of Tamil printing that developed, the new perceptions that came to emerge after the arrival of the printing press need to be investigated in depth. Tamil palm-leaf manuscripts saw the new light of printing along with missionary Tamil compositions. A great turn appeared when the natives themselves established their printing presses. Tamil society witnessed knowledge transformation with the diffusion of information through rapid development of the printed word. The printing industry received a boost and the technology contributed its might towards the cause of education of Tamils in an unprecedented manner. Textbooks in Tamil language got prepared and printed for the first time and all these added to the key elements of change in the social order.

It is significant to learn how the Tamil literary tradition broke away from the past and came drastically to move from manuscript to print and how the conquest of the British Raj in Tamil country and the French rule in

Pondicherry came to establish command over the intellectual space. There is a need to learn how printing in Tamil had been embedded in the wider global discourses across the world in the overseas particularly in Sri Lanka and Europe through the impact of the Europeans in the age of commerce, missionary expansion and empire.

The printing technology in Tamil, its social environment, news about authors, capital raised and used for printing, the contents of the printed works and how it reached the audience have been therefore planned to be adequately covered in this book. While documenting the rise of Tamil printing it explores how reaction to this nouvelle printing enterprise had been at the royal courts of the king of Thanjavur and Ramanathapuram.

The book provides a comprehensive account of the various faces of printing. It explores the role of the publisher observed at five different stages such as production, assessment, reproduction, distribution, and consumption. It examines whether the development of print in Tamil was an innovation or a revolution. It evaluates how the missionary publishers like the Protestants produced a large turnover of books including the Bible in Tamil printed time and again. The volume addresses the proliferation of native printing press which exposed Tamil literatures to get into the print media. It explains how the religious literature and the rivalry between religious groups led to polemical writings and printing pamphlets. It outlines the importance of the native authors and publishers who entered into the new profession of printing. It traces how print had increased literacy and reading habits of the Tamils in the region. The study holistically looks at the various stages of the production of the books, the design, the format, the founts used including the editing, printing, binding and marketing.

Chapter Outline

Chapter one introduces the subject proper. The second chapter deals with the art of printing Tamil books in the letter press of the Jesuits in South India between 1578 and 1679. It reports the Tamil early printed text in Portugal on 2 February 1554 and next examines the preparation of Tamil fonts in Goa and Quilon for printing. The establishment of the first Tamil printing Press began in Quilon and the coming of the first Tamil book called *Thambiran Vanakkam* from the Jesuit printing press happened on 20 October 1578. The Jesuit printing press functioned in Cochin enabled publication of *Krisiththiyani Vanakkam* on 14 November 1579 and *Confessionairo* on 28 May 1580. Followed by this, the lives of saints in Tamil got printed in Goa in 1586. The chapter examines the style and structure of Tamil language in these printed books of the sixteenth century. After a long gap the Jesuit printing press at Ambalakaadu had printed *Gnaanopadesam* (Catechism)

Part I and II in 1677 and Part III and IV in 1678. The Tamil-Portuguese dictionary of Antão Proença got printed at Ambalakaadu in 1679. The chapter critically examines the active role of the various Jesuits missionaries in printing Tamil books.

Chapter three highlights the role of the letter press that functioned in Tranquebar and the landmarks in printing Tamil books, pamphlets and calendars by the Danish-Halle mission between 1712 and 1799. It traces the preparation of Tamil fonts in Leipzig and Tranquebar for printing. The first printed Tamil book in Tranquebar happened on 17 October 1712. The first Tamil pamphlet was printed in Tranquebar on 25 October 1713. The establishment of a paper mill at Poraiyar and the activities between 1716 and 1722 had been outlined. Printing Tamil books and pamphlets on Protestantism in Tranquebar had developed. Reprinting Tamil books and pamphlets continued. Tamil books printed had been found in the catalogues issued from the printing press at Tranquebar in 1714 and 1733. Books on Christianity were largely printed in Tamil at the printing press in Tranquebar during 1733 and 1799. Printing the Tamil Bible was assigned priority and we find the Old Testament and the New Testament from the press in Tranquebar between 1714 and 1796. Hymn books got printed in Tamil at Tranquebar during 1713 and 1756. Printing books on Tamil grammar and Portuguese-Tamil dictionary happened between 1731 and 1739. Text books in Tamil composed by the Protestant missionaries were printed. Translated books in Tamil from German and Portuguese at Tranquebar were printed. Tamil calendars were also printed at the press in Tranquebar. Thus the functioning of the printing press and its problems had been analyzed.

Chapter four traces the functioning of the letter press in Madras, Palayamkottai and Nagercoil and the printing of books, pamphlets, journals, newspapers and advertisements in Tamil under the English Company and the Protestant missionaries between 1766 and 1857. Early efforts were made for the preparation of Tamil fonts in Madras between 1766 and 1769 and thereafter printing books in Tamil on Protestant Christianity developed at the press in Vepery near Madras from 1766 to 1806. Printing grammar, English-Tamil dictionaries, Tamil-English dictionaries and Tamil story books happened between 1766 and 1812. Advertisements came to be printed in Tamil during 1802 and 1813. Printing Tamil pamphlets and books had developed by the Religious Tract Society in Madras during 1812 and 1845. Printing Books in Tamil was developed by the Madras Book Society between 1824 and 1836. Journals, Newspapers and Tender Notices were printed in Tamil from Madras during 1831 and 1852. The Fort St. George College Press was set up in Madras and Tamil books got printed during 1813 and 1833. Printing Tamil books at the Government press developed in Madras between 1816 and 1845. The American mission press was established in Madras and books were printed in Tamil during 1820 and 1857. Improved Tamil typography developed in Madras during 1838 and 1857 and helped in printing. Funds were raised by the English for Tamil translation and so printing had spread at Neyoor, Nagercoil and Palayamkottai during 1823 and 1856. Geography books in Tamil were printed in Palayamkottai, Madras and Nagercoil and so an analysis of the contents had been undertaken. Textbooks were printed on astronomy, oceanography, mathematics and algebra in Tamil during 1844 and 1857. Books on medicine and chemistry in Tamil got printed from Madras, Nagercoil and Palayamkottai during 1850 and 1857. Almanacs prepared by Tamils were printed in Madras during 1848 and 1852. The study examines the role of the copyright act of 1847 introduced in Madras and the impact of European printing at the royal court of the Raja of Ramanathapuram and the Raja of Thanjavur.

Chapter five dwells on the Tamil authors, editors and print capitalists in Madras and printing the books, journals and newspapers between 1812 and 1857. It traces the migration of Tamil scholars to Chennaipattinam @ Madras and the rise of polemical literature and printing in Tamil. Gnaanapragasam Pillai of Thanjavur owned the first printing press in Madras and he printed books in Tamil and brought out the newspaper in Tamil in 1812. The study traces founding of the Tamil literary institutions by the natives in Madras and Madurai. Many Tamil authors, editors, printers and publishers rose in Madras and we find also the emergence of print capitalists. Printing books of Islamic Tamil literature happened besides books of Hindu theology. Tamil grammar and dictionaries printed in Madras were noticed by Karl Graul the German missionary who visited Madras in 1853. Many books of drama, ethics and stories in Tamil, books on science, mathematics and history in Tamil were purchased by him and he took them to Leipzig in Germany.

Chapter six highlights the significance of the letter press in Pondicherry and the role of the Catholic missionaries in the diffusion of the printed word in Tamil during 1778 and 1873. In the beginning printing books and tracts in French and English only took place in Pondicherry between 1778 and 1793. Thereafter printing Government orders and journals took place in French and Tamil in Pondicherry during 1817 and 1850. A letter press was set up by the Foreign Mission Society of Paris in Pondicherry and printing Catholic Christian literature in Tamil developed from 1841 and 1873 when Louis Savinien Dupuis became the first manager of the Catholic press. We find request for supply of paper, ink for printing and leather for binding the book for use in Pondicherry from France. In the meanwhile development of Tamil typography took place in Pondicherry. *Saathaaranam*, the short catechism was printed in 1841. *Gnaanamirdham* the prayer book was printed in 1841 and it got reprinted again in 1858. *Gnaanamirdha Thadaagam*, the large prayer book was printed in 1842, also got reprinted in 1847 and 1858. Printing *Sarithirathuukuaduththa Gnaanopadesa Surukkam* and *Sarithirathuukuaduththa Gnaanopadesathin Vinaa Vidai* the two books were printed in 1858. *Gnaanopadesa Surukkam, Padangalaal Vizhlagappapatta Gnaanopadesam* and *Sugirtha Mandirangalum Gnaanopadesa Kurippidamum*, the three catechism books were printed in 1861, 1863 and 1865. *Gnaanopadesa Surukkam* the catechism of Fr. Miguel in Vepery got printed in 1872. Further the child's prayer books of *Vaalar Pokkisham* and *Vaalar Thunai* were printed in 1844 and 1861. We find printing the litany of saints in various books in 1842, 1844, 1847, 1853, 1858, 1859 and *Praarthani Maalai* a litany book was published in 1867. Interestingly printing the books of monthly devotion had developed and we notice *Devamaathavin Vankka Maatham* (Devotion to Mother of God) in 1850, *Archsishta Susaiyappar Vanakka Maatham* (Devotion to St. Joseph) in 1867 and *Uththarikkira Aathumaakalin Vanakka Maatham* (Devotion to All Souls) in 1870. *Siluvai Paathai*, the stations of the cross got printed in 1842 and also it was reprinted in 1856. *Thirunaatkalin Vizhlakka Surukkam* the treatise on Christian feasts authored by Joseph Auguste Chevalier was printed in 1859. The book of liturgy called *Pusai Udhavi Mandiram* authored by Louis Marie Mousset got printed in 1859. The book called *Karunaakara Kadal* was printed in 1868. Printing *Beschi's Gnaana Unarthuthal* happened in 1842 and it was reprinted in 1846. Charles Michele Bertoldi's *Gnaana Muyarchi* was printed in 1843. *Gnaana Oduukangalukku Niyamikkapatta Archishta Ignaciyar Dhyaanagal* (St. Ignatius's Spiritual Exercises) authored by Charles Michele Bertoldi was printed in 1848. St. Alphonse Maria de Ligouri's book was translated into Tamil titled *Aathuma Nesam* (On the Passion of Our Lord) got printed in 1860. Again Thomas Kempi's Imitation of Christ translated was printed in 1863. *Archsishta Ignaciyar Gnaana Dhyaanagal* (St. Ignatius's Method of Meditation) authored by James Thomas Rossi was printed in 1864. Pierre Mauduit's *Divya Maathrigai* (Divine Model) got printed in 1866. Life of the Blessed John de Britto was printed in 1853 and it got reprinted in 1857 and 1858. *Devasagayam Pillai Sarithiram* (Life of Devasagayam Pillai) authore by Louis Saint-Cyr was printed in 1858. *Archsishta Gnaanapragaasiyaar Sarzithiramum Archsishta Sthanislausudaya Sarithira Pirasangangalum-maavana* authored by Louis Saint-Cyr got printed in 1862. Lives of St. Antony, St. Martin, St. Sebastian and St. Lawrence got printed. The Manual of the Society of the Immaculate and Sacred Heart of the Holy Mother of God (*Maasillammal Urpavitha Archsishta Devamaathavin Thiru Irudhaya Sabhai Anusaaram*) was printed in 1847 and got reprinted in 1856.

The history and rules of the society for good death (*Nanmarana Aaytha Sabhai*) was printed in 1860. Beschi's the catechist's guide (*Vethiyar Ozhukkam*) and Pierre Mauduit's manual for catechists (*Gnaana Kannaadi*) were printed in 1858. *Vetha Vizhlakkam* (Catholic Religion Explained) of Beschi was printed in 1842, and got reprinted in 1855 and 1868. *Lutherinithiyalbu* (The Character of the Lutherans) of Beschi was printed in 1842 and got reprinted in 1847 and 1869. *Pethaga Maruththal* (Denial of Alleged Aberrations) was printed in 1842 and got reprinted in 1855 and 1868. *Dushana Maruthalaagiya Tharkka Kummi* of Anthoni Nathar was printed in 1865. The books of Roberto Nobili on Religion such as *Sathiya Vetha Paritchai* was printed in 1842, reprinted in 1846 and *Deyva Paritchai* printed in 1843 got reprinted in 1863. *Sathiya Vetha Bhodhaga Surukkam* earlier printed in Colombo was reprinted in Pondicherry in 1846. *Poorviga Marai Vizhlakkam* (An Explanation of the Ancient religion) was printed in 1856. Biblical writings like *Sathiya Vetha Sarithira Surukkam* of C. Gnaanapragaasa Nathar got printed in 1865. *Meymarai Uththiyaanam* (Guide to True Religion) of L.S. Dupuis was printed in 1873. The New Testament in Tamil was printed in 1857. We find also printing the calendar of church festivals in 1844 and 1849. L.S. Dupuis authored many books in Tamil Prose and we find printing of *Vethapurattalai Maruththalaagiya Sathiya Thirusabaiyin Surkkamaana Vizhlakkam* in 1840, *Vethapurattalai Neekum Sanjiviyaagiya Meyyaana Thirusabaiyin Vizhlakkam* in 1841, *Nanraai Ninai: Maatha Anudhina Dhyaanam* in 1844, *Ainthukaaya Varampetra Archsishta Franciskuvin Sarithira Surukkam* in 1859, *Archsishtavargalin Sarithiram* in four volumes in 1866-7, *Ainthu Thirukaaya Varam Petra Archsishta Franciskuvin Thavathukkuriya Moonram Sabhai Ozhukkam* in 1859, *Illara Uththiyanam* in 1867 and *Thuravara Uththiyanam* volume one in 1869 and volume two in 1872.

Chapter seven explores printing Tamil grammar, dictionary, poetry and textbooks in the mission press, at the Government press and in the college printing press in Pondicherry between 1838 and 1873. Textbooks for learning Tamil language like *Aathi Chuvadi*, *Paramaartha Guru Kathai Muthaliyavai* were printed in 1844. Again textbook for learning European languages like *Paramaartha Guru Kathai Lathinilum Thamzhilillum* got printed in 1863 besides *Sambaashanai Anusaaram* (Manuel de la Conversation) in 1865. Printing grammar books for learning Tamil, French and Latin happened between 1845 and 1863. Printing dictionaries for easy learning of Tamil, French and Latin happened between 1846 and 1870. Production of C.J. Beschi's works through reproduction by Dupuis in the epic space took place by printing *Thembaavani* in 1851, 1852 and 1853. Printing books of Tamil poetry like *Thembaa Maalai* (1851), *Thiruppaavani* (1856), *Tiruvalluvar Seytha Kurat Sanghiragam* (1860) and *Vedhapuri Andhaathi* (1863) also happened. Books on mathematics in Tamil like *Vaalar Kanidham* (1853) *Siruvar Yen Chuvadi* (1863) and *Vaalar Kanidha Noolaathaaram* (1870) were printed. Books on geography and Tamil Language like *Bhumi Saasthira Padangal* (1861), *Bhumi Saasthira Surukkam* (1862), *Anda Vizhlakka Sathirathin Sangsebangkoodiya Bhumi Sathira Noolaatharam* (1864), *Siruvar Chuvadi* (1863) and *Siruvar Kalvi Puthaiyal* (1864) were printed. The study also explores the marketing strategy and sale of printed books in the overseas and local. The college printing press in Pondicherry printed stories and morals like *Kathaa Manjari*, *Neethisaara Vaakiyam Theriyalaanavaiyum* in 1864 and *Panchathanthira Kathai* in 1865. The Tamil poems of Savarrayalu Nayagar (1829-1911) in Pondicherry had been compiled by Solai Appaa Samy Mudaliar and the book was printed by A. Saligny, the manager of the Government press in Pondicherry in 1869. The study examines the regulations issued for printing by the French government in Pondicherry and the functioning of the press between 1852 and 1872.

Chapter eight dwells on the litho press in Pondicherry and Madras. It examines the expanding horizon of printing books in Tamil during 1859 and 1869. Lithography was introduced in Pondicherry in 1859 and we find *Gnaana Aarudhal* (Spiritual Consolation) the first book lithographed in 1859. Thereafter many books of Catholic Tamil literature were printed and we find *Archshista Ignaciyar Dhyaanagal* (St. Ignatius's Meditations), *Vellikilamai Puthumai* (Friday Miracles), *Sanikilamai Puthumai* (Saturday Miracles), *Karumpaambin Vishakadikku Marunthu* (Medicine for the bite of black Cobra) authored by Benoit Brisard, *Aayatham* (Preparation to Sacraments) and nine books on devotion to Mary the Mother of God got printed at litho press in 1860. Later *Thingalkilamai Puthumai* (Monday Miracles) *Sevvaykilami Puthumai* (Tuesday Miracles) and *Puthankilamai Pirasangam* (Wednesday Sermons) were printed in 1861. *Viyaalakilamai Puthumai* (Thursday Miracles), *Gnaayittrukilamai Puthumai* (Sunday Miracles) and *Paavasangirthana Pirasangam* (Sermons on Confession) were printed in 1865. *Karumpaambin Vishakadikku Thailam* authored by Benoit Brisard (An oil medicine for black snake's poisonous biting) was printed in 1868. *Kaanaa Vishakkaddikku Marundhu* authored by Benoit Brisard (Medicine for the poisonous bite unnoticed) was printed in 1869. Lithographed Tamil book had also appeared in Madras in 1865.

Chapter nine explores printing in Tamil that developed in the overseas particularly from Halle, Hamburg, Dresden, Erlangen, London, Colombo and Jaffna between 1671 and 1873. *Gnaana Mandira Selva Pungaavanam* was printed in Halle in 1749-50. The catechism book in Tamil was printed in Halle in 1750. *Gnaana Kannaadi* was printed in Halle in 1751. *Kalvi Ozhukkam* was printed in Halle in 1791. Printing Tamil books had also spread to Hamburg, Dresden and Erlangen during 1855, 1856 and 1865. Printing Tamil books developed in London between 1790 and 1873. The study also deals with the advent of the printing press in Colombo and the preparation of the Tamil fonts during 1732 and 1739. Thereafter Christian literature books in Tamil were printed by the Dutch at the printing press in Colombo between 1739 and 1789. Printing the Bible in Tamil by the Dutch had gained priority at the printing press in Colombo and Jaffna during 1741 and 1790. The study explores printing Tamil periodicals in Sri Lanka under the British during 1802 and 1870. The American mission press was established at Manippay and it printed calendars, books, dictionary and grammar in Tamil between 1835 and 1851. Books and booklets on Protestant Christian literature in Tamil developed between 1814 and 1861. The Catholic printing press functioned in Colombo and Tamil books were published at the *Vyagula Mari Naayagiyin Dharuma Sambradhaaya Achchukudam* during 1846 and 1849. Some Tamils began to set up their printing press in Sri Lanka and we find pamphlets and books printed during 1849 and 1851. Many polemical writings were also published in Tamil from Sri Lanka during 1836 and 1857.

Chapter ten deals with conclusion and it brings out the findings of research. The bibliography contains the books printed and the details of the various repositories and it serves as a useful tool to the readers. The book thus highlights the role of printing and technology in Tamil and the impact on language and society ushering into the modern world.

Notes

1. Ma. Su. Sambandham, *Achchu Kalai*, Madras. 1959; Ma. Su. Sambandham, *Achchum Pathippum*, Madras, 1980; Ma. Su. Sambandham, *Ezhuththum Achchum*, Madras, 1981; Ma. Su. Sambandham, *Tamil Ithaliyal Varalaru*, Madras, 1987; Ma. Su. Sambandham, *Tamil Ithaliyal Chuvadugal*, Madras. I990.
2. Stuart H. Blackburn, *Print, Folklore and Nationalism in Colonial South India*, New Delhi, 2003.
3. Sascha Ebeling: *Colonizing the Realm of Words: The Transformation of Tamil Literature in Nineteenth Century South India*, Albany, 2010; V. Rajesh, *Manuscripts, Memory and History: Classical Tamil Literature in Colonial India*, Delhi, 2014; V. Rajesh, 'Patrons and Networks of Patronage in the Publication of Tamil Classics, c 1800-1920', *Social Scientist*, Vol. 39, No. 3/4 (March-April 2011), pp. 64-91.
4. A. R. Venkatachalapathy, *The Province of the Book: Scholars, Scribes and Scribblers in Colonial Tamilnadu*, Permanent Black, New Delhi, 2012, p. 5.
5. P. Uma Maheswari, *Advent of Print Culture in Colonial Tamil Region: Technological, Cultural and Social Changes from 1712 to 1947*, Ph.D. Dissertation, Pondicherry University, 2013, pp. 153-253, 371-401 .

2

The Art of Printing Tamil Books in the Letter Press of the Jesuits in South India, 1578-1679

The oldest printed work is a wood-block of the Buddhist scripture by a Chinese during the Wu Zetian period (AD 684-705) now preserved in the Calligraphy Museum in Tokyo. The oldest surviving book on paper is the Phi Yu Ching (AD 250) on 'liu-ho' paper made in northern Chiang Su and it is made from six different materials. The use of paper was known in India as early as in AD 671 noticed by It-sing the Chinese traveller. The earliest evidence of paper manuscript in India is dated as belonging to 1105 AD and it is titled Pancaraksa and it is at the Ashutosh Museum in Kolkata.[1] The art of printing was transplanted from China to Europe through Marco Polo's description of it.[2] The Arabs were the agents who prepared the way by carrying the making of paper from China to Europe and the first steps towards printing had been made in Europe and the invention of the principle and honour is unquestionably due to Lawrence Coster, a native of Harlem who first found out the method of impressing characters on paper by means of carved locks of wood. Johannes Gutenberg (AD 1400-1480) of Metz and Peter Schaeffer in conjunction with John Faust invented the type mould which made printing from moveable metallic type practical for the first time.[3] Printing was first introduced in Portugal in 1495. Three years later Vasco da Gama had set sail on a voyage to India and the printed books from Europe were brought in the ships of the Portuguese to Malabar for use.[4]

Tamil Early Printed Text in Portugal, 2 February 1554

Tamil was the first language (among the Indian languages) to be learnt by Portuguese and it was the first language of India in which a book had been printed in 1554 in Lisbon, Portugal.[5] Tamil was the first non-European language to appear in print. The first little book in Tamil containing 38 pages was published in Lisbon on 2 February 1554. An original copy of this tract (discovered by Fr Xavier Thaninayagam in 1954) is preserved at the Belem Museum in Lisbon.[6] How this printed book found its way to the museum is itself an interesting story. This museum was originally part of the Library of the Carthusian monastery. This religious house was founded by Teotonio de Bragança in 1598, who was a distinguished Jesuit scholar born in Coimbra in 1536, educated in Rome and Paris. He later became the Archbishop of Evora. He possessed this book and gifted it to the monastery before his death in 1602. It was preserved there until it was disbanded in 1902. This is evident from a handwritten note on the book. In 1909 this book seems to have passed into the hands of an individual (name unknown) who eventually brought it to Belem Museum.

The text of the book is in Latin script, it has the distinction of being the first printed Tamil book, even though the script was not Tamil. The text is in a Tamil word-by-word transliteration, printed in red colour. Below that was given the Portuguese version in small letters printed in black colour. The title of the book runs as follows: *Cartilha que conte brevemete hoq todo christão deve aprender pera sua saluacam, a qual el rey dom Joham terceiro deste nome nosso senhor mandou imprimir e lingoa Tamul e Portugues co ha declaracam do Tamul por Cima de Vermelho* (Primer which contains in brief all that a Christian should know for his salvation and which Our Lord, the King Dom John III, had ordered to be printed in the Tamil language and in Portuguese with the Tamil meaning printed above in red).

The book was printed through an order issued by the king of Portugal. It was intended to teach the Christian religion to Hindus as an aid to the missionaries and so it was written in Portuguese and in Tamil, the most widely spoken language in south India at that time. Each line in 'thick print' in Tamil is followed by the Portuguese translation 'in fine print'. Above the two lines there is a 'statement' in Portuguese printed in red.

This book gives the Latin alphabet, the diphthongs, the syllables. It shows the Tamil pronunciation. It taught the missionaries to speak Tamil, but also served to learn Portuguese. The book was drafted by three Tamils, with the help of João da Villa do Conde the Franciscan missionary of the province of piedade.[7]

This book was printed two years before the introduction of printing press in Goa (the machine arrived at Goa on 6 September 1556 in the ship and started functioning in October 1556) by the Portuguese. This Tamil book was mainly intended to be used by the Portuguese missionaries in Portugal who were preparing to come to the Tamil coast for apostolic work.

This was the first book used by the missionaries for the propagation of the Christian faith among the natives on the Tamil coast. All of this confirms the great efforts made by the Portuguese missionaries to master the Tamil language and their dedication and commitment to learn Tamil before they could leave Lisbon for India. The relationship between the Christian conversions and Tamil language development was permanently encoded in the age of Portuguese expansion during the sixteenth century. The inaugural moment of the Tamil print-culture had witnessed the first book of cartilha. As this printed work is the transliteration it is concluded that Tamil scripts for printing were not invented by 1554. Those who knew Portuguese alone could use this book.

As the three Tamils had pointed out in the prologue, the Tamil language had two limitations in the printed book. The first relates in the pronunciation (*pronunciação*). The language of the book is poor in vocabulary and it could not explain certain things by its own words and speaking styles (*estilos de falar*) especially that in which the matter contains (*que esta obra leua*) and of which nothing was earlier known in Tamil country. The sentence in the book begins sometimes where the Portuguese end theirs sentence and in some cases it begins where they end it and also sometimes in the opposite. We also search for circumlocutions that correspond to the sentence, without being in discord as can be seen in the declaration (*declaração*) placed on top in red. The second limitation is that Tamil language expressed in the book is so barbaric that certain elocutions (*dições*) cannot be pronounced by any of the Latin characters (*com nenhums carateres latinos se podem pronunciar*). In addition, Tamil is also accused of not having adequate terms of theological content and phonological substance. The passage from oral Tamil into written Portuguese was indeed resolved quite successfully, but without any reference to the Tamil writing system and script. The sounds that the three Tamils axed upon for their Portuguese audience were, however, not simply auricular. They were completely difficult and unpronounceable sounds such as (ta, na) and semivowels (la, l) were therefore converted and normalized for regular Indo-European sounds.

The Tamil scripts are printed in larger letters, and the Tamil spreads along the lines without leaving any empty spaces, as the two Portuguese lines do. Red and black horizontal lines are, therefore, introduced to all in the void between Portuguese words. The visual effect is that the Tamil transcription looks as if imprisoned by Portuguese lines, as if making sure that no Hindu substances transgress into the pages of this Christian book. On the other hand, in spite of the empty spaces between Portuguese words, the Portuguese sentence appears to contain an excess of spoken sounds compared to the Tamil, or rather the Tamil sentence seems to be talking more and saying less.

The Preparation of Tamil Fonts in Goa and Quilon for Printing

In a letter dated 20 November 1545 addressed to his Superiors in Rome, Joannes de Beira, a Jesuit who lived in Casa de Santa Fe in Goa suggested that the Christian doctrines could be published in all the languages of the East.[8] Francis Xavier, the Jesuit on the pearl fishery coast also expressed the same view in 1549 confirming that the work of Christian literature should be printed.[9] However it took more than ten years for a printing press to be sent in a ship that left Lisbon on 29 March 1556 to reach Goa on 6 September 1556.[10] The first proposed printed work was the Catechism of Francis Xavier which summarized the doctrines of Christianity to be taught by the missionaries. A letter written by Fr Luís Frois on 30 November 1556 tells that the *Doctrina Christa Ordenada a Maneira de Dialogo Para Ensinar os Meninos* composed by Francis Xavier in Tamil for the benefit of the children had been also included in the future programme of printing.[11] Tamil fonts-making started in 1558 to print a book. João Gonçalves (Bastamante) a Jesuit scholastic in Goa undertook the work. This happened only after six years of Francis Xavier's death (2 December 1552).[12]

Anrique Anriquez became the Jesuit superior of the missions on the Tamil coast in 1549 and he headed it for more than a quarter century. He felt the need to print the liturgical books in Tamil. When he accompanied Alessandro Valignano the Jesuit visitor to Goa to attend the meeting of the superiors in December 1575 they discussed together about it. In the chapter meeting held there, this agenda was placed and a decision was taken to print books on catechism, confession, Christian doctrine and the lives of saints in Tamil. At the same time Anriquez was relieved of his administrative responsibility and asked to undertake the translation and composition of these books from Portuguese and Latin into Tamil. He also humbly accepted the assignment and applied his mind, time and talent to write these books. Further the Jesuit Visitor Valignano had also directed João Gonçalves to make Tamil types at the earliest for the use of printing books. In a letter dated 24 December 1576 we find that Pero Luíz, a brahmin convert who was admitted as a member of the Society of Jesus on the Tamil coast was chiefly sent to Goa to acquaint João Gonçalves more with the knowledge of typesetting the Tamil letters.[13] As a result we find making Tamil types for printing had been made ready in 1577.[14]

It is important and necessary to know how the method of printing began in Tamil while writings were made in palm-leaf first. It had been mentioned as early as 1548, Anriquez had transliterated a palm-leaf manuscript from Tamil to Latin script and he wrote above each word the declaration (*la declaración*) so that when it is read in the church, the missionary present, could have a translation and could hear what was read out.[15] Eventually the Jesuit missionaries on the pearl fishery coast having used palm-leaf in Tamil in which Christian doctrine had been written, shifted to make writings in paper and later moved over to printing Tamil books for use in the church.

The Establishment of the First Tamil Printing Press in Quilon and the Coming of the First Tamil Book: Thambiran Vanakkam from the Jesuit Printing Press, 20 October 1578

The credit for preparing the first Tamil metal types goes to João Gonçalves who was then in Goa. Fr Francisco de Sousa wrote: João Gonçalves was the first who made in India the types of Malabar (Tamil) letters with which the first book was printed.[16] Thambiran Vanakkam (Worship of the Lord) was the book titled in Portuguese *Doctrina Christam em lingua Malauar Tamul* got printed at the *Collegio do Saluador* of the Jesuits in Quilon (Kollam) on 20 October 1578 (3 Aypasi).[17] Further Francisco de Sousa wrote that this *Doctrina Christam* was the first printed book which India saw being born in its own land.[18] This small text can thus claim to be the first book printed in an Indian language. It contains seventeen pages of 10 x 14 cm size. We have a reference at the end of the book which says that the Tamil letters used in printing was made as per the model that was in use. Fr Fonseca in Rome who received this book which was sent from India has affixed his signature on it sometime in November 1579. In the last page i.e., sixteen we find the Tamil letters made in Goa in 1577 (*esta letra se fez e Goa no ano de LXXVII*) and the Tamil letters made in Cochin in 1578 (*letra tamul feita Coula ano de LXXVIII*) on folio 17. We find the following writing i.e., *Portata d'all Indie Hauuta dal padre Fonseca del mesme di Novembro MDLXXIX* (Fr. Fonseca in Rome received this book which was sent from India some time in November 1579). The book ends with the phrase *Soli Deo Honor & Gloria, Amen* (All Praise and Glory to God, Amen). The first page even carried the picture of Palm Sunday. An original copy donated by Curt. H. Resinger in 1951 is now available in the Harvard University Library, Cambridge, Massachusetts, USA.[19]

The missionaries seem to have continued their efforts to improve the Tamil types. In 1578, Fr João de Faria devised an improved version of the Tamil types in Kollam. In a reference dated in the year 1582 the following passage is found: 'Died at Goa, the Rev João de Faria who built the arches of St Paul and who was the first to start the press at the Fishery Coast for the great glory of God engraving and casting alphabets of the Tamil language'.[20] This Fr João Faria appears to have learnt the art of making types from Gonçalves in Kollam.

As both the Tamil types prepared by Gonçalves and Faria were found to be identical, both were used in printing the book. It was clearly stated on page sixteen of the Doctrina Christam that the Tamil types used in the first line were prepared in Goa in 1577 and those used in the subsequent lines were prepared in Kollam in the year 1578.

Regarding the style adopted for printing the books, we find that the *pulli* (dot) was not used on top of the consonants. Further, the long and short consonants called *kuril* and *nedil* were also not indicated. The long consonants (*nedil*) were sometimes found joined in printing. Alphabets such as aa, noo, too had no double loop symbol in printing. Moreover there was little gap between words. A careful scrutiny of Thambiran Vanakkam shows that many Portuguese words were used. To show that they were not Tamil words, double dagger signs were used before and after the word. The book has imprimatur the official permission. Thus it is understood that there was somebody to read and verify the theological orthodoxy of the Tamil text before publication. The Inquisition was working in Goa to suppress the heresy when no books could be published without the permission and authorization from the Church. The printed book had a title in Tamil and Portuguese and it is important to read and note the contents because they are different. The book was allowed to be printed by the Inquisition and it is mentioned in the Portuguese title of the book '*Doctrina Christaa tresladad em lingua Tamul pello padre Anrique Anriquez da Companhia de IESV, & pello padre Manoel de Sao Pedro. Com approuacao do Ordinario, & Inquisidor; & co licenca do Superior da mesma Companhia: Impressa em Coulam no Collegio do Saluador: aos vinte de Octubro de MDLXXVIII.* According to the second page of Thambiran Vanakkam, the co-author of the sixteen-page book was Padre Manoel de São Pedro.[21] Thus it is known Anriquez was not a single author of the book as opined by the scholars till date.

The Jesuit Printing Press in Cochin: Krisiththiyani Vanakkam Printed on 14 November 1579 and Confessionairo on 28 May 1580

Krisiththiyani Vanakkam was the second Tamil book printed on Saturday, 14 November 1579 (28 Aypasi) at the *Collegio da Madre de Deos* of the Jesuits in Cochin (Kochi). The actual size of the book was 10 X 14 cm. An examination of the original shows three pages that were left blank. This included the back side of the first leaf and both the pages of the last leaf. This book titled *Doctrina Christaa, a maneyra de dialogo: feyta em Portugal pello padre Marcos Iorge da Companhia de IESV: Treslada em lingua Malauar Tamul, pello padre Anrique Anriquez da mesma Companhia. Impressa co approuacao do Ordinario, & Inquisidor, & co licenca do Superior. Em Cochim no Collegio da Madre de Deos, aos quatorze de Novembro do anno de MDLXXIX*. The book running to 127 pages was the first Tamil book in prose written by Fr. Anriquez. The author signed his name in Tamil as Andriku Paadriyar.

The original discovered by Robert Streit in 1928 was available in Bibliothéque de la Sorbonne, Paris, although it is now said to have been lost. Mr Graham Shaw discovered another copy of Krisiththiyaani Vanakkam at the manuscript department in the Bodleian Library, Oxford in 1979.[22]

The printing of this book was paid for by the paravas. In the preface to the book Anriquez addressed the paravas thus: You desired that you and your descendants should achieve salvation in heaven, and you have desired many kinds of printed books and contributed large sums of money toward a printing press. We, therefore, give this book to you as a gift. Your financial support for this press has earned you public respect and praise.[23]

Printing the two books of Kirisiththiyaani Vanakkam and Thambiran Vanakkam had been helped by a native Tamil. It has been acknowledged by Anrique Anriquez vide his letters. Pero Luis the brahmin convert helped in arranging and understanding the Tamil alphabets and he had overseen personally the printing of the two books in Tamil.[24]

Confessionairo titled in Portuguese is the third Tamil book printed on 28 May 1580 (14 *vaikasi*). Its original Tamil title is mentioned Kompeciyonaayaru. The printed book is preserved at the Bodleian Library, Oxford. The size of it was 9 X 13.5 cm and the total number of pages was 107 recto and verso. The book has the text printed on 216 small pages. The logo of the Jesuits IHS (*Iesus Humanis Salvador*) is found there.[25] Thus three Tamil books were printed in three consecutive years

Portuguese missionaries on the Tamil coast during the sixteenth century desired to teach catechism, Christian doctrine and the treasures of heavenly knowledge through Tamil to the new converts. Hence they wrote prayers and the catechism in Tamil language with the apostles' creed, the ten commandments of God, the precepts of the church, Our Father, (the Lord's prayer), Hail Mary, Hail Holy Queen, Act of Contrition, Articles of faith, the sacraments of the church, capital sins or vice, the works of mercy, both the corporal and the spiritual, five senses, theological virtues, cardinal virtues, enemies of the soul, final ends and the eight beatitudes.

The Lives of Saints in Tamil Printed in Goa in 1586

Portuguese missionaries brought Flos Sanctorum the famous book on the lives of saints published in 1513 in their mother-tongue. It may be recalled here that Nicholas Lancillotto, a Jesuit had written a letter from Kollam as early as on 6 January 1551 to Ignatius Loyola that Fr. Anriquez had begun translating the lives of the saints in Tamil. Before the publication of this Tamil book the author had shown the full text to a few natives who were well versed in Tamil and had received valuable suggestions and comments and he carried out the corrections as suggested. This book had therefore far less grammatical errors and was very neatly written although its printing was delayed very much.[26]

After taking a long time for translation, this book was printed in 1586. The place of printing had been unknown since the original title page of Flos Sanctorum is missing. Some scholars have ascribed it to Punnaikayal an important centre of the Portuguese missionary activities on the pearl fishery coast where the Jesuits had a residence.[27] It is known from Jesuit records that printing press had functioned at Cochin. Hence Graham Shaw ruled out the possibility of Punnaikayal and he called the view of scholars into question. It has been reported in Jesuit records that in 1582 a Jesuit by name João Rodrigues (Bustamante) from the pearl fishery coast was sent to Goa in order to oversee the printing of the Flos Sanctorum.[28] Hence it may be concluded that the place of printing was Goa and the book was printed.

The printed Flos Sanctorum book was of moderate size (20.5 X 14 X 3.5 cm, 342 folios) and handy enough to be carried. An original book discovered by Rev. Xavier Thaninayagam in 1954 is still available in the Vatican Library. The preface and the table of contents are also missing in that book.[29] This book containing 334 leaves i.e., 660 printed pages is the magnum opus of Anriquez. There is also another original book preserved at the Royal Library in Copenhagen, Denmark.[30] This printed book is incomplete because leaves 1-18, 56-67, 74-76, 144, 224-228, 323, 326-334 (in total 49 leaves) are missing. The book has only leaves from 19-55, 68-73, 77-143, 145-223, 229-322 and 324-325.

In the first folio of the book in Vatican Library we find recorded that "to be given to the Vatican Library". Printing done in this book is without gap at the end of the words. There is a full stop used at the end of the sentence. The pages are serially numbered in Tamil. There are errors of omission in some pages of the book such as page numbers 39, 67 and 328. There are also errors of commission. While the page number 91 is printed instead of page number 61 and the page number 326 in the book is printed instead of page 327.

After the prologue in the book we find the readings for the great feasts of the liturgical year, with some feasts of our Lady and of the Apostles (which were held as feasts of obligation) and of various saints. In this book Anriquez had introduced the Tamil calendar to mark the Christian festivals and feasts as found correspondingly in the Gregorian calendar. He had used the Tamil months by finding out the equivalent months used in the Roman calendar. The tenth month of *Thai* in the Tamil calendar corresponded to the first month of January and the other months were equally made to agree with each other. He gave the table of corresponding days and months between the Tamil and Western calendars on page 668. He had also published the dates of movable Christian feasts of Ash Wednesday, Easter, etc., for the period from AD 1587 to 1614. The author has admitted that he had translated the lives of all saints found in three Portuguese books and that it took more than three years to complete. The publication of this Tamil book was generously sponsored by the paravas who paid 400 *cruzados* on one occasion to Fr. Anriquez.[31]

The testimony of Fr. Sebastião Gonçalves regarding Tamil publications is worthy of consideration here. He mentioned in the annual letter of the Jesuits in 1600 that all those books got printed in Tamil were made by the Jesuits alone. He further mentioned that there was no need any more to get either the matrices or the letters for printing the books from Venice in Italy. He revealed that these printed books could be found not only in the hands of the Christians on the pearl fishery coast but also with Hindus in the interior places of the hinterland. The Tamils were greatly astonished about the way in which good Tamil types were made and books printed in their language. The Tamil *pundits* and brahmins were highly impressed by the novelty and mysteries of printing.[32] There was no freedom of the press because restrictions for the missionaries came from the Catholic Church particularly the Holy Inquisition in Goa and also permission from the Bishop and the Jesuit Provincial with imprimatur and censor liborum.

The Style and Structure of Tamil Language in the Printed Books of the Sixteenth Century

A comparison of the sixteenth century Tamil language style and structure found in the texts of the epigraphs and in the printed Tamil books by the Portuguese can be quite revealing. We may compare the works of the Portuguese in Tamil and understand the improvements introduced in the language style. In this case we may compare the cartilha published in Lisbon under the supervision of Fr. João Villa de Conde and Flos Sanctorum published in 1586 by Anriquez in Goa. At the very outset it becomes evident that the language style of cartilha is inferior and the work of Fr. Anriquez was definitely an improvement in terms of language, vocabulary and style. The names of ecclesiastical authorities, liturgical ceremonies and Christian festivals came to be used in Tamil as they were found in the Portuguese language, for example *Bispo, Padre, Vigario, Apostolo, Compadre, Comadre, Missão* and Catholic. Significantly the names of Jesus, Mary and Joseph were pronounced in Tamil as *Esu, Mari* and *Soosai* almost exactly as in the Portuguese.

A detailed examination of the cartilha is taken up here to understand the style and language of Tamil. Although the *manipravaalam* style was very common in the sixteenth century, we find in the printed Tamil text several Portuguese words used verbatim as given below:

Page-Line	Word	Meaning
5-4	Iesu christo	- Jesus Christ
5-5	Cruz	- Cross
28-1	Sacramentos	- Sacraments
29-6	Comunhao	- Communion
29-5	Padrigalodu	- Among the priests

Further, we find that Anrique Anriquez who wrote and published the Krisithiyaani Vanakkam in 1579 had used Latin and Portuguese terms in Tamil characters while explaining the Christian mysteries of faith.[33] The following table gives a sample of words:

Portuguese/Latin word	Tamil word	English meaning
Gratia	kiraasai	grace
Missa	meesai	holy mass
Averea	Averaesai	avarice
Castidade	Kasithithathe	chastity
Baptismo	Vavatheesvumu	baptism

There were a number of names, verbs and ideas in the new religion of Christianity for which there were no Tamil equivalents. As they had to be made well known to the people at large, many Portuguese words came into usage. Thus new Christian names were coined for use in the cartilha when it was printed:

Page-Line	Names adopted	Equivalent English into Tamil Names
16-6	Pedro	Peter
17-1	Andre	Andrew
17-7	Poncio pilato	Pontius Pilot
18-1	Thome	Thomas
16-8	Bertholeomeu	Bartholomew
19-1/2	Matheus	Mathew
19-3	Simon	Simon
19-5	Judas	Judas
19-6-7	Mathias	Mathias
16-5	Sisser	Caesar

There were however several errors in the printed Tamil text as mentioned below:[34]

Page-Line	Word	Correction
6-1	Aralayathal	Adayalathal
9-6	Vicetapattavale	Visheshapatttavale
14-4	Vixessapatta	Visheshapatta

The Tamil language thus underwent some changes like other languages of the world and it did not remain the same throughout its history. The study of the evolution of Tamil language had been the field of investigation for some scholars. They opine that the literary language did not always reflect the changes in the spoken Tamil. A comparison made between the literary Tamil language with that of the inscriptional records shows that two distinct varieties were used in the sixteenth century itself. The spoken variety was mainly found in the prose developed by the Portuguese. The spoken Tamil is also found in inscriptions since they were used to convey simple messages to the public. The literary variety was for poetic works alone. While the spoken language had changed gradually, the language of the poetic compositions remained unchanged. The language of the inscriptions does not provide us a complete picture of the spoken language because the linguistic forms and contents of the inscriptions comprised a limited stereotype range of ideas and thoughts. However the language of Tamil inscriptions in the sixteenth century represented an admixture of spoken Tamil with occasional literary flourishes.

The Tamil language was in close contact with the Sanskrit language for a long period of time. The influence of Sanskrit has been found in the medieval period. Regarding the style of the Tamil language, the bilingual admixture of Tamil and Sanskrit called *manipravaalam* continued in the sixteenth century as evident from the Tamil publications of the Portuguese. Sanskrit words were introduced and profusely used in Tamil by the Vaishnavites in the Tamil country in the medieval period and Vira Chozhliyum, an eleventh century Tamil grammar speaks at length about this *manipravaalam* style.[35] If Sanskrit had been kept at a distance not allowing to interfere with the Tamil linguistic system it could not have influenced Tamil very much. The following are some of the Sanskrit words found in the Tamil printed works during this period:

Page/Line		Sanskrit words used in Tamil texts	Tamil	Meanings
5	3	racxica	ratcikka	to redeem
6	3	puthiran	makan	son
7	7	namaskaram	namaskaram	wishing
8	2	rajyam	arasu	kingdom

9	6	strigalil	penkalil	women
11	1	carvamum	ellamum	all
11	5	cannihastri	kanni	virgin
15	3	logathillude	ulagathilae	in the world
15	5	thosham	tosam	sin
20	1-2	manushan	manidhan	man
25	1-2	snehichu	nesithu	loving
31	2	ahangaram	aangaram	pride

The colloquial words were faithfully used by the Portuguese missionaries in the written form. They did not adopt the equivalent Tamil literary form when they printed the Tamil books. Some of the differences between the spoken and written forms of Tamil as found in the text of catechism used by the Portuguese may be noted below:

Page-Line	In colloquial	In Tamil meaning	In English
7-2	mulichen	vilizchen	awake
8-4	appan	thanthai	father
8-5	curucra	kodukira	give
8-1	iriquarray	irukira	seated
9-3	racxichi	ratchitittu	redeemed
28-3	pacradu	parkirathu	looking
21-7	kudukkirvan	kodukkiravan	giving
16-5	iiriquiran	iriukiran	sitting
33-5	codukkuradu	kodukirathu	giving
37-6	irriquiren	irukiran	sitting
37- 6	pillachen	pilathithen	alive
39-1	cholichi	cholli	said
16- 2	usur kondan	usuru	resurrection
25-7	ettavathu	ettavathu	eighth

Tamil in the sixteenth century was a diglossic language since it indicated the coexistence of two varieties of language style with two distinct sets of phonological, lexical and syntactic features. People used Tamil complementarily in specified domains of its use. The formal variety was mostly the written forms of Tamil while the other variety, considered as the informal one, was the spoken one. Portuguese language had a continuous influence only on the Tamil dialect of the low or the informal variety in the age of expansion of the Portuguese on the Tamil coast.

Thambiran Vanakkam of 1578 presents Portuguese as a curious intermediary language. We find on the second page, a diamond-shaped sign is introduced in order to shelter Portuguese and Latin words appearing in the text, i.e., all except titles such as 'Pello Sinal', 'Credo', and 'Os Mandamentos' which stand alone and apart from the Tamil text. The same principle of demarcation is found in all the four printed Tamil books too. It may be noted that Anriquez used redundant words to mean the words given with brackets and we find pathikumaapoley (Pathiyumpadi), yapadiey (Appadiey) and Avarodey ketka (Avaridam ketka).

The Jesuit Printing Press at Ambalakaadu: Printing Gnaanopadesam (Catechism) Part I and II in 1677 and Part III and IV in 1678

The Jesuit printing press of Cochin was shifted in 1663 when the Dutch captured the port from the Portuguese. The Jesuit seminary of Cochin was transferred to Ambalakaadu near Tiruchur in 1667 where the Jesuits had installed the printing machine.

Andre Freyre the Jesuit was asked by the superior of the Malabar mission to edit and publish the catechism composed by Roberto Nobili. Hence he went from Madurai to Ambalakaadu and began the work and he supervised the printing of the first two parts of the catechism in 1674. The Tamil title of the book is Gnaanopadesam and the Tamil name of Nobili is mentioned as Thathuvapothaga Swami. It was printed at the Jesuit Press in Ambalakaadu in 1677.[36] The Latin title of the book is *Catechismus Padre Roberti Nobili, Tamulico idiomate scriptus, Pars prima et secunda*. It has xiv +51+ 200 pages containing part one and two of Gnaanopadesam.

Andre Freyre gave a Latin introduction to this printed book. We find Sanskrit words are abundantly found in Roberto Nobili's prose. A sample of the first three printed pages of part one of the catechism show words such as *avasiyam, viseshamundu, kaariyam, kaaranammananthu, vissarikirathu, anurupa kaaranam, aupaavam, kalasa paathiram, bhumi, suryan, buddhi, belam* and *paathiram*.[37] Further a sample of the first three printed pages of part one of the catechism have been examined and it is learnt that spoken Tamil words have been used such as *kudukiirathu* (give) *sonnomay* (told) *senippikum* (born) *kuraisalaay* (little) *aththai* (that) *arinju* (understood) and *kusavan* (potter). The first three sample pages of the second part of the printed catechism have also been taken up for examination and we find Sanskrit words such as *sthree, manushan karthar, jalam, push-pangal, pravaagum, mathuram, virushangal, varnam, pakshigal, dushta, raathiri, belam* and *paripooranam* have been used.[38]

Rodrigo d'Abreu the Jesuit was asked by the superior of the Malabar Mission to monitor the activities of editing Roberto Nobili's part three of the catechism. He went from Madurai to Ambalakaadu and began the work and the third part of the catechism was printed at the Jesuit Press in Ambalakaadu in 1678.[39] The Latin title of the book is *Catechismus Padre Roberti Nobili, Tamulico idiomate scriptus, Pars tertia*. It has xi +336 pages containing part three of Gnaanopadesam. Simons Martins the Jesuit was appointed by the inquisition censor of this catechism and he gave his expression of assent in writing on 21 April 1677. An examination of the first three printed pages of the catechism shows that several Sanskrit words such as *dhaanam, visesham, sornam, rathinam, pragasam, anthasthu, upadesam, seeshan, manushan* and *subhaavam*.[40] Thus Tamil language style and structure in the printed books of the seventeenth century had been to known to us.

The Gnaanopadesam (part four of the catechism) was also printed from the Jesuit press at Ambalakaadu in 1678.[41] The Latin title of the book is *Theologi Catechismi Romani Quarta Pars*. The date mentioned is 9 September 1678. Roberto Nobili had himself mentioned that the brahmins used many Sanskrit words when they spoke. As he was in the midst of the company of brahmins and led the life of a sanyaasi it is natural that Sanskrit words are found abundant in his work Gnaanopadesam. Nobili had borrowed freely from Sanskrit mainly for the philosophical and theological ideas for expressing in Catholic doctrines. It is also known to us that Christians began to address each other when they met saying *sesunatharukku managalam* (praise be the Lord Jesus Christ) which shows that spoken Tamil of the times had Sanskrit words among the brahmins.[42] Nobili himself was called Iyer by the Christians. As a result we find all those Jesuits who followed and adopted the life style of sanyaasis began to write and use Sanskrit words in their spiritual works in Tamil. They began to minimize the use of foreign words and were also inspired to coining of new Tamil words in the seventeenth century. Nobili in his Gnaanopadesam had cited Valluvar's Thirukural, Thirumular's Thirumandiram, Tholkappiyam and Kachchiyappa Sivaachariyar's Kanthapuranam.[43]

Printing Tamil-Portuguese Dictionary of Antão Proença at Ambalakaadu in 1679

Antão Proença the Portuguese Jesuit had noted the existence of high and low Tamil, pure and corrupt Tamil, according to various classes and castes of the Tamil society during 1665 and 1679. He compiled a Tamil-Portuguese dictionary and testified the fact that Tamil Brahmins used Sanskrit words even in their ordinary conversations. A manuscript copy of his dictionary is available at the State Central Library in Goa.[44] It contains 16,546 main entries against which Tamil words and meanings have been given in Portuguese. It has 16208 non-lemmatized bilingual entries on 508 pages. In his preface to the dictionary he had provided guidelines for the Portuguese readers to read Tamil correctly by giving the transliterations of the Tamil words in Portuguese. Words given as subsidiary entries under one main entry have not been counted as separate entries. Hence the total nominal, verbal and adjectival besides composed forms and idioms in the dictionary if counted separately would increase the total of words more. He mentions that he had collected Tamil words from the dictionary of Ignacio Bruno who lived and did missionary work in Jaffna Pattanam but omitted words mostly used in the poetical works since they were not much in vogue in the spoken Tamil. Further Proença mentions that he had included many Sanskrit words in this dictionary since they were commonly used in the ordinary conversation of the Tamil Brahmins. He says that he used these Sanskrit words to help those who would read the books of Roberto Nobili and Manoel Martins, in which these Sanskrit words were found numerous.

Proença's dictionary was published by the Jesuit press at Ambalakaadu on 30 July 1679, posthumously i.e. thirteen years after his death. The Tamil portions seem to have been made from engraved wooden blocks while the Portuguese portion has been made by using the moveable type. Fr Xavier Thaninayagam mentioned the printer was an Indian, Ignacio Aichamoni probably Accamani a Tamil name.[45] This opinion is called into question now for we find his name is mentioned as Patre Ignatio Archamone and also as Ignacio Arcamone in records who was a Jesuit. He was the manager of the college press of Rachol in Goa in 1663, and in 1670 his name figures in various publications.[46] However, the press at Ambalakaadu is called the Tamil press of the province of Malabar. This printed dictionary original is available and preserved at the Vatican Library.[47]

In this printed dictionary we find twelve reports and letters documenting the lengthy process of censoring the dictionary by the Catholic Church authorities in Ambalakaadu, Cochin and Goa during the four months period between 20 September 1678 and 6 December 1678. These no-objection certificates firstly relate to the teaching of the Catholic Church and secondly to the complete identity of Proença's original manuscript dictionary with the printed version. In this process four censors of Goa who are explicitly named as Tamil experts, give their opinion on the dictionary. The most important among these is João de Magalhaens, the procurator of the Jesuit province of Malabar and Goa who is described as reviser in Goa. On 21 February 1679 he writes that he has examined again the book called Tamil-Portuguese dictionary by Antão Proença which he used intensively for many years in studying Tamil language and practice. He states that he copied it with his own hand and used it for teaching and translation. The three more Jesuit Tamil experts are mentioned in the censor's section viz., Antonio Perreira at Ambalakaadu, Valeriano Caetano, also at Ambalakaadu and João Pessoa, professor of theology at the colleges in Goa and Cochin. Proença had selected and used only such words of those words in the Tamil-Portuguese dictionary as would meet the requirements of the people in all walks of life to learn the Tamil language although it was mainly intended for the use of the Portuguese missionaries.[48]

The printing press in Ambalakaadu must have continued to function but we have no clues as to when the Jesuit press actually came to a complete halt. Jean Calmette (1693-1740) the Jesuit in Pondicherry in his letter dated 28 September 1713 mentioned that the Protestant missionaries in Tranquebar had a new printing press and it had placed the Danish at a clear advantage. The Jesuit mission press was not printing anything by then and so he lamented. Yet the difficulties of multiplying books by handwriting by the Jesuits was no small obstacle in their zeal.[49]

To conclude it may be said that the journey of book printing in Tamil had made a remarkable progress under the Jesuits. The King of Portugal had extended his continued support to the Jesuits through supply of paper for printing. Though the book in Tamil in Portugal appeared in Roman Script and not in Tamil script in 1554, the missionaries had made sincere efforts through development of Tamil fonts and the first book in Tamil fonts appeared only in 1578 after a gap of 24 years. Owing to scarcity of paper the Jesuits have carefully selected to print important books needed for the use of people and the missionaries. They have published only eight books in total over a century (between 1578 and 1679). The expression '*Thamizhiley piriththeyezhuthina*' had been used to mean 'translated in Tamil'. No printing of Tamil books happened between 1587 and 1677 and we find a long gap of 90 years. The quality of printing Tamil books by the Jesuits is admirable. The binding is also equally good. The price of the printed books had not been fixed and cited. The title pages of some Tamil books were printed in Portuguese and other books at times in Latin so as to make it easy identification for the European readers. The press was primarily used to publish the ecclesiastical works. Printing was considered the domain of the Jesuits. Tamil books printed were sent to Goa, Lisbon and Rome. The secrets related to Tamil typography, typesetting, printing and binding were well guarded by the missionaries and largely remained unknown to Tamils.

Notes

1. Joseph Needham, *Science and Civilization in China*, Vol. V: Paper and Printing, Cambridge, 1985; P.K. Gode, *Studies in Indian Cultural History*, Poona, 1960; J. Trier, *Ancient Paper of Nepal,* Copenhagen, 1972.
2. *The History of Printing*, Society for Promoting Christian Knowledge, London, 1855, p. 17.

3. Graham Shaw, *The South Asia and Burma Retrospective Bibliography, Stage 1: 1556-1800*, London, 1987; Graham Shaw and John Randall, *From Conversion to Subversion: 250 Years of the Printed Book in India*, Sussex, 2014.
4. Affonso de Albuquerque, *Cartas de Affonso de Albuquerque*, eds., Raymundo Antonio de Bulhão Pato and H. Lopes de Mendonça, Academia das Ciências de Lisboã, Lisboã, 7 vols., 1844-1935, vol. I, pp. 44-5.
5. Biblioteca da Cartuxa, Evora, E.2098; Biblioteca Municipal, O Porto, Portugal, MSS Codice no. 143; Xavier S. Thaninayagam, 'Tamil Manuscripts in European Libraries', *Tamil Culture,* vol. III, October, 1954, pp. 210-88; Xavier S. Thaninayagam, 'The First Printed Books in Tamil', *Tamil Culture*, vol. VII, no. 3, pp. 288-308.
6. Fernando de Almeida, ed., *Cartilha em Tamul e Português: Impresa em 1554*, Ministerio da Edução Nacional, Direção-Geral do Superior do Ensino Superior e da Belas-Artes, Lisboã, 1970. P. Uma Maheswari had mentioned the date of publication of Cartilha as 11 February 1554 and it is incorrect. The date is 2 February 1554 because in print we find ii (II) and not XI. See, P. Uma Maheswari, *Advent of Print Culture in Colonial Tamil Region: Technological, Cultural and Social Changes from 1712 to 1947*, Ph.D. Dissertation, Pondicherry University, 2013, p. 281.
7. Ibid., pp. 24-7; Jean Filliozat, *Un catéchisme tamoul du XVIe siècle en lettres latines*, Pondicherry, 1967.
8. Jose Wicki and J. Gomes, *Documenta Indica* (hereafter DI), 18 vols., Roma, 1948-88, vol. I, p. 58.
9. George Schurhammer and Jose Wicki, eds., *Epistolae S. Francisci Xaverii alliaque Eius Scripta*, Roma, II vols., 1944-45, vol. II, p. 211.
10. DI, vol. III, p. 508.
11. Francisco de Sousa, *Oriente Conquistado a Jesus Christo pelos Padres da Companhia de Jesus da Provincia de Goa,* III vols., Lisboa, 1710, Porto, 1978, see, Con I-1-23, p. 18; DI, vol. III, p. 514.
12. C.G., Rodeles, 'Early Printing in India', *Journal of the Royal Asiatic Society of Bengal*, vol. IX, April 1913, pp. 153-155, see p. 155.
13. Josef Wicki, 'Pedro Luis Brahmane und Erster Indischer Jesuit (ca.1532–1596)', *Neue Zeitschrift für Missionswissenschaft*, 6, 1950, pp. 115-26; Ines G. Zupanov, *Missionary Topics; The Catholic Frontiers in India, 16th-17th Centuries*, Ann Arbor, 2005.
14. Biblioteca Apostolica Vaticana (hereafter BAV), Città del Vaticano, VAT Baago 3; Flos Sanctorum, p. LXX.
15. DI, vol. I, pp. 286–8, see the letter written from Vembar dated 31 October 1548.
16. Francisco de Sousa, Oriente Conquistado, Con I-2-33, p. 81.
17. Harvard University Library, Cambridge, Massachusetts, USA, Doctrina Christaa tresladad em lingua Tamul pello padre Anrique Anriquez da Companhia de IESV, & pello padre Manoel de Sao Pedro. Com approuacao do Ordinario, & Inquisidor; & co licenca do Superior da mesma Companhia, Impressa em Coulam: no Collegio do Saluador, aos vinte de Octubro de 1578. See also, Thamizh Naadaan, *Thamizh Mozhhiyin Muthal Achchu Puththagam*, Salem, 1995, pp. 1-12.

18. Francisco de Sousa, Oriente Conquistado, Con I-2-12, p. 67.
19. DI, vol. VII, pp. 426-7. In light of the above, the contention of Georg Schurhammer that Malayalam types were first prepared by Gonçalves may not hold ground. See, Georg Schurhammer and G.W Cotrell, 'The First Printing in Indic Characters', *Harvard University Library Bulletin*, vol. VI, no.2, Spring 1952, pp. 147-160.
20. Francisco de Sousa, Oriente Conquistado, Con II-2-3, p. 157.
21. Mo. Nevis Victoria, *Thambiran Vanakkam: Thamizh Mozhiyin Muthal Achchu Puthagam*, Chennai, 2011.
22. Bodleian Library, Oxford, Doctrina Christam or *Krisithiyani Vanakkam*, Cochin, 1579, Vet. Or. f.Tam.1.*Doctrina Christaa, a maneira de dialogo: feyta em Portugal pello padre Marcos Iorge da Companhia de IESV: Treslada em lingua Malaur Tamul, pello padre Anrique Anriquez da mesma Companhia. Impressa co approuacao do Ordinario, & Inquisidor, & co licenca do Superior, Em Cochim: no Collegio da Madre de Deos, aos quatorze de Nou mbro, do anno de 1579.*
23. Ibid., pp 6-7. The Tamil text runs thus: '*Pala pala posthagangal achchiley undaaga venumenu anega muthal achchundaaga silvazhithirgaley, agaiyinaaley intha pusthagm ungalukku nankodaiyaaga varavittom. Anega muthal silav-zhthithu achcundakkiviththathinaaley sangaiyum kirthiyum logar munpaaga pettirgaley*'.
24. DI, vol. XI, p. 790. Pero Luis wrote from Kollam in 1580 to Everard Mercurian, the Superior General of the Society of Jesus, that he had spent the whole month of October in Cochin for the love of printing in Malavar (Tamil) (*por amor de empresão malavar*).
25. Bodleian Library, Oxford, Anrique Anriquez, *Kompeciyonaaru* or Confessionario, 1580, Vet. Or. f.Tam.1. Ines G. Županov, 'I Am a Great Sinner: Jesuit Missionary Dialogues in Southern India, (Sixteenth Century)', *Journal of the Economic and Social History of the Orient*, vol. 55, 2012, pp. 415-446.
26. DI, vol. X, pp. 269, 372, 801.
27. Roth E. Muller and Roth J. Muller, *Aussereuropaische Druckerein in 16 Jahrundert*, Baden-Baden, 1969.
28. DI, vol. XII, p. 716.
29. Jose Wicki, *IV Centenario da Primeira Imprensa de Goa*, Lisboã, 1956, p. 11.
30. Det Kongelige Bibliotek (hereafter KB), Kobenhavn, Orientalske Afdeling, 1531. Graham Shaw, 'The Copenhagen Copy of Henriques' Flos Sanctorum', *Fund og Forskning i Dei Kongelige Biblioteks Samlinger*, vol. 32, 1993, pp. 39-50.
31. DI, vol. XI, p. 292; Jose Wicki, 'O Flos Sanctorum do P. H. Henriques, Impresso na Língua Tamul em 1586', *Boletim do Instituto Vasco da Gama,* vol. 73, 1956, pp. 42-9.
32. BAV, Flos Sanctorum, p. XII; Jose Wicki, 'The Confraternity of the Charity of Fr. Henriques', *Indian Church History Review,* vol. I, 1967, pp. 3-8.
33. S. Rajamanickam, *The First Oriental Scholar*, Palayamkottai, 1972, p. 87.
34. Bodleian Library, Oxford, Anrique Anriquez, Doctrina Christam or *Krisithiyani Vanakkam*, Cochin, 1579, Vet. Or. f.Tam.1, chapter 2.

35. K. R. Govindaraja Mudaliar, *Vira Chozhliyum: Mulamum Peruntevanar Iyattrriya Uraiyum*, Madras, 1942, p. 180. The text runs. 'Idaiye vadaveluthu, eithil viraviyal eendi edugai neadiyethumilla *maniparavalam*'.

36. SCL, Goa, Shelf mark 1-1a and 1b, *Gnaanaupadesam: Thathuvapothaga Swamigal Udayathu, Muthal Kaandam*. Ambalakaadu, 1677. The Portuguese title is *Catechismo Madurense: Escripta em Tamul pelo Padre Robert Nobili S.J. em 1674 e divido em duas partes, Impressoe em Ambalacatta no officina de Ignacio Archamanio em 1677.*

37. S. Rajamanickam, ed., *Gnaanopadesam, Kaandam Onru*, Tuticorin, 1966, pp. 1-3.

38. SCL, Goa, *Gnaanaupadesam, Rendaam Kaandam*: *Catechismo Madurensa em lingoa Tamulica, por Pe. Roberto Nobili da Companhia de Jesus*, e 2a parte, *Impressoe em Ambalacatta no officina de Ignacio Archamanio em 1677*; S. Rajamanickam, ed., *Gnaanopadesam, Kaandam Rendu*, Tuticorin, 1966, pp. 1-3. The reprint of 1891 mentions the year wrongly in the title page as 1675. Gnaanopadesa Kaandam: Ihuthu R.P. Robert de Nobili yennum Thathuvapodha gaswamingaliyattri, Athisreshtariyargal Parisothithu azhlitha uthaarapadi Madurai missionai saarntha sesu sabhai madathil 1675am Varushathil achchittriundha 1-2 kaandnagalin prathikkinanga rendaam pathippaga melor uthaarapadi Ma. Saa. Iyagappa pillai avargalaal Chennai arch. Susaiyappar achchukodathir pathipikkapattathu, 1891.

39. Joseph Bertrand, *La Mission du Madure d'après de Documents in Edits*, 4 vols, Paris, 1847-1854, vol. III, p. 264; S. Jeyaseela Stephen, *Letters of the Portuguese Jesuits from Tamil Countryside, 1666-1688*, Pondicherry, 2001, pp. 242-7.

40. SCL, Goa, *Gnaanaupadesam: Thathuvapothaga Swamigal Udayathu, Munram Kaandam*: *Catechismus P. Roberti Nobili, Tamulico idiomate scriptus ... Pars Tertia*, Ambalacatta: no officinal de Ignacio Archamonio, 1678, pp 1-336, see pp 1-3.

41. Bibliothèque Municipale de Chalon-sur-Saone, France, Livre Patrimoine-GT6216, *Gnaanopadesam: Thathuvapothaga Swamigal Udayathu, Naankaam Kaandam*: R.P. Roberti Nobili Romani Societate Iesv, *Catechism Romani Qvarta Pars, Ambalacatta, no officinal de Ignacio Arcchamonio*, 1678.

42. S. Rajamanickam, *The First Oriental Scholar*, p. 27.

43. Anand Amaladass, 'Early Jesuit Mission Methods in Asia With Special Reference to the Nanopatecam (the Catechism) of Roberto Nobili', Anand Amaladass and Ines G. Zupanvo, eds., *Intercultural Encounters and the Jesuit Mission in South Asia, 16th-18th Centuries*, Bangalore, 2014, pp. 88-112, see, pp. 101-2.

44. State Central Library (hereafter SCL), Goa, MS 34, Antão de Proença, *Vocabulario Tamulico Lusitano precedido de uma Arte em Tamul e seguido da termos poeticos*, dated 1670. There is another copy of this dictionary that exists but undated. SCL, MS 38. The dictionary is titled *Vocabulario Tamulico-Lusitano* with 223 folios in two columns.

45. Biblioteca Apostolica Vaticana (hereafter BAV), Città del Vaticano, Borgiano Indiano 12, *Vocabulario Tamulico com a significaçam Portugueza composto pello p. Antam de Proença da Companhia de Jesu, Missionario da Missam de Madurey, com todas as licencas necessaries da Santa Inquizicao e dos superiors,*

na impressa Tamulica do provincia do Malabar, por Ignacio Archamoni impressor della, Ambalacatta em 30 Julho 1679 annos, see, the preface, paragraph 2; Xavier S. Thaninayagam, *Antão de Proença's Tamil-Portuguese Dictionary, AD 1679*, Kuala Lumpur, 1966; Xavier S. Thaninayagam, 'Antão de Proença's Tamil-Portuguese Dictionary, 1679, An Introduction', *Tamil Culture*, vol. XI, no.2, April-June 1964, pp, 117-127, see p.121.

46. Biblioteca Casanatense, Roma, *Purgatorii Commentarium Concannice Compositum*, Goa, 1663; Bodleian Library, Oxford, *Conciones per Annum Concannice Compositae a Patre Ignatio Archamone e Societatis Iesu*, Goa, 1670.

47. Edgar C. Knowlton, 'Antão de Proença's Vocabulario Tamulico Lusitano: Indo-Portuguese Elements', *Tamil Culture*, vol. XI, 1964, pp.135-64; E.C. Knowlton, 'Portuguese-Tamil Linguistic Contacts', in *Proceedings of the First International Seminar-Conference of Tamil Studies*, 1966, pp. 607-17; Thomas Malten, 'Antam de Proença's Tamil-Portuguese Dictionary, Printed in Índia in 1679', in Charles J. Borges and Helmut Feldmann, eds., *Goa and Portugal: Their Cultural Links*, New Delhi, 1997, pp. 271-79.

48. BAV, MSS Borgiano Indiano, no. 12, fl.10.

49. Leon Besse, *Father Beschi: His Times and his Writings*, Trichnopoly, 1918, p. 93.

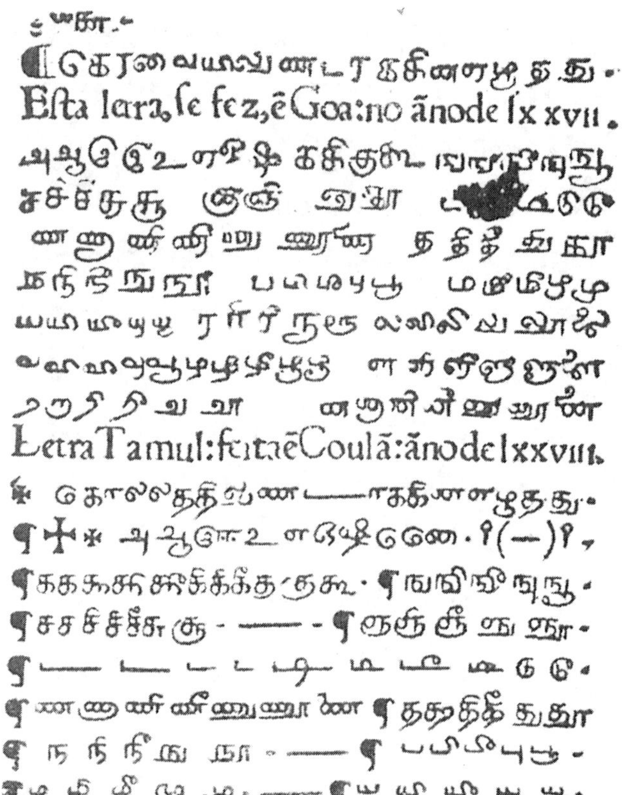
Esta lera, se fez, ẽ Goa: no ãno de lx xvii.

Letra Tamul: feita ẽ Coulã: ãno de lxxviii.

Soli DEO honor, & gloria. Amen.

2.1. The Tamil fonts made in Goa and Quilon mentioned in Thambiran Vanakkam printed at Quilon in 1578.* (Courtesy*: Houghton Library, Harvard University, Cambridge, Massachusetts, USA).

Doctrina Christaã, a maneyra de
Dialogo: feyta em Portugal pello
padre Marcos Iorge da Companhia de
IESV: Tresladada em lingua Malauar
Tamul, pello padre Anrique Anriquez
da mesma Cõpanhia. Impressa cõ appro-
uação do Ordinario, & Inquisidor,
& cõ licença do superior. Em
Cochim, no Collegio da
Madre de Deos, aos
quatorze de Nouẽ-
bro, do Anno de
M . D . L X X I X

Vão nesta doctrina algũs vocabulos,
os quais, pera se conhecerẽ não serẽ Malaua-
res, se lhe pos este sinal, † †: assi como,
†Graça† : †Igreja†. &c.

2.2. The Portuguese title page of Krisiththiyaani Vanakkam printed at Cochin in 1579. **(Courtesy*****: Bodleian Library, Oxford, Vet.Or.f. Tam.1).***

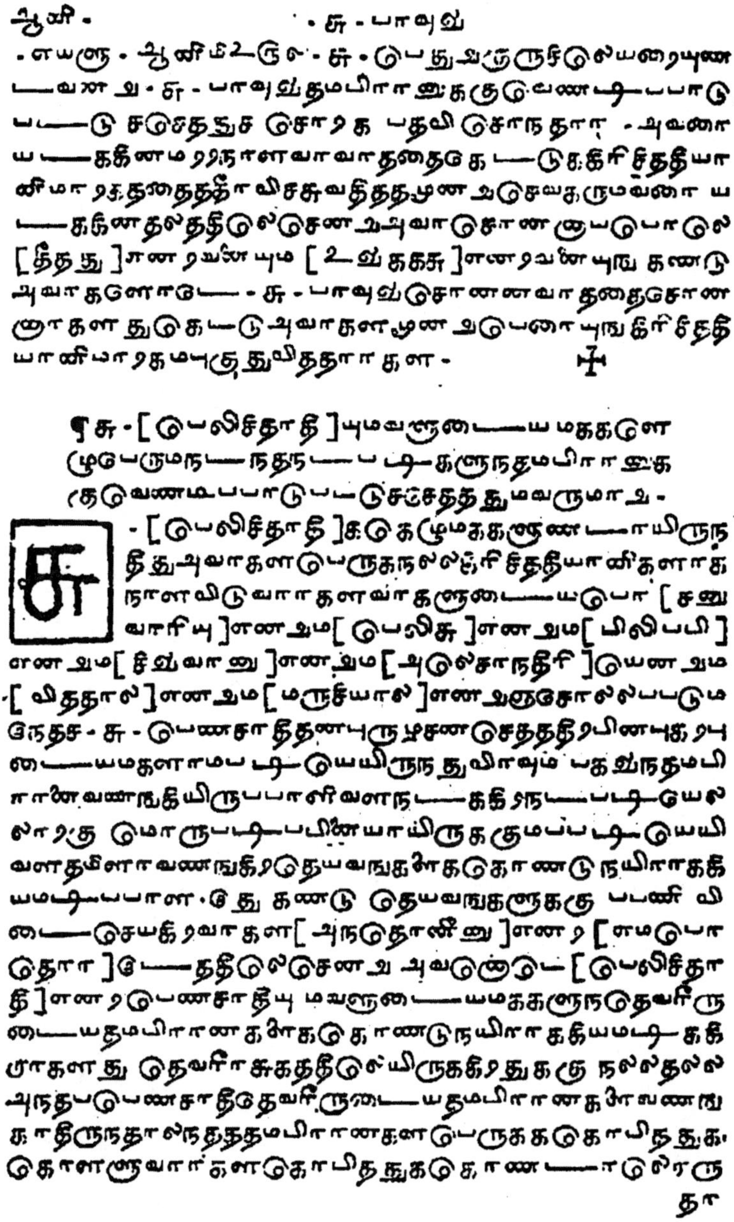

2.3. *A page from Flos Sanctorum printed in Goa in 1586.*
(Courtesy*: Biblioteca Apostolica Vaticana, VAT Baago. 3*).

3

The Letter Press of the Danish-Halle Mission in Tranquebar and the Landmarks in Printing Tamil Books, Pamphlets and Calendars, 1712-99

The Protestant missionaries boarded the ship which left Copenhagen on 30 November 1705 arrived at Tranquebar on the Tamil coast on 9 July 1706. They began to do evangelical works among the Tamils. Bartholomäus Ziegenbalg the missionary in Tranquebar wrote on 22 August 1708 to the missionaries in Halle demanding for a printing press with Tamil and Portuguese fonts. In 1709 he again appealed to all the Protestant European countries to help in their missionary work.[1] Johann Ernst Grundler another missionary in Tranquebar appealed again for printing press and supply of paper. The appeal became fruitful in 1711 through the efforts of Rev. Anton Wilhelm Boehme the German chaplain to prince George of Denmark when the Society for Promotion of Christian Knowledge (SPCK) in London sent a printing press in 1711 to Tranquebar with fonts of Latin types both Roman and italic and 100 reams of paper, under the care of Jonas Finck a printer along with 213 copies of the New Testament in Portuguese.[2] The ship which carried the printing machine was captured by the French and taken to Brazil. The machine was lying concealed in the vessel. The SPCK with the help of the English Governor of Fort St. George at Madras ransomed the ship. Jonas Finck had died in the meantime at the Cape of Good Hope. The printing machine, types and paper reached Tranquebar in June 1712. A German soldier who was educated as a printer helped the press to start functioning.[3]

The Preparation of Tamil Fonts in Leipzig and Tranquebar for Printing

A Tamil translation of the Apostles' Creed printed in Tamil characters in 1710 by the Protestant missionaries at Halle in Germany as an experiment was sent to Bartholomäus Ziegenbalg the missionary in Tranquebar and he received it in 1711. Tamil fonts cast at Leipzig in 1712 were sent from Halle in Germany to Tranquebar with Mr Alder a printing expert. This is mentioned in the letter of Bartholomäus Ziegenbalg dated 18 August 1715. The printing press at Tranquebar thereafter began to function on 11 June 1713 but installation works were completed by 6 October 1713. A sample printing work began for the first time was completed on 25 October 1713.[4] As the size of the Tamil types sent from Halle were too large, it was felt that more quantity of paper would be consumed if printing done. Since paper being a very costly commodity then, it was felt that smaller type Tamil fonts should be cast for printing. Ziegenbalg who left for Europe from Madras in 1714, took with him these Leipzig-cast Tamil letters so as to have his book *Grammatica Damulica* printed in Halle. H. J. Elers, Johann Peter Artopaus, Reuter, Peter Michelsen, Wolfgang Dietrich Erhardt, Gessner were a few printing and type-casting foundry technicians, and they were associated with the printing works of the Danish-Halle Mission both in Halle and Tranquebar. Attempts were made by these printing foundry experts who revised their style of cutting of the Tamil letters. Besides Tamil fonts, Telugu letters were also cast in metal, and they were planned to be used by Benjamin Schultze to print in Telugu. Thus, efforts were made to have the technical input for printing. The samples prepared with fonts were printed twice (in 1712 and in 1713) and it consisted of the Tamil consonants and vowels numbering 229 in total. The *Symbolum Apostolicum* that had been printed was a tri-lingual publication and it had the first line in Tamil, the second line in Latin and the third line in German language.[5]

The First Printed Tamil Book in Tranquebar, 17 October 1712

According to missionary records, on 17 October 1712 the first print in Tamil appeared from the printing press in Tranquebar. It was the Tamil catechism manual called *Retchippin Ozhukkam*. The book also had a title in Portuguese called '*A ORDEM da salvação, ou doutrina Christaa Brevemente en perguntas e repostas declarada e provada com principaes testemunhos da escritura Sagrada. Juntamente com alhuas Oraçoens e Cantigas, Tranquebar em India Oriental na Costa de Coromandel, na Estampa dos missionarios del Rey de Dennemark, anno 1712*'.[6] The next print came from the press was a small Portuguese ABCD on 8 November 1712.[7]

In the mean while, Friedrich IV the king of Denmark issued a royal letter to the commander of the Danish fort and trading factory in Tranquebar and he informed the arrival of three men who would be employed in the printing press. These individuals were Johann Berlin, Johann Gottlieb Adler together him with a fourteen year old brother of Adler whose name is not recorded.[8] The commander was ordered to let the press and the men arrive at the Danish-Halle mission's premises undisturbed and he was asked to extend full support for the installation of the press and the commencement of the printing works.[9] The king of Denmark gave the missionaries permission to print in Tranquebar without being subject to censor. Berlin and Adler brothers arrived in Tranquebar and they began to do the works related to printing by September 1713.

The First Printed Tamil Pamphlet in Tranquebar, 25 October 1713

The Tamil text prepared by the missionaries at Tranquebar was also ready by then for printing. It was titled '*Akkiyaanam yeththanai aruvarakkap padathakka kaariyam yendrum, athile nikkikra pergal yeppadi retshikkappattu karai yeralam yendrum vezhlippaduthugira vetha pramaanam*' (How abhorrent is heathenism and how those who are a follower it can be redeemed and saved). It was successfully printed on 25 October 1713.[10] This pamphlet printed was in octave. In the short preface, the Protestant missionaries addressed the Tamils as friends and appealed to them the real purpose for which they were sent by the king of Denmark. They also mentioned they were unable to speak with them individually about the situation of their life and show them the way to salvation. Hence they wrote and printed this book. They indicated that in the near future they would print more with similar contents.

This pamphlet of *Akkiyaanam* (Ignorance of the knowledge that leads to salvation) printed was distributed free of cost by Ziegenbalg to the people in the area of Nagapattinam, Karaikal and Tranquebar. Tamils had also well responded to the contents of this first printed pamphlet.[11] It has been mentioned that not being able to write anything against the printed pamphlet of *Akkiyaanam* a person had sent a reply to Ziegenbalg. The individual had stated that he had read the whole pamphlet, but not able to find any contradictions in its teachings. On the contrary everything written in it seems well reasoned and readily understandable. He said that he was incompetent either to respond to it or write anything against it. Only those who are as learned as Ziegenbalg and those who are solely devoted to teaching would be able to give him a fitting response. Indeed, he found it very difficult to comment further. If he were to write something, it would not be very worthwhile. If he expressed himself inappropriately Ziegenbalg could not tolerate him any longer. We find thus the honest and open-minded expression on the subject matter and contents of the pamphlet published by the Protestant missionaries in Tranquebar.[12] Print in Tamil had thus come to create the possibility of wide circulation of ideas, and also introduced a new world of debate and discussion. Even those Tamils who disagreed with European missionaries could communicate their ideas and respond. The Protestant missionaries could also print the message, and they could persuade Tamils to act, react and think differently and make them move in action. This is something found new and novel in the field of religion and life in Tamil country.

The next and the second printed work in Tamil was the catechism. It contained an explanation of the Christian doctrine translated from the Portuguese version with necessary modifications based on the Holy Scripture with the catechism of Martin Luther.[13] The book was printed on 13 November 1713 under the Tamil title '*Oru Kristhavana vethapramaanathinpadiye ariya vendina mandirangalaiyum padichu seyyavendina gnayangaliyum pothichivikkira gnaana upadesam, Tharanganpaadi achiley pathikka-pattathu, Kristhu pirantha 1713 varusham*'.[14]

The Establishment of a Paper Mill at Poraiyar, 1716-22

The word *kaakhitham* was referred to paper in Tamil in the early modern age. Paper-making by hand in Tamil country is reported during the early seventeenth century. But the paper produced near Nagapattinam was used for wrapping the bales of cloth for export by Tamil traders. Paper was manufactured by a Chinese paper-maker and the paper was also un-sized and found useless for printing and adhered to the type. Hence the Danes in Tranquebar decided to have a paper mill and it was related to the development of printing books. [15]

It was planned to set up the paper mill at Poraiyar by Alder the employee of the printing press in Tranquebar. He and Johan Sigismund Hass the commander of the fort of Tranquebar entered into an agreement and signed that a paper mill to be erected on a fifty-fifty basis. The Danish-Halle mission should have all the paper it needed, free of cost, and the rest of the production should be sold. For the paper which was sold the mission was supposed to pay one *panam* per ream to the Danish East India Company. On 13 January 1716 the foundation stone was laid for the paper mill. The power for the stampers of the mill was obtained from a tread mill driven by bullocks. The staff of the paper mill consisted of 22 persons. In the autumn of 1722 the missionaries decided to sell the buildings of the paper mill because the mill ran into difficulties.[16]

The missionaries decided to print the letters to be sent in Portuguese, Tamil and English at the printing press. A letter in Portuguese dated 7 April 1713 to Reverend George Lewis, the Anglican chaplain to the Honourable English East India Company at Fort St. George giving an account of the method of instruction used in the charity schools of the church called Jerusalem in Tranquebar by the Protestant missionaries got printed at the Tranquebar Press. Ziegenbalg had mentioned in this letter that the printing press which the Danish mission had received from the Society for Promotion of Christian Knowledge. He wrote 'We may remember on this occasion, how much the art of printing contributed to the manifestation of divine truths, and the spreading of books for that end, at the time of the happy Reformation, which we read of in history, with thanksgiving to Almighty God'.[17] Further another letter addressed to the Tamils by the missionaries of Tranquebar was printed in 1717. Again yet another letter from William Wake, the Archbishop of Canterbury to Ziegenbalg and Grundler was printed in 1719 for wide circulation.[18]

Printing Tamil Books and Pamphlets on Protestantism in Tranquebar

The missionaries in Tranquebar used the feathers of the Turkey-cocks for writing on paper with ink. They sharpened the feather according to their needs. Benjamin Schultze in his letter dated 3 December 1720 from Tranquebar to Neubeuer in Germany requested to send feathers of the Turkey-cocks for use. He also said that one-hour running sand clock was urgently needed to note the timings. The sand clocks sent earlier from England were used for long and so they had become useless. He wrote these were essential for doing their missionary work. Johann Ernst Grundler the Protestant missionary in Tranquebar learnt Tamil well and he wrote a sermon in Tamil. Benjamin Schultze therefore took efforts and he saw to the printing of the same in 1720. It was titled '*Visuvamullapergalukku varugira pakkyangalai vezhipaduthugira pirasangam: Intha pirasangamaanathu tharan-ganpadiyile navamaay kuttapatta yerusalem engira kovilukk utpatta kirisithavargalukku kuruvaay iruntha makisatta yovannak eranesathuk kirintalar. Kristhu pirantha ayirathu elupathi irupatham varusamaagira pothu ithu tharanganpadiyile irukkira paathirimargaluday achiley pathipikkapattuthu*'.[19]

In 1721 the book of Christopher Wilkens's Preparation to Lord's Supper in German was translated by Malayappan and it was checked and revised by Benjamin Schultze. It appeared in print. The Tamil title was '*Narkarunai Posthagam: Archayasista Narkarunaikku Paathiram Ullavanaka, Kristhu pirantha 1721 varum Tharangapaaddi achchile pathipikkapattathu*, and the Latin title was '*Solidissima Instituto Sanctae Coenae: inqua ostenditu qua praeparatione ante: Qua exteriorum interiorumque morum observationae circa: et qua novitiate vitae post usum sanctae coenae digne sacramentum celebraturus se probare debeat in gratiam christianae gentis Damulorum exhibita a missionaria Danica Benjamin Schultze, Trangambariae, Typis ac sumptibus Missionis Danicae, MDCCXXI*'.[20]

The missionaries prepared writings in Tamil in the mode of dialogues. Such dialogues prepared also got printed owing to their plan to distribute the same amongst the people. In 1728 we find a small book '*Islamaana-vanum kristaananum karai yerugira vazhiyin periley onrukkonru pannugira pirasangam*' (A common dialogue between a Muslim and a Christian) and it was composed by Christoph Theodosius Walther. The printed book had a Latin title '*Dialogus inter Moslimun et Christianum de ia ad salvtendeus est unus, mediator dei et hominum unus, homo Jesus Christus*'.[21]

The work of August Hermann Francke was translated from German to Tamil and the book was published in 1728. The Tamil title was '*Paavika-laana manusar yentha ozhungunpadiey retchikapattu pakkiyam ullavarga-lumaay motchavaangalumaay pogaveneum engira vetha padippinai*'. The printed book had a Latin title '*Doctrina de ordine quo Homines Peccatores Salvari atque Felicis immortalitatis participes fieri debent, editio secunda*'.[22]

The missionaries printed *Retchithalin Ozhlungu*, the catechism in 1730. The printed book had a Latin title '*Ordo Salutis methodo Catechetica, pro divierso Catechumenorum captu trifaria froma exhibitus, & notis quisbusdam instructus*. It had 72 pages.[23]

Reprinting Tamil Books and Pamphlets

Reprinting the pamphlet *Akkiyaanam* was planned by the missionaries and this they felt very important. Ziegenbalg in the meantime wrote at length on denouncing Hinduism. He therefore composed a book on the topic in Tamil titled '*Akkiyaanaththai vezhipaduthugira vetha pramaanam*' and it was printed on 25 October 1713. A new edition later appeared in November 1728 with an altered title. The reason for the same was that two of the words in the original title had contemptible sound to the native ears. 300 copies were printed at that time.

Reprinting the catechism of Martin Luther in Tamil was felt necessary and so earlier what was printed in 1713 got reprinted on 27 July 1715. The Tamil title is *Oru Kristhavana vethapramaanathinpadiye ariya vendina mandirangalaiyum padichu seyyavendina gnayangaliyum pothichivikkira gnaana upadesam, Tharanganpaadi achiley pathikkapattathu, Kristhu pirantha 1715 varusham.*[24] Once again this catechism along with Portuguese text got printed separately on 7 October 1715. The title in Portuguese has been '*Summario das doutrinas Chistaaas por use dos catechumens, Tran-quebar: na estampa dos missionaries del Rey de dennemarck, no anno de christo de 1715*'.[25]

The catechism in Tamil and Portuguese again was reprinted with a different Tamil title '*Karaiyerukirathukku surukkamaaha ariyavendina gnaana upadesathinyudaya kuripidam*' and the printing was completed on

14 September 1717.[26] Philipp Jakob Spencer's catechism translated and printed in 1713 was planned to be reprinted in 1718. Reprinting the book was completed on 14 January 1719 at Tranquebar with the title *Gnaanu-padesthainyuda kurippidam*. It has 178 pages.[27]

The book titled '*Motchathukku pora vazhiyai vezhlipaduthugira gnaana upadesam: Naalaam pathithal*' was reprinted in 1726 for the fourth time.[28] The catechism of Martin Luther was reprinted again in 1730. The Tamil title is '*Mandira Chuvadi: Ithiley vethapiramaanathinpadiey padikka vendiaya anju mandirangalum athugalin viyratikalum anthantha vezhalihaley seyvikka padathakka sepangalum adangi irukkudhu, Rendaam visai*'. The title of the same book in Portuguese has been given. It was called '*A verdadeira religião em hum compendio summariamente compre-hendida, E com testemunhos da escritura sagrada provada segunda impressão, Trangambar, na officina da Real Missão de Dinamarca.*[29]

Printed Tamil Books Found in the Catalogues Issued from the Printing Press at Tranquebar in 1714 and 1733

The publishers in Europe printed the catalogues of the books along with the price for the purpose of marketing. It was also done with a view to facilitate the readers. This practice came to be adopted in Tranquebar with a view to promote the book trade. There are two catalogues of all the books printed from the printing press at Tranquebar which include the list of printed books in various languages. The first catalogue of books of 1714 has twelve pages. We find 1 book in Hebrew, 1 book in Greek, 1 book in Latin, 3 books in Portuguese, 4 books in Spanish, 4 books in French, 4 books in English, 6 books in German, 11 books in Tamil, 12 books in Armenian and 12 books in Malaysian.[30] There were 22 Tamil books printed in Tranquebar between 1712 and 1731.[31]

According to the second catalogue of the list of books printed in 1733 we find that that no book was printed in any language at Tranquebar against the year 1728.[32] There are 74 titles in total printed at Tranquebar between 1712 and 1731. Books were printed in German, Portuguese and English. We find 33 Tamil books printed in total between 1712 and 1731.[33] No Tamil book was printed in the year 1725.

It is very important to note the number of copies of the printed works meant for wide circulation. *Akkiyaanam* the book printed at Tranquebar from the printing press in 1728, the second edition had 300 copies.[34] The Tamil catechism manual with the Portuguese title '*A ordem da salvação, ou doutrina Christaa Brevemente en perguntas e repostas declarada e provada com principaes testemunhos da escritura Sagrada. Juntamente com alhuas Oraçoens e Castigas, Tranquebar En India Oriental na costa de Coromandel Na Estampa dos missionarios del Rey de Dennemark*' printed in 1728 had 200 copies.[35] Thus a minimum of 200 or a maximum of 300 copies were printed in the beginning as per the availability of paper and the nature and content of the book.

Books on Christianity Printed in Tamil at the Printing Press in Tranquebar, 1733-99

Though Protestant missionaries had used palm-leaf manuscripts in Tamil in the beginning by following the local tradition yet they printed books of importance. The book *Retchithalin Ozhlungu* was printed in 1731. It had 72 pages. The Latin title is *Ordo Salutis*. The same was reprinted in 1748.[36] The book then had 102 pages because the missionaries had revised and enlarged the version. The printing of the book was completed on 25 February 1748.

The Christian doctrine was felt important to reach out to the people. Hence the work of August Hermann Francke was translated and it was printed in 1734. The Tamil title is *Kristhumaarkathina Surukkamaana Vizhlakkam*. The Latin title is *Doctrinae Christiane Rudimenta olim ab autore Beato A.H. Franckio theologo Halensi Germania edita: Nunc in lingual Tamulicam translata: Accessit brevis notitia de S. Scriptura religione*.[37]

Christoph Theodosius Walther wrote a book in Tamil on the history of the church and it was printed in 1735 from Tranquebar.[38] It was a translation and revision of an earlier Portuguese history of the Christian church. The Tamil title is *Vaiyam thonriya nazhl muthal innaal varaiyum thirusabaiyil nikazhlantha karaana viseshangalai therivikkum sarithira vilakkangkazhlin posthagam*. The book has the Latin title which runs: *Historia Sacra: Rerum in eccelesia inde ab orbe condition ad nostrum usque aetatem gestarum notitiam exhibens Historia Sacra, quae per septem peridoes et veteris et novi testamenti, regni lucis ac tenebrarum originem, progressus certamina et vicisittudines, nec nou eclessiae regimen et disciplinam atque primas origines particularium doctrinarum et rituum in compendio tradit: Illustrantur subinde vaticinia prophetarum, ex historiarum monumentis; addunturque synchronossimi historiae exoticae, praefertim indicae: in gratiam exercitatiorum in Ecclesiae Tamulicae.*

Some books were reprinted again and again. The book titled '*Tharangambadiyile irukkura Gurumaargal Thamizh saathiyaar ellorukkum ezhuthina nirupam, Naalam pathithal*' was published as the fourth edition in 1744.[39] The third edition of *Akkiyaanam* was printed and it has 56 pages. After throwing away the printed waste and doing the neat binding we find 1136 copies were available on 2 October 1745. Thus more copies of books had come to be printed. The book was titled in Tamil '*Mennana millamaiye thanaiya aruvarukkapadathakka kariyam enrum athiley nikkira pergal yeppadi retcshikapattu karaiyeralam enrum vezhipadugira vetha piramaanam*'.[40] It has a Latin title called '*Regula didascalica de gentilitate abominda et quomdo gentiles liberari atque salvari possint edito tertia*'.

Motchathukku pora vazhiyai vezhipaduthugira gnanna upadesam the Tamil catechism first printed in 1716 was reprinted again in 1750. The title is '*Oru Kristhavana Motchathai adairathukku vetha paramaanathina padiye ariya vendina vizhlakkangalaiyum mandirangalaiyum padichu seyya vendina nayayangalaiyum pothichivikkira gnaana upadesam*'.[41] The book earlier had only 24 pages. The missionaries had revised and enlarged the contents and so the book when reprinted had 48 pages. We find its eighth edition in 1777 printed at Tranquebar.[42] This book had spiritual instruction, with prayers composed by the Lutheran missionaries. The title of the eighth edition is *Motchathukku pora vazhiyai vezhipaduthugira Gnanna upadesam: Yettam pathithal*.[43]

The pastoral letters in Tamil composed and circulated by the missionaries to the natives were also again and again got reprinted. The famous one titled '*Tharangambadiyile irukkura gurumaargal thamizh saathiyaar ellorukkum ezhuthina nirupam*: *Aintham visai*, was reprinted in 1752 and it was the fifth edition.[44]

The missionaries of Tranquebar had targeted the Tamil Muslims for conversion. Hence they wrote and published such a literature and printed it in 1727. This was reprinted as the third edition in 1753. The book has 48 pages. It was composed by Christoph Theodosius Walther. The Tamil title is *Islamaanavan krisithamaanavan karai yergira vazhiyin peril onruk konru pannugira prasangam*. There is a biblical quotation from 1, Timothy, 2:5 in Arabic woodcut and we find mention '*ala allah wahid wasit allah wa-al-nas wahid al-insan yasu al-masih*'.[45] We find a Latin title in the printed book which runs '*Dialogus inter-Moslimum et Christianum de via ad salvtem dues est unus mediator dei et hominum unus nomo Jesus Christus*'.

The books of Apocrypha in the Old Testament printed in 1727 got reprinted in 1761. Its title in Tamil is *Sirakku engiravar ezhuthi vaitha Gnaanam*.[46] Another book titled '*Kirisithamaana Upadesathin surukkamana vizhlakkam: Ithiley aynthu mandirangalum athugalin viyarathigalum anthantha vezhaikaliley sebika padathakka sepangalum adangi irukkuthu- Aaraam visai*' was reprinted as the sixth edition in 1761.[47] The Bible quotations and selection of texts were made in Tamil to reach out to the people. The book in Tamil titled '*Vetha Vaakiyangal: Ithil Paraaparan aruliseytha vethamaanhalin ezhuthu adangi irukkudhuthu*' was printed in 1762. The Latin title is '*Dicta Biblica, ex codice sacro slectaa, secundum ordinem articulorum theologiae thetica collecta, in usum scholarum ecclesiae Tamulicae ad perdiscendum spatio LII. Hebdomadum, accomodata, et in duas partes repartita*'.[48]

Benjamin Schultze's work titled '*Meyyana Sarvesuranum meyyana manushanum onnaairukkira yesu kristhu naatharaanavar intha bhoologathiley sagala manusargalai paavathinudaya adumaithanuthuleyum yenyennaikkum nirkira naragathinudaya akkiineyulum ninru meelkkathakathaga thammudaya sarirathileyum thammudya aathumathulayeum yeththinai ninaivulagaiyum vethanaigaleyum kadaisiliey maranathilum nangu sollappadaatha porumaiyodu paddupattaryenru surukkamaaga vezhipaduthugira sarithira posthagam*' printed in 1723 was reprinted in 1766. The Latin title is *Historia passionis, mortis resurrectionis et ascenscionis Jesu Christi. Fili Dei et Mariae Virginis, Tamulice, ex IV Evangelis Conscripts, Editio tertia.* The book in duodecimo, has a new and revised title *Yesukristhu naatharaanavar Paadupattaarenru vezhipaduthugira kathai posthagam.*[49]

The fourth edition of *Akkiyaanam* was printed in 1772 at the press in Tranquebar.[50] Christian Friedrich Schwartz the missionary composed a work on a dialogue between a heathen and a Christian. It was titled '*Akkiyannikum kristhavanukkum undaana sampaashanai*'.[51] It was reprinted at Tranquebar in 1783 and also again in 1791.

The book titled '*Mokshattukku pora vazhiyai vezhipaduthugira gnaana upadesam*' was printed in 1777. It had spiritual instruction, with prayers composed by the Lutheran missionaries.[52] In 1781, a Protestant liturgy cum ritual book titled *Tharangambadi thiruchabayil vazhangum gnaana muraimaigazhin vizhlakkam* was printed at the Tranquebar press in a type apparently derived from the fonts at that time used in Sri Lanka.[53] The book has the Latin title called *Rituale Trangambaricum*. It has 141 printed pages. Some of the pages printed were also issued as separate pamphlets and we find the baptism ritual in Tamil titled '*Sirupillaikalukku gnaanasnanam kodukkira varthamaanam*. The Latin title '*De Baptismo infantum*' is also added and bound for use as a pamphlet.[54]

Reprinting of Tamil books continued in 1783 and we find the second edition of *Gnaana upadesathina kurippidam: Irandaam pathithal.*[55] Further we also find printing of new books. Christian Friedrich Schwartz's work titled 'Vikkiraha *pattikkaaranukkum kristhavanukkum undaana sampaasanai*' was printed in 1783.[56] The third edition of '*Gnnaana Sangeethangaludaya posthagam: Ithiley Daavidenpavarum veru sila archaysistavargalum paadina 350 sangethhangal adangi Irukkuthu: Muntram Pathithal*' was printed in 1785.[57] The missionaries published a book on explaining Christian religion in 1796. It was in Tamil titled *Kirisithamarkathina surukkamana vizhlakkam*.[58]

In 1799 '*Thiruchabaiyin Sarithira Posthagam: Ithil sindhu mudaliya pala raachiya sarithirangalum sangirika pattathu*' composed earlier by Christoph Theodosius Walther was reprinted. It is the second edition and has 316 pages. The Latin title is *Historia ecclesiastica. Cui adduntur Synchronismi Historiae Exoticae, praesertim Indicae, Editio Secunda*.[59] This book on Protestant church history contains Beschi's unpublished *Vetha Vizhlakkam* of 1728 and writings of Roberto Nobili the Jesuit.[60] Thus whatever was found useful from the Catholic writings were freely came to be used by the Protestants.

Printed books at the printing press in Tranquebar were bound well and it was done in the binding unit of the press. The work in the beginning was carried out by Timothy and after his death some native Christians were trained. They were employed in the press. Leather was used for binding the books of the Danish mission's own use and also for the use of the Europeans. Three natives were found employed as book-binders in 1748. We find the same three persons had continued to work as book-binders even in 1769.[61]

Printing the Tamil Bible: The Old Testament and the New Testament from the Press in Tranquebar, 1714-1796

The missionaries were eager to print the New Testament (the first part) in Tamil and it was printed on 23 September 1714 with Halle sent type font. The second part of the New Testament was finished with Adler's smaller types of font cast locally from the lead wrappings of imported Cheshire Cheese at Tranquebar and it was printed on 13 July 1715. The first leaf of this book and the contents page is printed in the larger Leipzig Tamil font. The types used in Ziegenbalg's New Testament are clear and they run like long chains without any space between words. The types were exact reproductions of the characters of the Tamil inscriptions of the seventeenth century. There were no dots on the consonants and no extra symbol to denote the long vowels. The New Testament printed was dedicated to King Friedrich IV of Denmark.

The first Tamil Bible translated had appeared in print in 1714 had the four Gospels and the Acts of the Apostles and it was called the New Testament Part I. The Tamil title is '*Suthanaagiya Sarvesuranaanirukkira yesukristhu naatharaanavar indha bhulogathiley manushanaai pirantha viseshangalaiyum bhoduvicha upadesangaliyum seytha arputhangalaiyum manusharukku vendi paadupattu yellaraiyum moondu raetchithuvitha vaanagalaiyum uyirodey ezhunthiruinthu paralogathiley magaimaiyaga yerinathaiyum avarudaya seshargalagiya apostalarmaargal logam yengum poey ippadikothavichu viseshangalai sagala senangallukkum pirasangam panninathaiyum vezhipaduthugira puthu yerpaadinudaya muthalam vaguppagiya Anju veda posthagam, Kristu piratha Ayirathu yezhunuthu pathinaalam varushamgairapothu Tharanganpadiyiley irukkira paathrimaargaludaya achiley pathipikka pattathu'*. The Latin title printed is '*Novum Testamentum Domini Nostri Jesu Christi, ex Originali Texte in Linguam Damulicam o Versum, in Usum Gentis Malabaricae, opera et studio Bartholomrei Ziegenbalg et Joan. Ernesti Grundleri Serenissimi Danise Regis Friderici IV ad Indos Orientales Missionariorum, Tranquebariae, MDCCXIV*'.[62]

In 1715 the letters of St. Paul to the Romans to Revelations of the New Testament Part II by Bartolomaeus Ziegenbalg and Johann Ernst Gruendler was printed. The Tamil title is '*Archasishta aposthalarmaargalaay irukkira pavulos engiravar romaa pattanathaarukku yezhuthi anuppina nirupamum, korinthiya engira pattanathaarukku yezhuthi annupina rendu nirupamum, kalaachiya engira thesatthaarukku yezhuthi annupina nirupamum, yebesiyaa engira pattanathaarukku yezhuthi annupinna nirupamum, philippa engira pattanathaarukku yezhuthi anuppina nirupamum, kolossey engira pattanatharukku yezhuthi anuppina nirpamum, thessaloniya engira pattanathaarukku yezhuthi anupinna rendu nirupamum, thimotheus engiravarukku yezhthuthi anuppina rendu nirupamum, filiomin engiravarukku yezuthi annupina nirupamum, yebireya saathiyarukku yezuthi anuppina nirupamaum, yakobus engiravarukku yezhuthi anuppina nirupamum, pedurus engiravarukku yezuthi anuppina rendu nirpamum, yoennans engiravarukku yezuthi anuppina moonu nirupamum, yudasengirvar yezhuthi anuppina nirupamum, yoyannansengiravrukku vantha arivippinudaya parama ragasiya posthagamamumagira puthu yerpaatinudaya rendaam vaguppagira irupathi rendu vetha posthagam*'.[63]

In 1719 we find the re-issue of New Testament in Tamil of 1715 that appeared in print. The Tamil title was '*Suthanaagiya Sarvesuranaanirukkira yesykristhu naatharaanavar inda bhulogathiley manushanaai pirantha viseshangalaiyum bhoduvicha upadesangaliyum seytha arputhangalaiyum manusharukku vendi paadupattu yellaraiyum moondu raetchithuvitha vaanagalaiyum uyirodey ezhunthiruinthu paralogathiley magaimaiyaga yerinathaiyum avarudaya seshargalagiya apostalarmaargal logam yengum poey ippadikothavichu viseshangalai sagala senangallukkum pirasangam panninathaiyum vezhipaduthugira puthu yerpaadinudaya muthalam vaguppagiya Anju veda posthagam. Kristu piratha Ayirathu yezhunuthu pathonpathaam varushamgairapothu Tharanganpadiyiley irukkira paathrimaargaludaya achiley pathipikka pattathu*'.[64]

In 1722 the New Testament revised by Benjamin Schultze with a Latin preface dated 16 October 1722 is a second edition of Ziegenbalg and J.E. Grundler appeared in print. The Tamil title was '*Suthanaagiya Sarvesuranaanirukkira yesukristhu naatharaanavar inda bhulogathiley manushanaai pirantha viseshangalaiyum bhoduvicha upadesangaliyum seytha arputhangalaiyum manusharukku vendi paadupattu yellaraiyum moondu raetchithuvitha vaanagalaiyum uyirodey ezhunthiruinthu paralogathiley magaimaiyaga yerinathaiyum avarudaya seshargalagiya apostalarmaargal logam yengum poey ippadikothavichu viseshangalai sagala senangallukkum pirasangam panninathaiyum vezhipaduthugira puthu yerpaadinudaya muthalam vaguppagiya Anju vetha posthagam*'. The Latin title was '*Novum Jesu Christi Testamentum, ex originali textu in linguam damulicam versum opera & studia Bartholomaei Ziegenbalgi & Jo. Ern Grundleri–Daniae Regis Friederici IV, Ad Indos orientles missionariorum, Editio secunda correctior et accessione summariorum, cujusvis capitis auctior, Tranquebariae, Typis Damulicis missionis Danicae, MDCCXXII*' and the book was in octavo.[65]

In 1723 the Old Testament from the book of Genesis to Judges by Ziegenbalg, Part I was printed. The Tamil title was '*Sarvathukkum vallavarumaay anaadhiyaai irukkiravarmaay yengum niranjavarumaay irukkira parraapara vasthuvaanavar poorva kaalathiley paramadalithil irunthu thiruvilampathina sathyama veda posthagathin muthalaam vagauppu: ithiley atchshista mosesengiravar sarvesuranyadaya thiruvaayile ninru ketta gnayangalayum kartharaanavar adiilay paralogathayum bhoologathayum yeppadi undaakinar yengirathayum avar sagala senanga-lukkiley oru kolaithirathai thammudaya sonthamaana senangkallaga therindu kondaar engirathayum vezhipaduthugira mosesuvin anju posthagangalaiyum, yousuvaa vengiravarudaya gnaana posthagamum, neethikaaragaludaya vaththamanangalay kaanpikkira posthagamum, adangi irukkudhu: Kristu pirandhu ayriath yezhuthnuthi irupathu moonam varushamgira poedhu, ithu thatanganpaadiiley irukkira paathrimar-galudaya achiley pathipikka pattudhu, 1723* : The Latin title was '*Biblia Damlica, seu quod Deus est locutus Veteris Testamenti, pars prima, in qua Mosis libri quinque, Josuae liber unus atque liber unus Judicum, studio & opera Bartholomaei Ziegenbalgi, Missionarii, ad Indos orinetales in lingua Damulicam versi continentur, Tranquebariae, in littore Coromnadelino typis et sumtibus Missionis Danicae, MDCCXXIII*' and the book was in quarto.[66]

In 1724 the book of Psalms by Benjamin Schultze was printed under the Tamil title '*Daavidengiravar yezhuthivaitha gnaana sangeethan-galudaya posthagam'*. The Latin title was '*Liber Psalmorum Davidis regis et prophetae, ex originali textu in lingua damulicam versus opera et studio*

Benjamin Schultze ad Indos orientales Missionarii, Tranquebariae, MDCCXXIV and the book was in octavo.[67]

In 1726 the Old Testament, from the book of Ruth to Song of Songs by Benjamin Schultze, Part II was printed. The Tamil title was '*Azhavillatha gnnanamullavarumaay azhavillatha kirubaiullavarumaay azhavillatha deivigiamullavray irukkira parraapara vasthuvaanavar pazhaya yerpaatinyudaya kaalathiley thiruvilampathina veda posthagathin rendaam vagauppu: ithiley archiyasishta ruth engiravzhludaya posthagamum, archiyasishta samuyel yengiravrudaya muthalaam posthagmum, rendam posthagamum Maarassakaludaya muthalam posthagamum, rendam posthagamum, paralipomvenru sollapatta muthalaam posthagamum, rendam posthagamum, echcheruvengiravarudaya posthagamum, neyemiya-vengiravrudaya posthagamum, yesther engarivaludaya posthgamum, yobu engiravaruday posthagamum, Daavidengriavar ezhuthi vaitha gnnana sangeethngalengira posthagamum, Salamon engiravr pesina vaakiyam-galudaya posthagamum, ekkeilsesiyesh engira naamathai kondirukkira posthagamum, unnathamaana paatinuduaya posthagamum adangai irukkudhu.Kristu pirandhu 1726 varushamagira poedhu, ithu thatanganpaa-diiley irukkira paathrimargaludaya achiley pathipikka pattudhu.* The Latin title was '*Biblia Damulica, seu quod Deus Sapientissimius in sua Divina oeconomia cumn Populo Israelitico et Egit t et Locutus est. Veteris Testanenti Pars Secunda, in qua Libellus Ruth, Samnzelis Liber Prior et Posterior, Liber Nehemiae, Liber Esther, Liber Jobi, Liber Psalmorum Davidis, Liber Proverbium, Liber Ecclesiastae, et Liber Cantici Canticorum, studio et opera Bartholomaei Ziegenbalgii et Benjamini Schultzi Missionariorum ad Indos orientalis, in linguam Damulicam versi continentur, Tranquebariae- MDCCXXVI'* and the book was in quarto.[68]

In 1727 the Old Testament, from the book of Isaiah to Malachi by Benjamin Schultze, Part III was printed. The Tamil title was '*Anju kanda seeraay irukkiravarumaay, yellathayum arinthu irukkiravarumaay, azha-villatha parisuthamullavarumaay irukkira parraapara vasthuvaanavar pazhaya yerpaadu irukkirapothu puthu yerpadinyadya magimaiayai vezhipaduthapora yesu kristhuvin periley thiruvilampathina veda posthagtahin moonam vagauppu: Ithialey archiyasishta theergatharisi-galagira yesaypiyavengairavr kanda therisanthaninudya posthagamum, yeremiyavengiravar pannina pirasangathinyudaya posthgamum, avar paadina pulambalinyudaya posthgamaum, ysekkiyelengiravrakku kaan-pikka patta therisanathinyadya posthagamum, Daaniyelengiravar therisanamaaga kanda vathamaanagaludaya posthagamum, oseyaasum, yoyellum, Aamossum,obaadiyaavum, yonaasum, mikkavum, naahummum, abakukkum, sepaaniyavum, aakkayum, sakarayaasum, malayosum engira-*

vargal theerkatharisanamaaga solli, ezhuthi vaitha posthagangalum adangi irukkudhu, Kristhu pirandhu 1727 varushamagira poedhu, ithu thatanganpaadiiley irukkira paathrimargaludaya achiley pathipikka pattadhu. The Latin title was '*Biblia Damulica, seu quod Deus Omnniscius de gratia in Jesu Christo tempore Novi Testamenti Revelanda per Sanctos suos Prophetas est Vaticinatus. Veteris Testamenti Pars Tertia, in qua Prophetae Majores, Esaias, Jeremias, ejusdemque Lamentationes, Ezechiel, Daniel; Prophetae Minores, Hoseas, Joel, Amos, Obadia, Jona, Micha, Nahum, Habacuc, Zephania, Haggai, Zacharias, et Malachias, studio et opera, Bartholomaei Ziegenbalgii et Benjamini Schultzi, Missionariorum ad Indos orientalis, in linguam Damulicam versi continentur, Tranquebariae, MDCCXXVII'* and the book was in quarto.[69]

In 1728 Apocrypha from the book of Tobit to the Prayer of Manasseh, the Old Testament Part IV was printed. The Tamil title was *Pazhaya yerpattin kaalathinudya theerkatharisagalikku pirakaalam undaayiruntha yuthasamayathayaragiya punniyathumakkal dharma nadakkaigalin perilleyum, akkaalam thuvakki Yesunaathar bhulogathiley manushanaga vanthu pirantha mattukkum thirusabaiiley nadantha kaaranagalin perilleyum yeuzthi vaitha apocripha yengira naamamulla gnaana posthangalagiya gnaathinudaya posthagamum seeraakengirvarudaya posthagamum, yesderengiravar ezhuthina posthagamum, thobiasne-giravarduaya posthagamum, yudithengirvazhludaya posthagamum, Estherengiravazhludaya posthagathodey sernthuirukkirathum, Baaruchengiravarudaya posthagamum, eremiya ezuthina nirupamum, Soolaiiley iruntha moonupergal Isha thothirathinduaya vaarthaigalum, Susaanengiravazhlukku sambuvicha sethiyum, bellengira vikkirathinuda-yavum, dhiraakonvengira malaipaambinudayavum vaththammanamum, makkabeyengiravargaludaya muthalaam posthagamum, rendaam posthagamum, moonaam posthagamum, manassessengiravarudaya sepamum adangi irukkudhu, Kristhu pirandhu 1728 varushamagira poedhu, ithu tharanganpaadiiley irukkira paathrimargaludaya achiley pathipikka pattadhu*'. The Latin title was '*Libri Apocryphi, seu Libri a quibusdam Piis Viris Ecclesice Antiquce Judaicaepost Prophetas Veteris Testamenti Scripti, continentes partim Varias Regulas Vitce Utiles,partim Supplemen-tum Historic Ecclesiasticae Veteris Testamenti, scilicet Liber Sapientiae, Ecclesiasticus sive Sirach, Liber Esdrce, Liber Tobice, Liber Judith, A djectiones ad Librum Esther, Liberaruch, Epistola Jeremice, A djectiones ad Danielem seu Trium Virorum Hymnologia, Historia Sosannae, item Belis et Draconis, Maccabaeorum Liber Primus, Secundus, et Tertius, denique Oratio Manassis, studio et opera, Ziegenbalgii et Schultzii in linguam Damulicam versi, Trangambariae, Typis & Impressis Missionis Danicae, MDCCXXVIII*' and the book was in quarto.[70]

In 1739 the Gospel of St. Mathew, third edition titled '*Yesu Kristhu Swamiyin Seensanagiya aposthalum suviseganumaayiruntha archaysishta Mathei enbavar ezhuthivaitha suviseshath aagamam*' was printed. The Latin title was '*Evangelium Matthaei de Domini Nostri Jesv Christi, qui est Filius Dei, nativitate humana, doctrina miraculis adserta, conversatione inculpate, morte expiatrice, gloriosa resurrectione et, instiuta in terries ecclesia, in coelos adscencu./ Matthaeus, Editio Tertia, prioribus ad genium linguae Tamulicae textumque originalem curatius exacta, succinstisque summaries atque parallelismo historico et exegetico adornata, Editio Tertia), Trangambariae, Missionis Danicae, MDCCXXXIX*' and it was in octavo.[71]

In 1747 the Book of Psalms, second edition titled '*Raasavum Thirgatharisiyumayiruntha Archisista Dhavidengiravar ezhuthi vaitha Gaana snageethangaludaya Posthgam: Ithilaye Dhavid enbavarum vaeri sila archisitavargalum paadina 150 sangethangal adangiirukuthu, Randaam pathithal*, Kristhu pirantha 1747ile ithu Tharanganpaadiile achadikapattathu' was printed. The Latin title was '*Liber Psalmorum Davidis, Regis et prophetae: ex originali textu in linguam Tamulicam versus, opera & studio Benjamin Schultze, ad Indos orientalesmissionarii, Editio secunda, Trangambariae: typis missionis danicae, anno MDCCXLVII*' and it was in octavo.[72]

In 1758 the four gospels of the New Testament volume one printed earlier in 1714 and 1715 were again printed for the third time. The Tamil title was *Ualga Retchakaraaana Yesu Swamiyin Muttinar manusharagiya Mathei, Maarku, Lukka, Yovan enpavargal avar peril yezhuthi vaitha naalu suviseshamath aagamangal, Munraam Visai*'. The Latin title was '*Domini Nostri Jesu Christi, qui est servitor mundi, noui foederis libri: S. Matthaei, Marci, Lucae et Joannis Evangelia, Apostolorum Jesu Acta revelation, editio tertia, Trangamabriae typis sumtibusque missionis Danicae, anno MDCCLVIII*'. Further the New Testament, volume two containing the Acts of the Apostles was also reprinted in 1758 under the Tamil title '*Ulaga retchakraana yesu kristhu sami undu pannina puthu udanpadikaiyin agaamangal*' and it had no Latin title which was normally found in books.[73]

In 1760 reprint of Apocrypha of 1727, earlier translated by Benjamin Schultze, the Old Testament appeared under the Tamil title *Siraakku engiravr yezhuthi vaitha Gnaanam-Irandam Visai*.[74]

Seventeen years later (in 1777) the revised version of Ziegenbalg and Schultze's Old Testament from Genesis to Judith was done by Johann Philipp Fabricius and it got printed under the Tamil title '*Manushasaathi Ratchikaapattu varathakka sarvalogathaya Paraaparanaana Karthar aruli seytha Sathya vetham, Muthalam Pangu*'. The Latin title was '*Librorum Sacrorum Veteris Testamenti Pars prima, continens Libros Mosis, Josuae et Judicum,*

Editio secunda Correctioner, Trangambariae, Typis sumptibus Missionis Danicae, MDCCLXXVII'.[75]

In 1782 the revised version of Old Testament of 1726 and the translations from Ruth-Job by Johann Philipp Fabricius was printed under the Tamil title '*Manusaathi ratechikka padavrakathakka sarvalogathaya paraaparanana Karthar aruliseytha sathya vedam, Irandaam pangu*'. The Latin title was '*Librorum Sacrorum Veteris testamenti pars secunda: continens Libros Ruth, II. Samuelis, II. regnum, II. Chronicorum, Esrae, Nehemiae, Esther et Jobi, Editio secunda Correctioner, Trangambariae, Typis sumptibus Missionis Danicae, MDCCLXXXII*'.[76]

In 1785 the third edition of Psalms of the Old Testament appeared in print under the Tamil title '*Gnnaana Sangeethangaludaya posthagam: Ithiley Davidenpavarum veru sila archaysistavargalum paadina 350 sangethhangal adangi Irukkuthu, Muntram Pathithal, Kristhu pirantha 1785 varushathiley ithu tharangapadiyile missiyon achchukudathileypathika pattaththu*'.[77]

In 1788 the fourth edition of New Testament part I of 1715 got printed under the Tamil title '*Ulaga Ratchagraraana Yesu Swamiyin Muthinar manusharagiya Mathei, Marku, Lukaa, Yovaan yenbavargal peril yezhuthi vaitha naalu suviseshath thaagamangal*'. The Latin title was '*Domini Nostri Jesu Christi qui est Servator Mundi Novi Foederis Libri Pars Prima S. Matthei, Marci, Lucae et Johannis Evangelia, Editio Quarta, Trangambariae, Typis Sumtibusque Missionis Danicae, Anno MDCCLXXXVIII*'.[78]

In 1791 the translations of Psalms-Song of Songs, by Johann Philipp Fabricius appeared in print under the Tamil title '*Manushasaathi retchikapattuvarathakka sarvalokathaya paraaparanana kartar aruli seydha sathya vedam, Munraam pangu*'. The Latin title was '*Librorum Sacrorum Veteris, pars tertia, Continens Libros psalmorum, Proverbiorum, Ecclesiastae et Cantici Canticorum, Editio secunda Correctioner, Trangambariae, Typis sumptibus Missionis Danicae, MDCCXCI*'.[79]

In 1796 the Old Testament from Isaiah to Malachi translated by Johann Philipp Fabricius got printed under the Tamil title '*Manushasaathi retchikapattuvarathakka sarvalokathaya paraaparanana kartar aruli seydha sathya vetham, naalam pangu*'. The Latin title was '*Librorum Sacrorum Veteris Testamenti, Pars Quarta, In qua Libri Prophetarum Majorum & Minorum continentur, editio secunda Correctioner, Trangambariae, Typis sumptibus Missionis Danicae, MDCCXCVI*'.[80]

It must be stated that the titles of the Tamil Bible printed had been long like Hanuman's tail. The Latin titles had also been always accompanied except once. There are three different sizes of the printed Tamil Bible while some are quarto, some in octavo and some in duodecimo.

Hymn Books Printed in Tamil at Tranquebar, 1713-1756

Ziegenbalg with the assistance of Grundler aimed to translate songs in Tamil and we find 48 hymns successfully made from German to Tamil in 1713 and they were set to Tamil music. These hymns for translation were taken from the song book of Johann Anastasius Freylinghausen in German.[81] In 1715 we find songs were printed in a hymn book titled 'the book containing 48 songs that are sung by the Christians belonging to the newly erected Church of Jerusalem in Tranquebar' and this was the first Tamil hymnal printed. Grundler began to revise the hymnal and he carried out the work since 22 November 1714. It is noticed in records that the hymnal with 48 songs got printed at Tranquebar on 24 January 1715.[82] The Tamil title of the book was *Pirathani Posthagam* and it was in octavo and the print order was 300 copies.[83]

Again a hymn book was printed at Tranquebar in 1719.[84] The translated hymns of 48 from German into Tamil for worship were again reprinted in a book in 1721. This was the next hymn book (second edition) published. This had 48 songs in Tamil meter and also according to the Tamil music scale.[85] Schultze had successfully translated by 1723 various songs i.e., 112 hymns from German into Tamil and the book titled '*Gnaanap-paatukalin posthaham*' was printed in Tranquebar in 1723.[86] This was the third edition of hymns that appeared with 160 songs compiled by him.[87] It contained such well known German hymns such as '*Wach auf mein hertz und singe*', '*Christus der ist mein heben*' and '*Dancksei gott in der Hohe*'.[88] Schultze's *Hymnologia Tamulica* containing 112 hymns was again printed in 1725.

Christian Friedrich Pressier and Christoph Theodosius Walther the missionaries also translated hymns from German into Tamil in 1747. The Latin title of the book is '*Hymnologia Tamulica*'. It contained 307 songs. This is the fifth edition of hymns appeared in 1756 The Tamil title is *Puthithaay thamizha paduthapatta gnaana paatukkal adangiirukkira posthagam*. The Latin and the Tamil titles have been partly printed in red.[89] The sixth edition of '*Gnaana paattugalin posthagam: Aaraam pathiththal*' appeared in 1787 and it contained 58 hymns.

Printing Books on Tamil Grammar and Portuguese-Tamil Dictionary, 1731-1739

The Jesuits had printed Tamil-Portuguese Dictionary of Antão Proença at Ambalakaadu in 1679. It was widely used by people. However there was no Portuguese-Tamil dictionary. Hence Nikolaus Dal (1690-1747) the missionary in Tranquebar composed Portuguese and Tamil vocabulary with Portuguese grammar. This book appeared in print in 1731. It was titled

'*Quarta parte da grammatica Portugueza, convem a saber hum vocabulario em portuguez e Malabar, que contem os nomes, verbos e adverbios de ambas as lingoas, que sao mais usados no trata cotidiano, e dos quaes os Vocabulos Malabares vao impressos com o carcater Tamul, e juntamente com letra Portugueza para o uso da escola Portugueza de Trangambar, Trangambar, Na Officina da Real Missao de Dinmarca, Anno de MDCCXXXI*'.[90]

Costanzo Giuseppe Beschi the Jesuit had composed *Kodunthamizh* (Spoken Tamil grammar) in 1728. The Protestant missionaries found it very useful and so they approached him and sought the consent for publication. Hence *Kodunthamizh* was printed in Tranquebar in 1739. It was titled '*Grammatica Latino-Tamulica: Ubi de Vulgari Tamulicae Linguae Idiomate, Kodun-Thamizh dicto, ad Usum Missionarum Soc. Ise/ Auctore P. Constantino Iosepho Beschio, eyjusdem Societ, In regno Madurensi missionario, A.D. MDCCXXVIII, Trangambariae: Typis Missionis Danicae, MDCCXXXIX*'.[91]

In the same year Christoph Theodosius Walther's observations of Tamil grammar was printed. It was titled '*Observationes Grammaticae quibus Linguae Tamulicae Idioma Vulgare in usum operariorum in messe Domini intergentes Vulgo Malabares Dictas illustratus/ Christophoro Theodosio Walthero, Trangambariae, Missionis Regiae, MDCCXXXIX*'.[92]

Printing Text Books of Geography in Tamil Composed by the Protestant Missionaries

The missionaries got printed a book in Tamil titled *Bhoologathinudaiya Mudhalaam Pangaagira Europa* (Europe, the first part of the world) at the Tranquebar press in 1732. It has 48 pages. This book appears to be the Tamil-English dictionary of various places in Europe. It is difficult to identify the present names of the cities and countries mentioned in this book because, nearly 300 years ago, those cities and countries in the European continent bore different names. Such subject books were published by the missionaries to impart geographical knowledge to the children at the mission schools in and around Tranquebar. This is yet another proof to show that the German missionaries evinced keen interest to develop the knowledge of the native converts about world geography and also on earth science.[93]

The missionaries had printed a geography book in Tamil from the Tranquebar press in 1732. It is titled *Bhuvana Saasthirathin Per Posthagam: Idhilae Airopa, Aasia, Aprica, America vendrum, pinnai Arachista Pau-luvinudaiya Payanangalae vendrum Paalastheenavendrum Sollappatta Desappayangalilae Adangi yulla Pradhana Desangal Pattanangaludaiya per naamangal vaasik kappadum. Kadaisiyilae Bhuvana Sasthirathukku Aduththa Siridhu Sulogangal Serkkappattirukkudhu* (Heritage book of World Geography). In this, the names of cities are mentioned which are in Europe, Asia, Africa, America besides the names of places visited by Apostle Paul. At the end, we have some data about the universe and a few verses related to the heritage world geography added.[94] The book has 64 pages. We have the title page in Latin and in Tamil.

Printing the Translated Books in Tamil from German and Portuguese at Tranquebar

Translating the book of Johann Anastasius Freylinghausen (1670-1739) titled *Grundlegung der Theologie: Darin die Glaubens-Lehren aus Göttlichem Wort deutlich fürgetragen und zum thäthigen Christenthum wie auch Evangelischen Trost angewendet werden zum Gebrauch des Paedagogii*, printed in Halle in 1703 from German to Tamil was done. The first part of the book translated was titled *Vetha Sasthiram* in Tamil and it was printed at Tranquebar in 1717.[95] The second and the third part of the translation in Tamil on completion had also been printed at Tranquebar.[96]

Translating Johann Wilke's *Communions Buch* from German to Tamil was done by Catechist Malayappan in Tranquebar in 1721-22. The printing of this book began at Tranquebar on 14 June 1721 and completed on 13 February 1722.[97] Malayappan took the assistance of Benjamin Schultze in the course of translation.

Schultze translated the book in Portuguese on the passion and death of Jesus Christ for he thought that it would be useful to natives. He had begun the translation in August 1713 and completed the work later.[98] The book titled '*Meyyana sarvesuranum meyyana manushanum onnaairukkira yesu kristhu naatharaanavar intha bhoologathiley sagala manusargalay paavathinudaya adumaithanuthuleyum yenyennaikkum nirkira naragathinudaya aakkineyulum ninru meezlkkathakathaaga thammudaya sarirathileyum thammudya aathumathulayeum yethinai ninaivugalaiyum vethanaigaleyum kadaisiliey maranaththaium sollappadaatha porumaiyodu paadupattuirunthathu surukkamaaga vezhipaduthugira sarithira posthagam*' (The history book which describes how the lord Jesus Christ, who is the true god and true man in one person bore with indescribable patience, much pain and torment in his body and in his soul and finally died, so that the people of the whole world might be saved from the slavery of sin and from eternal hell) was printed in Tranquebar in 1723.[99] The same book was again reprinted as a second edition with the title '*Manushavathaaram pannina devasuthanaagira yesu kiristhu swami manusha jathiyai retchikka paadupattu marithathanri uyirthu paralogathuku ezhuntharliya sarithiram: Irandaam pathithal*' from Tranquebar in 1740.[100]

Printing Tamil Calendars at the Press in Tranquebar

Anrique Anriquez the Jesuit was the first to examine and introduce the Tamil calendar to the Europeans. He noted Tamil months corresponded to Gregorian calendar. *Thai*, the Tamil month more or less corresponded to January and so he made it identical with January giving it the same number of days. Similarly other months were made to correspond to each other. The table of correspondence was given by Anriquez in his Flos Sanctorum book printed at page 668 in Goa in 1586. He also saw to it that Tamil calendar began in April and made to agree with the Gregorian calendar. Thus the western and Tamil calendars were made to agree.

The Protestant missionaries in Tranquebar printed the calendar in Portuguese from the printing press in Tranquebar in 1712.[101] The missionaries also printed the calendar in Portuguese for the next year (1713) and so it was widely circulated and sent out all over India as an advertisement for the printing press. The Protestant missionaries in Tamil country did not adopt the calendar introduced by Pope Gregory in 1582. They followed the Julian calendar. Even in Europe it happened so until the English adopted the new style of calendar in 1752. The Danish missionaries also followed the same in their diaries thereafter. Europeans did not enforce and impose the Christian calendar system upon the Tamils.[102]

However, we find calendars in Tamil continued to be printed in Tranquebar. The calendar for 1789 was prepared and printed at the end of the year 1788. It is titled *Ulagathin retchakaraana kristhu pirantha aayiraththi yennoothi yenpatthi onpathaam varushaththukku sellum panjangam: Intha panjangam tharanganpayil irukkum misiyon achchukudathil pathipikkapattathu.*[103] It had 14 printed pages. The Tamil calendar for the year 1791 was prepared also by making computations to match the Tamil New Year that began on 10 April 1790 and ended on 9 April 1791. This calendar also had the equivalent months of the western calendar. It had 14 printed pages.[104] Further the calendar for the next year 1792 was also printed in December 1791.[105]

Functioning of the Printing Press and its Problems

A report in 1751 had mentioned the troubles caused by insect ravages in the printing press premises. The white ants had eaten through and damaged the first two sheets of a book printed. The printing press was obliged to have these pages printed once again. It has been noted that such insects were liable give trouble in the hot climate like Tamil country and so they have taken proper and adequate measures to separate the books to facilitate the passing of fresh air between them.[106]

Johann Schloricke was in-charge of the printing press till his death in 1731. Johann Adler set up the type-foundry to produce small Tamil fonts. It has been said that since 1748 the printing work was only looked after by a single native Christian printer well trained by the missionaries and skilled. He was assisted by a soldier who was on his days off. The printing works commenced in 1745 were not finished until 26 August 1751.[107] The printing of a new edition of the shorter catechism commenced in 1761 also had not been completed and the works were still printing even after a gap of one year (in 1762). Further it was reported in 1763 that they were still printing the larger catechism which was going on for more than three years. Thus printing works were moving very slow at the press in Tranquebar.[108] The main reason was lack of manpower.

In 1737 the missionaries of Tranquebar had sent the Danish type-caster to Colombo where he prepared new Tamil types for the Dutch.[109] The Dutch East India Company (VOC) printed Lord' Prayer in Tamil and another book of catechism with this new fonts in 1739. The Gospel of St. Mathew also got printed in Colombo in 1741. The orthographical peculiarities of the scribes of the period under consideration are found. We find that the consonants are not dotted. The short vowels e and o and the long vowels and short are printed alike. The dot characterizes the short vowels 'e' and 'o' as written in this period had been absent. Similarly, the dot which characterized the combination of consonants with the short vowels e and o had also been absent. The numerals representing the year 1743 is printed in Tamil characters. The word for month in Tamil is *maatham* and this is abbreviated and printed as *mii*. The western style punctuation has not been found in the Gospel according to St. Mathew printed in Tamil by the VOC at Colombo in 1741 by Adolphus Cramer. Thus there had been exchange of knowledge on printing between the Danes and the Dutch from Tranquebar to Colombo.

Johann Meissel became the superintendent of the press in Tranquebar in 1755 and later Wilhelm Becker became the superintendent in 1777. Absence of required fonts had been mentioned as the major problem for the printing press. Type founding which was so much important had been previously been attached to the printing press earlier in order to keep the printing press supplied with necessary renewals. But it was separated and very much neglected. In 1748 type required was cut by a soldier when on leave and he was trying to teach another person at the same time.[110] On 12 February 1770 it was reported that printing work in the press was stopped owing to the shortage of types. The former founts cut and cast did enough and more service for several years but they needed to be replaced by newer ones. The ships that sailed from Europe had brought Portuguese and Tamil types and so the printing works had resumed.[111] In 1773, it was mentioned that paper scarcity for printing was a problem. In 1775 paper came from England and Denmark for printing the Tamil Old Testament. The press was highly reliant on the imported paper from Europe since locally produced varieties did not prove suitable for printing purposes.

Johann Christian Meisser from Copenhagen arrived at Tranquebar on 2 July 1755 as the overseer of the printing press. Later Savari Rajan the head-printer succeeded him as the overseer of the press on 23 October 1771 on the death of Meisser. It has been mentioned that Savari Rajan possessed considerable skill in casting the large ornamental initials in a special kind of Indian wood.[112] Becker reached Tranquebar in 1777 as the new overseer of the printing press from Europe and with his assistance the press began to function in a better condition than before.[113]

The printing machine in Tranquebar was operated by the foot.[114] We have also have come to know from records that there was a printing machine operated by both arms and it was a tedious and fatigue to the printer.[115] Thus there were two models of printing presses in use while one by hand and the other by foot driven. Innovations came in printing technologies and wooden printing presses had given way to cast-iron machines. The Tamil types used at the Tranquebar printing press were elegant but conformed to the Tamil then current in palm-leaf writing and inscriptions. Over the years, new versions of the types cut with much difficulty by German engravers at Leipzig and Halle found way to Tranquebar and they were used for decades. With changing economic and political fortunes, the printing press saw a steady decline. There were no Tamil books printed after 1799.[116]

The printing press was dormant and the reasons for not functioning are many. The British had occupied Tranquebar in 1801. James Johnson the traveller had mentioned in 1805 that Tranquebar had lost its importance and it declined.[117] The Danish settlement during the Napoleonic wars had been was under the occupation of the British troops between 1808 and 1815.[118] The Danes were but still liable to yearly payment of *pescush* (tribute) of 2000 *chakarams* to the ruler of Thanjavur in 1815. They did not hold the surrounding villages of Tranquebar at all in sovereignty.[119] The Danish Asiatic Company was finally dissolved in 1843 and King Christian VIII sold Tranquebar to the British in 1845 for a sum of 1,250,000 rupees. The Protestant missionaries had moved over to Madras to work under the patronage extended by the English East India Company.

To conclude it may be mentioned that publication of Tamil books from the printing press in Tranquebar were mostly repeats since 1745 and there were a few exceptions. Many Tamil pamphlets like *Akkiyaanam* were reprinted from time to time. Tranquebar press had printed a total of 338 titles in several languages (bibles, gospels, catechisms, grammars, dictionaries, calendars, etc.,) during the eighteenth century and I have included some of the books like *Meyyana Sarvesuranum meyyana manushanum onnaairukkira yesu kristhu naatharaanavar intha bhoologathiley sagala manusargalai paavathinudaya adumaithanuthuleyum yenyennaikkum nirkira naragathinudaya akkiineyulum ninru meelkkatha-kathaga thammudaya sarirathileyum thammudya aathumathulayeum yeththinai ninaivulagaiyum vethanaigaleyum kadaisiliey maranathilum nangu sollappadaatha porumaiyodu paddupattaryenru surukkamaaga vezhipaduthugira sarithira posthagam*' printed in 1723 and reprinted in 1766, which has escaped the attention of Graham Shaw. Tamil books printed were sent to the library of Fort St. George in Madras, London, Halle and Copenhagen.

Notes

1. Bartholomäus Ziegenbalg, *Propagation of the Gospel in the East: Being a Collection of Letters from the Protestant Missionaries, and other worthy Persons in the East-Indies, & c. Relating to the Mission; the Means of Promoting it; and the Success it hath pleased God to give to the Endeavours used hitherto, for Propagating True Christianity among the Heathen in those Parts, but chiefly on the coast of Coromandel with a map of the East-Indies. III Parts, Published by the direction of the Society for Promoting Christian Knowledge*, London, Printed and Sold by J. Downing, 1709-1718, Part II, p. 15.
2. Ibid., Part III, pp. 1-17.
3. Rosenkilde Volmer, 'Printing in Tranquebar 1712-1845' *The Library Series 5*, vol. 4, 1949, pp. 179-195.
4. Ove K. Nordstrand, 'Some Notes on the Foundation of the Royal Danish Mission Printing Press and Paper Mill at Tranquebar' *Proceedings of the First International Conference-Seminar on Tamil Studies*, 1966, pp. 364-8.
5. Gérald Duverdier, 'Über die Bedeutung Unbedeutender Drucke-Die Ersten Tamilischen Drucke zu Halle (1712-1713)', *Wissenschaftliche Zeitschrift der Martin-Luther-Universität Halle-Wittenberg-Halle*, Jahrgang XXIV, Heft 5, 1975, pp. 103-126.
6. Det Kongelige Bibliotek, Kobenhavn, (hereafter KB), Hjelmst, 486c, *Retchippin Ozhukkam*: *A Ordem da Salvação, ou Doutrina Christaa Brevemente en Pergun-tas e Repostas Declarada e Provada com Principaes Testemunhos da Escritura Sagrada, Juntamente com Alhuas Oraçoens e Castigas,* Tranquebar en India Oriental na Costa de Coromandel, na Estampa dos Missionarios del Rey de Dennemark, Anno 1712.
7. KB, 47-460.
8. Ove K. Nordstrand, Some Notes, p. 366.
9. Ibid.
10. Bibliothek der Franckesche Stiftungen (hereafter BFSt), Halle, C: 38:84; BFSt, C: 38:85; Hans-Werner Gensichen, 'Abominable Heathenism: A Rediscovered

Tract by Bartholomäus Ziegenbalg', *Indian Church History Review,* vol. I, no. 1, 1967, pp. 29-40.

11. *Der Königl. Dänischen Missionarien aus Ost-Indien eingesandter ausführlichen Berichten, Von dem Werck ihrs Ams unter den Heyden, angerichteten Schulen und Gemeinen, ereigneten Hindernissen und schweren Umstanden; Beschaffenheit des Malabarischen Heydenthums, gepflogenen brieflicher Correspondentz und mundlchen Unterredungen mit selbigen heyden*, Teil 1–9, (Continuationen 1–108) Waiserihaus, Halle, 1710–1772 (hereafter HB), vol. I, pp. 635-43; Daniel Jeyaraj and Richard Fox Young (translated, introduced and annotated), *Hindu-Christian Epistolary Self-Discourses: 'Malabarian Correspondence' between German Pietist Missionaries and South Indian Hindus (1712-1714)*, Harrassowitz Verlag, Wiesbaden, 2013, see the twenty sixth letter, pp. 273-7.
12. Daniel Jeyaraj and Richard Fox Young, Hindu-Christian Epistolary, pp. 272-3.
13. BFSt, C: 38:94; *A Expliҫão da Doutrina Christaa Segundo a Ordem do Catecismo do B. Luthero, em Perguntas e Repostas Proposta, e com Necessarias Testemunhos da Escritura Sagrada Provada: Traduziada em Lingoa Portugueza pelos Ministros da Palavra de Deus e Missionarios delrey de Dennemark*, Tranquebar em India Oriental na Costa de Coromandel, na Estampa dos dittos Missionarios, no Anno de 1713.
14. BFSt, 190F:21.
15. Ove K. Nordstrand, Some Notes, pp.367-368.
16. Ibid, p. 368.
17. KB, Hjelmst, 456; Bartholomäus Ziegenbalg, and Johann Ernst Gründler, *A letra a o muy reverendo senhor George Lewis, o ministro da palavra de Deus em Madraspatnam, naqval se da aviso da ordem e instruiçaõ, que se trata nas escolas da charidade da igreja, chamada Jerusalem, em Tranquebar*, Tranquebar, Com letras dos missionarios Reaes de Dennemark, 1713; Bartholomäus Ziegenbalg, Propagation of the Gospel in the East: p.105. See the German translation sent to Halle, HB vol. 1, p. 630.
18. KB, Hjelmst, 459; *Epistola quam venerabilis societas de promvenda Christi Cognitione, in Anglia Propagandi evangeli causa, instituta, ad viros reverendos, dominum Bartholomaeum Ziegenbalg et Dn. Joh. Ernestum Grundler, Danie Regis Missionarios in India orientali*, Tranquebariae, Typis Missionis Danicae, Anno 1719.
19. AFSt, Letter of Benjamin Schultze dated 3 December 1720 from Tranquebar to Neubeuer in Germany; BFSt, C: 38:90; C: 38:96.
20. KB, HJ, 484.
21. KB, 7-212; KB HJ 486.
22. KB, 3-471; KB HJ 375.
23. British Library, London (hereafter BL), no. 14170.a.29; BL, or.90.a.65; KB, 3-470.
24. KB, HJ, 376.
25. KB, HJ 486.
26. *Karaiyerugiradhukku Surukkamaaha Ariya Vendina Gnaana Upadesathinudaya Kurippidam*, Tranquebar, 1717, KB, 3-472; KB, HJ 376.

27. *Gnaana Upadesathinudaya Kurippidam*, Tranquebar, 1718, KB, HJ 441; BFSt, C: 64.1.
28. KB, HJ, 376; BFSt, C: 38:92
29. KB 3-471; KB, HJ, 376.
30. Bodleian Library, Oxford, Range 8752, pp. 1-12; *Catalogo dos Livros que se Achao na Biblioteca da Igreja Chamada Jerusalem en Tranquebar*, Tranquebar, na Estampa dos Missionarios Reaes de Dennemarck, Anno de 1714.
31. HB, vol. III, continuation 33, pp. 927-36. Ziegenbalg gave a list of 38 Tamil books printed at Tranquebar.
32. Ibid.
33. Subbiah Muthiah, 'Giving India the Printed Word' in Andreas Gross, Y. Vincent Kumara Doss and Heike Liebau, eds., *Halle and the Beginning of Protestant Christianity in India*, Halle, 2006, vol. III, pp. 1241-8; See also the chronological list of books published at Tranquebar, 1712-1731, pp. 1383-90.
34. HB, vol. III, continuation 26, pp. 67-8.
35. Ibid.
36. KB, 3-471.
37. BFSt, 54: H:30.
38. KB, 2-2; School of Oriental and African Studies Library (hereafter SOASL), London, EB.73.40; BFSt, MISS C:6; Christoph Theodosius Walther, *Thiruchabaiyin Sarithira Posthagam: Historia Ecclesiastica Cui adduntur Synchronismi Historiae Exoticae, Praesertim Indicae*, Editio Secunda, Trangambariae, 1799, BL, London, no. 14170b.60. The book contains 316+xxxiv pages.
39. BFSt, C: 38:88; C: 38.87, C:77.
40. KB, 3-471; KB, HJ, 490; Rosenkilde Volmer, Printing in Tranquebar, p. 185.
41. BFSt, C: 38:89.
42. KB, 3-471.
43. BL, no. 14170.a.41.
44. KB, 3-471.
45. KB, 7-212.
46. KB, HJ, 36.
47. HB, vol. IV, continuation, 105, p. 998.
48. BFSt, C: 81; KB, HJ 444.
49. Graham Shaw, *The South Asia and Burma Retrospective Bibliography, Stage 1: 1556-1800*, London, 1987, pp. 129-30. Graham Shaw has not mentioned these printed books.
50. KB, 3-471; KB, HJ 472.
51. BL, no. 14170.a.41. *Mokshattukku Pora Vazhiyai Vezhipaduthugira Gnaana Upadesam*, Tharanganpadiyil, 1777. The book contains 48 pages. The year is mentioned in Tamil characters.
52. Bodleian Library, Oxford, Drav.f.17; Royal Asiatic Society Library, London, 177E; KB, 7-107; *Tharangambadi Thiruchabayil Vazhangum Gnaana*

Muraimaigazhin Vilakkam: Rituale Trangambaricum, Tharanganpadiyil, 1781. The book contains 141 pages. The year is mentioned in Tamil characters.

53. BL, no. 3425.d.20; KB, 7-107, *Sirupillaikalukku Gnaanasnanam Kodukira Varthamaanam*, Tranquebar, 1781. This book has 18 pages.
54. KB, 7-107.
55. KB 1-459.
56. KB, 3-471.
57. KB, 1-111.
58. KB, 3-471.
59. BL, no. 14170b.60.
60. BL, no.or.90.a.59, *Thiruchabaiyin Sarithira Posthagam*, Trangambariae, 1799.
61. Rosenkilde Volmer, Printing in Tranquebar, p. 192.
62. American Bible Society, New York (hereafter ABSL), accession no. 25060; New York Public Library (hereafter NYPL), OLB 1728, -II vol; Lambeth Palace Library, United Kingdom, call number E 1099.D2; BFSt, 12D 7, pp. 1-494.
63. ABSL, accession no. 12226b; NYPL, OLB 1728,-II vol. 42; BL, Or.70.b.21.
64. Society for Promoting Christian Knowledge Archives, London, The Latin title of the Tamil Bible is '*Novum Jeşus Christi Testamentum ex Originali Textu in Usum Gentis Malabaricae in Linguam Damulicam, Vulgo Malabarica Dictam, Versum, Opera & Studio Bartholomei Ziegenbalgi & Joh. Ernesti Grundle, Serenissima Daniae Regis Frederici IV ad Indos Orientales Missionarium, Tranquebariae in Littore Coromandelino: Typis Damulicis Missionis Danicae, 1719*'.
65. BL, Or.71.c.18; KB, 1-188; KB, Hj 46a-b.
66. ABSL, accession no.15291; NYPL, OLB 1723 I vol; BL, Or.70.b.21; KB, 1-41, KB, HJ, 7.
67. KB, 1-111; BL, Or.71.c.21.
68. BFSt, 12D 6, pp.799-1070; NYPL, OLB 1723-I vol; KB, 1-41; KB, HJ 9, BL, Or.70.b.21.
69. BFSt, 12D 7, pp. 1-396; NYPL, OLDB 1723-I vol.; BL, Or. 70.b.21.
70. BFSt, 12D7, pp 1-302; NYPL, OLB 1728- II vols; KB, HJ 10; KB, HJ 1-163.
71. KB, 1-209.
72. Biblioteca Nacional de Lisboa (hereafter BNL), Cota Res. 248v; KB, 1-111; KB, HJ 490.
73. KB, 1-189; KB, HJ 47a-b; KB, HJ 490.
74. KB, HJ 36.
75. BL, Or. 71.d.6(1); KB1-41.
76. KB 1-41; BL, Or. 71.d.6(2).
77. KB, 1-111.
78. Ostereichische Nationalbibliothek, Vienna, 5.M.29; KB, 1-189.
79. BL, Or.71.d.6 (3); KB, 1-41.
80. BL, Or.71.d.6 (4); KB, 1-41.

81. BFSt, C: 70.
82. Rosenkilde Volmer, Printing in Tranquebar, p. 185.
83. Daniel Jeyaraj, ed., *Olai Chuvadigalil Thodakakaala Thamizh Kristhava Iraineri Paadalgal, 1714: Mulamum Vizhakkamum*, Chennai, 2014; Rosenkilde Volmer, Printing in Tranquebar, p. 186.
84. HB, vol. II, continuation 13, p. 35; J.E. Gründler, *Piratthanai Posthagam*, Gesang-Buch Den 24 Jan 1715, in HB, vol. III, continuation 33, pp. 929, 933.
85. KB, Kobenhavn, Hjelmst, 1314, *Hymnologia Sagrada: Isto he, Espirituaes Cantigas Para Excitação da Christaa Devoção, E para Edificação em Fe e Piedade, Com Real Licenca, Tranquebar, Em India Oriental na Costa de Coromandel,* em a Estampa da Real Missão de Dennemark, no Anno 1719.
86. Arno Lehmann, Es begann in Tranquebar, pp. 26, 61.
87. BL, 14170b.17; see also, Or.90.8.61; *Gnaana Paatugalin Posthagam*: *Hymnologia Damulica, Sive ex Germanico in Damulorum Idioma, Observatis usque et Melodiis et Rhythmis Odarum, Translatorum Centum et Sexaginta Hymnorum Spiritualium Fasciculus, in Gratiam Juventutis Damulicae Aeque ac Ecclesiae Hujus Gentis, Christo Nomen Dantis, Exhibita a Benjamin Schultze*, Tranquebariae, MDCCXXIII. The book has xii+200 pages.
88. BFSt, 54 G5, *Gnaana Paatugalin Posthagam*: *Hymnologia Damulica, Sive ex Germanico in Damulorum Idioma, Observatis usque et Melodiis et Rhythmis Odarum, Translatorum Centum et Sexaginta Hymnorum Spiritualium Fasciculus,* Tranquebariae in Littore Coromandelino, Typis & Sumptibus, Missionis Danicae Edito Tertia. The book has viii+ 200 pages.
89. Ibid.
90. KB, HJ, 2037.
91. SOASL, EB.73.20; EB 73.15/1; KB, 47-525; BL, 621.c.27(1) ; 621.c.28 (1).
92. SOASL, EB.73.15/2; EB 73.19; KB 47-525.
93. BFSt, C: 80/1, *Bhoologathinudaiya Mudhalam Pangaagira Europa*, Tranquebar, Typis Missionis Danicae, MDCCXXXII.
94. BFSt, F3, INDEX GEOGRAPHICUS exhibens nomina REGIONUM & URBIUM PRAECIPURUM, in tabulis EUROPAE, ASIAE, AFRICAE, AMERICAE, item ITINERARII S.PAULI APOSTOLI & PALASTINAE obvia. Accesserunt aphorismi quidam Cosmographici, TRANGAMBARIAE, Typis Missionis Danicae, MDCCXXXII.
95. KB, 3-470; KB, HJ 485; BFSt, 54 G1. The book is titled in Latin *Theologia Thetica: In qua Omnia Dogmata ad Salutem Cognoscendi Necessaria Perspicua Methodo Tractantur ac Dictis Classicis Probantur, ad Propagationem Evangelii Christi intergentes Orientales in Lingua Damulica Scripta a Bartholomaeo Ziegenbalgio & Johanne Ernesto Grundlero*, Tranquebariae 1717.
96. BFSt, 54 G1, pp. 173-735.
97. KB, HJ, 484, *Archayasista Narkarunaikku Paathiram Ullavanaka*: *Solidissima Instituto Sanctae Coenae: Inqua Ostenditu qua Praeparatione Ante: Qua Exteriorum Interiorum que Morum Observationae irca: et qua Novitiate Vitae post Usum Sanctae Coenae Digne Sacramentum Celebraturus se Probare Debeat in Gratiam Christianae Gentis Damulorum Exhibita a Missionaria Danica*

Benjamin Schultze, Trangambariae, Typis ac Sumptibus Missionis Danicae, MDCCXXII.

98. HB, Vol. II, continuation 19, p. 342; Vol. III, continuation 33, p. 928

99. BFSt, 63F 28; BL, Or.90.a.67; BL, no. 14170.a.24; The book is titled in Latin '*Historia Passionis, Jesu Christi Fili Dei et Mariae Virginis Damulice, ex Quatuor Evangelistis Conscripta a Benjamin Schultze Mission Danico'*, Tranquebariae, Offic. Missionis Danicae, MDCCXXIII. The book has 77 pages.

100. BFSt, 63F 33, The book is titled in Latin '*Historia Passionis, Mortis, Resurrectionis et Ascenscionis Jesu Christi Fili Dei et Mariae Virginis, Tamulice, ex quatour Evangelistis Conscripta. Editio Secunda, Penitus Recognita Er Ad Textum Graecum Conformata'*, Trangambariae, Missionis Danicae, Anno 1740.

101. Graham Shaw, *The South Asia and Burma Retrospective Bibliography,* p. 41.

102. S. Jeyaseela Stephen, *A Meeting of the Minds: European and Tamil Encounters in Modern Sciences, 1507-1857*, Primus, Delhi, 2016, p. 704.

103. KB, 19-192.

104. KB, 19-193. Tamulisk calendar for aaret sathaarana varusham fom begynder den 10 April 1790 og endes den 9 April 1791, Trankenbar. MDCCXC.

105. KB, 19-192. Ulagathin retchakaraana kiristhu pirantha aayiraththi thonnoothi rendaam varushaththukku sellum panjangam: Intha panjangam tharanganpadiyil irukkum missiyon achchukudathil pathipikkapattathu, MDCCXCI.

106. Rosenkilde Volmer, Printing in Tranquebar, pp. 193-4.

107. Ibid., p.193.

108. Ibid., p. 194.

109. Graham Shaw, The South Asia and Burma Retrospective Bibliography, p. 8.

110. Rosenkilde Volmer, Printing in Tranquebar, p. 193.

111. Ibid., p. 194.

112. Ibid.

113. Ibid., p. 195.

114. Tamilnadu State Archives (hereafter TNSA), Chennai, *Tanjore District Records* (hereafter TDR) vol. 3492, p. 481 (19 November 1807).

115. Ibid.

116. Rosenkilde, 'Printing at Tranquebar', pp. 194–5.

117. John Johnson, *The Oriental Voyager or Sketches and Remarks on a Voyage to India and China in 1803*, London, 1807, p. 306.

118. Martin Kreiger, *Kaufleute, Seeerauber und Diplomaten der Danische Handel auf der Indische Ozean, 1620–1868*, Bohlau verlag, Koln, 1998, p. 200.

119. TNSA, Foreign Department: Sundries, *Correspondence Relative to the Restoration of the Danish Possessions, 1815–1816*, vol. 2, 10 July 1815.

A BCDEFGHI
KLMNOPQR
STUVWXYZ

A B C D E F G H I K L M N
O P Q R S T U V W X Y Z.

a b c d e f g h i k l m n o p q r
s ſ ſſ t u v w x y z.

A B C D E F G H I K L M N
O P Q R S T U V W X Y Z.

a b c d e f ff g h i k l m n o p q r
s ſ ſſ t u v w x y z.

ab. ç. ch. j. ſt.
1 2 3 4 5 6 7 8 9 0.
JE-SU CHRI-STO.

ANNO 1712.

3.1. *The first sample of printing with Portuguese ABCD in Tranquebar in 1712.*
(Courtesy: *Det Kongelige Bibliotek, Kobenhavn, KB, 47-460*).

A ORDEM DA SALVAÇAÕ,
OU
A DOUTRINA
CHRISTAÃ
BREVEMENTE
EMPERGUNTAS E REPOSTAS
declarada e provada
COM PRINCIPAES TESTEMUNHOS
DA ESCRITURA SAGRADA.
Juntamente com alhuãs Oraçoens e Cantigas.

TRANQUEBAR
Em India Oriental na Costa de Coromandel
Na Estámpa dos MISSIONARIOS
del REY de DENNEMARK.
Anno 1712.

3.2. The Portuguese title page of Retchippin Ozhukkam,
The first Tamil book printed in Tranquebar on 17 October 1712.
(Courtesy*: Det Kongelige Bibliotek, Kobenhavn, Hjelmst, 486c).*

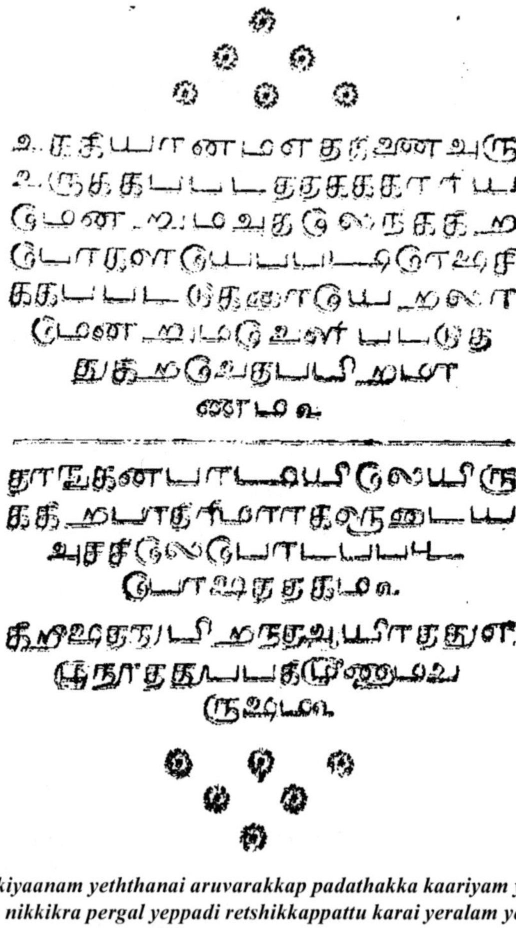

3.3. Akkiyaanam yeththanai aruvarakkap padathakka kaariyam yendrum, athile nikkikra pergal yeppadi retshikkappattu karai yeralam yendrum vezhlippaduthugira vetha pramaanam, the first Tamil pamphlet printed in Tranquebar on 25 October 1713. **(Courtesy*****: Bibliothek der Franckesche Stiftungen, Halle, C:38:84).***

SUMARIO

DAS

DOUTRINAS

CHRISTÃAS

POR USO DOS

CATECHUMENOS.

TRANQUEBAR,

No Anno de Christo

de 1715.

3.4. Oru kristhavan motchaththai adaigiraththukku vethapiramaanath in padiye ariyavendiya vizhakkangalaiyum mandirangalaiyum padichchu seyyavendia gnaayangaliyum bhodivikkira gnaana upadesam, the catechism of Martin Luther in Tamil printed in 1715. (Courtesy: *Det Kongelige Bibliotek, Kobenhavn, HJ, 376. 25; HJ 486)*

EPISTOLA,

quam

VENERABILIS

SOCIETAS

DE PROMOVENDA CHRISTI COGNITIONE, IN ANGLIA

PROPAGANDI EVANGELII CAUSA,

inſtituta,

AD VIROS REVERENDOS,

DOMINUM

BARTHOLOMÆUM

ZIEGENBALG

ET

DN. JOH. ERNESTUM

GRUNDLER,

Daniæ Regis Miſſionarios in India Orientali,

ſcripſit.

TRANQUEBARIÆ,

Typis Miſſionis Danicæ. Anno 1719.

3.5. The letter from William Wake, the Archbishop of Canterbury to Ziegenbalg and Grundler printed at Tranquebar in 1719.
(Courtesy: Det Kongelige Bibliotek, Kobenhavn, Hjelmst, 459)

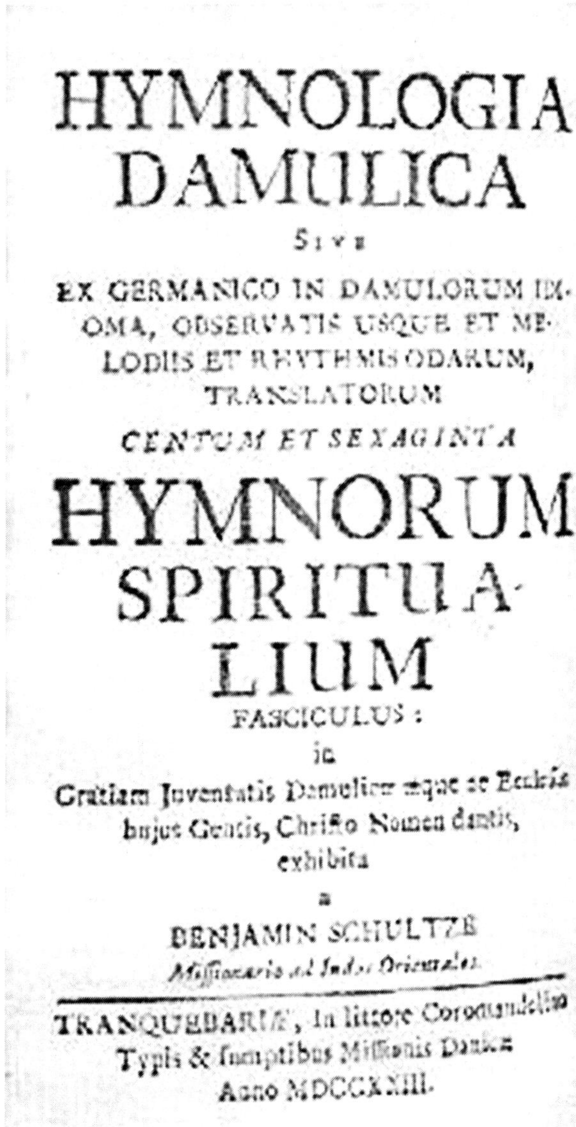

HYMNOLOGIA
DAMULICA
Sive
EX GERMANICO IN DAMULORUM IDIOMA, OBSERVATIS USQUE ET MELODIIS ET RHYTHMIS ODARUM,
TRANSLATORUM
CENTUM ET SEXAGINTA
HYMNORUM
SPIRITUALIUM
FASCICULUS:
in
Gratiam Juventatis Damulicæ atque ac Ecclesiæ hujus Gentis, Christo Nomen dantis,
exhibita
a
BENJAMIN SCHULTZE
Missionario ad Indos Orientales.

TRANQUEBARIÆ, In littore Coromandelino
Typis & sumptibus Missionis Danicæ
Anno MDCCXXIII.

3.6. The Latin title page of hymns translated from German to Tamil and printed in Tranquebar in 1723. (*Courtesy*: Bibliothek der Franckesche Stiftungen, Halle, 54 G5; British Library, London, 14170b.17; Or. 90. 8.61).

3.7. The title of Gnaana Paatugalin Posthagam printed in Tranquebar in 1723 (*Courtesy*: Bibliothek der Franckesche Stiftungen, Halle, 54:G5, British Library, London, 14170b.17; Or.90.8.61)

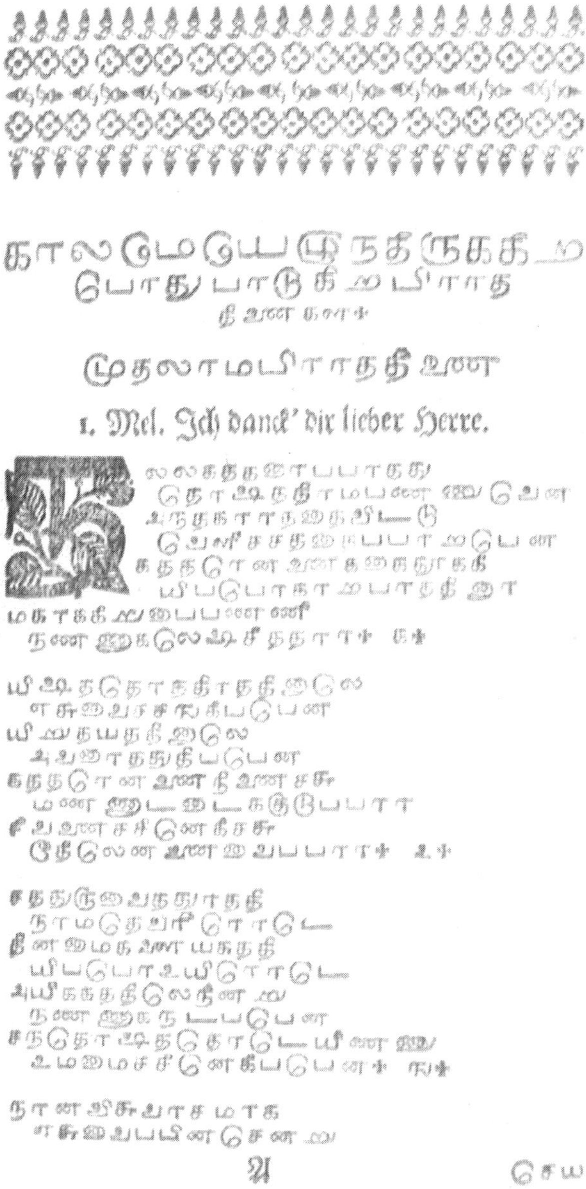

3.8. A page from the book of hymns printed in Tranquebar in 1725. (Courtesy: British Library, London, 14170b.17; Or.90.8.61; Bibliothek der Franckesche Stiftungen, Halle, 54:G5).

A VERDADEIRA
RELIGIAO
EM HUM
COMPENDIO
SUMMARIAMENTE
COMPREHENDIDA,
E COM TESTEMUNHOS
DA ESCRITURA SAGRADA
PROVADA.
Segunda Impreſſaõ.

TRANGAMBAR,
Na Officina da Real Miſſaõ de
DINAMARCA.
Anno de 1730.

3.9. The Portuguese title page of Mandira Chuvadi: Ithiley vethapirama anathinpadiey padikka vendiaya anju mandiran-galum athugalin viyratikalum anthantha vezhalihaley seyvikka padathakka sepangalum adangi irukkudhu, Rendaam visai, the catechism of Martin Luther reprinted in Tranquebar in 1730.
(Courtesy*: Det Kongelige Bibliotek, Kobenhavn 3-471; HJ, 376)*

DOCTRINA

DE

ORDINE

QVO

HOMINES PECCATORES

SALVARI

ATQVE

FELICIS IMMORTALITATIS

PARTICIPES FIERI

DEBENT.

EDITIO TERTIA.

TRANGAMBARIÆ,

Anno Chriſti

MDCCXXXIII.

***3.10. The Latin title of Paavikalaana manusar yentha ozhungunpadiey retchikapattu pakkiyam ullavargalumaay motchavaangalumaay pogaveneum engira vetha padippinai, the book of August Hermann Francke translated from German to Tamil and the third edition printed in Tranquebar in 1733.* (Courtesy*: Det Kongelige Bibliotek, Kobenhavn, 3-471; HJ 375*)**

DOCTRINÆ CHRISTIANÆ

RUDIMENTA

OLIM AB AUTORE

BEATO A. H. FRANCKIO

Theologo Halensi

GERMANICE EDITA: NUNC IN

LINGUAM TAMULICAM

TRANSLATA.

Accessit brevis notitia de S. Scri-

ptura & religione.

DICIT ILLI JESUS: EGO SUM VIA,

ET VERITAS, ET VITA: NEMO VENIT

AD PATREM, NISI PER ME.

JOAN. XIV, 6.

TRANGAMBARIÆ,

TYPIS MISSIONIS DANICÆ,

MDCCXXXIV.

3.11. The Latin title page of the Christian doctrine of August Hermann Francke translated from German to Tamil and printed in Tranquebar in 1734. (Courtesy: Bibliothek der Franckesche Stiftungen, Halle, 54:H:30).

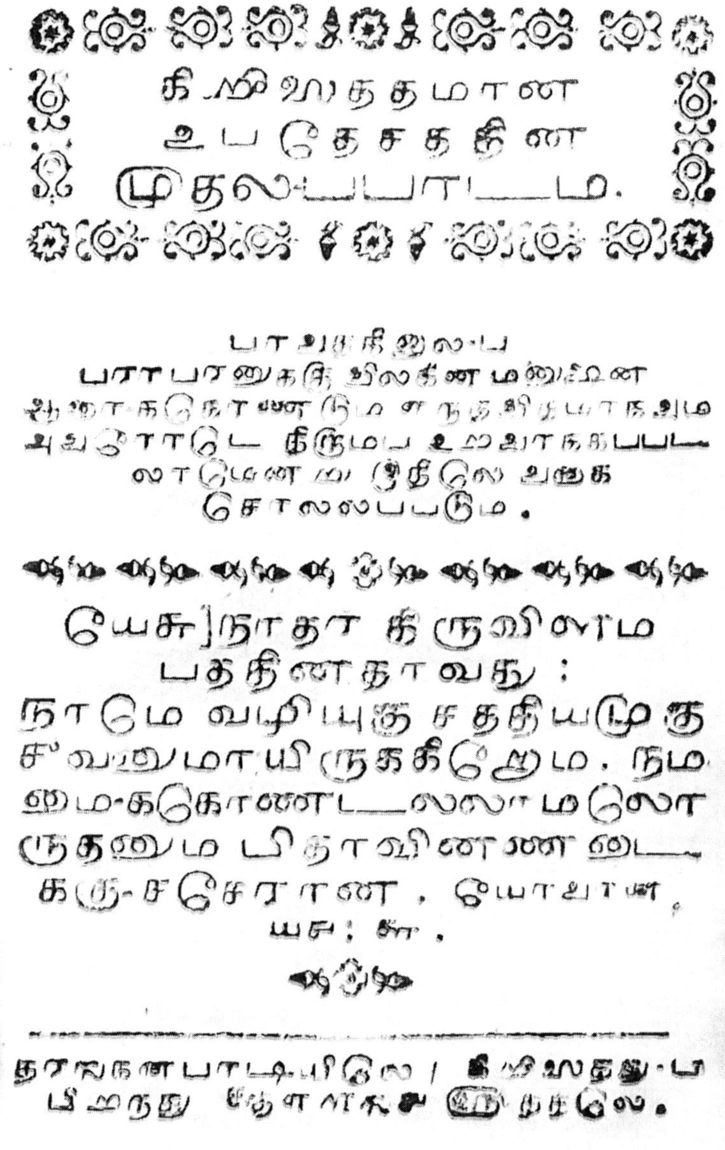

கிறிஸ்தத்தமான உபதேசத்தின் முதல் பாடம்.

யேசுநாதர் திருவுளம்பற்றினதாவது:
நாமே வழியும் சத்தியமுமாயிருக்கிறோம். நம்மைக்கொண்டல்லாமல் ஒருத்தரும் பிதாவினண்டைக்குச் சேரார். யோவான். 14: 6.

3.12. The Tamil title page of Krisiththamaana Upadesathin Muthal Paadam printed in Tranquebar in 1734
(Courtesy: Bibliothek der Franckesche Stiftungen, Halle, 54:H.34)

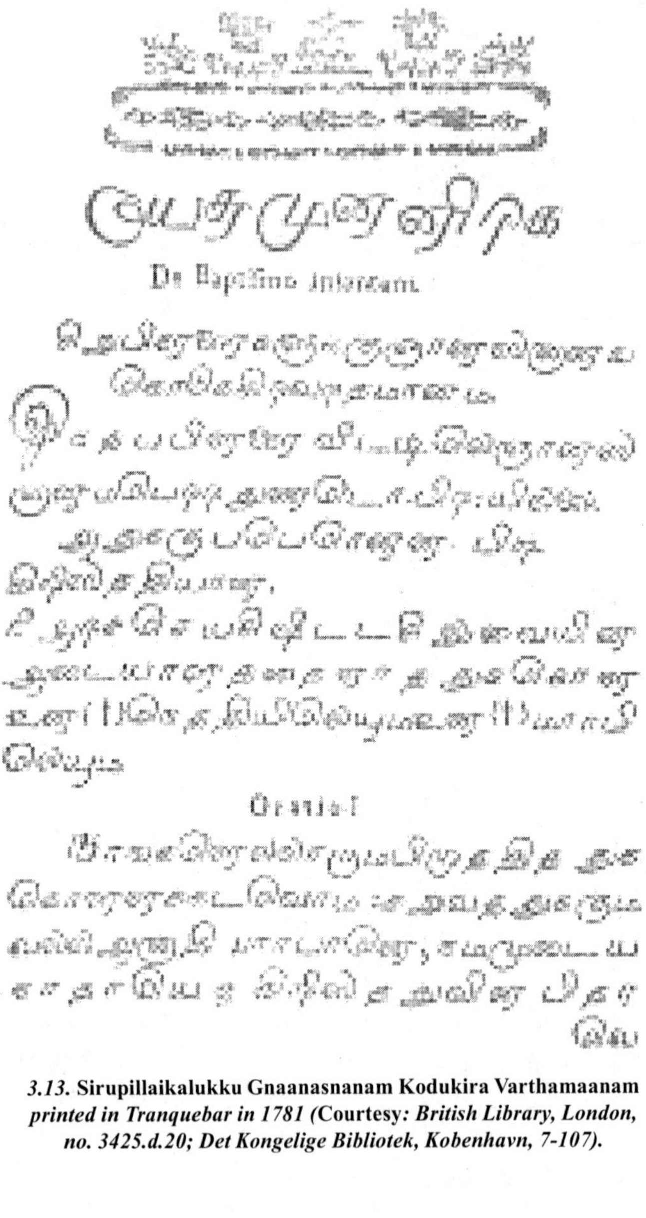
De Baptismo infantum

Oratio I

3.13.* Sirupillaikalukku Gnaanasnanam Kodukira Varthamaanam *printed in Tranquebar in 1781* (Courtesy*: British Library, London, no. 3425.d.20; Det Kongelige Bibliotek, Kobenhavn, 7-107).

4

The Letter Press of the English Company and Protestant Missionaries in Madras, Palayamkottai and Nagercoil: Printing Books, Pamphlets, Journals, Newspapers and Advertisements in Tamil, 1766-1857

The printing machine operated by hand was confiscated in January 1761 from the French Governor's palace by the English during the siege of Pondicherry. It was taken to Madras along with some font types available accompanied by Charles Delon the French printer. Thereafter the English company was planning to put it into proper use. Johann Philipp Fabricius the Protestant missionary at that time in Madras convinced Sir Eyre Coote to give the printing press and the font types to him, with the understanding that requests for printing from the English Company at Fort St. George would take priority over missionary work.[1] Thereafter the press was set up at Vepery in Madras in 1762 and in the beginning it issued a calendar in English for the year 1763.[2]

The Preparation of Tamil Fonts in Madras, 1766-1769

Johann Philipp Fabricius desired to have Tamil fonts cut. In his letter to Sebastian Andreas in 1761 he had mentioned the usage of the letters 'Kee' and 'See' in Tamil. He gave the specification of Tamil font types.[3] Further again in his letter dated 10 April 1768 he mentioned the Tamil alphabets in two separate lines to be made for the preparation of printing his Tamil-English dictionary. The first line included the letters, ka, tha, pa, ma, ya, la, short kombu, laa, long kombu, ra, yi, va, yee, u, mi, mee, mu, moo, si, na, A, na, vu, zha, ru, ye, yae, nu, zha, ra, thu and da. The second line included the alphabets of vu, na, mi, roo, ir, ku, ka, zha, nu, noo, yee, o, zha, ka, noo and yoo. The sample of letters were cast and printed in a sheet in Madras on 2 January 1769.[4]

Printing Books in Tamil on Protestant Christianity at the Press in Vepery in Madras, 1766-1806

The Protestant missionaries in Madras had successfully set up a printing press of their own by 1766 which they had received from Europe. It was called with alternative names as the Lutheran mission press, Madras Lutheran mission press and Wepery mission press. Johann Philipp Fabricius had prepared by then the Tamil catechism and it was the first book to be printed in Tamil (stated as *Chennapattanathukkutpatta Veperiyile Miciyo Achchukkudathil Pathipikkapattathu*) in the mission press at Vepery near Madras in1766.[5] The translations of the four Gospels and Acts of the Apostles by Fabricius got printed six years later (in 1772) at the same press under the Tamil title '*Nammuda kartharum iratchakarumaahiya yesu kristhuvinaal undaana kirupayin udanpadikaiyaagiya puthu yerpaadu: Kristhu pirantha (1772 numeral in Tamil) Chennapattanathil achchadikappattathu*'.[6]

Fabricius wrote a polemical work against Catholicism and it got printed at the Vepery press in 1774 under the title '*Paappu maarkam innathenru kaanpikkira thezhlivaana vizhlakkam*'.[7] The Tamil hymnal translated by Fabricius from German was also printed in the same year.[8]

Christian Friedrich Schwartz the missionary had composed a work on a dialogue between a heathen and a Christian. It was titled '*Akkiyannikum kristhavanukkum undaana sampaashanai*'. This book was printed from the mission press at Vepery in 1776. It had 89 pages.[9]

The translation of John Bunyan's Pilgrims' Progress was completed and the book was published from the Vepery press in 1793. The Tamil title is '*Oru Paradesi intha logathaivittu marumaikku nadantherinathu sorpanamenru uvamaiyiley kaanpikka pattirukkuthu*'. The book had 137 pages.[10] In English it is titled 'The Pilgrims' Progress from This World to That which is to come: Delivered under the Similitude of a Dream'.

The second edition of the Tamil hymnal of Fabricius translated from German appeared in print from the Vepery press in 1797.[11] Again in the next year (1798) the second edition of '*Paappu maarkam innathenru kaanpikkira thezhlivaana vizhlakkam*' of Fabricius got printed.[12]

Carl Heinrich von Bogatzky's work was translated into Tamil by Daniel Pillai of Tranquebar titled '*Paramandalangalil thangal pokkisham undenru irukkira paraaparanudaya pillaigalin aabarana petti*' (The golden treasury, comprising texts, hymns, and prayers for every day in the year) and it was printed in the Vepery press in 1800.[13] The Malabar New Testament of our Lord and Saviour Jesus Christ by J.P. Fabricius in Tamil was printed in 1806 from the press. Thus the missionaries had assigned priority to printing Tamil books on the doctrine of the Protestants, catechism and liturgy.

Printing Tamil Grammar, English-Tamil Dictionaries, Tamil-English Dictionaries and Story Books, 1766-1812

The missionaries further printed books on Tamil language and dictionary. In 1766 two volumes of Johann Philipp Fabricius' 'A Dictionary of English and Malabar' got printed in the Vepery press.[14] In 1779 Fabricius' *Thamizhlum Inglishumaay Irukkira Agaraathi* (A Malabar and English Dictionary, Wherein the Words and Phrases of the Tamilian Language, Commonly called by the Europeans the Malabar Language, are Explained in English) was printed.[15] Johann Philipp Fabricius and Johann Christian Breithaupt had compiled the 'Dictionary of the English and Malabar Languages' and it was printed in 1786.[16]

Fabricius prepared in 1778 'A Grammar for Learning the Principles of the Malabar Language, Properly Called Tamul or the Tamulian Language', and the book was printed at Vepery press.[17] In 1789, the second edition of his book 'A Grammar for Learning the Principles of the Malabar Language', appeared in print from the same press.[18]

Many story books got printed in Madras. *Vikkiramaathithan Kathai* in verses was printed in 1804. This is a prolix history of the devil vedhaazhlam who served the Tamil king Vikkirmaadiththan and performed many cunning tricks. This devil had at first been one of the god's priests in the other world and when the goddess Parvathi had an occasion to speak in private with the god Siva the priest consented and heard their secret discourse, but made it public, in consequence of which, Siva became angry and cursed him so that he became a devil on earth, where he has been playing tricks ever since. The book 'A Vocabulary of English and Tamil words', by I. Nicholas was printed in 1807. *Sathamukha Raavanan Kathai* another story book in verses was printed in 1808. *Mariyaathai Raman Kathai* was printed in 1812. *Tamil Ariyum Mantai Kathai* was also printed in the same year.

The Vepery mission was connected with the Church of England, and it carried out the work under the auspices of the Society for the Propagation of the Gospel conducted by the Lutherans of the Royal Danish mission. The Vepery mission press continued to print books mainly in Tamil language. We find a book *Oru Paththira Thirattu* printed in 1839 and it contained stories. In the printed book some terms have dots over consonants and some words do not have dots over the consonants. In the preface it has been stated that Tiruvencatachella Moodeliar who had been attached to the College of Fort St. George and *munshi* for 25 years had helped in the preparation of the book.[19]

Advertisements Printed in Tamil, 1802-1813

There were many printing press functioning in Madras (like the Courier press in Court House Street, Fort St. George from 1785-1793 under Joseph

Martin and Hicarrah press) and they printed mostly in English. A Journal in English called *Madras Gazette* appeared in print in 1792. It is reported by S. Samuel, the manager of this Madras Gazette that Tamil fonts had been prepared at huge expense of the government and advertisements in Tamil would be introduced in 1796. A Tamil newspaper (weekly) appeared in print in 1802 in the Ceylon Government Gazette (in trilingual, Tamil Singala and English) and there was a separate sectional heading in Tamil titled '*Arasaanga Vathamaani*'. It was printed on all Mondays from Colombo. The first issue appeared on 15 March 1802.[20] The advertisement on pearl fishing given by the Ceylon Government in Tamil appeared in print in the 'Madras Courier' on 7 December 1813. The Tamil types for printing still had continued to come from London to Madras. They were though said to be coarse and bulky but were used at the printing press. We find notices of advertising like the sale of printing machines in Madras but they were few and far. Heefke, Faure & Company auctioned four Watt & Company printing machines, printing boards, paper and ink in 1804.[21] The letter-copying presses invented by James Watt were used mainly for making copies of outgoing correspondence. However, many printing machines and types had gradually come through the ships that sailed from London to Madras.

Printing Tamil Pamphlets and Books by the Religious Tract Society in Madras, 1812-1845

31 October 1822 (Reformation Day), Rhenius established a Religious Tract Society for the publication of Tamil tracts. He became the first secretary of the society. It was engaged in preparing and publishing not only religious tracts, but also larger volumes in the vernacular as well as school-books. Some members of the Religious Tract Association at Madras (organized in 1818) became members of the Religious Tract Society.[22] Tracts and bibles were distributed to people, openly and freely in the street.[23] The primary object was the circulation of religious tracts in Tamil on the same principles with those of the Religious Tract Society in London. The secondary object was the publication of school-books and other elementary and useful works in Tamil.[24] Religious Tract and Book Society of Madras published considerable quantities of literature. *Vetha Sasthira Surukkam* was composed in Tamil by C.T.E. Rhenius and it was printed in 1838 and it had 612 pages. It was reprinted and the third edition appeared in 1845 and had 588 pages. It was out of print even after reprint and so the fourth edition appeared in 1852.[25]

The Religious Tract and Book Society in Madras printed in Tamil regularly handbills, hymn-books, lyrics and devotional material for evangelistic and church purposes. The society also printed tracts dealing with science in the course of time. The tract number 74 in Tamil general series was on cholera. The tract attributed the fearful plague to the crime of idol worship.[26] We also find brief chapters on scientific and literary subjects in the tracts. It is interesting to note that the names of sciences mentioned in Tamil such as Urigai (meteorology), Thathuva sastram (physics), Yennavu saathiram (mathematics), Rasavadha saathiram (chemistry), Vaan sastram (astronomy), Bhumi saathiram (geography), Thaavara saathiram (botany), Suranga saathiram (mineralogy) and Bhumi bandha saathiram (geology). Further, the names of arts (viththai) were also mentioned such as Uzhavu viththai (agriculture), Anga sethana viththai (anatomy), Vaagada viththai (medicine), Panchaloga viththai (metallurgy), Kappalottum viththai (navigation) Acchu viththai (printing) and Rana vaythiya viththai (surgery). One tract dealt with the human body: udhiram (blood), secretions, bones and colours of the skin.[27] Another tract dealt with pulan (the senses) and vyadhi (diseases).[28]

The Tract and Book Society in Madras in 1843 had a stock of 3500 Tamil volumes and out of which 1795 Tamil volumes were bound and kept in its depository.[29] Again in 1844 it had a stock of 5500 Tamil volumes at the depository out of which 2055 Tamil volumes were bound as reported in the society's publications.[30] Copies of these tracts and books were sent for circulation to various places in Tamil country and the details had been furnished for the year 1844 as follows in its report.[31]

Place	*Number of copies*
Aranai	1700
Coimbatore	8400
Kumbakonam	8000
Cuddalore	4300
Madras	43592
Madurai	32350
Mannargudi	950
Mayavaram	3000
Nagapattinam	2200
Palayamkottai	500
Poonamallee	1060
St. Thomas Mount	4150
Salem	2300
Thanjavur	3500
Tiruchirapalli	6400
Wallajabad	310

Printing Books in Tamil by the Madras Book Society, 1824-1836

The Madras Book Society formed in 1820 had set up a printing press of its own in 1824. Ramasami's Arithmetic, in Tamil, 1200 copies had been printed. The works in the press and under review during the year 1823–24 included: (1) Abridgement of Ancient History, revised and adapted for Indian students accompanied with a translation in familiar Tamil and two lithographic maps illustrative of the subject-one in English and one in Tamil; (2) Abridgement of the History of Hindustan from the first invasion of the Mussulmans to the subversion of their power; (3) translation in familiar Tamil, Mrs. Trimmer's edition of Aesop Fables, Part 1-revised; and (4) Mrs. Trimmer's edition of Aesop Fables, Part 2-revised. The works in hand reported during 1823–24 included: Tamil translation of Pleasing Tales, Tamil translation of Joyce's Scientific Dialogue with lithographic plates, Tamil Grammar, Tamil Dictionary and Abridgement of Wilk's History of Mysore with a Tamil translation.[32] The works published by the Madras Book Society were used extensively by schools in Tamil country. The Public Consultation of 1836 noted that 13 titles totaling to 147 copies were sold to six schools under government control.[33]

Journals, Newspapers and Tender Notices Printed in Tamil from Madras, 1831-1852

Tamil Magazine a journal came to be published in Madras in 1831 by Madras Christian Tract Society for the growth and development of knowledge. Essays on science and medicine in Tamil were published in the journal. The editor was Iswara Chandra Sat, who went to England and did not return. The periodical came out regularly for six months, but then failed. The editors of the journal had been frequently changed and this seriously affected the publication but continued to be published for fifteen years.[34]

The monthly periodical Tamil Magazine was under the editorial care of Rev. A. Leitch in 1844. It continued to be the repository of a large amount of very valuable matter original and translated. To quote the language of Rev. A. Leitch, 'the Tamil Magazine was a great blessing to the infant church of India. It diffused a literary taste along with its information among the people, and every year was adding to its efficiency. During the last one year it had been well supported. Its literary character was far superior to that of some Hindu periodicals. The new arrangement by which a sermon written by a missionary, and unanimously approved of by the Tamil Revision Sub-Committee, was issued in every number, was giving it access to new spheres, and adding new interest to its present walks of usefulness'.[35] Lengthy religious instructions issued had caused a problem for the readers. In 1846 efforts were made to merge Tamil Magazine with a new journal that appeared in print called *Sathiya Thuthan* a bi-monthly, but it was highly unsuccessful.

Rasa Vriddhi Bhodini the newspaper in Tamil was printed thrice a month from Madras in 1833. News that appeared in English journals had been translated and it got printed. Government subsidy was given for the publication. In 1835 Madras Chronicle a weekly newspaper was printed. The same name appeared also in the Tamil title of the newspaper.[36] *Sana Snegan* a bimonthly from Madras was printed in 1841. *Madhiyam* a newspaper had come to be published monthly thrice in 1844. Karl Friedrich Leberecht Graul (1814-1864) the German missionary purchased and he took the periodicals like *Rajadhani*, the Tamil journal, 1844-45 and *Kalvi Kalangiyam*, another Tamil journal, a few volumes printed in 1843-44 to Germany.[37] *Dhina Varthamaani* a weekly newspaper was printed in 1855 by Rev. Peter Percival. This was a weekly and had 8 pages. The local price in Madras for the natives was 3 rupees and it was 5 rupees for the Europeans. The outstation sale price including postal charges had been fixed at 5 rupees. Literature, science and essays had appeared in the newspaper.[38]

Saint George Gazette was published from Madras in 1832. The same name in Tamil also appeared in the title. It was a bi-weekly and appeared in Tamil and English, on Tuesdays and Fridays. The first issue came out on 4 January 1832. The page numbers had appeared in this bi-weekly serially for six months and so they were bound together and sold separately.[39] It may be worthwhile to note and examine a tender notice appeared in print on 8 January 1852 in the Saint George Gazette. The text runs thus: '*Ithanaal arivikkira thennavenraal, black townil meethiyaay nirkum thaneer pazhaiya naatramaana kaalvaay vazhiyaay pogaamal Chennai pattanang kottai melpaarisaththil uzhlla palsatti (Esplande) vazhiyaay kuvam attrukku pagumpadiyaay merpadi (in abbreviation) sengpoovil irunthu dharkas-thugal (tenders) 1852 varusham (varu in abbreviation) janavari maasam (mee in abbreviation) 23 thethi (thee in abbreviation) velli kilamai varaikkum intha aappisil vaangappadum,* A.H. Vopp, Aakting sekretri, Military board aappisu, W.H. B. BAYLEY, Tamil Translation of Govt. Gazette, 6.1. 1852'.[40] We find English words were freely used in Tamil advertisements. Further equivalent English terms for translated Tamil words were found in brackets for easy understanding of the public.

The Fort St. George College Press in Madras and the Tamil Books Printed, 1813-1833

The English East India Company founded *Chennai Kalvi Sangam* (literally Chennai Education Society), the College of Fort St. George in 1812 through the efforts of Francis Whyte Ellis (1777-1819) who became the first superintendent of the college. It gave priority to the teaching and production of knowledge of Tamil and other languages spoken in the Madras Presidency. The main purpose of the college was to ensure that incoming junior civil servants destined for administrative positions in the countryside would be able to communicate easily with the local populace. The pundits taught Europeans, conducted oral examinations in reading, constructing and conversing and in the grammar and construction of several languages, subjects of revenue and judicial system of administration or having reference to common dealings and familiar dialogue with natives.[41]

A printing press was established at the College of Fort St. George in 1813 and Tamil literary and grammatical works were planned to be printed. The *pundits* were involved in editing and publishing with the active patronage of the Madras Government.[42] When Sir John Malcolm visited the College in 1817 F.W. Ellis showed him at that time the Thembaavani manuscript in palm-leaves composed by Beschi. John Malcolm desired to have a copy and so it was made in palm-leaves to take it to England.[43] The two boards at the beginning and the end of the manuscript were ornamented with gold and silver. It was sent by the Governor of Fort St. George to place it in Lord Spencer's Library.[44]

Mr. William Urquhart of the Madras Courier, 1795 had acquired from his friends in England, a very extensive indent of types and other printing materials in 1817 at a great expense, which then surpassed every other printing because it included Tamil types.[45] In 1822 William Church of Boston patented a typesetting machine consisting of a keyboard. Notices of Protestant Church's printing machine of a most curious and novel description had been found and it promised to be highly useful in Tamil country where new types that were not readily obtained had appeared in the government gazettes of Madras.[46]

Thomas Munro, the Governor of Madras Presidency encouraged the formation of Madras School Book Society in 1820. It was a voluntary body helped to grow education and came to publish books in English and Tamil. The Fort St. George College in Madras took keen interest to provide schools with suitable text books in Tamil.[47] The books on Tamil grammar, translation of Tamil poetry and textbooks in Tamil came to be composed and were printed between 1813 and 1819 from Fort St. George College Press in Madras.

1. *Kodunthamizh*, by Beschi, Fort St. George College Press, Madras, 1813.
2. *Ilakkana Surukkam*, by Thirusittrambala Desikar, Fort St. George College Press, 1813.
3. *Ramayanam: Uththara Kaandam*, translated from Sanskrit, by

Thirusittrambala Desikar, Fort St. George College Press, Madras 1815.

4. *Thirukural* translated by F.W. Ellis, Fort St. George College Press, Madras, 1816.
5. *Nedung kanakku*, Fort St. George College Press, Madras, 1816.
6. *Purva Chakravarthi Kathai,* Fort St. George College Press, Madras, 1819.

In 1815 we find a 'List of books printed, printing or preparing for the press' was issued from the Fort St. George College press.[48] It contains the following details on Tamil books.

1. J.C. Beschi, *Kodunthamizh* grammar in Latin, printed
2. Chidamabara Vaaththiyaar, *Ramayana Uththara Kaandam*, Tamil translation, textbook for civil servants, printed
3. J.C. Beschi, Tamil-Latin dictionary, *Kodunthamizh*, under printing
4. J.C. Beschi, *Chaturagaraathi*, Tamil-Latin dictionary, *Senthamizh*, under printing
6. Chidambara Vaaththiyaar, *Thamizh Surukka Vizhlakkam*, in prose for Tholkaappiyam, for the use of Indian students, under printing
7. J.C. Beschi, *Senthamizh* grammar in Latin, preparing for press
8. Perur Vaaththiyaar & Chidambara Vaathiyaar, Vignaaneswara and Mithakashara's Vyaavahaarakandaavi translation in Tamil, preparing for the press.

It may be mentioned that the College Board in Madras had reprinted Beschi's *Kodun-Thamizh* in Latin in 1813 which was formerly printed first by the Danish-Halle missionaries at the Tranquebar Mission Press in 1738.

There is another 'List of books printed, printing or preparing for the press' issued from the Fort St. George College press in 1819.[49] We find F.W. Ellis' *Thirukural* English translation again began printing in 1818 and the two-thirds of thebook had been stated to have printed. J.C. Beschi's *Kodunthamizh* grammar in Latin and Chidambara Vaaththiyaar's *Thamizh Surukka Vizhlakkam* half of the books had been stated to have been also printed.

The Fort St. George College Press had published books on education. The Tamil classical original texts were collected and the manuscripts of great importance came to be published for the first time. The pundits employed were great scholars, and they were paid very well and they taught Tamil language, grammar to the English civil servants and so their books were also published between 1820 and 1833.

1. *Ilakkana vinaa vidai*, Villipakkam Thandavaraya Mudaliar, Fort St. George College Press, Madras, 1820.
2. *Kathaa Manjari*, Villipakkam Thandavaraya Mudaliar, Fort St. George College Press, Madras, 1820.
3. *Chathuragaraathi* of Beschi, Fort St. George College Press, Madras, 1824.
4. *Thamizh Arichuvadi*, 6 books, by Captain Henry and Visvambara Sastri, Fort St. George College Press, Madras, 1825.
5. *Kathaa Manjari* by Villipakkam Thandavaraya Mudaliar, reprinted at Fort St. George College Press, Madras, 1826.
6. *Panchathanthira Kathai*, translated by Villipakkam Thandavaraya Mudaliar, Fort St. George College Press, 1826.
7. *Kalvi Eni*, translation of Mrs Trimmer's tales, by Saamiyappa Mudaliar and Kandasami Pulavar, Fort St. George College Press, Madras, 1827.
8. Thamizh Arichuvadi, Captain Henry and Venkatachala Mudaliar, Fort St. George College Press, Madras, 1827.
9. *Ilakkana vinaa vidai*, by Villipakkam Thandavaraya Mudaliar, the second edition, Fort St. George College Press, 1828.
10. *Ilakkana surukka vivara vidai*, Fort St. George College Press, Madras, 1828.
11. *Bughola sathira sangiraham* (A textbook of geology), Fort St. George College Press, Madras, 1828.
12. *Kathaa Chinthaamani*, by Villipakkam Thandavaraya Mudaliar, Fort St. George College Press, Madras, 1833.

Printing Chathuragaraathi during 1819-1824 in Madras is important to note. Chathuragaraathi, the outstanding work of lexicography by C.J. Beschi remained in manuscript after being composed at Tirukkovalur in 1732. The credit for printing and publishing the second part goes to F. W. Ellis who got it printed with the assistance of Thirusittrambala Desikar in 1819. The second part namely *Porulagaraathi* and the entire work as a single volume got published by Richard Clarke first in the year 1824. *Chaturagaraathi*, of Beschi was reprinted by J. Smith at the Church Mission Press at Madras, 1835.

The English Company made efforts to produce elementary textbooks on European science and literature too. This pursuit was driven by the recommendations of Lord Auckland, the Governor-General, who, in his minute of 1839, argued for the use of vernacular medium in such schools.[50] He reasoned that after the first expense of preparing school books had been incurred, instruction in that manner must be made more economical than through English, which required the employment of an English master on a salary at least two or three times as high as would be adequate for a native teacher who had received an English education, at the same time perfectly conversant with his own mother-tongue. He also advocated that the government should be especially invited to cooperate, through the bodies charged with the control of public instruction under their superintendence, in the common object of aiding the preparation of a useful and comprehensive set of class books to be afterwards rendered into the vernacular languages of the regions.[51] The minute of Munro dated 10 March 1826 emphasized that anyone can produce Tamil books without European's ideology. Further, the minute of the Board of Governors of the Madras University on the preparation of class-books dated 26 July 1841encouraged printing books on the natural sciences in Tamil language. Hence books in Tamil largely were printed for learning and teaching in Madras.

Printing Tamil Books at the Government Press in Madras, 1816-1845

The East India Company's solicitor Robert Williams and John Goldingham the English company's astronomer and engineer, both started 'The Madras Gazette' run by the former and 'The Government Gazette' started in the year 1795 by the latter, were printed at the first Government Press established in 1800 by enlarging Male Asylum Press. Government printing, by order of Lord Clive in 1800 was produced by the Madras Male Asylum press. It also published under special arrangements an official and general newspaper called the Government Gazette. In 1831 the monopoly of the Asylum press was terminated and Government printing was divided among various private firms. The Fort St. George Gazette press was at the same time opened in the Government office. The first new Gazette consisting of 12 pages was issued on Wednesday, 4 January 1832. Subsequently the printing of the Commander-in-Chief's General Orders was introduced, together with English and Vernacular Acts. In 1845 the establishment consisted of 40 persons, with three Columbian presses of English manufacture, and a few wooden presses. Later, printing the Proceedings of Government had begun in 1855, and the press establishment was increased to a staff of 95 persons. A binding section was also added about this time. We find many Tamil books of Christian literature and spiritual readings published.

1. *Pothuvaana Sepa Posthagam*, by Johann Peter Rottler, Government Press, Vepery, 1816.

2. *Pothuvaana Sepa Posthagam*, Second edition, by Johann Peter Rottler, Government Press, Vepery, 1817.
3. The book of common prayers with the occasional services & Psalter translated into Tamil by J.P. Rottler, Government press, Madras, 1819.
4. *Pothuvaana Sepa Posthagam*, Third edition, by Johann Peter Rottler, Government Press, Vepery, 1820.
5. *Pothuvaana Sepa Posthagam*, Fourth edition, Johann Peter Rottler, Government Press, Vepery, 1822.
6. *Visuvasaththukum uraiyattikum ututta pirathaana vetha vaakiyangal*, by Johann Philipp Fabricius, Vepery, Third edition, 1822.
7. *Vikkiraha bhakthikkum deyva bhakthikkum sambaashanai*, by Christian Frederick Schwartz, Vepery, Madras, 1823.
8. *Gnaana posana vizhlakkam: Gnaanasnanam Narkarunai yenbavaigalin magimaiyai solliyathu*, Karl Theophilus Ewald Rhenius, Vepery, Madras, 1825.
9. *Kristhuvin gnaana paadalgal*, Johann Philip Fabricius, Fourth edition, Vepery, 1825.
10. *Vikkiraha pattikkum Deyva pattikkum sambaashanai*, Second edition, by Christian Frederick Schwartz, Vepery, Madras, 1827.
11. *Thirumandirangal* (prayer book) Vepery, Madras, 1829.
12. *Thothitra Maalai: Muthalam Pangu; Munnanth Tharumapuram Adheenam Vidwan Arumuga Thambirannenru sollapattu ippozhuthu Wesley Abrahammennum peyar pettravar sangikikkapadathakka Robert Karwaar Iyeralye Gnaanasnaanam pettra naalil yesu retchagar perile paadiyathu*, Part I, Sixth edition, Madras, Church Mission Press, 1836.
13. *Sathya Vetham* by Ziegenbalg (A short treatise on the most important teachings contained in the true veda, i.e., the Bible), reprint, Vepery, 1844.
14. *Kristhu matha kandanam* (Criticism of Christian religion), Vepery, 1845.[52]

The American Mission Press in Madras and Printing Books in Tamil, 1820-1857

The American mission founded in Madras functioned at *Thanga Saalai* (Mint Street), in Pedda Nayakkan Pettai in 1820. It had a printing press and further purchased again a new printing machine from the church mission in 1838 and set up its own printing establishment at Broadway in Madras.

Many books in Tamil were printed from the press since its inception. The printing press had been using Tamil types cast at Halle in Germany. These types were known as 'the square upright typefaces'.

We also find the church mission printing press in Nellore publishing Tamil books in 1830. The First lessons and idiomatic exercises in English and Tamil designed to assist Tamil youths in the study of English language got printed in Nellore, at the Church Mission Press in 1830.[53] Christian literature books continued to be printed in Madras on a large scale. *Vetha Uthaarana Thirattu* by Rhenius was printed in Madras in 1835. It got revised and printed in Madras in 1852.[54] *Gnaana Upadesam*, a Roman Catholic catechism for the use of Tamils was slightly modified from James Butler's catechism for the instruction of children and it was translated by Manikkam Royappa Swami and the book was printed in Madras in 1839 and it had 110 pages.[55] *Vethiyar Ozhukkam* of Beschi containing instruction to catechists in 20 chapters with an appendix of eight chapters preceded by a biography of Beschi in English and Tamil was printed in Madras, It was abridged and adapted to the use of Protestant missionaries.[56] A book in Tamil and English titled Practical Expressions of the Parables of Christ got printed in Madras in 1844.[57] John Christian Arulappan translated Mrs. Favell Lee Martimer's book 'Line upon Line' from English to Tamil titled *Satta Thittam* and it was printed in Madras in 1845. He also wrote *Sathya Vetha Kanaadi* and the book was printed in Madras in 1846 which had 258 pages.[58] *Deva Aarathaniyiley Paadugira Gnaanapaatum Adangiya Sangeetha Thirattu,* was printed in Madras in 1848 and it had 136 pages.[59] *Patha Manjari* a vocabulary English & Tamil comprehending terms relating to Christian theology & the religion, philosophy and mythology of the Hindus was printed in 1852 and it had 100 pages.[60] *Gnaana Paatukal* a book of 146 pages was printed at the American Madras Mission press in 1853.[61] *Saathi Viththiyaasa Vizhlakkam*, dealing with caste as it existed among Hindus and native Christians with an appendix containing passages on caste from the Rig Veda in Sanskrit and Tamil was printed in 1857 and the book had 155 pages.[62]

Improving Tamil Typography in Madras, 1838-1857

The American Mission Press functioned under the superintendence of P. R. Hunt in 1838 and he improved the Tamil typography and raised the standard of printing. He taught some of his workmen the very difficult art of cutting type punches by hand and he designed also a new type Tamil type face. He gave the letters a more regular slope, and even spacing, with better alignment. This new types greatly added to the beautiful appearance of Tamil books. P.R. Hunt introduced three fonts of type in pica, long primer and brevier sizes. He published the smallest Tamil edition of the Bible.

The Tamil types were next in superior to the Roman characters which were imported in the period. G.U. Pope, the author of Tamil handbook printed in 1855 had mentioned in his preface that he would have scarcely ventured to publish in Tamil country, a book requiring such peculiar attention to accuracy in type and arrangement, had he not been zealously seconded by P.R. Hunt, the able superintendent of the American Press, whose efforts helped to improve Tamil typography and to whom the people are certainly indebted.[63]

Tamil typography in Madras reached its excellence and a glance at the pages of Miron Winslow's 'A Comprehensive Tamil-English Dictionary' printed in 1862 with 67,452 words is a witness to the printing enterprise and the craftsmanship. P.R. Hunt had taken extraordinary care in cutting the smallest Tamil letters for this purpose. John Murdoch had praised him and said that the American Mission had raised the standard of Tamil printing.[64] Later many type foundries like A.K. Manicka Mudaliar and Nelson type foundry had come to be located in Madras. K. Namasivaaya Mudaliar had assisted in the printing of books for women and he published a series of books under the title 'Mary Rani'. He greatly assisted in evolving a type between a 12 point and a 14 point and this series had been named after him called *Namasivaaya Yezhuththu Varisai.*[65]

Gnaana Desaanthari: Than Paavangalai Nivaaranam Pannum Vagaiyum Motch Gathiyayum Thedik Kandarindhu Paakiyanaarathai Solliya Sarithiram was printed in 1841 at the American Mission Press (for the Madras Tract and Book Society) in Madras.[66] In the same year another bilingual book (in Tamil and English) was printed titled 'Good Instruction Called Spiritual Milk and Spiritual Lamp in English and Tamil' (*Narpothagamaagiya Gnnanapaalum, Gnaana DeepikaiyumIngilisum Thamizhumaaga Achchadikapattathu*).[67] In 1842 a Tamil book titled *Pala Thirattu containing Tharsamayatchi, Mey Vazhi, Vazhakka Kannaadi, Sathya Vetha Menmai* and *Gnaanapal* was printed.[68]

The American Mission Press in Madras continued to print many books in Tamil during 1843–47 which were used for teaching. These include *Bhuvana Sasthiram: Muthal Pangu* (Geography of Hindoostan, Part I), *Mana Kanidham* (Mental Arithmetic), *Tamil Muthal Puthagam*, *Tamil Irandaam Puthagam* (Tamil series, I and II), *Tamil Instructor*, I, II, III, and IV, *Thiruttantha Sangiragam* (Collection of Proverbs), Geography Part I with Questions and Cliff's First Geography for Natives. *Ingilisum Tamilumaana Agaraathi* (An English and Tamil dictionary or Manual Lexicon for schools giving in Tamil and important English words and the use of many in phrases) got printed in 1844. Abridgment of Rhenius' *Tamil Grammar* was printed in 1845. Scripture textbook (English and Tamil) for each day in the year got printed at the American Mission Press in Madras in 1845.[69] A Tamil reading book was printed in 1845 and a second edition was brought out (for the Madras Christian Knowledge Society) in 1848.[70] The fifth edition of the Tamil first book was again published and later it was printed (for the Christian Vernacular Education Society) at the American Mission Press.[71] The English East India Company laid emphasis on Tamil and English language teaching and so many books came to be printed.

Raising Funds for Tamil Translation: Printing at Neyoor, Nagercoil and Palayamkottai

Printing had been recorded in Nagercoil in 1827. Oriental Translation Fund of Great Britain & Ireland was raised by the English and it facilitated the translation and printing of the Tamil books. It is gleaned that the first volume of the miscellaneous translations was printed under the title *Sagaadevan Sasthiram*. It was translated by Rev. Joseph Roberts and got printed in 1831 and the book had 68 pages. We also find details of all the Tamil books printed under miscellaneous translations.[72]

Tirunelveli Tract and Book Society came to be established by the Protestant missionaries and the printing press started functioning at Neyoor, Nagercoil and Palayamkottai. Many Tamil books were printed and they were circulated. *Vetha Sasthira Surukkam* of Rhenius was printed at Neyoor in 1838 and it had 612 pages.[73] *Suvisesha Sambandha Attavanai* of A.P. Caemmerer was printed at Nagercoil and it had 44 pages.[74] *Gnaanapaatu Puththagam* was printed at Nagercoil. It had 188 pages.[75]

The printing press at Palayamkottai functioned very well and some Tamil books got printed. *Kaanaan Desa Vizhlakkam*, the geography of the land of Cannan was printed in 1849 and it had 264 pages.[76] Edward Sargent's *Pooriviga Sarithiram* was printed in 1850. The translation of Stephen Hobbs that dealt with an outline of ancient history to the birth of the lord Christ was printed. The book had 205 pages.[77] *Madurai Seemai Viruththaantham*, a geographical and historical account of Madura Country got printed at Palayamkottai in 1863.[78]

A report sent by Rhenius and L.B.E. Schmid to Halle in 1823 mentions a geography textbook printed in Tamil for the seminary (Part I: Introduction and Asia), besides other book such as an outline of world history, a chronology of world history, a treatise on different natural phenomena, and a treatise on the main religions and a Tamil grammar printed at Palayamkottai.[79]

An Analysis of the Contents of Geography Books in Tamil Printed at Palayamkottai, Madras and Nagercoil, 1823–56.

Bhoomi Sasthiram, a book in Tamil by Karl Theophilus Ewald Rhenius, dealt with earth science. It had six sections. The first section dealt with the nature of the earth and the Asian continent. The second section dealt with continental Europe. The third section explained about the continent of Africa. The fourth section dealt with the American continent. The fifth dealt with the islands in the southern ocean including Australia. The last section carried an index and errata. It was an exhaustive study of all the continents, their locations, climate and vegetation. Many technical terms in Tamil were used by him, which helped Tamil readers become familiar with such words. Equator, horizon, zenith, meridian, zodiac, ecliptic, constellation, the tropics, summer solstice, winter solstice, torrid zone, temperate zone, frigid zone, latitude, longitude, etc. were explained in Tamil language. The purpose of writing this book, as stated by Rhenius, was the creation of knowledge among the Tamils. The book was printed in Chennaipatnam in 1832 and had 728 pages.[80]

There was a need for a new book on geography, and a book titled *Bhoomi Sasthira Surukkam* (Short Notes on Geography), was printed by Church Mission Press (established by Charles Mault), at Nagercoil in 1846. A textbook on geography for Tamil students, World Geography–First Book, was published at Nagercoil in 1856.[81] Thus knowledge of geography was spread in Tamil through books printed at Madras and Nagercoil between 1832 and 1856.

Textbooks Printed on Astronomy, Oceanography, Mathematics and Algebra in Tamil, 1844-57

The English in Madras printed reading lessons, arranged for everyday in the year, comprising leading facts connected with theology, astronomy, geography, mineralogy, metallurgy, philosophy, natural history; with selections made from *Thirukural*, *Naaladiyaar*, *Moothurai* and *Nanneri*. In 1844, the reading lessons contained historical facts concerning India and England, anecdotes illustrative of moral and religious duties, vocabulary of English adjectives, fables, and a variety of other miscellaneous matter.[82] The titles of the reading lessons were given from 1 January to 31 December.[83] It was followed by *attavanai* (index) from *Thai*, till *Margazhi* (Tamil months).[84]

Reading lessons, arranged for everyday in the year had a chapter on the sun and astronomy in the book for 1844. It stated that the sun was the largest and most magnificent object that came within the range of human observation. Its nature, shape, movements, and other phenomena, had in every age and country awakened inquiry and elicited speculation. The following were the opinions of the wisest of modern astronomers. The sun, the planets, with their moons, and the comets, formed one collection of worlds called the solar system. Of this system the sun was the centre and imparted to the other bodies that moved around it light and heat. The form of the sun was nearly that of a sphere or globe. Its diameter was about 886,000 miles, and its circumference about 2,700,000 miles, its distance from the Earth was about 95,000,000 miles, and its magnitude more than a million times larger than our planet. The sun was generally considered by the ancients to be a globe of pure fire, but the opinion entertained then was, that it was, an opaque body surrounded by an atmosphere of a phosphoric nature. One of the modern philosophers computed the light of the sun on each square foot of the earth turned towards it as equal to 6,500 lamps placed at one foot distance. Though the sun appeared to people as one bright body, yet when seen through a telescope, it was found to have dark spots which were supposed to be openings in the phosphorescent fluid that surrounded it. Though the sun was the centre of a vast number of revolving spheres it was itself ever moving: first, round the common centre of all bodies belonging to our system; second, on its axis; third, towards the constellation Hercules. The science which treated of the forms, distances and appearances of the heavenly bodies was called astronomy. It was a very noble and useful science—noble, for it treated of the most magnificent of the Creator's works;—useful, for it assisted the mariner when voyaging upon the sea, the traveller when traversing foreign and unknown countries, and the historian in ascertaining the dates of events that were past. The sciences of geography, chronology, and navigation were intimately connected with astronomy. People would commend this science to all who can give it their attention. They would derive from it both pleasure and profit.[85]

There was a chapter on earth, its nature and form dealing with geography. It was mentioned that earth in which we live was a large body composed of land and water. Its diameter was about 7,925 miles, and its distance from the sun was 95,000,000 miles. It moved round the sun once in 365 days and 8 hours. The idea was entertained by many ignorant persons that earth was flat like a board. The falsity of this notion would be manifested if we considered the four following facts. (1) If a traveller turned his face to the east or west and journey straight forward, he would after a lapse of time return to the place he had left. This would not be the case were the earth flat like the top of a table. (2) When a ship was voyaging towards land, the first part of it visible to those on shore was the top of the mast, then the sails, and at length the hull. Were the world flat, the whole ship would be visible at one and the same time. (3) When earth came directly between the sun and the moon, the shadow cast upon the moon was circular—which showed conclusively that earth was round. (4) If we journey towards the north-star, that body which was at first just above the horizon would at length be seen above our heads. These facts showed conclusively that the earth was globular. As earth moved round the sun, sometimes one part was turned towards that orb and sometimes another part. This was the cause of day and night. All the time that a certain place was next to the sun, to the inhabitants of that place it was day, when by the earth's motion it was turned away from that place it was night. The length of day and night was different in different parts of the year, and different parts of the world. The science that treated of the nature and form of earth, as also of the various countries, seas, etc. upon its surface, was termed geography. It was a science which the young should study with great care, for without the knowledge of geography, books that treat of other nations could be read with, little interest or profit. With geography readers should connect history and chronology. An opportunity would thus be afforded of bringing to the notice of the readers a greater number of facts relative to the events of all ages and countries which would be found, interesting and instructive.[86]

The phenomena of the sea were also given at length. It was stated that about two-thirds of the surface of earth was covered with water. This water was congregated sometimes in large and sometimes in small portions. The large bodies of water were called oceans while the smaller ones were called seas, gulfs, lakes and rivers. There were five oceans—the Atlantic, Pacific, Indian, Northern and Southern. There were several phenomena connected with the ocean worthy of notice. These were its extent, its strength, its restlessness, its taste, its colour, its invariableness, its depth, its tides, its currents, its phosphorescence, its inhabitants and its utility. Each of these phenomena was briefly noticed. First, the extent of the ocean was mentioned. It was stated that we could look across the widest rivers with the naked eye, by the aid of a magnifying glass we could see across many lakes and bays; but though we ascend the highest mountains and had the assistance of the most powerful telescopes, we cannot see across the ocean. The Atlantic Ocean was 2,300 miles broad. The Pacific Ocean was 10,000 miles wide. The Indian Ocean was 4,000 miles broad. These oceans were also many thousand miles in length. The second phenomenon was that the strength of the ocean, and it was said that when a ship was on the land it required all the strength of many strong men and beasts even to stir it, but when launched into the ocean it sat like a bird on the surface of the water, and was tossed up and down with perfect ease. The ocean could hold up all the ships, even those most heavily laden that could be placed upon it. Besides this, if a ship after being finished must be taken to pieces, it required the labour of many persons for a long time to do it; but the ocean could in a few hours break to pieces the strongest ships. The power and strength of the ocean was great. The third phenomenon was the restlessness of the ocean, and it was said that nowhere was the water of the ocean for an instant still. Its movements were different in degree at different times, but they always existed. The

Prophet Isaiah compared the heart of a wicked man to the sea, because it was never peaceful and never happy.[87] Thus, the subject of science was treated in the reading lessons. The details were given with a view to make the subject of science popular among the people in Madras with scientific information and facts provided in a manner that was easily understandable.

A bilingual (Tamil and English) book titled the elements of Algebra was published for the use of students in the government schools, as per the orders of the Director of Public Instruction in Madras. The basic concepts of algebra, the western system of a special branch of mathematics, were for the first time printed and made available to Tamil students in 1857.[88] A book entitled Elements of Geometry in Tamil Part I was meant for school children. This was the first book on measurements. Since all mathematical concepts were learnt by heart by school children in the Tamil region, the English had printed the book with geometrical drawings and algebra concepts.[89] Thus, the knowledge of mathematics was spread by means of printed books in Tamil.

Books on Medicine and Chemistry Printed in Tamil from Madras, Nagercoil and Palayamkottai, 1850-57

Samuel Fisk Green (1822–84) began to define medical terms in Tamil, and he undertook the task of creating a medical nomenclature in Tamil in 1850.[90] He published *Angaathi Paatha Sugarna Vaatha Urpaalana Nool* from Madras in 1857. This was a translation of Calvin Cutter's book in English titled Anatomy, Physiology and Hygiene. It was translated into Tamil by S.F. Green with the help of some Tamils. The book had 204 pages.[91] Tamilized English words were used to suit Tamil pronunciation. Many Sanskrit words were interspersed in this book. In 1855 S.F. Green started a dictionary of Tamil medical science and another work on medical synonyms in English and Tamil.[92] The American Mission in Nagercoil printed a book titled Chemistry, Practical and Theoretical in 1857.[93] The missionaries and the English Company in Madras made efforts to print science books. The Christian Vernacular Literature Society in Madras and the Madras Tract Book Society played a key role in this regard.

The Almanacs Prepared by Tamils and Printed in Madras, 1848-52

A bilingual almanac (Tamil and English) for the year 1848 was worked out by Somasegaram Pillai and it was printed at Madras.[94] The pages are numbered in the Tamil numbering system. The almanac dealt with the astronomical knowledge of the Tamils giving details of the solar and lunar eclipses, new moon and full moon formations, besides several other celestial data. The contents of the book included diagrams illustrating the nature of solar and lunar eclipses, the solar system, the waning and waxing of the moon, the Earth, tables of days, *tithies* and *yugas*, tables of months and signs, explanations of astronomical symbols, fixed and movable festivals, lunar eclipse, the reason why they had discontinued astrology in this almanac, a new planet and ephemeris of the planets.[95]

Another bilingual book of almanac (Tamil and English) for the year 1852, the Bissextile or Leap Year, was worked out as a technical almanac by Vaithiyalinga Pillai. It was printed at Madras in 1852. The almanac provided certain technical, astrophysical and astronomical data about the solar system. There was information about the size of the sun and also those of a few other planets. Taking the size of earth as one unit, the author gave in English the size of Mercury, Venus, Mars, Vesta, Jupiter, Saturn and Herschel. He also gave the distance from the sun and the period of revolution of several planets in Tamil in a tabular form.[96] Thus, astronomical and astrophysical knowledge was spread among the public by printing calendars and almanacs in Tamil at Madras between 1848 and 1852.

The Impact of European Printing at the Royal Courts of the Rajas of Ramanathapuram and Thanjavur

Tamils did not know the art of printing even during the third decade of the eighteenth century and it is attested by the fact that Kumara Muthu Vijaya Raghunatha Sethupathi @ Katta Thevan the ruler of Ramanathapuram (17 September 1729-12 August 1735), contacted the Protestant missionaries of Tranquebar in 1730, and he tried to enlist the support of the missionaries to have the Raamayanam in Tamil to be printed. The missionaries were not interested to print Hindu texts and so they politely refused.[97] The ruler was though willing to finance the complete expenditure, the technology unknown to him was a great barrier. The missionaries did not wish to print and circulate the Hindu sacred text. However, Tamils had come own printing press in Madras only by 1812.

Printing in Tamil by the Protestant missionaries had paved way for an interest in publishing and owning a printing press by Serfoji II, the Raja of Thanjavur (1798-1832). He had desired to have a printing machine and we find in a correspondence of 7 June 1803.[98] Directions were given by the British and Foreign Bible Society for procuring a printing press, a font of Tamil types, together with a considerable quantity of printing paper to be supplied to the Raja in 1809. The English East India Company had permitted the Raja to have the printing machine and Benjamin Torin the former British resident of Thanjavur was asked on 30 September 1811 to arrange for sending a printing machine.[99] It was finally shipped from London free of freight to Thanjavur. As no Tamil types were available for purchase locally, the idea of cutting types at the palace in Thanjavur was mooted. The Raja made efforts to establish a Devanagari press. The superior and elegant Devanagari types were cast for Serfoji and these were not simply crafted out of a European template, but were the result of a five-year long typographical experiment funded and directed by the Thanjavur court involving several kinds of expertise.[100]

The High School in Madras evolved into the Presidency College and the Madras University was established by Lord Elphinstone the Governor with the University Board on 12 December 1839 necessitated preparation and printing of several textbooks and handbooks for the use of students and it is altogether a different phase in printing. The battle of books took place with special reference to the contents in the textbooks prepared. In a Tamil poem, a portion of which was prescribed for examination by the Madras University, there was a glowing description of what cannot be named. The scenes which took place in the bridal chamber were related at length in another part of the poem. Murdoch's criticism was specially focused on textbooks, and he even authored a pamphlet, titled 'The Idolatrous and Immoral Teachings of Some Government and University Text Books'. In it, he advocated the expurgation of objectionable passages, and suggested making selections instead of prescribing the full text.[101] Under these circumstances Tamil poems of love and war and the texts of *Aganaanuru* and *Puranaanuru* could not be printed. The ethical and religious texts in Tamil therefore saw the light of printing on large scale.

In England a free copy of every book, which was published, must be presented to the British Museum but this was not the case in Madras or throughout India.[102] The English Company in Madras did not have any systematic way of keeping track of the publishing activity of the Tamils till 1856. There was no statement of books printed in Madras and there was also no official catalogue of books registered for the years. At the outbreak of the Sepoy Mutiny in 1857, Lord Canning, the Governor-General of India (1856-1862), passed the Licensing Act of 1857 and according it, licenses were required to be taken for keeping printing presses.[103] All applications were to be made to the Governor-General in Council, who might grant licenses on any conditions they pleased or refuse to grant without assigning any reasons. No observation impugning the motives or designs of the British Government, whether in England or in India, or in any way tending to bring it into contempt, weaken its authority or that of its servants, civil or military were to be published. There was a standing order in all printing establishments that a copy be filed at once of every sheet printed, and preserved for reference. Every press was compelled, under the penalty of having its license withdrawn, to send to the authorities, before the end of

January, a list of all the works printed during the year, filled up in the form prescribed. There were few lithographic presses belonging to European merchants used solely for commercial purposes and so such were excluded from the above rule.[104]

Our investigation shows that there were 13 printing presses actively engaged in printing in Madras city between 1766 and 1857. It is gleaned that 212 books in Tamil language and 27 bilingual books (in English and Tamil) were printed from Madras between 1766 and 1857. We find 19 books in Tamil and 16 books in Tamil respectively printed from the towns like Palayamkottai and Nagercoil. There were 8 journals and 3 newspapers in Tamil published in Madras besides innumerable number of pamphlets in Tamil issued in Madras between 1766 and 1857. Translation society established in Madras helped the preparation and printing of school textbooks. The preparation of Tamil fonts in Madras developed and P.R. Hunt of the American Mission Press improved the Tamil typography between 1838 and 1857. We find interestingly Tamil texts being printed with even spacing, punctuation marks like the semicolon, colon, the question mark and the exclamation mark introduced for the first time. In the expanding English East India Company rule the development of Tamil prose took place with a lot of English words freely mixed. The institutions like the Madras School Book Society, the Religious Tract Society, Fort St. George College in Madras had contributed towards printing in Tamil. The British introduction of printing helped develop written Tamil language with the publication of grammars, vocabularies and Tamil literary texts with the founding of new type fonts to meet the requirements of the Tamil language structure. The periodicals published were the forerunners of modern Tamil journalism. Before the arrival of Europeans, periodicals did not exist in Tamil country. The periodicals printed acted as outlets for the intellectual Tamil communities and began to act as a communication network. Some of the individuals who printed books were extremely dedicated to Tamil. In Madras city the printers were trained, printing equipments were collected and Tamil type fonts were invented and cast, to be put at the disposal of press. The *Ayutha Yezthu* or *Muppar Pulli* letter (mentioned in Tholkaapiyam, Muthal Paagam, Yezhthu Athigaaram Sirappu Paayiram) was cast in Tamil in Madras and it came to be used in printing in 1826 in the book titled *Dharuma Nool* by the College of Fort St. George press. It is important because the Jesuits and the Protestant missionaries in Tranquebar had not adopted it earlier in their printing.

Notes

1. E.W. Grinfield, *Sketches of the Danish Mission on the Coast of Coromandel*, London, 1831, pp. 89-90.

2. Graham Shaw, *The South Asia and Burma Retrospective Bibliography, Stage 1: 1556-1800*, London, 1987, p. 9.
3. Archiv der Franckesche Stiftungen (hereafter AFSt), Halle, M2 B6:1.
4. AFSt, M2 B6:16.
5. *Der Königl. Dänischen Missionarien aus Ost-Indien eingesandter ausführlichen Berichten, Von dem Werck ihrs Ams unter den Heyden, angerichteten Schulen und Gemeinen, ereigneten Hindernissen und schweren Umstanden; Beschaff-enheit des Malabarischen Heydenthums, gepflogenen brieflicher Correspondentz und mundlchen Unterredungen mit selbigen heyden*, Teil 1–9, (Continuationen 1–108) Waiserihaus, Halle, 1710–1772 (hereafter HB), continuation 105, p. 998.
6. British Library, London (hereafter BL), Or.72.b.11.
7. Georg Christian Knapp, et.al., *Neuere Geschichte der evangelischen Missions-Anstalten zu Bekehrung der Heiden in Ostindien aus den eigenhändigen Aufsätzen und Briefen der Missionarien erausgegeben*, Teil 1–8, (Stück 1–95) Waisenhaus, Halle, 1770-8/ 1795-1848, (hereafter NHB), XIII, p. 48.
8. NHB, XII, p. 1474; NHB, XIII, p. 48.
9. BL, no. 14170.a.41. *Mokshattukku Pora Vazhiyai Vezhipaduthugira Gnaana Upadesam*, Tharanganpadiyil, 1777 (year is mentioned in Tamil characters). The book contains 48 pages; see also, Bodleian Library, Oxford, Drav.f.17.
10. BL, 14170.cc.1.
11. NHB, Continuation, 52, pp. 379, 382.
12. Bayerische Staats Bibliothek, Munich, A.or.5646, Johann Philipp Fabricius, *Paappu maarkam innathenru kaanpikkira thezhlivaana vilakkam, Irandam Pathithal*, MDCCXCVIII.
13. BL, no. 14170.c.26, Carl Heinrich von Bogatzky, *Paramandalangali Thangal Pokkisham Undenirukkira Paraaparanudaya Pillaigalin Aabarana Petti*, Translated into Tamil by Daniel Pillai, Vepery, 1800.
14. Johann Philipp Fabricius, *A Dictionary of English and Malabar*, II vols., Mission Press, Vepery, Madras, MDCCLXXVI, Archives of the Gurukul Lutheran Theological College and research Institute, (hereafter AGLTC), microfilm, accession no. 578, Roll no. 51.
15. BL, 622.k.9; 621.1.29; Bodleian Library, Oxford, Drave.d.4; Library of the School of Oriental and African Studies, London, EB.77.16; Universitats Bibliothek Gottingen, Ling.II.7345.1, Johann Philipp Fabricius, *Tamilum Inglishumaay Irukkira agaraathi: A Malabar and English Dictionary, Wherein the Words and Phrases of the Tamilian Language, Commonly called by the Europeans the Malabar Language, are Explained in English by the English Missionaries of Madras*, Wepery, near Madras, 1779.
16. Library of the School of Oriental and African Studies, London, EB.78.177, EB.78.29; BL, London, 621.1.29; Det Kongelige Bibliotek (hereafter KB), Kobenhavn, 72-1113; Royal Asiatic Society Library, London, 175B; Universitats Bibliothek Gottingen, Ling.II.7345, Johann Philipp Fabricius and Johann Christian Breithaupt, *A Dictionary of the English and Malabar Languages, Printed and Completely done at Vepery, near Madras*, 1786.
17. Johann Philipp Fabricius, *A Grammar for Learning the Principles of the Malabar Language, Properly Called Tamul or the Tamulian Language, by the English*

Missionaries of Madras, Printed at Wepery near Madras in the year MDCCLXXVIII; Bodleian Library, Oxford, Drav.e.80.

18. KB, 167-1665; Bodleian Library, Oxford, Drave.e.90; BL, 1609/4372.
19. *Oru Paththira Thirattu: A compilation of papers in the Tamil language including general or public business to which is added a glossary in Tamil & English of many words used chiefly in the business of the courts & public cutcherries*, edited by Andrew Robertson of the Madras Civil Service, Printed at Vepery Mission Press of the Society for Promoting Christian Knowledge, 1839.
20. A. Maa, Sami, *Paththonpatham Nuttrandu Thamizh Ithalgal*, Madras, 1993, p. 57.
21. Government Gazette, Madras, 21 November 1804.
22. *The First Report of the Religious Tract Association at Madras*, 1819.
23. *Twenty Fifth Report of the Madras Tract and Book Society with an Abstract of the Society's Publications for the Year Ending December 1843*, Madras: American Mission Press, 1844, pp. 1, 8.
24. *Twenty Sixth Report of the Madras Tract and Book Society with an Abstract of the Society's Publications for the Year Ending December 1844*, Madras: American Mission Press, 1845, p. 1V.
25. BL, 14170.b.42, Rhenius, *Vetha Sasthira Surukkam*, Neyoor, 1838; BL, 14170.b.43, *Vetha Sasthira Surukkam*, Third edition, 1845; *Vetha Saasthira Surukkam, Iraniusaiyaraaley Seyyapattathu: Summary of a Body of Divinity in the Tamil Language by the Late Reverend CTE Rhenius Missionary*, Fourth edition, Madras The Tract and Book Society, The American Mission, Madras, 1852.
26. *Twenty Sixth Report of the Madras Tract and Book Society with an Abstract of the Society's Publications for the Year Ending December 1844*, Madras: American Mission Press, 1845, p. 2.
27. Ibid., pp. 16–19.
28. Ibid., pp. 19–20.
29. *Twenty-fifth Report of the Madras Tract & Book Society with an Abstract of the Society's Publications for the Year Ending December 1843*, Madras, Published at the American Mission Press, 1844, p. 6.
30. *Twenty-Sixth Report of the Madras Tract & Book Society with an Abstract of the Society's Publications for the Year Ending December 1844*, Madras, Published at the American Mission Press, 1845, p. 4.
31. Ibid., p. 5
32. BL. 14170.k.32, *Kattu Kathaigal: Aesop's fables, containing instructive morals, translated into Tamil by A. Theroovengada Pillay, (together with the English text) and revised by C. Rajah Sooboroya Moodeliar*, Madras, 1853; *Nedungakannkennum Yen Chuvadi*, ed. T. Kuppan Iyengar, Madras, 1859; S. Jeyaseela Stephen, *A Meeting of the Minds: European and Tamil Encounters in Modern Sciences, 1507-1857*, Delhi, 2016, p. 812.
33. BL, *Public Consultations*, no. 12, Entry dated 23 February 1836.
34. A. Maa, Sami, Paththonpatham Nuttrandu, p. 59. Murdoch had not mentioned Tamil Magazine. See, John Murdoch, *A Classified Catalogue of Tamil Printed*

Books with Introductory Notes, Madras, 1865. S. Jeyaseela Stephen, A Meeting of the Minds, p. 815.

35. *Twenty-fifth Report of the Madras Tract & Book Society with an Abstract of the Society's Publications for the Year Ending December 1843*, Printed at the American Mission Press, 1844, pp. 5-6.
36. A. Maa, Sami, Paththonpatham Nuttrandu, pp. 60-62.
37. Karl Graul, 'Notizen, Correspondenzen und Vermischtes. Die tamulische Bibliothek der evan. luth. Missionsanstalt zu Leipzig', *Zeitschrift der Deutschen Morgenländischen Gesellschaft*, H.VII, Leipzig, 1853, pp. 558-568.
38. A. Maa, Sami, Paththonpatham Nuttrandu pp. 404-41.
39. Ibid., p. 60.
40. Ibid., p. 295.
41. BL, *Madras Public Consultations*, (hereafter MPC) 13 February 1816.
42. Sascha Ebeling, 'The college of Fort St .George and the transformation of Tamil philology during the nineteenth century', in Thomas R. Trautman, ed., *The Madras School of Orientalism: Producing Knowledge in Colonial South India*, New Delhi, Oxford University Press, 2009, pp. 233-260.
43. A. Muttusami Pillai, 'A Brief Sketch of the Life and Writings of Father C. J. Beschi or Viramamuni Translated from Original Tamil with a Portrait', *The Madras Journal of Literature and Science*, Vol. XI, January-June 1840, pp. 250-300,
44. Ibid., p. 257.
45. BL, Government Gazette, Madras, 9 October 1817.
46. BL, Government Gazette, Madras, 7 December 1824.
47. Robert Caldwell, *Records of the Early History of the Tinnevelly Mission of the Society for Promoting Christian Knowledge and the Society for the Propagation of the Gospel in Foreign Parts*, Higginbotham & Co., Madras, 1881, p. 185; See also, Robert Eric Frykenberg, 'Modern Education in South India 1784-1854: Its Roots and its Role as a Vehicle of Integration Company Raj', *Journal of Historical Review*, vol. 91, no.1, 1986, pp. 37-65.
48. BL, Oriental and India Office Collection (hereafter OIOC), *Madras Public Consultations*, 22 December 1815, List of books printed, printing, or preparing for the Fort St. George College Press.
49. BL, OIOC, *Madras Public Consultations*, 4 December 1819, Inventory of books printed, printing, or preparing for the Fort St. George College Press.
50. 'Minute by the Right Honourable Lord Auckland the Governor General dated 24 November 1839', in H. Sharp, ed., *Selections from the Educational Records, 1781–1839*, Calcutta, 1920, p. 162.
51. Ibid., p. 169.
52. BL, 14170.cc.4; BL, 14170.b.48; BL, 14170.bb.5. Stuart Blackburn, *Print, Folklore and Nationalism in Colonial South India*, New Delhi, 2003, pp. 191-194; S. Jeyaseela Stephen, A Meeting of the Minds, pp. 787-94, 803-4. It may be mentioned that Pothuvaana Sepa Posthagam, Tamil translation by Christian David was printed at Serampore, in the Mission press in 1818. It had 378 pages. See, BL, 14170.b.51.

53. *First Lessons and Idiomatic Exercises in English and Tamul with Forms of Petitions and C Designed to Assist Tamul Youths in the Study of English Language*, Nellore, Church Mission Press, Nellore, 1830.
54. BL, 14170.e.16, *Vetha Uthaarana Thirattu*, Madras, 1835; BL, 14170.b.41, *Vetha Uthaarana Thirattu*, revised edition, Madras, 1852.
55. BL, 14170.a.6, *Gnnana Upadesam by Manikkam Royappa Swami*, Madras, 1839.
56. BL, 14170.c.23, *Vethiyar Ozhukkam*, Madras, 1844.
57. *Analysis of a Volume in Tamil entitled Practical Expressions of the Parables of Christ*, Madras, American Mission Press, 1844.
58. BL, 14170.aa.27, , John Christian Aroolappan, *Satta Thittam*, American Madras Mission, Madras, 1845; BL, 14170.b.25, John Christian Aroolappan, *Sathya Vetha Kannaadi*, Madras, 1846.
59. BL, 14170.a.7, *Devaaarathaniyiley Paadugira Gnaanapaatum Adangiya Sangeetha Thirattu*, Madras, 1848.
60. BL, 14170.c. 18, *Patha Manjari*, Madras, 1852.
61. BL, 14170.c.5 (1), *Gnaana Paatukal*, American Madras Mission, Madras, 1853.
62. BL, 14170.b.54, *Saathi Viththiyaasa Vizhlakkam*, Madras, 1857.
63. George Uglow Pope, *Tamil Hand Book*, First edition, 1855, Preface, p. iv. See also his other books BL, 14172h.39 (1), George Uglow Pope, *Thamizh Ilakkana Noor Surukka Vinaa Vidai*, fifth edition, Madras, 1855; BL, 14172.h.40, George Uglow Pope, Introductory Tamil Grammar: Thamizh Ilakkana Noor Surukka Vinaa Vidai, second edition, Madras, 1846; BL, 14172.h,81, Pope's Third Tamil Grammar, *Ilakkana Nool*, 2 parts, Madras, 1858.
64. John Murdoch, *Papers on Indian Reform – Is India becoming Richer? With the Proposed Remedies for the Existing Poverty*, Vepery, Madras, 1887, p. 67.
65. Ma. Su. Sambandan, Achchum Pathippum, p.136.
66. *Gnaana Desaanthari: Than Paavangalai Nivaaranam Pannum Vagaiyum Motch Gathiyayum Thedik Kandarindhu Paakiyanaarathai Solliya Sarithiram. Ithu Ingilisu Bhashayilirundhu Thamizh Bhashaiyile Thiruppiyathu,* Madras, Printed at the American Mission Press for the Madras Tract and Book Society, 1841.
67. *Good Instruction Called Spiritual Milk and Spiritual Lamp in English and Tamil: Narpothagamaagiya Gnnanapaalum, Gnaana Deepikaiyum Ingilisum Thamizhumaaga Achchadikapattathu*, Madras, Printed at the American Mission Press for the American Madras Mission, 1841.
68. *Pala Thirattu: Ithiley Tharsamayatchi, Mey Vazhi, Vazhakka Kannaadi, Sathya Vetha Menmai, Gnaanapalum Serkkapattirukirathu: Select Tracts Containing Hinduism's Own Witness, The True Way, Mirror of Custom, Excellency of the Bible and Spiritual Milk,* Madras, Printed at the American Mission Press, 1842.
69. *Second Brief Report of the American Madras Mission, 1843–1847 with an Appendix*, American Mission Press, Madras, 1848.
70. *Tamil Reading Book, Pallikudangalrir Payittruvikka Vendi Tamil Vasaga Puthagam, 1845,* 2nd edn., Madras Christian Knowledge Society Press, Vepery, 1848.
71. *Tamil First Book, Tamil Mutharpusthagan*, Fifth edition, Madras, Christian Vernacular Education Society, Madras: American Mission Press, 1860.

72. BL, 14003.d.5, *Sagaadevan Sasthiram or Book of Fate* Translated by Rev. Joseph Roberts, Madras, 1831.
73. BL, 14170.b.42, *Vetha Sasthira Surukkam*, Neyoor, 1838.
74. BL, 14170b.14 (2), *Suvisesha Sambandha Attavanai*, Nagercoil, 1854.
75. BL, 14170.b.18, *Gnaanapaatu Puththagam*, Nagercoil, 1848.
76. BL, 14170.c.11, *Kaanaan desa Vizhlakkam*, Palayamkottai, 1849.
77. BL, 14170.h.17, Edward Sargent, *Pooriviga Sarithiram*, Palayamkottai, 1850.
78. BL, 14172.h.66, *Madurai Seemai Viruththaantham*, Palayamkottai, 1863.
79. NHB 72. St., 1277.
80. Karl Theophilus Ewald Rhenius, *Bhoomi Sasthiram*, Chennaipatnam, 1832.
81. Bibliothek der Franckeschen Stiftungen, Halle (hereafter BFSt), BFSt/C:38:49; *Thamizh pillaigalukkkaha yerpaduthappatta bhumai sasitram muthalam puthagam*, South India Christian School Book Society, The London Mission Press, Nagercoil, 1856.
82. *Dhinamari Vizhlakkam*: *Reading Lessons, Arranged for every day in the year: Comprising the leading facts connected with theology, astronomy, geography, mineralogy, metallurgy, philosophy, natural history: Selections from Cural, Naladeyar, Mootheri, Nanneri (Historical facts concerning India and England–Anecdotes illustrative of moral, religious duties and vocabulary of English adjectives–Fables and a variety of other miscellaneous matter)*, Madras, Asylum Press, 1844.
83. Ibid., pp. i-x.
84. Ibid., pp. 1–26.
85. Ibid., pp. 6–7. Against Sunday, 3 January 1845 and Tuesday, 5 January 1845, the sun and its dimensions and phenomenon were printed.
86. Ibid., p. 8. On Wednesday, 6 January 1845, the subject of Earth had been treated.
87. Ibid., p. 10. On Friday, 8 January 1845, the phenomena of the sea had been given.
88. BFSt/ C: 38:5; *The Elements of Algebra*, Director of Public Instruction, Scottish Press, Madras, 1857, pp. 1–98.
89. BFSt, C:38:74; Thomas Lund, *Alavu Nool, Mudhalam Puthagam*, Madras, 1857, pp. 1–165.
90. Ebenezer Cutter, ed., *Life and Letters of Samuel Fisk Green*, London, 1891.
91. BL, 14172.h.55, *Angaathi Paatha Sugarana Vaatha Udarpaalana Nool*, Second edition, Madras, 1857.
92. K. Meenkashisundaram, *The Contribution of European Scholars to Tamil*, Madras, 1974, p. 42.
93. *Chemistry, Practical and Theoretical*, American Ceylon Mission, Nagercoil, 1857.
94. Bibliothek der Evangelisch-Lutherisches Missionsanstalt, Leipzig (hereafter BELM), Somasegaram Pillai, *Thiri yaangam 1848*, The American Mission Press, Madras, 1848, pp. 1–60.
95. Ibid., pp. 1–12.

96. BELM, Vaithiyalinga Pillay, *Thiri Yaangam 1852*, Madras Tract and Book Society, Madras, 1852, pp. 1–188.
97. HB, vol. III, continuation 31, p. 704.
98. Tamilnadu State Archives, Chennai, (hereafter TNSA), *Tanjore District Records*, vol. 3477, pp. 1001-10.
99. TNSA, *Tanjore District Records*, vol. 3503, p. 213.
100. Savithri Preetha Nair 'Of real use to the people: The Tanjore printing press and the spread of useful knowledge', *The Indian Economic and Social History Review*, vol. 48, no. 4, 2011, pp. 497–529.
101. John Murdoch, 'Duty of Government with respect to Vernacular Literature in India', Nos. 45-48, Educational, 19 March 1867; see Nos. 16-18, Educational, 10 December 1874.
102. BL, G. O. no. 49, Home, 1866.
103. BL, G. O. no. 50, Home, 1866.
104. BL, G.O. no. 51, Home (Public Branch), 1866.

ELLIS' CURAL,

ABRIDGED.

எல்லிஸ் குறள்.

அறப்பால்—ON VIRTUE.

CHAPTER I.

கடவுள்வாழ்த்து—The Praise of God.

அகரமுதலவெழுத்தெல்லாமாதி
பகவன்முதற்றேயுலகு.

As ranked in every alphabet the first,
The selfsame vowel stands, so in all worlds,
The eternal God is chief.

கற்றதனாலாயபயனென்கொல்வாலறிவ
னற்றாடொழாஅரெனின்.

What is the fruit that human knowledge gives,
If at the feet of Him, who is pure knowledge,
Due reverence be not paid.

மலர்மிசையேகினான்மாணடிசேர்ந்தார்
நிலமிசைநீடுவாழ்வார்.

They who adore His sacred feet, whose grace
Gladdens with sudden thrill the fervent heart,
High o'er the earth shall soar to endless joy.

வேண்டுதல்வேண்டாமையிலானடிசேர்ந்தார்க்
கியாண்டுமிடும்பையில.

To Him, whom no affection moves nor hate
Those constant in obedience, from all ill
In this world and the next, are free.

4.1. Ellis Kural translated into English and printed in Madras in 1814. (Courtesy: Bodleian Library, Oxford).

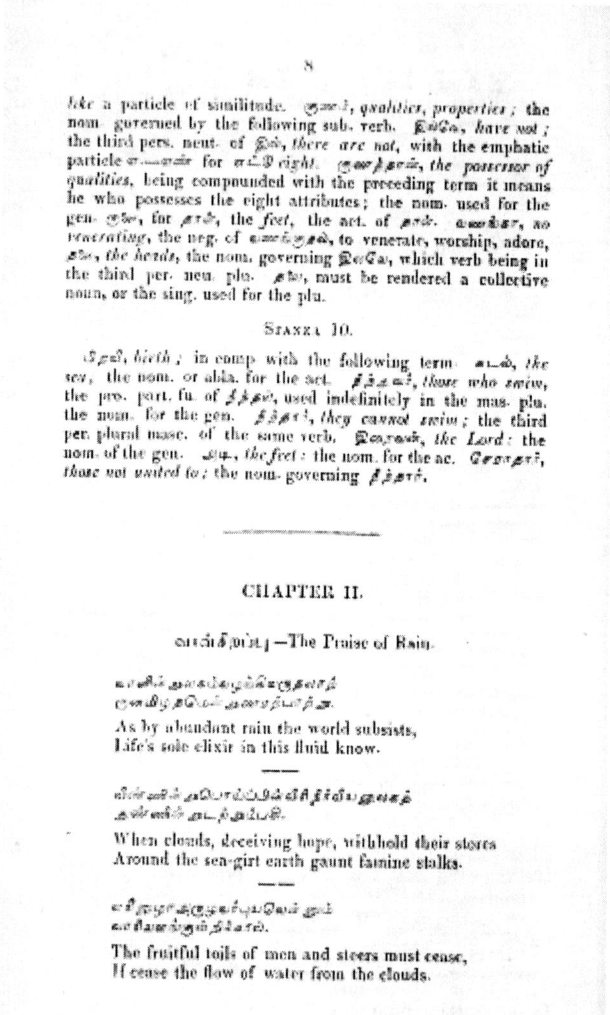

8

like a particle of similitude. [illegible], *qualities, properties;* the nom. governed by the following sub. verb. [illegible], *have not;* the third pers. neut. of [illegible], *there are not*, with the emphatic particle [illegible] for [illegible] *eight.* [illegible], *the possessor of qualities*, being compounded with the preceding term it means he who possesses the eight attributes; the nom. used for the gen. [illegible], for [illegible], the *feet*, the act. of [illegible]. [illegible], *no venerating*, the neg. of [illegible], to venerate, worship, adore, [illegible], *the heads*, the nom. governing [illegible], which verb being in the third per. neu. plu. [illegible], must be rendered a collective noun, or the sing. used for the plu.

STANZA 10.

[illegible], *birth;* in comp. with the following term [illegible], *the sea*, the nom. or abla. for the act. [illegible], *those who swim*, the pro. part. fu. of [illegible], used indefinitely in the mas. plu. the nom. for the gen. [illegible], *they cannot swim;* the third per. plural masc. of the same verb. [illegible], *the Lord:* the nom. of the gen. [illegible], *the feet:* the nom. for the ac. [illegible], *those not united to;* the nom. governing [illegible].

CHAPTER II.

[illegible]—The Praise of Rain.

[illegible]
[illegible]

As by abundant rain the world subsists,
Life's sole elixir in this fluid know.

[illegible]
[illegible]

When clouds, deceiving hope, withhold their stores
Around the sea-girt earth gaunt famine stalks.

[illegible]
[illegible]

The fruitful toils of men and steers must cease,
If cease the flow of water from the clouds.

4.2. Page eight from Ellis Kural printed in Madras in 1814. (Courtesy: Bodleian Library, Oxford).

TEXT.

Translation.

The symptoms of the Sidángum are—general coldness of the body, looseness of the bowels, pains in the joints, great thirst, flatulency affecting the lungs and causing a difficulty in breathing, cough, swooning, hiccup, a general weakness of the body, delirium. The Sidánga-sannidon, usually fatal in fifteen days, is accounted incurable; but when Medicine is demanded, the gift of a Cow having been previously made, it may be administered, relying on the mercy of God.

The remedy prescribed for it, in the Chintamani is the composition called *Rasa Ananda B,hairavam* of which the formula is contained in the following extract.—

SANSCRIT.

Translation.

Rasa Calyána B,hairavam is a medical composition formed of the following Ingredients; namely,

1.	Rasam	Mercury.
2.	Visham (1)	A poisonous Root.
3.	Valham	Venom of a Serpent.
4.	Gand,ham	Brimstone.
5.	Nága	Calx of Zinc.
6.	Vengam	Do. of Lead.
7	Caná	Long Pepper.

All these should be of equal weight. Grind them together with the juice of Chittramúlam (a medicinal root "CeylonLeadwort, Plumbago Zeylanica," it is of a very hot nature, and in medical works, therefore, is known by all the synonymes of Fire) for 12 hours, make them into pills and letting them dry in the air, put them into a strong crucible, place it in a sandbath and calcine for 12 hours; then grind the mass with the gall of fish and form it into pills of 2 grains each. This, the Rasa Calyána B,hairavam may be given in the species of convulsion called Carnica, the diet being carefully attended to and confined to milk with Rice boiled and mixed with sugar; the drink to be the syrup of Sugar-Candy.

The species comprehended under the class *Ajirna* are four, which are thus enumerated in the Chintámani.

DISEASES.	DISTINGUISHING SYMPTOMS.
1. Rasa Sésham.	Dyspepsia, in which the Head is chiefly affected—Megrims; it takes its specific name from its being often caused by the excessive use of Mercury.
2. Viswash'tam.	This is the common Dyspepsia, affecting the whole body, attended by pains in the limbs and joints.
3. Vidhámam.	Vishúchi, attended by the symptoms hereafter explained is comprehended under this term—*Vil,hamá cha Vishúchy sntu.*
4. Dhámam.	Dyspepsia attended by *spontaneous coldness*, but neither so rapid in progress nor virulent in degree.

4.3. *The Tamil text and its translation printed in the Madras Courier of 12 January 1819.* (Courtesy: *British Library, London).*

4

The	அநத	His	அவனுடைய
Get	வாஙகுகிறது எடுததுககொளளுகிறது	Her	அவளை அவளுடைய
Run	ஓடுகிறது	See	காணகிறது பாரககிறது

Get my old hat — என பழைய தொபபியை எடுததுவா
I see her — அவளைக காணகிறேன
The hat is his — அநத தொபபி அவனுடையது
See my new box — என புதிய பெடடியைப பார
Run & get his bad ink

May	ஆம	Ask	கேடகிறது
Can	கூடும	Him	அவனை
Fly	பறககிறது	You	நீ—நீர

Ask him — அவனைக கேள
Can you fly? no — நீ பறககக கூடுமோ? இலலை
An ant may fly — ஒரெறும்பு பறககலாம
You may go — நீபோகலாம
If he ask, he may go

She	அவள	Pen	தூவல
Can-not	கூடாது	Eye	கண
Cry	அழுகிறது	But	ஆனாலும

I cry,but you cannot நானழுகிறேன ஆனாலுநீயழககூடாது
It is my pen — அது என தூவல
She sees my pen — அவள என தூவலைககாணகிறாள
You may see my eye
My pen but her ink

Cut	வெடடுகிறது	Far	தூரமான
Say	சொலலுகிறது	All	எலலாம
Lie	பொயசொலலுகிறது	Eat	தினகிறது

He cut her hat — அவன தொபபியை வெடடினான
I say no — இலலையெனறு நான சொலலுகிறேன
You lie — நீ பொயசொலலுகிறாய

***4.4. Page four of First lessons and exercises in English and Tamul designed to assist Tamul Youths in the study of English printed at the Church Mission Press in Nellore in 1830.* (Courtesy: *Bodleian Library, Oxford*).**

HEATHENISM REJECTED AND CHRIST RECEIVED.

SONGS OF PRAISE,

BY WESLEY ABRAHAM,

A NATIVE POET, FORMERLY CALLED ARUMUGA TAMBIRAN, SOMETIME OVERSEER OF TARMAPURAM, NEAR TANJORE, WHO, AFTER BEING ENGAGED FIFTY YEARS IN VISITING HOLY PLACES, AND IN INSTRUCTING DISCIPLES, WAS PUBLICLY

BAPTIZED IN THE WESLEYAN CHAPEL, MADRAS, ON THE FIRST SUNDAY IN AUGUST, 1836.

ISAIAH XII. 1, 2.

AND in that day thou shalt say, O Lord, I will praise thee: though thou wast angry with me, thine anger is turned away, and thou comfortedst me.

Behold, God is my salvation; I will trust, and not be afraid: for the Lord JEHOVAH is my strength and my song; he also is become my salvation.

தோத்திரமாலை.

முதலாம்பங்கு.

முன்னேதருமபுரம் ஆதீனவித்துவான்

ஆறுமுகத்தம்பிரானென்றுசொல்லப்பட்டு

இப்போது

வெஸ்லி ஆபிரகாமென்னும்பெயர்பெற்றவர்,

சந்திக்கப்படத்தக்க ரோபர்ட் கார்வர் ஐயராலே

ஞானஸ்நானம்பெற்றவராகிய

இயேசுஇரட்சகர்பேரிலேபாடியது.

PART I.

SIXTH EDITION.

MADRAS, PRINTED AT THE CHURCH MISSION PRESS.

1836.

4.5 Thothira Maalai printed at the Church Mission Press in Madras in 1836.* (Courtesy: *Bodleian Library, Oxford).

A

COMPILATION

OF PAPERS IN THE TAMIL LANGUAGE.

INCLUDING SEVERAL ON PUBLIC BUSINESS,

TO WHICH IS ADDED

A GLOSSARY IN TAMIL AND ENGLISH

OF MANY WORDS USED CHIEFLY IN THE BUSINESS OF THE COURTS

AND PUBLIC CUTCHERRIES.

EDITED BY

ANDREW ROBERTSON,

OF THE MADRAS CIVIL SERVICE.

ஒரு

பத்திரத்திரட்டு

தமிழ்ப்பாஷையில் அதிகாரதோரணமாயெழுதப்பட்ட, அரமனை அலுவல்களில் முக்கியமாய்வழங்குகிறபலமொழிகளுக்கு

ஒரு அகராதியும்சேர்க்கப்பட்டு, சென்னபட்டணத்துக்கிராணியுத்தியோகஸ்தர்களில்,

ம. ா. ா. ஆன்றியு - ரோபர்ட்சன்

துரை அவர்களாலே அச்சிற்பதிப்பிக்கப்பட்டது.

MADRAS:

PRINTED BY R. W. THORPE,

AT THE VEPERY MISSION PRESS, OF THE SOCIETY FOR PROMOTING CHRISTIAN KNOWLEDGE.

1839.

4.6. The title page of Oru Pathirathirattu edited by Andre Robertson printed at Vepery Mission Press in Madras in 1839. (Courtesy: *Bodleian Library, Oxford*).

Good Instruction,

CALLED

SPIRITUAL MILK,

AND

SPIRITUAL LAMP.

In English and Tamil.

நற்போதகமாகிய

ஞானப்பாலும்,

ஞானதீபிகையும்,

இங்கிலீசும், தமிழுமாக

அச்சடிக்கப்பட்டது.

MADRAS:

PRINTED AT THE AMERICAN MISSION PRESS, FOR THE AMERICAN MADRAS MISSION.

1841.

4.7. The title page of Gnnanapaalum gnaana deepikaiyum printed in English and Tamil at the American Mission Press in Madras in 1841.* (Courtesy*: Harvard University Library, Cambridge, Massachusetts, USA).

பல திரட்டு.

இதிலே

தற்சமையசாட்சி.-மெய்வழி.-வழக்கக்
கண்ணாடி.—சத்தியவேதமேன்மை.—
ஞானப்பாலுஞ் சேர்க்கப்பட்டன.

SELECT TRACTS,

CONTAINING

HINDUISM'S OWN WITNESS,

The True Way,

MIRROR OF CUSTOM,

Excellency of the Bible,

AND

SPIRITUAL MILK.

MADRAS:

PRINTED AT THE AMERICAN MISSION PRESS.

1842.

4.8. The title page of Pala Thirattu printed at the American Mission Press in Madras in 1842. **(Courtesy:** ***Harvard University Library, Cambridge, Massachusetts, USA).***

READING LESSONS,

ARRANGED FOR

EVERY DAY IN THE YEAR,

COMPRISING THE LEADING FACTS CONNECTED WITH

THEOLOGY—ASTRONOMY—GEOGRAPHY—MINERALOGY—METEOROLOGY—PHYSIOLOGY—NATURAL HISTORY, (WITH CUTS.)

SELECTIONS FROM

THE CURAL—NALADEYAR—MOOTHERI—NANNERI.

HISTORICAL FACTS CONCERNING INDIA AND ENGLAND—ANECDOTES ILLUSTRATIVE OF MORAL AND RELIGIOUS DUTIES—VOCABULARY OF ENGLISH ADJECTIVES—FABLES—AND A VARIETY OF OTHER MISCELLANEOUS MATTER.

தினமறிவிளக்கம்.

இப்புத்தகத்திலே

[illegible]

MADRAS:

PRINTED AT THE AMERICAN MISSION PRESS.

1844.

4.9. The title page of Dinamari Vizhlakkam printed at the American Mission Press in Madras in 1844. (Courtesy***: Bodleian Library, Oxford).***

TAMIL READING BOOK.

பள்ளிக்கூடங்களிற்

பயிற்றுவிக்கவேண்டிய

தமிழ்

வாசகபுத்தகம்.

௲௮௱௪௰௮.

இது

திருநெல்வேலியிலுள்ள

சார்சென்றையராலே

செய்யப்பட்டது.

இவற்றுள்ச் சிலமுன் எழுதப்பட்டுஞ் சில திருப்பப்பட்டும்
மற்றவை புதிதாய் எழுதப்பட்டுமிருக்கின்றன.

Second Edition.

MADRAS: PRINTED BY REUBEN TWIGG, AT THE CHRISTIAN KNOWLEDGE SOCIETY'S PRESS, VEPERY.

1848.

4.10. The title page of Tamil reading book for schools printed at Vepery Press in 1848.* (Courtesy: *Bodleian Library, Oxford).

வேதசாஸ்திரச்

சுருக்கம்,

இரேனியுசையராலேசெய்யப்பட்டது.

SUMMARY OF A

BODY OF DIVINITY.

IN THE TAMIL LANGUAGE.

BY THE LATE

REVEREND C. T. E. RHENIUS, MISSIONARY.

FOURTH EDITION

MADRAS:
THE TRACT AND BOOK SOCIETY
AMERICAN MISSION PRESS.
1852.

4.11. The title page of Vetha Saasthira Surukkam by Rhenius printed at the American Mission Press in Madras in 1852. **(Courtesy*****: The New York Public Library).***

5

Tamil Authors, Editors and Print Capitalists in Madras: Printing Books, Journals and Newspapers, 1812-57

Tamils were not mute to the development of printing by the Europeans and they did not remain as idle and silent spectators. They began to edit the old manuscripts and continued to write commentaries besides composing new works. Printing machine in India was not that easily available and so they began to buy the imported machine and established their own printing press and invested their funds. Thereafter books, journals and newspapers in Tamil were printed. Hence this chapter explores the role of the natives as authors, editors, printers and publishers and their contribution to the growth of printing and literary development in society.

The Migration of Tamil Scholars to Madras

Pondicherry was under the occupation of the English East India Company from 1793 to 1815. Hence it was easy for the Tamil scholars to migrate to Madras by finding employment.[1] Vidwan Saminatha Pillai was born of a *vellala* Catholic family at Pondicherry in the eighteenth century. Having removed his residence to Madras he was introduced to the notice of F.W. Ellis and he became his preceptor in the Tamil language. He wrote *Nasarai Kalamabagam* and *Saminathan Pillai Thamizh*. He wrote *Gnnadhikkarayar Kaapiyam* and commanded general admiration and so his name got spread far and wide. In the *Gnaadhikiarayar Kaapiyam* he has introduced many historical passages from the Bible by way of episodes in the life of the hero of the poem, in a style and language highly creditable to him. As usual with the writers of epics in Tamil he opens his poem after the invocation with the eulogy on rain and the stanzas were quoted by F.W. Ellis in his comments on the Kural which formed the first part of it.[2]

Appavu Muthusami Pillai was born of a Catholic *vellala* parents in Pondicherry. He learnt several languages and was familiar with Tamil, Sanskrit, Telugu, Latin and English. He obtained the offices of manager of the college of Fort St George and *munshi* to the Tamil translator to the English East India Company at Madras. In 1816 at the desire of Mr. F.W. Ellis the senior member of the College Board he made a journey to the south of Tamil country of procuring useful Tamil manuscripts for the college. He composed *Attrum Uthiyaanam* for private devotional reading by the Roman Catholics and it was compiled from various sources. The book was printed in the commercial press in Madras in 1817 and it had XX + 512 pages.[3]

Muthusami Pillai published the life of Beschi the Italian Jesuit in Tamil and in English. He wrote a work titled '*Vetha Vikarpaa Dhikkaram*' partly in prose and partly in poetry to refute the publication of Ponnambalam a Hindu *vellala* who lived at Purasaiwakkam near Madras titled *Vetha Vikarpaa* (The Misunderstanding of Vethaa) which made a sensation amongst the Protestants and the Catholics for it dealt with condemnation of the Bible. *Vetha Vikarpaa Dhikkaram* of Muthusami Pillai printed in 1840 was received with great applause before the assembly of the learned men in Madras. Muthusami Pillai wrote a commentary on F.W. Ellis stanzas called *Tharavu kochaga kalippaa*. This he did in order to refute an idea which was prevalent amongst the Hindus that Ellis having ended each of his stanzas with the words of *Namasivaaya*, he had therefore become a convert to their religion. Muthusami Pillai proved that these words were never intended to present the pentagramation, but only conveyed the meaning reverence to the only God'. According to records Muthusami Pillai died on 23 September 1840.[4]

Nayanappa Mudaliar born of a *vellala* family in Pondicherry in 1779 left Pondicherry and he found employment as a Tamil pundit in the college of Fort St George. He revised and edited the poems of *Siththambala Kovai*, *Thanjaivaanan Kovai*, Raghunatha Sethupathi's *Oru Thurai Kovai*, *Naaladiyaar*, the ninth and tenth parts of *Dhivaagara Nigandu*, and the eleventh part of *Chudaamani Nigandu* with their explanation in prose. When a committee was formed at Madras amongst the principal Tamil gentlemen in the place for the purpose of publishing an edition of Villiputturar's Mahabharatham the editorship was entrusted to Nayanappa Mudaliar and while collating the different manuscripts of the work he died on 25 January 1845.[5]

Gnaanapragaasa Mudaliar hailing from Pondicherry migrated to Madras. He translated the sketch of ancient Mediterranean history from English to Tamil. It was printed at the American Mission Press in Madras in 1828 and had 39 pages.[6] He also translated the history of India from the time of the Muslim invasion from English into Tamil and the book was printed for the Madras School Book Society in 1830 and it had 89 pages.[7]

Tamil scholars who migrated from Pondicherry to Madras were both authors and publishers. *Thiruvaranga Pathitrupaththandadhi* was composed by Thiruvengadasala Mudaliar of Puthuvai. We find *Iru sol alangaram, Mutchol alangaram* (two words beautification and three words beautification), had been edited by Kuppu Iyer of Thanneerkulam and the book was published by Narayanaswami Mudaliar of Puthuvai.[8]

Polemical Literature and Printing in Tamil by the Natives

Polemical writings between Tamil Hindus and Christians began to develop in Madras in this period. Muthu Kumara Kavirayar wrote *Gnaana Kummi* (Song on Wisdom) and it appeared in print in Madras in 1827. Armuga Thambiran the Saivite of the Dharmapuram Adheenam who embraced Christianity, baptized in Madras by Wesley Abraham in 1836 wrote *Agnaana Kummi*, against the book of *Gnaana Kummi* and it was published in Madras in 1837.[9]

Vethanayagan of Thanjavur wrote Christian literary works. His work *Kuruttu vazhi* (Blind path), a Christian polemic against heathenism was printed in Madras in 1847. He wrote *Sasthira Kummi* (a satire on the superstitious beliefs of the Hindus) and it was printed in Madras in 1840. It got reprinted at the American mission press in Madras in 1850 and also again in 1862.[10] Polemical literature in Tamil had come to be continuously circulated widely. Shanmuga Kavirayar edited *Mei gnana botham* (Teachings of true wisdom) and it was against Christian Missions. This book was printed in Madras.[11]

Gnaanapragsam Pillai of Thanjavur: The First Owner of the Printing Press in Madras and the Books and Newspaper Printed in Tamil, 1812

Gnaanapragasam the son of Malayappa Pillai hailing from Thanjavur had established a printing press in Madras in 1812. It was called *Maasa Thinasarithaiyin Achchukudam*.[12] Thiruvengadam had set up another printing press and it was called *Iyal Thamzih Vizhlakka Achchukudam* in 1819 at Kanchipuram. Hence it is learnt that there was no ban for setting up the printing press in Madras under the English East India Company administration. The view that natives were allowed to own printing press after the Act of 1835 passed by Charles Metcalfe as stated by many scholars repeatedly is therefore called into question and it needs revision.[13] The early colonial policy of the English company in Madras was cautious and it was not aimed towards antagonizing the Hindus.

The court of Directors in London had raised the question of the freedom of the press in 1830 and at that time Lord William Bentinck was apprehensive of the effect of the agitation on the army which recalled to him the circumstances which led to the mutiny of Madras officers in 1809. His minute embodying the decision to impose restrictions on the press, in this behalf, has been an important one because he drew comparison between the state of the press in Madras in 1809 and 1830. The Adjutant-General of the Madras army who was at the time in Calcutta, described the angry feeling and language so loudly expressed, and all the signs of the times, to be precisely similar to those which prevailed before the Mutiny of Vellore, and he anticipated a similar explosion in Calcutta. He said let it be remarked that the mutiny did take place at Vellore in Madras region and though there was not a shadow of liberty belonging to the press there, the communication and interchange of sentiment and concert was as general as if it had passed through medium of a daily-press, without the reserve which the responsibility of the editor more or less required for his own security. His firm belief was that more good than harm was produced by the open and public declaration of the sentiments of the army. There was vent to public feeling, and the mischief was open to public view and the result was so far confirmatory of opinion given, that no overt act had taken place. Sir Charles Metcalfe held the view that any restrictions imposed on the press would cause fresh irritation and provide a new grievance. These regulations remained in force up to 1835 when they were cancelled by Sir Charles Metcalfe in spite of the fact that he was merely acting as Governor-General till Lord William Bentinck was appointed. He showed a great courage in passing, with the help of Lord Macaulay, the Act XI of 1835 abolishing for the whole of India the system of licence and censorship for the press and replaced them by one simple registration as in England. For this step, he incurred the wrath of the Court of Directors of the English Company in London and he was immediately recalled from India.

Maasa Thinasarithai was the first newspaper in Tamil appeared in Madras for the first time in 1812. The news for each month had been collected and printed as monthly as the title suggests. Gnaanapragasam the son of Malayappa Pillai hailing from Thanjavur was the editor of the *Maasa Thinasarithai*.

Thirukural the classical Tamil text was printed in Madras. The title was *Thirukural moola paadam*, and it got published at *Maasa Thinasari-thaiyin Achchukudam* in 1812. The title page of *Thirukural* printed in Tamil mentions Tirunelveli Ambalavaana Kaviraayar had corrected the mistakes and he sent it to Chennapattinam. It was sent again by Ambalavaana Thambiran the Thiruvaavaduthurai Adheena Vidwan from there to Sirkaazhi Vaduhanatha Pandaaram for re-examination and scrutiny. Thereafter the book of Tirukural was printed in paper. It was published in *kaliyuka* 4900, in the year *angirasa* in Tamil printed by Gnaanapargasan, at the *Maasathina Sarithaiyin* printing press in the city of Chennaipattanam situated in Thondaimandalam in the year 1812 (given in Tamil numeral). There are no dots over the Tamil consonants printed in this book.[14] Some more books came to be printed from *Maasa Thinasarithaiyin* printing press. *Naaladiyaar* and *Thiruvaluvamaalai* got printed at the *Maasa Thinasarithai Achchu-kudam* in Madras in 1812.

The increasing role of the Tamil pundits played in composing and printing Tamil books in Madras is important to note. We find the creation of a new literary culture. *Thamizh Vizhlakkam* (Tamil Expositor) authored by Subburaya Mudaliar hailing from Tiruverkadu near Madras was printed in Chennaipattanam in 1811.[15] It was the first Tamil grammar book composed in prose for Tamil audience. It was prepared in the question-answer format. The title page runs thus: '*Thamzhiludaya viyalppai kezhviyumuthaaramumaa yezhuthapatta oru surukkamaana vayamai adangiya Thamizh Vizhlakkam. Thirverkaadu Subbaraya Mudaliyaaraal undu panni ingilisi bhashaiyil mozhi peyarkkapattathu. Chennaipattanaththil achchu pottathu*'. This printed Tamil book is of great literary significance, which is of 97 pages and it had Tamil idioms. The second edition of *Thamizh Vizhlakkam* was printed at *Maasa Thinasarithai Achchukudam* in Madras in 1817.[16] Subburaya Mudaliar had also composed *Manitha thozhil vizhlakkam* and it got printed in Madras in 1812.

Founding Tamil Literary Institutions in Madras and Madurai by the Natives

Tamils established two literary institutions at Madras and Madurai to promote Tamil literature. Saravana Perumal Iyer born of a Jangama family at Tirutthanigai near Madras, studied under his father Kandappa Iyer. He became the president of the *Vivekha Kalvi Saalai*, a literary institution established at Madras by certain native gentlemen for the promotion of Tamil literature.[17] Vethagiri Mudaliar born of a *Tuluva vellala* family at Kuzhlathur in AD 1795 moved over to Madras and studied under Ramanuja Kavirayar. He became the president of a Tamil literary institution at Madurai and he presided over the institution for a period of seven years.[18] Thus abiding interest had been shown by Tamils for the study of Tamil literature in the age of English expansion in Tamil country.

Tamil Authors, Editors and Printers in Madras

Saravana Perumal Iyer is a notable figure in printing books. Sivapragasa Desikar's Pazhamalai Andhaathi was edited by Saravana Perumal Iyer and the book got printed in Madras in 1832.[19] Visaaka Perumal Iyer (the eldest son of Kandappa Iyer hailing from Thirutthani) and Saravana Perumal Iyer (the younger brother of Visaaka Perumal Iyer) established *Kalvi Vizhlakka Achchukkudam* (Knowledge Elucidation Press) in Madras. It functioned at Otteri, Kusapettai in the suburbs of Madras in 1834.

Saravana Perumal Iyer wrote commentary for Avvaiyar's two works called Vaakundaam and Nal Vazhi and the book was printed in Madras in 1841.[20] Athiveera Rama Pandiyar's Naidatham cantos one to six attracted the attention of Saravana Perumal Iyer and so he wrote a commentary and he published the book in Madras in 1842.[21] The same book was reprinted in 1859.[22] Paranjothi Munivar's Thiruvizhayaadar Puranam was edited by Saravana Perumal Iyer and the book was printed in Madras in 1850.[23] Thayumaanavar's hymns on Siva were published by him in Madras in 1851.[24] Thiruvaasagam was also edited by Saravana Perumal Iyer and the book was printed in Madras in 1857.[25]

Saravana Perumal Iyer wrote a commentary on the kural and it was the first and the most prominent of his works of which he published under the title *Thiruvalluva nayanar tirukkuralin urai* (with the text with interpretations and prolegomena) in 1830. The next treatise on grammar had been under the title *Iyattamil surkkam* and yet another on rhetoric he published under the title *Aniiyel vizhlakkam*. He engaged himself in editing many of the Tamil classical works which were circulated then in manuscript which had many errors and rendered by the carelessness of the copyists. This included the moral teachings of the poetess Avvaiyaar.[26] *Prabhu linga leelai* (a work on Veera Saivism), was commented by Saravana Perumal Iyer along with his father Kandappa Iyer. *Avivega purana guru kathai* was edited by Saravana Perumal Iyer.[27] He published also *Arunagiri Andhaathi* in 1830. Pazhamalai Andhaathi of Duraimangalam Sivapragasa Desikar was edited by Saravana Perumal Iyer and the book was printed in 1832 which had 19 pages.[28] He edited *Thirukkaruvai Pathitrandhaathi Moola Paadam* in 1835 and *Kanthar Alangaaram* in 1836. He published *Nalvazhi Urai* in 1841. Thus many *prabhandam* works came to be printed but mostly incomplete. However books printed are small and do not have a lot of pages. The reason may be that sufficient quantity of paper required for printing could not be procured in the local market. Further needed capital amount required for investment was not possible.

Visaaka Perumal Iyer published *Ilakkana Surukka Vinaa Vidai* in 1828. *Thirukkural* with the commentary of Parimelazhagar was edited by Visaaka

Perumal Iyer and it was printed in Madras in 1830. *Baala Bhodga Ilakkanam* was published in 1852. The second edition of *Nannul Mulamum Kandigai Uraiyum* was published by Visaaka Perumal Iyer at the *Kalvi Vizhlakka Achchukudam.*

Kuzhlathur Vethagiri Mudaliar owing to his ill health relinquished his post of the president of the Tamil literary institution in Madurai and he migrated to Pondicherry where for some time he was employed as a Tamil pundit in the Catholic college. Then again he went to Madras and established a printing press of his own and commenced publishing manuscripts with a learned prose commentary of his own. It is found that Vethagiri Mudaliar was a frequent contributor to the *Udhaya Tharagai* (Morning Star) journal published from Jaffna from 1841 to 1843. His contributions were chiefly on grammar and classics tended very much to enhance the value of that periodical and drew forth to him from the editors high tribute of thanks.[29] Vethagiri Mudaliar composed four didactic poems respectively titled *Manu Neethi Sathagam*, *Manu Viyyakiyaana Sathagam*, *Needhi Chintamani* and *Sanmaarka Saaram* of which the first three contain a hundred stanzas each, and the last a hundred and ten stanzas. These poems were inscribed by him to a friend of his in Sri Lanka whose name he has introduced at the end of every stanza. The addendum to the Tamil dictionary was done by Vethagiri Mudaliar and it was published at the American Mission press at Manippay in 1842. Further his production as well as the stanzas marked with asterisk in the 11th part of Mandla Purudar's Nigandu was also published by the American Mission press in Manippay in 1843.[30]

Vethagiri Mudaliar was a leading figure in editing and publishing various Tamil manuscripts. *Arichuvadi, Athichudi, Kondrei venthan* and *Vetriverkei* had been edited and published by him and got printed in Madras in 1829-30. *Oru Sol Pal Porul Thoguthi Naanuru Paadal Mulamum Uraiyum* composed by Vethagiri Mudaliar had been printed in 1839. *Naladiyar Moolamum Uraiyum* of Jain scholars had been commented by him. *Neidham mulamum uraiyum* was published by him. The story of Nala and Dhamayanthi with commentary of Athiveera Rama pandithar was commented by Vethagiri Mudaliar. *Tiruvasagam* (Siva hymns) of Manikkavasagar was edited by him. He published Thirukural in 1849. *Thogai Peyar Vizhlakkam* of Vethagiri Mudaliar appeared in print in 1849. *Thiru murugartruppadai* of Nakkiradevar was edited by him and it was published by Madurai Mudaliar in 1850. *Peragathiyam* (A grammar book authored by Agasthiyar) was revised by Vedhagiri Mudaliyar and it was printed in Madras in 1850. *Thogeipper vizhlakkam*, in prose form, was composed by Vethagiri Mudaliar was also printed. *Aanpudhi malai* and *pennpudhi malai* was edited by him and it was published by Arunachala Mudaliar in 1850. *Panchadasapiracharanam* (Fifteen Chapters, a treatise of Vedantha philosophy in dialogue form) was edited by Vethagiri Mudaliar. *Siva vakkiyam* was also edited by him and it was published by Madurai Mudaliar in Madras in 1851. *Kandhar alangaram* of Arunagiri nadhar was edited by Vethagiri Mudaliar and it was published by Ilatchumana Mudaliar in 1851. *Kaarigai Mualamum Viruthiuraiyum* got printed in 1851.[31] *Akkapai Siddhar Paadal* was edited by Vethagiri Mudaliar and it was published by Veerabadhira Chettiar in Madras in 1851. *Kabilar agaval* was edited by Vethagiri Mudaliar and it was published by Madurai Mudaliar and Saminatha Desikar.[32] *Bhavargeethai Moolamum Uraiyum* was done by Vethagiri Mudaliar and the book printed in 1852 had 231 pages.[33] He finally died in 1852.

Villipakkam Thandavaraya Mudaliar (1790-1850) became a teacher in the college of fort St George in Madras. He was well versed in Tamil and Marathi. He began to compare and examine the various manuscripts of *Senthan Dhivaagaram* of Dhivvagarar and he published the first eight parts in 1819.[34] A Tamil grammar titled *Ilakkana Vinaa Vidai* was composed by Thandavaraya through an order of the Board of the Chennai Kalvi Sangam. The book containing 330 pages had been printed in Madras in 1820.[35] He produced a series of instructive fables. In 1826 a collection of tales had been compiled by Thandavaraya and the book titled *Kathaa Manjari* containing 84 pages was printed in 1826.[36] The second edition of *Kathaa Manjari* appeared in print in 1846 and the book had 80 pages.[37] *Chudaamani Nigandu* of Mandalapurudar ten parts was published by him in 1835.[38] *Nannul* of Pavanandi, Narkavi Rajar's *Agapporul Vizhlakkam* and Aiyanar Idanar's *Venbaa Maalai* the three texts on grammar and rhetoric had been edited by Thandavaraya. The book containing 119 pages was printed in 1835. It is found that the first 89 pages had been printed on light blue paper.[39]

There are many scholars who also did their best in editing and printing Tamil manuscripts. Rajanallur Ramachandra Kavirayar revised and edited the three first parts of Beschi's *Chaturagaraathi* and it was printed in 1824.[41] *Urichol Nigandu* by Kangeyar was printed in 1840. *Kandasamiyam* by Subramania Desikar was printed in 1844.[40]

Kottaiyur Sivakolundu Desikar (1770-1860) was a notable Tamil scholar and pundit who found employment in Madras at the Chennai Kalvi Sangam founded by the English. He edited Thiruvaasagam and it was printed in Madras in 1857.[42] Chidambara Pandaram was another scholar who became the first head of the college.[43] Venkatachala Mudaliar was employed in the college of Fort St. George since 1814 and he assisted Alexander Robertson, who was the college *munshi* (translator).[44]

Madurai Mudaliar is an important figure in printing and publishing Tamil books. He published *Kandhar Anubudhi* the work of Arumuga Thambiran. *Thiruvengada Maalai* edited by Arumuga Thambiran was published by Madurai Mudaliar in Madras in 1829. *Thiruvarangak Kalambgam* of Divya Kavi Pillai Perumal Iyengar was edited by Madurai Mudaliar. *Thiruppadal Thirattu* of Pattinathu Pillaiyar from Kaveripattinam was edited by Singaara Mudaliar but it was published by Madurai Mudaliar. *Suttukkavi Thirattu* was edited by Arumuga Thambiran and it was also published by Madurai Mudaliar.[45] Thus many Tamils edited several literary manuscript texts for printing. Some of them sponsored and became the publishers and contributed towards the growth of printed books.

Muniappa Mudaliar took interest in editing manuscripts. *Njana Vottiyan*, a psychological-mystical poem was edited by him. *Sasivarna Bhodham* of Tathuvaraja Swami was edited with a commentary by Muniappa Mudaliar but it was published by Ramasami Pillai in Madras in 1829.[46]

Sabapathi Mudaliar was another Tamil scholar and he played his own role and contributed in editing manuscripts and printing books. He owned his printing press called *Kalvi Vizhlakka Achchukudam*. *Needhi Venbaa* was edited by Sabapathi Mudaliyar and it was printed in Madras in 1830. *Sadhuragiri arappalee sura sadhagam* of Ambalavaana Kavirayar was edited by Sabapathi. *Needhi neri vilakkam* of Kumaragurupara swami was given a commentary by Sabapathi. *Bala Puthagam* was edited by him but it was published by Madurai Mudaliar in 1850.[47]

The Emergence and Growth of Print Capitalists in Madras

Several printing presses had sprung up in Madras and they were owned by Tamils. This is an important feature which contributed to printing Tamil books. *Iyal Thamizhl Vizhlakkam* a press in Kanchipuram was owned by Thiruvenkatachala Mudaliar. His yet another printing unit was the Saraswathi Achchukkudam. The book 'A Garland of Advice for Men and Women' came out from the Saraswathi printing press. *Kalvi Kalanjiya Achchukkudam* was founded in 1839 by Umapathi Mudaliar and it was located in George Town in the vicinity of Madras.[48]

Hindu religious Tamil books gradually came to be poured out in increasing number from the printing press of the natives. Tharangapuram Shanmuha Kavirayar published *Ithikasamahiya Sri Mahabharatham* in 1842. *Gnaana Vaasittavamala Raamayanam, Thamizh Mulamum Uraiyum* appeared in print in Madras in 1851. *Kambaraamayanam* evinced interest of the Hindus for publication. It was printed at *Kalvi Kalanjiya Achchukudam* in Madras in 1842. The Tamil title was *Pragalaathan Sarithiram*

Yenra Narasinga Vijayam. It contained *Yuththa Kaandam and Iranyavathai padalam*. In the next year (1843) *Kambaraamaayanam Bala Kaandam* in original was published by Venkatachala Mudaliar and the book had 218 pages. Semangalam Narayana Sami Mudaliar and Venkatachala Mudaliar published *Srimat Kambaraamayanam, Aaranya Kaandam* at *Saraswathi Achchukkudam* in 1844. The book had 156 pages. Mazhavai Mahalinga Iyer published *Baalakaandam* text in original in 1845. Vidwan Soobroya Moodeliar published *Srimat Kambaraamaayanam, Baala kaandam* in 1857 at *Kalvi Vizhlakka Achchukudam* owned by Sabaapathi Mudaliar in Madras.

Books on Tamil grammar had continued to be printed. We find Mazhavai Mahalinga Iyer publishing *Yezhuthadhigaaram* of *Tholkappiyam* with the commentary of Nachinaarkiniyar in 1847.[49] Some Tamil Brahmins made efforts to edit the manuscripts and made commentaries with a view print. *Satchidhanandha Maalai* of Palaianandha swami was edited by Sinivasa Iyengar and it was published by Muthuswami Mudaliar. *Thiruvengadaththandadhi* (100 stanzas in praise of Vishnu in Tirupathi) of Divya Kavi Pillai Perumal Iyengar was edited by Annaswami Nayagar. *Thiruvallikkeni Parthasarathi Peril Pancha Rathnamum Viruthamum was* published by Ragava Achariyar in 1829. *Veerasami Iyer* wrote *Kasi Yathirai Sarithiram* and it was printed in Madras in 1835.[50]

Many Tamils worked laboriously and devoted their time and energy in editing manuscripts and printing Tamil books. *Azhwar Nootrandhadhi* of Kambanattawar was edited by Venkatachala Mudaliar. *Thiruvadha voorar puranam* was commented by Kumaraswami Desikar. *Muudhurai* of Avvaiyar, *Nal Vazhi* (the good way) and *Nanneri* (the good motivation), of Sivaprakasa Swamigal was edited by Arunachala Mudaliar and it was published by Ilatchumana Mudaliar. *Thiruppul vayal kumaresa sadhagam* (hundred stanzas of moral contents, all of which are addressed to Karthikeya) of Gurupada Dasar was edited by Shanmuga Mudaliar. *Saidhapura maalai* edited by Ponnambala Kavirayar was published by Umapathi Mudaliar and Ayyasami Vaathiyar. A medical text *Sitter aruda nondi chindu* (study of poisonous animals and of their treatment in the form of verse) was edited by Chandirasekara Kaviraya Pandithar and it was published by Vengadasala Mudaliar.[51]

It is interesting to note that some Chettiar financiers had begun to invest their funds in the printing industry. Veerabadhra Chettiar was a publisher of books in Tamil. *Vivega Chinthamani* edited by Arumuga Thambiran was published by Veerabadhira Chettiar in 1829. *Arunagiri Andhadhi* edited by Devagiri Mudaliar was also published by Veerabadhira Chettiar.[52]

Printing Books of Islamic Tamil Literature

In this expanding age of Tamil printing the Muslims in Tamil country had also begun to make efforts to publish books of Islamic literature. *Siraapuranam* the biography of Mohammed the prophet in Tamil was printed in 1842 by Syed Mohammed Hassan in Madras. Again *Sirra Vengira Puranam* was reprinted in Madras in 1850 and this was for the use of the Tamil speaking Muslim Labbais. *Thirupaadarthirattu* of Poet Kunangkudi Abdul Khader Musthaan Sahib was printed in Madras in 1847. *Nagai Andhaathi* composed on the Sufi saint of Nagore was printed by Abdul Khader Nayinar Lebbai of Kayalpattinam in 1850. A civil law book was translated into Tamil by Syedshaw Ali Sahib and it got printed at Mutbhai Kursheed printing press at Mirsahib Pettai in Madras in 1850. *Muhammadiya Samaya Vizhlakkam* composed by Raayavelur Khader Mohaideen Sahib was printed in 1851 at Prabhaakara printing press owned by Kesava Mudaliar at Swami Naayakan Street that functioned in Chintadripettai near Madras. *Vivekaaram* a story book was translated from Persian into Tamil by Rasaa Hussai Khan at the request of Ettayapuram Venkatesa Vattappa Nayaakar and it was printed also at the Prabhaakara printing press.[53]

Printing Kitheriammal Ammaanai the Catholic Tamil Literature in Madras, 1849

Kitheriammal Ammaani is the poem of Beschi and this he sung in 1730 in the folk rhythm. He expounded the greatness of St. Quiteria through this work. Beschi had mentioned about it in his *Thonnul Vizhlakkam* completed in 1731. The poem contains 2342 verses in the ammaanai form and it dealt with virgin martyr St. Quiteria of the fifth century. Three women join together and cast dice in turn as part of a game. Before the dice is cast one among them sings the exploit of a hero or deity and then throws the dice. The next women would then interrogate her in verse and then flings the dice. The last assails the doubts of the second in a verse and then flings the dice. The verses thus sung are called *ammaanai* in Tamil literature and are set in folk rhythm. The miraculous deeds of St. Quiteria had been narrated along with her life sketch by Beschi. The ballad has 1100 strophes of two verses each, and 132 of four. Beschi did not adhere strictly to the original version of the saint's story but he altered the story of this virgin saint to suit his ends. In the original only the last twin girls were ordered to be flung into the river. In Beschi's version the mother produces simultaneously nine girls and being ashamed of it, she requests her maid—who was a catholic—to drown all the nine children in the river. One among these girls is Kitheriammal who outshines all her other sisters. These girls are not drowned. They survive and later offer themselves to God. Kitheriammal performs a number of miracles. Belief in miracles is common. The whole plot centred around heroine Kitheriammal who is equally chaste and completely at the disposal of the Lord. Thus Beschi had composed this poem and popularized the cult of Quiteria. The book was printed at Gnaanodhaya press in Madras in 1849.[54]

Printing the Books of Hindu Theology

Karl Friedrich Leberecht Graul (1814–64), the German missionary took interest in the Tamil books printed by the natives. He purchased and took with him many books to Germany in 1853. He had written a small note about them in German.[12] He had mentioned some Hindu theological works printed in Tamil. (1) *Periya puranam* of Sekkizhar, commented by Mahalinga Iyer (2) *Thiri Sira Malai puranam* of Siva Ellappa Navalar edited by Meenatchisundaram Pillai (3) *Viruthaachala Puranam* of Nyanakutta Swamigal, commented by Muniappa Mudaliar and (4) *Kandhar purana vasagam* of Parasurama Mudaliar. Karl Graul also purchased the book of *Sooriya namaskaram, varkka maalai*, published by Appaswamy Mudaliar and Periyasami Mudaliar and *Thiruthondar puranam* of Umapthi Sivachariyar printed in Madras in 1836.[55]

According to Karl Graul, *Srimadh Kamba Ramayanam* was edited by Venkatachala Mudaliar. *Sri Krishna Swami Thuthu* of Villiputhur Alwar was commented by Kumaraswami Desikar of Kanchipuram. *Kalinga-thupparani* was published by Suppuraja Mudaliar in Madras in 1841.

Thirukkovaiyar of Manikkavasagar was edited and corrected by Narayanappa Mudaliar as per the commentary of Nachinarkiniyar. *Muthu-thandavar keerthanam was* edited by Subramaniya Pandithar. *Thirupugazh* of Arunagirinadhar was edited by Palanandha Swamigal. *Tandaliar sadhagam engira pazhamozhi vilakkam*, of Santhalinga Kavirayar, was also edited by Palanandha Swami. *Arichandra Sarithiram* was edited by Palanandha swamigal. Further *Gnaana Kummi*, of Palanandha swami, was edited by Munisami Mudaliar and the book was printed in Madras 1850.[56] *Manavala narayana sadhagam* of Narayana parathiyar was printed in Madras. *Govindha sadhagam pazhamozhiyodu mula padam* of Narayana parathiyar was edited by Vengadasala Mudaliar and it was printed in Madras.[57]

Tamil Grammar and Dictionaries Printed in Madras Noticed by Karl Graul in 1853

Karl Graul noted that Tamils had made commentaries on Tamil grammar texts and some of them had made revisions. As a result, many books came to be printed in Tamil in Madras. The list of printed books include (1) *The first part of Tholkappiam,* with the lessons on letters and with the commentary of Nachinarkiniyar, revised by Mahalinga Iyer (2) *Ilakkana panjangangalil Nannul moolamum agapporul mulamum purapporul ilakkiyatthodu venba malai mulamum*, revised by Thandavaraya Mudaliar (3) *Karigai* of Amirtha sagara munivar, with a detailed commentary by Guna saagara munivar, revised by Vethagiri Mudaliar of Kuzhlathur and (4) *Karigai moola padham* (Prosody), of Amudha Saagara Munivar and Dhandi Alangaram of Dhandi Aasiriyar revised by Vethagiri Mudaliar of Kuzhlathur.[58]

We also find Tamil grammar works composed by European missionaries and the books printed like (a) *Grammatica-Latino-Tamulica,* Kodunthamizh by Beschi, Madras, 1813, (b) *A grammar of the Tamil language* by C.T.E. Rhenius, Madras, 1836 and (c) *Tamizh ilakkana nul surukka vina vidai* (a short treatise on the Tamil learning in question and answer form), of G.U. Pope, the English missionary in Tirunelveli, printed in 1846 at Madras carried by Karl Graul. These are available in the Bibliothek der Evangelisch-Lutherisches Missionsanstalt, Leipzig.[59]

Karl Graul had mentioned (a) *Nannurkandigai Urai* (short commentary of Nannul), of Vethagiri Mudaliar of Kuzhlathur, Madras, 1829, (b) *Uvamana Sangiragam-Rathina Churukkam,* of Thiruvengada Iyer, revised by Arumuga Pillai of Thiruchirappalli and published by Varadhappa Mudaliar of Thiruvallikkeni, Madras in 1837.[60]

Karl Graul refers to Tamil dictionaries and the list includes (1) *Chudamani Nigandu*, text and commentary edited by Muniappa Mudaliar (2) *Pathinoravathu nigandu*, text and commentary edited by Mamu Pillai (3) *Pannirendavadhu nigandu*, (the 12th to the Chudamani nigandu) edited by Mamu Pillai. Graul cites the printed books like (a) *Dictionary, Tamil and English*, by J.P. Rottler, Madras, 1830 (b) *Manual lexicon for schools*, by Rev. J. Knight and Rev. J. Spaulding, Madras, 1844 and (c) *Malai agarathi* (a botanical dictionary), of Simon Kasi Chetti, Madras, 1844.[61]

Printing Books of Drama, Ethics and Stories in Tamil

The ethical texts in manuscript had attracted Tamils for printing books. *Needhi mozhi thirattu*, a selection from the writers of Tamil moralists for the use of schools got printed in Madras in 1841. *Neethi saara vakkiyam*, collected by Ramasami Pillai was printed in 1844.[62]

Some manuscripts on drama had been edited and printed in Madras. *Rama Naadagam* of Arunachala Kavirayar was edited by Venkatachala Mudaliar and Ramasami Nayagar. *Thirukkadavur Nondi Nadagam* of Mathura Kavirayar was edited by Muniappa Mudaliar. The book *Poom Paavaiyar Vilasam* of Arumuga Vallal was printed in Madras in 1827.[63]

Panchathanthira Kathai was edited by Subburaya Ubadhiyar. It was also edited by E.N. Muthsami Mudaliar and it was printed in Ezhumur in

1847 and the book had 110 pages.[64] *Panchathanthira Kathai* was also edited by Srinivasapuram Srinivasa Iyengar and the book printed in Madras in 1852 had 84 pages.[65] *Sattapiracharanam* of Seshagiri Swami was edited by Arunachala Swami. *Ubanidadham* was commented and published by Sundara Asariyar. *Ozhuvilodukkam* of Kannudaiya Vallal was commented by Chidambara Swamigal. *Umaradevar's Sasthirakkovai* was edited and published by Sorubanandha Paradesi in Madras in 1830.[66] *Madana Kamarasan Kathai* was edited by Selai Ponnambala Kavirayar and the book printed in 1855 had 198 pages.[67]

Printing Books on Science, Mathematics and History in Tamil

Some books on science were published by the native publishers of Madras. These included instructional publications and some on native arithmetic, primarily for use in the indigenous schools. Saravana Perumal Iyer wrote a treatise on geography entitled *Kozhla Deepikai* in which he explored the Puranic knowledge and adopted the Copernican system establishing it by quotations from the ancient Hindu authors especially with regard to the rotundity of the earth. Except this work on traditional astronomy no other work related to science was found among the works printed in the native press before 1850.[68] Further, history of the world in Tamil was printed in Tamil in Madras in two volumes while volume one dealt with Europe and volume two dealt with Asia.[69]

The Tamils in Madras had taken interest in printing books on mathematics in Tamil. '*Enn Chuvadi*', the mathematical manuscript was edited by Mamu Pillai, and it was published by Annamalai Mudaliar in Madras in 1829. It was also reprinted in 1851. This work of mathematical treatise dealt with weights and measures. It also had details of cycles of the years. It came to be used as a general knowledge in the elementary schools.[70]

Many Tamil scholars began to edit and publish a particular manuscript. We find Nannul edited by many. At the same time commentaries composed were also plenty. We find Nannul Viruthiurai by Ramanuja Kavirayar got printed at Madras in 1847 while within three years Nannul with commentary of Sankara Namasivaayar was revised by Sivagnaanar also got printed in Madras in 1851.[71]

Owing to demand for paper in Tamil country for printing the art of paper-making industry had well developed particularly around the region of Thanjavur. A letter from a paper merchant Kutti Veerabhadran in 1814 reported that his shop had 21 kinds of papers manufactured and these were supplied to the English East India Company and the Raja of Thanjavur for use. These paper varieties were named after the places which included Mannargudi, Kumbakonam, Panthananallur, Tirukattuppalli and Tiruvarur.[72]

However, fine quality of paper for printing was purchased by the Thanjavur court from the English Company only in Madras in 1829. The reason was that imported paper from London had been found to be superior.[73] The natives had used and preferred the local variety of paper in their printing press in Madras.

To conclude it may be said that the transformation of Tamil classical texts and folklore had taken an important place by marking a departure from a manuscript tradition into print form in Tamil society. It was chiefly possible through the efforts of a number of people who were Tamil pundits and financiers who owned printing houses. These Tamils had observed clearly the fate of palm-leaf manuscripts in the longer run and so they had decided to give new life to the Tamil literary texts in paper through printing. Books composed by the Tamil authors newly also saw the light of printing. The printed books thus came to be widely circulated and they were read by the people. Thus there developed a new cultural movement of reading with the advent of the new technology of Tamil printing towards growth.

Our investigation shows that there were 13 native printing presses actively engaged in printing in Madras city between 1812 and 1857. It is gleaned that 212 books in Tamil language were printed from Madras between 1812 and 1857. There were 8 journals and 3 newspapers in Tamil published in Madras between 1812 and 1857. Literary institutions of the natives in Madras and Madurai established helped in the promotion of Tamil literature. The preparation of Tamil fonts in Madras developed by the natives had not been so elegant when compared to the English company. Books printed in Tamil by the natives were not superior when compared to the English with regard to even spacing, punctuation marks like the semicolon, colon, the question mark and the exclamation mark. However it must be admitted that Tamils had learnt the art of printing books and introduced Tamil literary texts to a wider audience than the English East India Company in Madras.

Notes

1. S. Jeyaseela Stephen, *Pondicherry under the French, Illuminating the Urban Landscape, 1674-1793*, Primus, New Delhi, 2018, p. 601.
2. Simon Casie Chitty, *The Tamil Plutarch: Containing a Summary Account of the Lives of the Poets and Poetesses of South India and Ceylon from the Earliest to the Present Times with Select Specimens of their Compositions*, Jaffna, 1859, pp. 55-56.
3. British Library, London (hereafter BL), call number 14170.a.13, A. Muthusami Pillai, *Attrum Uthiyaanam*, Madras, 1817.
4. Simon Casie Chitty, The Tamil Plutarch, pp. 55-56.
5. Simon Casie Chitty, The Tamil Plutarch, p. 61.

6. BL, 14170.k.11, *Aathikaala Sarithira Sangiraham, A sketch of ancient history with a version of the same in Tamil by Puthuvai Gnanapragasa Moodeliar*, Madras, 1828.
7. BL, 14170.k.12, *Tulakkar pithitta kaala mutal sollapadum Industhaani sarithira sangiraham, A summary of the history of Hindoostahan from the Muslim invasion in English with a Tamil translation by Gnanapragsa Moodeliar*, Vepery, 1830.
8. Karl Graul, 'Notizen, Correspondenzen und Vermischtes. Die Tamulische Bibliothek der Evan. Luth. Missionsanstalt zu Leipzig', *Zeitschrift der Deutschen Morgenländischen Gesellschaft*, vol. VII, Leipzig, 1853, pp. 558-568, see p. 566.
9. Albertine Gaur, *Catalogue of Tamil Books in the British Library*, London, The British Library, 1980, p. 11.
10. John Murdoch, *A Classified Catalogue of Tamil Printed Books with Introductory Notes*, Madras, 1865, p. 21.
11. Karl Graul, Notizen, Correspondenzen und Vermischtes, pp. 558-568.
12. Ma. Su. Sambandan, *Achchum Pathippum*, Thamizhlar Pathippagam, Madras, 1976, pp. 28-31.
13. V. Rajesh, 'Patrons and Networks of Patronage in the Publication of Tamil Classics, c 1800-1920', *Social Scientist*, Vol. 39, Nos. 3-4, March-April 2011, pp. 64-91, see p. 69.
14. A. Maa, Sami, Paththonpatham Nuttrandu, pp. 30-31, 80-85.
15. BL, 14172.f.6, *Thamizh Vizhlakkam*, Madras, 1811.
16. BL, 14172.f.7, *Thamizh Vizhlakkam*, Second edition, Madras, 1817.
17. Simon Casie Chitty, The Tamil Plutarch, p. 84.
18. Ibid., pp. 112-113.
19. BL, 14172.b.23.1, *Pazhamalaiyandthaathi*, Madras, 1832.
20. BL, 14172.a.1, *Vaakundaam*, *Nal Vazhi*, *Nanneri*, by Saravana Perumal Iyer, Madras, 1841.
21. BL, 14172.b.58, *Naidhtham Moolamum Uraiyum*, by Saravana Perumal Iyer and Kandappa Iyer, Madras, 1842.
22. BL, 14172.a.12, *Vaakundaam, Nal Vari, Nanneri, by Saravana Perumal Iyer*, Madras, 1859.
23. BL, 14170.ee.1, *Thiruvilaiyadar Puranam*, Madras, 1850.
24. BL, 14172.c.24, *Thiruppaadar Thirattu*, Madras, 1851.
25. BL, 14172.b.15, *Tiruvaasagam*, Madras, 1857.
26. Simon Casie Chitty, The Tamil Plutarch, p. 84.
27. Karl Graul, Notizen, Correspondenzen und Vermischtes, pp. 558-568.
28. BL, 14172.b.23 (1), *Pazhamalaiyandhaathi*, ed., Saravana Perumal Iyer, Madras, 1832.
29. Maraimalai Adigal Library, Chennai, *Morning Star*, vol. I, p. 230.
30. Simon Casie Chitty, The Tamil Plutarch, pp. 112-113.
31. BL, 14172.e.36, Vethagiri Mudaliar, *Kaarigai Mualamum Viruthiuraiyum*, Madras, 1851.

32. Karl Graul, Notizen, Correspondenzen und Vermischtes, pp.558-568.
33. BL, 14171.dd.7 (8), *Sri Thaandavaraya Mudaliar Sarithira Surukkam*, Rangoon, 1919, pp. 1-8; BL, 14170c.19, *Bhagavatgeethai Moolamum Uraiyum by Vethagiri Mudaliar*, Madras, 1852.
34. BL, 14172.e.4, *Senthan Dhivaagaram Edited by Thandavaraya*, Madras, 1877.
35. BL, 14172.f.3, *Ilakkana Vinaa Vidai*, Madras, 1820.
36. BL, 14170.k.23, *Kathaa Manjari*, Madras, 1826.
37. BL, 14170.k.69, *Kathaa Manjari*, Madras, 1846.
38. BL, 14172.e.9, *Chudamani Nigandu*, Madras, 1856.
39. BL, 14172.e.3, *Ilakkana Panchangangalil Nannul Moolamum Agapoorul Moolamum Purapporuatilakiyathodu Venbaamaalai Moolamum*, Madras, 1835.
40. Simon Casie Chitty, The Tamil Plutarch, p. 114.
41. BL, 14172.f.13, *Iguthu Veeramaamunivar Seytha Chaturagaraathi*, Madras, 1824.
42. BL, 14172, b.15, Kottaiyur Sivakolundu Desikar, ed., *Thiruvaasagam*, Madras, 1857.
43. BL, Madras Public Consultations (hereafter MPC), 11 September 1815.
44. BL, MPC, 9 July 1830, 20 April 1836, 17 July 1838.
45. Karl Graul, Notizen, Correspondenzen und Vermischtes, pp. 558-568.
46. Ibid.
47. Ibid.
48. Chengalvaraya Pillai, *History of the Tamil Prose Literature*, Madras, 1904, pp. 58-59.
49. BL, 14172.dd.2, Tharangapuram Shanmuha Kavirayar, *Ithikasamahiya Sri Mahabharatham*, Madras, 1842; *Gnaana Vaasittavamala Raamayanam, Thamizh Mulamum Uraiyum*, Madras 1851; BL, 14172.f.4, *Tholkaapiyam,* ed. Mahalinga Iyer, Madras, 1847.
50. Karl Graul, Notizen, Correspondenzen und Vermischtes, pp.558-568.
51. Ibid.
52. Ibid.
53. David Shulman, 'Muslim Popular Literature in Tamil: The Tamimmancari Malai' in *Islam in Asia*, Yohannan Friedman ed., Colo, 1984, vol. I, p. 176-77; Safiullah Syed, 'Urdu Journalism in Tamilnadu from 1840 to 1850', *Annals of Oriental Research*, XXVII, Part I & II, pp. 7-9.
54. *Kitheriammal Ammaanai*, Gnaanodhaya Press, Madras, 1849; see also, Bibliothèque Asiatique des Missions Etrangères de Paris (hereafter BAMEP), TA.202, *Dairiyanathaswamigalyennum Veeramaamunivar Aruliseytha Archisista Kitheriammal Ammaanai: Ithu Royapuram Archsista Royappar Aalayathil Mahasangaikuriya The. Mari. Gnaanaparagasanatha Swamigal Uthavipetru Merpadikovil Thamizh Kalvisaalai Upaathiyar Pavazhai Vai. The. Ma. Sinnasami Reddiyar Avargazhlaal Paarvai idapattu Mayilai Ponnuswami Muthaliar avargalaal Chennai Lakshmi Vilas Achchukudathil Pathipikkapattathu*, 1876.

55. Karl Graul, Notizen, Correspondenzen und Vermischtes, pp. 558-568.
56. Ibid.
57. Ibid.
58. Ibid.
59. Ibid.
60. Ibid.
61. Ibid.
62. BL, 14170.k. 16, *Neethisaara Vakkiyam*, A glossary of moral sentences compiled Kottamangalam Ramasami Pillai, Librarian of Madras College, Madras, 1844. Karl Graul, Notizen, Correspondenzen und Vermischtes, p. 566; Neethisaaraa Vaakkiyangalil Theriyalaanavai (Selections from the Neethisaara Vakkiyam of V. Thandavaraya Mudaliar is found in Kathaa Manajari, printed in 1864 vide pp. 114-176. See, BL, 14171, aa.15.
63. Karl Graul, Notizen, Correspondenzen und Vermischtes, pp. 558-568.
64. BL, 14170.k.26, *Panchathanthira Kathai*, ed., E.N. Muthusami Mudaliar, Ezhumur, 1847.
65. BL, 14170.k.21, *Panchathanthira Kathai*, ed., Srinivaspuram Srinivasa Aiyengar, Madras, 1852.
66. Karl Graul, Notizen, Correspondenzen und Vermischtes, pp. 558-568.
67. BL, 14170.k. 17, *Madana Kamarasan Kathai*, Madras, 1855.
68. S. Jeyaseela Stephen *A Meeting of the Minds: European and Tamil Encounters in Modern Sciences, 1507-1857*, Delhi, 2016, p. 807.
69. BL, 14172.h. 56, *Pala Desa Sarithira Surukkam*, Madras, 1857.
70. Karl Graul, Notizen, Correspondenzen und Vermischtes, pp. 558-568.
71. BL, 14172.f.1, (1847); see also, BL, 14172.f.2 (1851).
72. Saraswathi Mahal Library, Thanjavur, *Modi Bundles*, 72C/18-4; P. Subramanian, Venkataramaiyaa and Vivekananda Gopal, *Thanjai Maraattiyar Modi Aavana Thamizhaakamum Kurippuraiyum* (Modi Records of the Mahratta Rulers of Tanjore in Tamil Translation), 3 vols, Tamil University, Thanjavur, 1989, vol. I, part V, p. 211.
73. Saraswathi Mahal Library, Thanjavur, *Modi Bundles*, 160C/45; P. Subramanian, Venkataramaiyaa and Vivekananda Gopal, *Thanjai Maraattiyar Modi Aavana Thamizhaakamum Kurippuraiyum*, vol. I, part VIII, p. 394.

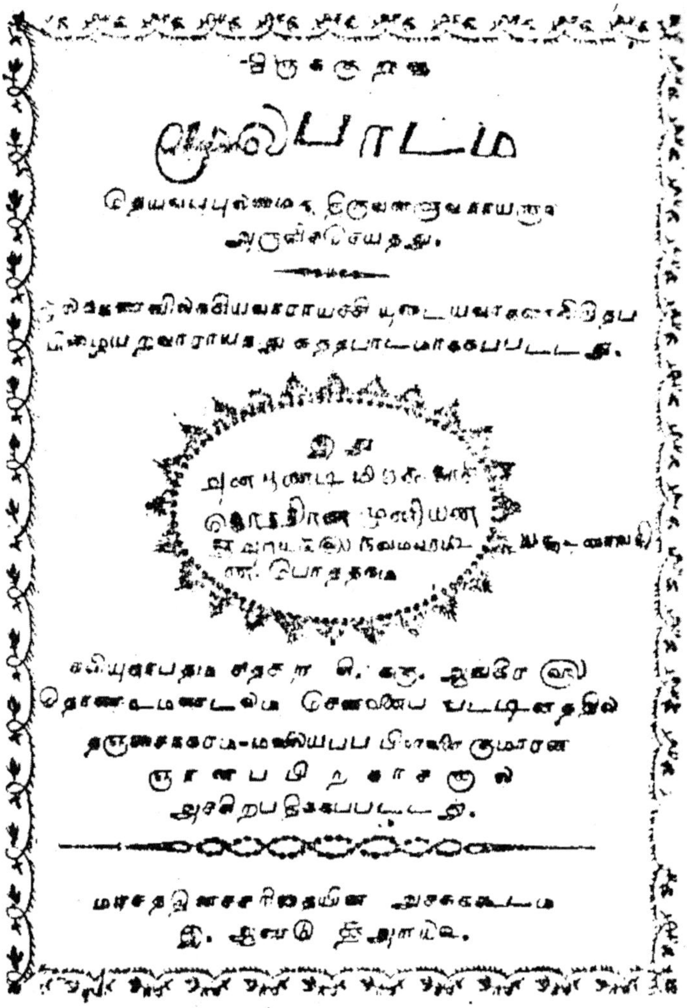
திருக்குறள்
மூலபாடம்

5.1. The title page of Thirukural Moolapaadam printed at Maasathinasarithaiyin Achchukudam in Madras in 1812 (Courtesy: *Aa. Ma. Samy*).

6

The Letter Press of the Catholic Missionaries in Pondicherry and the Religious Literature Printed in Tamil, 1841-73

Thomas Arthur Comte de Lally the new Governor of Pondicherry appointed had sailed from France in a ship in May 1757 reached Mascareigne Island in December, broke journey for forty days and sailing again on 26 January 1758 had reached Pondicherry on 28 April 1758. This ship brought a printing machine operated by hand. The printing press could not be put into operation immediately owing to the siege of Madras, the English settlement. Notes of credit were printed in the year 1760 at Pondicherry. With the ongoing Anglo–French struggle in the region, Pondicherry city was captured by the English when the French forces surrendered on 16 January 1761. Sir Eyre Coote confiscated the printing machine from the residence of the French Governor and he took it to Madras along with the French printer Delon and the founts available.[1] As the printing machine taken to Madras was never returned, another printing machine was brought from France in 1765 (after restoration of Pondicherry) along with Jean Fischer the printer.

Printing Books and Tracts in French and English in Pondicherry, 1778-1793

According to records the French Governor of Pondicherry had issued an order on 20 June 1778 and stated vide section 36 and 37 that no books, tracts or newspapers should be printed without his prior permission.[2] The press was working and we learn that the articles of surrender by the French to Sir Hector Munro dated 17 October 1778 had been printed from this press when the Indo–French town was captured by the English.[3] This is the earliest available imprint from Pondicherry. The press continued to be active even during the British occupation and in 1784 we find a book in French titled '*Manuel de Cipaye*' was printed in Pondicherry.[4] This book contains thirteen chapters and deals with the formation of sepoys in the battle, the strong foot exercises to be given to them, the general commands and manners to be followed in the battle, the different manners of defeating the enemy, the manner of entering the various points and direction during the march of the colonel and commandants with respective distances and sub–divisions of the group to be formed, the manner of serving as one group in a battalion comprising of 10 companies of sepoys, the march towards the battle field, the formation of a battalion of the second line with the required passages and the lines, the change of positions and the movements towards the centre, the various manners of the band of musicians, and finally the manner of passing during the time of honour and also during the inspection conducted by the commissioner-of-war.

A small catechism and an alphabet written in Thai (Siamese) characters had been printed from the press in Pondicherry in 1787. It was done by using Latin types at the request of Monsigneur Arnaud–Antoine Garnault while on the way to Bangkok to take up the post of Bishop Metellopolis.[5]

The press continued to function even during the French Revolution and it was called *L'Imprimerie Nationale*. It had printed the proclamations of the Civil Commissioner.[6] We also find the proceedings of the newly elected *L'Assemblee Constituante* published with 5 articles of the decree outlawing slave trading in the French territories in India from 1 November 1792. The text was signed by J.B.F. de Bury the president and it was approved for printing by the Governor of Pondicherry on 16 October 1792.[7] Again 40 articles approved for convening the next *assemblee constituante* on 2 December 1792 with the number of members, mode of their election, and the qualification required of candidates signed by J.B.F. de Bury the president had been printed from the press. It was approved for printing by the Governor of Pondicherry on 20 October 1792.[8] Further, we find the welcome speech of the president of the *assemblee* to Lescallier and Lescallier's speech to the *assemblee constituante*, the president's reply and the *aseemblee's* exhortation to the citizens of Pondicherry had been printed from the press.[9] Printing continued in 1793 and the text contains three decrees concerning the leasing of new farms, import duties on goods such as tobacco and betel–nut and the standardization of weights.[10]

Pondicherry was captured by the English and it was occupied by them on 23 August 1793. However, the printing press was still active and we find in 1795 a book printed in English on the practice of farriery by Captain Letang.[11] Printing in Pondicherry was still in its infancy stage since the town had remained under the English East India Company till December 1816.

Printing Government Orders and Journals in French and Tamil, 1817-1850

After the restoration of Pondicherry the government press was established by the French in 1817. Notifications of the government were printed and they were pasted on the streets. It is to be noted that Tamil printing had not developed because Tamil founts were not cast and they were not that easily made available for printing. In 1823 the Government decided to print government orders and notifications in a journal called *Archives Administratifs* and it was a weekly was published in French. However, in 1828 the news in Tamil printing was also included in the journal. The same journal was renamed and it appeared in print under the new name *Bulletin des Actes Administratifs des etablissmenets français de L'Inde*. It was bilingual printed in French and Tamil.[12]

In 1838 Camille Guerre who lived in Pondicherry was granted permission by the French Governor of Pondicherry to start publishing a journal with news of politics, literature and commerce. It was titled *Impartial de Pondichéry* and this was a weekly that came to be published in French and Tamil. Camille Guerre was the editor and publisher. The orders of the Government and the notifications were ordered to be published free of cost. The advertisements of the courts also appeared and the chief advocate of the French Government in Pondicherry had fixed the rates from time to time. Impartial de Pondichery had become bi-monthly in 1849. As requested by the publisher, the French government had increased and fixed the rates for advertisement and an order was issued in this regard on 14 August 1849. But the journal came to be stopped its printing and publishing in the next year (1850).[13]

Venkatarayar who approached the Government in Pondicherry was granted permission to publish a journal in Pondicherry in 1838. The title of the journal was '*Soleil Indien*'. Venkatarayar was the editor. The journal was officially registered and it got printed from the press of the Tamil pundit Lakshmanan who was accorded sanction by the French Governor to own a printing press. This was the first Tamil journal weekly printed in Pondicherry. It is surprising that the first Tamil journal was given French title. The French Governor in Pondicherry had ordered that the notifications and the orders of the Government should be published free of cost in *Soleil Indien* journal and this was the only condition then imposed. Advertisements of the courts had also appeared and the chief advocate of the government in Pondicherry had fixed the rates for it from time to time.[14] Thus the first Tamil printing press functioned in Pondicherry in 1838.

It appears that the Home Government was not averse to the establishment of printing-presses in Pondicherry by the local private individuals.

This broad-minded policy was followed towards the intellectual and moral advancement of the inhabitants of the French settlement.

The Letter Press of the Catholic Missionaries in Pondicherry: Louis Savinien Dupuis the First Manager, 1841

François Jarrige (1796-1889) the MEP missionary in Bangalore in 1828 noticed that the Protestants had printed books in English and they were also doing the same in Madras by printing books and tracts in Tamil to supplement the instruction given to the native Christians. Hence it was reported that the MEP mission in Pondicherry should set up a printing press to serve the needs of the Catholics in aiding evangelization.[15] Clement Bonnand the Apostolic-Vicar of Pondicherry in 1830 wrote to Jean Tesson in Paris that he understood and realized the significance of the Catholic publications and the printing press which could be the attempt to diffuse Catholic instruction and to counter balance the efforts of the Protestants in the region.[16] However finance was a serious matter of constrain to establish a printing press in Pondicherry. In 1837 Bonnand asked Jean Tesson in Paris for permission to print books and tracts in the local languages (in Tamil, Telugu and Kannada) of the Pondicherry mission. He said that writings in refutation of the Protestant claims of the ancient church should be made known to the public through printing and asked Tesson to take up seriously the matter with the other directors of the MEP seminary in Paris.[17]

In the mean while Bishop Bonnand had opened up a dialogue with the religious authorities in Paris and Rome. This decision was motivated by the fact that having the books printed elsewhere would be costly and also prove too much of a financial strain of Pondicherry mission. He therefore wrote a letter to Cardinal Fransoni of the Sacred Congregation for the Propagation of Faith on 20 December 1840 seeking permission for setting up a printing press.[18] He favourably received a reply on 9 February 1841 with the necessary permission from Rome to set up the printing press.[19]

Bonnand also received a reply dated 9 March 1841 wherein he was granted the necessary permission to publish Catholic books in Pondicherry.[20] It is mentioned in a Tamil book printed with the title *Vetha Purattalai Neekum Sanjivi*, that permission for printing had been granted from Rome vide an order dated 11 March 1841.[21] It was not very clear and explicit to Bonnand from the contents of the letter that he received from Rome and so he wrote again a letter on 20 August 1841 to Rome seeking the clarifications.[22] In this connection he received a reply on 20 November 1841 which mentioned the two clauses. It stated at first that these books should be free from all errors. Secondly copies of all printed books in Pondicherry should be forwarded from Pondicherry to the Sacred Congregation to the Propagation of Faith after printing.[23]

Bishop Bonnand in the mean while entered into negotiations with the French civil authorities in Pondicherry. He wrote to De Bourquer du Camper the French Governor for permission to set up the Catholic mission press. Monsieur du Camper authorized the mission press to be set up in Pondicherry on 6 July 1840 on condition that a copy of each of the works printed there should be deposited in the government archives. Bonnand made a further request to the Governor and the government gave him an old printing machine together with a certain quantity of ink. Bonnand also purchased the required the Tamil types and yet another printing machine for a sum of 2000 francs.[24] Later Bishop Bonnand purchased another printing machine and Latin types and other accessories and expressed in June 1841 the hope of the press that would have the types necessary for printing in the other European languages too.[25]

As early as on 8 April 1840 Bishop Bonnand had expressed his intention to Jean Tesson in Paris to appoint a suitable priest as manager of the Catholic printing press in Pondicherry. Bonnand had nominated Jacques Roger (1811-1857) the missionary and entrusted him with the preliminary work of organizing the press. Louis Savinien Dupuis was later appointed officially as the manager of the printing press by Bonnand when Roger left for parish work in the mission on 1 July 1841. Dupuis in his letter of 18 August 1841 had mentioned that a printing machine was purchased in 1840 and the Catholic press had come under his full charge and direction in August 1841.[26] Bishop Bonnand had also mentioned in his letter to Jean Tesson dated 21 October 1841 that printing in Tamil is assigned priority in the press.[27] Tamil characters used for printing were purchased by Bishop Bonnand from Camille Guerre for 711 rupees and 7 *panams* (2,000 francs). Marion Bressilac Melchior (1813-1859) wrote in 1842 that Dupuis the scholar who can compose books had been rendering great service to the Pondicherry mission through printing.[28]

Request for the Supply of Paper, Ink and Leather from France to Pondicherry for the Use of the Printing Press

Paper-making was mechanized in 1800, when the first paper-making machine was invented by Nicolas-Louis Robert, the Frenchman in the Didot paper mills near Paris. He used a moving belt, and paper was made one sheet at a time. Joseph Bramah the English engineer in 1805 devised a paper-moulding machine which used a rotating cylinder and this development led to the production of continuous reels of paper. L.S. Dupuis desired to get paper from France for use in the Catholic printing press in Pondicherry. He wrote his letter of 9 December 1839 to Jean Tesson in Paris and said that please do not forget to send him two hundred reams of paper for the use of the missionaries in Pondicherry.[29] Having become the manager of the printing press the supply of paper from France was the need of the hour. We find Dupuis thereafter continuously requesting for the supply of raw materials such as ink, letter types for printing, and leather for binding the books. On 21 March 1845 Dupuis wrote that the new printing machine purchased for use in the press was doing well and everything was perfect. Dupuis said that it was a good acquisition and requested Tesson to pray that the printing press might grow day after day. He added that if some good souls could supply paper it would be good. Currently the paper was too thin to accept printing the letters and it caused for the tearing off. This was the main defect that he found with regard to the quality of paper.[30]

Dupuis said in his letter of 11 October 1845 to Jean Tesson that an important topic that he wished to complain was that, about 100 hides of different colours that Tesson had sent. Dupuis found 24 hides were of very ugly colour and Tesson had not sent the bill. Hence, he had no idea of the price. Dupuis said that he could not use them and he was afraid, because the leather bound books might cost too much. On the whole if Tesson could send some articles, please see that he enclosed the bill, or at least give an indication about the value of the objects sent. Dupuis mentioned in the same letter (11 October 1845) that apart from the colour paper that had been sent for printing the jacket of the book through the last shipment, some sheets were found painted with a colour. He was sure that in the long run, the colour would fade. This colour paper within no time would get spoiled, and it would disfigure the book printed. Dupuis said that in the near future, if colour papers for the jacket of the books were sent, he asked Tesson to please verify the quality of paper because they were too thin. Dupuis said that he had not received the last consignment of paper. Hence he requested to send 150 reams of paper in the next shipment, to enable him to continue with the printing of the books at the Catholic press in Pondicherry.[31] Dupuis in his letter on the next day (12 October 1845) to Tesson said that if the reams of the paper which the gentleman was supposed to bring had been done during the last travel by ship, kindly don't send the 300 reams which he had now asked for. Please send some ink if it had not been already sent.[32]

Dupuis was time and again writing letters for the supply of articles from France for the printing press. He wrote on 11 January 1847 that though he had not asked for any paper to be supplied for the use of the printing press for the time being, please do not think that he had no intention of doing or stopping the printing works. He said that we are certainly deprived of paper as Tesson could understand from his letter sent earlier. He had got only some stock and so requested him to please send 300 reams of paper.

He said that he needed for printing during the course of the year 1847, 260 reams of paper that were not glued, and 90 reams of paper that were glued. He said again to send good quality, strong and beautiful paper and see also that it was not too expensive.

As Dupuis had already mentioned, many a time, the paper of Mr. Leroux sent from Bordeaux was too thin. Many pages had holes too and they have to be discarded. A minimum 20 to 26 sheets of paper per ream were useless and sometimes even the number was on the higher side. Moreover, many sheets of paper were missing while counting the reams. Dupuis said that he was sure, a better quality of paper existed, but Mr. Leroux did not think about it. Mr. Leroux had promised to refund the loss on papers. He asked Tesson to please remind him of his promise. Dupuis said that if Mr. Leroux wanted to do business and work with him, please ask him to send stronger and better quality of paper. Dupuis added that in his opinion Leroux did not give any discount or compensation. As he had to consider the freight and the taxes to be paid, Dupuis had somehow preferred the paper sent to him from Bordeaux than from Paris.[33]

Dupuis stated that colour paper that he had been sending for the use of jacket of the books was of poor quality, because it was very thin and did not hold. The jacket covers for the books could not be made with this paper. Hence he wrote and asked him to send two reams of colour paper for the use of book covers. This need not be of first grade, but it should not be either too thick. It need not be also too expensive and above all, it should be of good quality and strong. Dupuis requested also to send two reams of marbled colour paper, or of any other kind exclusively for the jacket of the books.[34]

Dupuis said that he had to complain to Tesson about the leather pieces, because he was not very happy with the quality of the colour. He said that make sure that next time that these leather pieces should be of better quality and good colour. All these could be sent through the missionaries coming by the ship to Pondicherry. Dupuis said that it was difficult for him to judge the quality of the stuff that he had received finally, and the good samples shown earlier while placing the order. He asked Tesson when he would get the opportunity next time he could send 100 to 150 reams of paper in advance in the quota of next year.[35]

Dupuis in his letter of 11 August 1848 to Tesson said that if he had not sent the quantity of paper that he had asked for, please send it at the earliest. The last ream of papers sent from Paris was better than those of Bordeaux. Dupuis preferred the one from Paris but had to pay 80 francs more for the roll of 100 reams. It was an extra expense. Therefore he would like to order less paper for he was not sure of the quality. Meanwhile he said that Tesson could wait for a better opportunity to send the papers.[36] Dupuis in his letter of 9 April 1850 said that he was very glad to mention that the printing of the French-Tamil Dictionary had been very successful and it had come out very well. He requested Tesson kindly to send 4 reams of colour paper for the jacket covers of the printed books and 4 reams of paper decharge.[37] Dupuis in his letter of 10 November 1858 wrote to Tesson that not to forget the requirements for the printing press which he had asked for.[38] In his letter of 10 April 1861 Dupuis said that he had asked Tesson in his last letter for the supply of 300 reams of paper and also he asked to send four reams of ordinary paper which was needed.[39] Dupuis said that he was writing his letter dated 20 March 1864 to enable Jean Tesson to dispatch the requirements he had asked for. He said that to see that all this reached in the fair season, if earlier possible before the monsoon. The colour papers were badly needed for the jacket use in the printing press and he asked to forward the same at the earliest, and all that he had mentioned to him in his earlier letter sent. He wrote that more paper might be sent as his needs were increasing. Nothing was to be forgotten and dispatched at the earliest so that printing press work would not suffer.[40]

Dupuis in his letter from Pondicherry dated 9 December 1869 asked Jean Tesson to send four reams of marble papers of different colours and the colour should be well conditioned so that the insects do not eat it. He also mentioned that two reams of decharge paper and five reams of epreuve paper. Further he said that if there was occasion to send paper without freight Tesson could send 50 reams of collage paper similar to that was sent to him lastly from Nantes.[41] Thus it is known that the Catholic printing press in Pondicherry was heavily dependent on the supply of raw materials from France.

The Development of Tamil Typography in Pondicherry

We have come to know the evolution of Tamil type design and the transformation of Tamil letter-forms from palm-leaf manuscripts to early letter press printing that developed after the advent of the Europeans.[42] Letter press is the method of printing, and the only process which can use type directly. Printing is done from cast metal type or from blocks on which the image or printing areas are raised (in relief) above the non-printing areas. Ink rollers touched only the top surface of the raised areas, and the inked image was transferred directly to the paper. The development of letter-types in Tamil scripts had developed because the Jesuits and Protestants had prepared and used the Tamil fonts. Establishing a foundry to produce smaller Tamil types was the need of the hour in order to save on that ever-precious commodity and good printing paper. A further spurt to the development of Tamil type-faces came during the end of the eighteenth century (both in Tamil country and Europe) in response to the growing economic and administrative interests of the Christian missions and the East India Companies. The smiths cut a punch in hard metal for every Tamil letter, accent and punctuation mark and struck it into a softer metal to make the mould for casting identical pieces of type. The type was made from an alloy of lead, antimony and tin. The finished characters were kept in compartmentalized type cases from which the Tamil text was assembled. With the development of movable lead type, hot metal came to be used in Europe for the production of printed works. The low cost of setting lead type, which could be melted down after printing so that the same metal was used over and over again, made this technique the mainstay of the printing industry for centuries. In tune with the times, in order to develop printing Dupuis felt that the letter types were to be cast in France and sent to him for use in the printing press. In his letter 21 March 1845 he wrote to Jean Tesson and he asked him please to request Mr. Heldoorn for the following number of characters.

Number	*Price (in Francs)*
566	5
585	5
335	5
611	6
491	4
498	4
490	4
499	4
497	4
601	7
676	4
935	5
767	5
850	8
488	4
Total	74 Francs

Dupuis also said that please send me these small things as soon as you can, since it would help him in printing the books and enable the faithful to pray. Mr. Heldoorn could have sent the exact price of the objects that he forwarded to him but Dupuis was astonished to find that no reference had been made either to his letter of information or about Mr. Heldoorn's previous correspondence. Dupuis said that may be that Heldroon felt that it was not necessary because he had just sent to Dupuis the quantity that had been asked for. Therefore in that case he had nothing to write to Heldroon.[43]

The huge number of characters in the Tamil language made the typesetter work difficult in the printing press and he had to walk between five or six cases of type and reach high and low in order to find and retrieve the required pieces. L.S. Dupuis in 1855 had mentioned that the English experts who saw such a clear and easy victory in his use of typography in the Catholic press in Pondicherry instead of confusion that existed previously have been amazed. He noted that no doubt that this reform would introduce among their ranks and Dupuis said that he reckoned that France would have to take the same path of making major improvements and reforms of typography, which originated with one of its subjects and overseas colonies. Dupuis sent the specimens of typography cast in the foundry in Pondicherry for the universal Expo held in Paris in 1855.[44] It is interesting to note Tamil characters for the use of the letter press in Pondicherry were cast in France in 1863 by M. Bertrand Loeulliet which he had supplied to Fr. Charles Dallet the director of the MEP in Paris. We find also a printed sheet containing a table of all the Tamil scripts which had been in 53 x 70 cm preserved well at the Archives of the MEP Society in Paris.[45] The ligatures used by the Tamil script in manuscripts occupied vertical space more on the bottom. But Dupuis had taken efforts cautiously and these ligatures are designed equal to make the Tamil more efficient regarding interlinear spacing. This equal sizing is designed carefully to avoid any jumps for the reader in both text and display conditions.

We have observed earlier that various missionaries in Tamil country had prepared books of catechism from time to time improving upon the subject matter. However, it has been reported that there were two types called *Chinna kurippidam* (the penny catechism) and *Periya kurippidam* the grand catechism. The two catechisms widely used by the catechists and the local people were composed by Roberto Nobili. There were also other catechisms composed by some Jesuit missionaries that were in use in various localities in Tamil country till the end of the eighteenth century. However, with the advent of the MEP missionaries in Pondicherry it was felt necessary to have a common single and uniform catechism. Hence the compilation and publication of it was planned which would help and bring about a certain form of uniformity of religious instruction–both in substance and form–in all areas of the Pondicherry mission.

Clement Bonnand the Apostolic-Vicar during his pastoral visit in Pondicherry mission had observed the disadvantages of having several catechisms in the same vicariate, and he decided to consult his missionaries and to obtain their views in this regard. In a letter dated 13 June 1837 he addressed the issues before his fellow missionaries. All the priests had complained about the differences found in Tamil catechisms that are taught to the faithful in the various communities of the same vicariate. They found them inaccurate, too long or too short or too verbose. They liked to see a single catechism which might be allowed and which might be in use all over the mission. A superior quality of catechism was planned to be composed which could be made the model everywhere. Bishop Bonnand said that he was fully willing to do all that depending on the missionaries to please them. He told that let each missionary send him a copy of the Tamil catechism which was in use in his district, if there were two let them send him a copy of the one and the other. Let each missionary put in the margin notes on the passage which he would like to have changes or which he found defective, and let the missionaries say that one might substitute or add or strike off. Let them also add by means of an appendix of all that they would like to see in the catechism to be made. That being done let missionaries send each one personally the copies and the works of which he had just spoken. Bonnand said that having received them all he would work in consultation with the missionaries who were present in Pondicherry to draft a summary of the doctrine which he would first send to the missionaries to know if they find it suitable and then to be learnt and taught everywhere Tamil language is spoken.[46]

Bishop Bonnand received reply only from eight missionaries. They had sent the details as requested by him. Bonnand thereafter drafted two catechisms one in summary form and the other containing the Christian doctrine in greater detail. In a letter dated 20 April 1841 he gave the reasons for the two catechisms the manner of teaching them as well as the practical guidelines for making it easier for them to be learnt by those who were not favoured by good memory.[47] Thus these two catechisms which were accepted by the missionaries were planned to be printed for circulation.

Saathaaranam: The New Catechism Book Printed in Pondicherry in 1841

The first catechism book was the penny catechism called in Tamil *Saathaaranam* (ordinary). It was mainly based on the writings of the former missionaries (*par plusieurs anciens missionaires*). The next book is *Gnaano-padesa kurippidam* and it is a book of catechism published at the printing press belonging to the big Church (cathedral) in Pondicherry in 1841. The title page mentions that it contained the *sugirtha mandiram* of the Catholic Church and *Gnaanopadesa kurippidam*. The text in the past was translated into Tamil by the missionaries and it was examined by the *vidyabarragar* and *virpannar* (theologians and scholars). The book was printed with the permission of Clement Bonnand Drusipare the Bishop.[48]

The synod held in Pondicherry in 1844 discussed the books to be propagated in Tamil country. It was decided that the Christians should use the *Gnaanopadesa kaandam*, of Roberto Nobili and the abridged history of the Old Testament and the New Testament (*purandima* and *patchima kaandam*) of Jacome Goncalves.[49]

Prayer Books Printed: Gnaanamirdham, 1841, 1858 and Gnaanamirdha Thadaagam, 1842, 1847, 1858

In 1841 L.S. Dupuis published a book titled *Gnaanamirdham* which contained catechism and prayers. The same book was later reprinted in 1858 and it was titled *Gnnaamirthamaagiya katholikku thirusabhaiyin sugirtha mandirangalum gnaanopadesa kurippidamum*. In French missionary records it is known as *Gnaannamirdham* (*Ambroisie spirituelle*) and also it has been mentioned by Dupuis. The title page of the book mentions that the book *Gnaanamirdham* containing prayers and catechism had been was published for the fourth time at the *senmavirakkini maatha kovil* printing press at Pondicherry in 1858 as per the orders that came from Rome with the permission of Bishop Clement Bonnand Drusipare.[50]

The preface of *Gnaanamirdham* mentions that the book is issued to know God and to follow his commandments by all Christians, both the children and the elders and also to attend the holy sacrifice of the mass in a devout manner. Hence in this book the *gnaanopadesa kurippidam* (penny catechism) had been included. It is believed that the people would learn the prayers well and would leave all sinful and evil ways and lead a virtuous life. It is mentioned that the book contains all the days of fast and abstinence to be observed during the liturgical year and mentions all feasts both moveable and immoveable days. The moveable feast days of Ash Wednesday, Easter, the feast of Holy Spirit, ascension of Jesus Christ and Corpus Christi from the year 1859 to 1883 (25 years) have been furnished. The book contains prayers of *Pater Noster*, *Ave Maria*, *Credo*, ten commandments, precepts of the church, act of contrition, St Bernard's prayer, litany of Our Lady, mysteries of the holy rosary, prayers for good death, prayers for the dead, burial besides *chinna kurippidam* and *periya* kurippidam. The book contains a total of 321 pages. A. Louis wrongly mentions that this book explains the Christian teachings.[51] In fact it is a prayer book.

In 1842 L.S. Dupuis had published another book titled *Gnaanamirdha Thadaagam* which contained catechism and prayers. The same book was later reprinted in 1847.[52] In French missionary records it is known as *Gnaannamirdha thadaagam* (*reservoir d'ambroisie spirituel*). L.S. Dupuis in his letter of 9 February 1847 to Jean Tesson in Paris requested him to forward a copy of this book *Gnaanamirtha Thadaagam* the catechism and prayer book to Rome. He stated that this book printed at Pondicherry had been also sent to Sri Lanka for the use of the Catholics.[53]

Gnaanamirdha thadaagam was again printed in 1858. The title page of the book mentions that the book *gnaamirdha thadaagam* containing prayers and catechism had been published for the third time at the *senmavirakkini maatha kovil* printing press at Pondicherry in 1858 as per the orders that came from Rome.[54] The title page also mentions that many prayers and meditations had been added in this book and the book had been examined by the MEP priests and printed by Clement Bonnand Drusipare the Bishop of Pondicherry. The *vivekam* (to the knowledge of the readers, vide pp. 19-25) mentions that prayer is important for saving the souls. Hence whatever works and occupations you may be employed it is necessary to set aside some time for prayer. Hence prayers are assembled and given in the book. The title is so aptly given *gnaanamirdha thadaagam* and it is very appropriate. It said that very important prayers and meditations have been included. Whatever was asked in the name of Lord Jesus Christ had been granted and all goodness would flow in the channel of grace. Hence one who does not pray would suffer and incurs loss. Never forget to pray. Daily pray. Continuously pray had been the slogans given. The book has an epilogue. At the end the quotation from Thessalonians chapter III, verse 1 is given. The moveable dates of feasts from 1851 to 1880 had been found in the book.

The book contains all the days of fast and abstinence to be observed during the liturgical year. It mentions all feasts both moveable and immoveable days. The moveable feast days of Ash Wednesday, Easter, feast of Holy Spirit, ascension of Jesus Christ and Corpus Christi from the year 1858 to 1897 (40 years) have been furnished. The book interestingly contains *amavasa* (no moon days) and *pournami* days (new moon days), solar and lunar eclipses and the details are given in Tamil. The feast days for the whole year had been given in Tamil calendar months. The book contains, *pathithari maruppatharkkuriya sankshebham* (refuting the Protestants) from *Thembaavani cheyyul* (poetry) of Beschi and *chinna kurppidam*. The book contains a total of 763 pages. A. Louis wrongly assigns that *Gnaanmirdha Thadaagam* explains the Christian teachings. In fact the book only contains prayers.[55]

Printing Sarithirathuukuaduththa Gnaanopadesa Surukkam, 1858 and Sarithirathuukuaduththa Gnaanopadesathin Vinaa Vidai, 1858

In 1858 *Sarithirathuukuaduththa Gnaanopadesa Kurippidam* a book on catechism in Tamil was printed by L.S. Dupuis. The title page mentions that it was printed with the permission of Bishop Bonnand, and an order that came from Rome. There are 38 lessons from creation to end. The Christian chronology of BC and AD is interestingly given (pp. 326-29) in the book. There is also another bilingual book that contains catechism in French and in Tamil in question answer format and it was prepared by Claude Fleury. The Tamil version is found along with French text. The book is titled, *Questions et reponses du petit catechisme Historique de Fleury, avec quelques lecons supplementaires par un member des la congregation des mission-etran geres* with Tamil title *Sarithiraththuk-kuaduththa Gnaanopadeaththin Vinaa Vidai*. The book was printed in 1858 and has 72 pages.[56]

Three Catechism Books printed: Gnaanopadesa Surukkam, 1861, Padangalaal Vizhlagappapatta Gnaanopadesam, 1863 and Sugirtha Mandirangalum Gnaanopadesa Kurippidamum, 1865

Gnaanopadesa Surukkam (*Abrege du catechism par demandes et responses*) in question-answer type was printed in 1861. The Roman Catholic catechism illustrated by pictures was printed in 1863 under the title *padangalaal vizhakapatta gnaanopadesam*. It had 21 pages. Prayers and catechism book was printed under the title *Sugirtha Mandirangalum Gnaaopadesa Kurippidamum* in 1865.[57]

Gnaanopadesa Surukkam of Fr. Miguel in Vepery Printed in Pondicherry in 1872

The catechism book titled *Gnaanopadesa Surukkam* was printed in 1872 and it contained morning and evening prayers. The preface of the book (p. 2) mentions that the book was based on *Mandira Maalai* (A collection of prayers) and *gnaanopadesa kaandam* (big catechism) of Roberto Nobili, Thathuva pothagar). It was prepared by Fr. Miguel the Capuchin who was the parish priest of St Andrew's church at Vepery in Madras in consultation with the necessary permission of Arulananda swami who was the Capuchin superior there. The book is the third impression and the prayers have been corrected and printed at the press in Pondicherry. The book contains 15 lessons. It has a total of 127 pages.[58]

Child's Prayer Book: Vaalar Pokkisham and Vaalar Thunai: 1844, 1861

The catechism book with daily prayers in Tamil was needed for use of the children in their spiritual exercise of piety and so it was printed in 1844.[59] This book titled *Vaalar Pokkisham* (Child's Treasury) contained morning and evening prayers of the Roman Catholic church and served well for hearing the Holy Mass besides having the shorter and larger catechism (*kaalai maalai vazhipaatirkaaga surukkamaagavum neend-athaaga paadal thoguthi kondathu*). The same book was reprinted later in

1861 and 1897.[60] A. Louis wrongly attributes *Vaalar Pokkisham* as a school textbook.[61] It has a total of 266 pages with six pictures. L.S. Dupuis had sent three copies of *Vaalar Pokkisham* to Paris and it is mentioned by him in his letter to Jean Tesson dated 3 December 1844.[62]

Vaalar Thunai (Child's Companion) was another book of prayers for the use of children. It contained prayers to be said in the afternoon and evening, and prayers to be said during the holy mass.[63] It was printed in 1844. A Louis wrongly again attributes *Vaalar Thunai* as a school textbook.[64] L.S. Dupuis had sent three copies of *Vaalar Thunai* to Paris and it is mentioned in his to Jean Tesson dated 3 December 1844.[65]

Printing the Litany of Saints in 1842, 1844, 1847, 1853, 1858, 1859 and the Book Praarthani Maalai in 1867

L.S. Dupuis had printed prayers and litany in the book titled *Siluvai Paathai* printed in 1842. We find (a) litany of the passion of Jesus Christ (b) litany of the holy face of Jesus (*Thirumugathin piraarthanai, litanies de la Sainte face*) (c) litany of Holy Eucharist (d) litany of the dolours of the Blessed Virgin Mary (e) Sacred Heart of Jesus (f) Sacred Heart of Mary (g) Mount Carmel and (h) *Motcha rakkini* (the Queen of Heaven).

In his book *Nanraai Ninai* authored and printed by L.S. Dupuis in 1844 he published the litany of the Guardian angel, St. Joseph, St. Antony, St. Francis Xavier and St. Sebastian. In the book of *Maasillammal Urpavitha Archsishta Devamaathavin Thiru Idhya Sabhai Anusaaran* printed in 1847 L.S. Dupuis published the litany of Blessed Virgin Mary.

In the book titled *Arulanandar Sarithiram* (life of John de Britto) printed in 1853 L.S. Dupuis published the litany of John de Britto. In *Gnaamirtha thadaagam* the third edition of 1858 we find 3 litanies that include the litany of the Holy name of Jesus, the litany of all saints and the litany of extreme-unction. In the book titled *Ainthukaaya Archsishta Franciskuvin Thavathukkuriya Moonram Sabhai Ozhukkam* printed in 1859 he published the litany of St. Francis and also the litany of Elizabeth.

All the above mentioned litanies printed in several books were assembled together and he published a book titled *Praarthanai Maalaiyum Gnaanamirthamum* (*Recueil de litanies*). L.S. Dupuis vide his circular dated 31 December 1867 to all priests in the Pondicherry mission mentioned about this book. He said needless to say that the month of March was dedicated to St. Joseph and the Jesuits in Tamil country had composed a book titled '*Praarthanai Maalai*'—a collection of litanies in honour of saints including St. Joseph. He wrote that a publication on the life of saints was about to be brought out from the Catholic printing press under his direction and he would be pleased to offer a copy of the publication to the priests. He said that these books may be of great help to them in their mission and for encouraging meditation.[66]

Printing the Books of Monthly Devotion: Devamaathavin Vankka Maatham (1850), Archsishta Susaiyappar Vanakka Maatham (1867) and Uththarikkira Aathumaakalin Vanakka Maatham (1870)

L.S. Dupuis felt the need to make available the books of monthly devotion. In 1850 the Devotion to Mary in the month of May was printed.[67] This book was composed by Louis Saint-Cyre the Jesuit (born in 1813, ordained priest on 13 June 1840 and left Bordeuax on 21 February 1841) who came to Nagapattinam in 1842. The Jesuits had started a school at Nagapattinam in 1844 and Louis Saint-Cyre was the principal. He wrote at that time the book titled *Devamaathavin Vanakka Maatham* (Devotion to Mother of God).[68] There is a preface by L.S. Dupuis and we find that the book was composed by a Jesuit. It states that in Italy the devotion to Mother Mary developed and spread in the churches and chapels of the famous cities and towns. Like mother pours hers love and affection and cares for her children, the divine mother she being the queen of the heaven does towards her people who are the children. Hence the month of May assigned for the devotion to Mary should be observed properly. What could be done during each day of the month is neatly explained. The book begins with St. Bernard's prayer (p. 21) and contains *gnaana paatugal, Thirukaavalur adaikala naayagimel venkalippa, adaikala malai, thevamaathvin thottiram, devamaathavin peri paatukkal, litanie beate marie virginis and hymnus S. Casmiri* in Latin (p. 440). The total pages of the book printed are 446.

L.S. Dupuis in his circular to the Immaculate nuns on Friday, 11 January 1867 he stated that he had planned to print the book *Archsishta Susaiyappar Vanakka Maatham* (Month of St. Joseph for Pious). The book got printed according to records in month of March 1867.[69]

L.S. Dupuis printed a book titled *Utharikkira Aathumaakal Vanakka Maatham* in 1870.[70] It was to encourage devotion to all souls during the month of November which has been assigned by the Catholic Church. The title page of the printed book mentions that it was composed by a Jesuit and printed based on an order issued from Rome and Bishop Laouënan of Pondicherry. It contains 474 pages in total. It is known that the author of the book was Louis St. Cyr, the Jesuit. The *paayirman* (preface) mentions that prayers to all souls and offering the holy mass and by making gifts to people can help the dead. It had been a practice of the Church since long as said by St. Augustine. The priests pray for the dead everyday in the holy mass. Every Monday is assigned to pray specially for the dead. November the month had been assigned for the devotion to the dead and all souls. It coincides with the Tamil months of *ayapasi-kaarthigai*. Hence all the 30 days we should pray for the souls and the importance had been explained in the book.

Siluvai Paathai Printed in 1842 and reprinted in 1856

L.S. Dupuis in his letter to Jean Tesson dated 18 April 1842 mentioned that as soon as the paper arrives through ship 'Tropique' he will reprint the book titled *Siluvai Paathai* (The Way of the Cross). He stated that the first edition of books printed had been sold. The book printed was well received for it depicted the sublime pathos of the crucifixion of Christ. Dupuis never expected that it would be so. He stated that the printed book had reached as far as Sri Lanka. He hoped that with God's grace that the printing press would be able to survive. He noted that he had a good distribution of books, thanks to the school teachers and other people helped in the religious mission.[71]

Siluvai Paathai (*Chemin de la Criox*) the book was printed for the second time in 1842 at the Catholic press at Pondicherry on arrival of paper from France. There is a *paayiram* (preface) which mentions that Christ took the form of human, i.e., God became man to redeem the people of the world from sin and he showed the way of the cross and reached heaven. Hence all Christians should carry the cross very patiently as he taught to reach the eternal paradise. The book was titled so because it helps to meditate on the passion of our lord Jesus Christ. The clock of the passion from Thursday onwards had been given on hourly basis (p.80). The pictures of the fourteen Stations of the Cross had been printed in the book. Prayers of the five wounds of Jesus had been also given. A special rosary is provided and the prayers had been furnished. The last seven sacred words of Jesus and the utterances along with the prayers and meditation had been given. The litany of the passions, the litany and prayers of the dolours of the Blessed Virgin Mary have been added. Devotion to the Blessed Sacrament, prayer and litany of the Immaculate Heart of Mary, litany of our Lady of Mount Carmel and the spiritual benefits of the prayers have been given (p. 370). It has been stated that the book is written in the style of both *senthamizh* and *kodunthamizh* so as to help all the faithful (p.12). The preface (p. 13) states only once on a Friday the way of the cross could be made. But during the lent all the Fridays the way of the cross should be observed. The book contains the manners of conducting the way of the cross and the prayers had been given both in Latin and Tamil. The songs in Tamil had been composed in Tamil *ragams* (tunes). The book contains in total 387 pages.[72] Five copies of *Siluvai Paathai* the book printed had been sent to Paris and the information is found mention in the letter of L.S. Dupuis to Jean Tesson dated 3 December 1844.[73] *Siluvai Paathai* was reprinted in 1856 and the book had 380 pages.

Thirunaatkalin Vizhlakka Surukkam Authored by Joseph Auguste Chevalier Printed in 1859

Joseph Auguste Chevalier born at Are et Senans on 16 March 1814 was ordained priest on 3 September 1837. He joined the MEP society on 13 October 1837 left France on 3 September 1838. He at first worked in the Pondicherry vicariate from 1839 to 1845 and then worked in Mysore area from 1845 to 1880. In 1852 he became the military chaplain in Bangalore and worked for 22 years. He wrote a book titled *Thirunaatkalin Vizhlakka Surukkam*. L.S. Dupuis printed this book and so an order was obtained from Rome. Bonnand the Bishop of Pondicherry also permitted the book to be printed in 1859.[74] There is a preface and it mentions that the feast days have to be observed very well and so in brief the author had given the details and information. It is stated that The Council of Trent had made three parts of the liturgical calendar year and it is normally followed. The first season is the advent to the birth of Jesus containing four weeks. The second is from the birth of Jesus to his ascension to heaven and the third is from the feast of the decent of the Holy Spirit to beginning of advent.

The author states, Dear brethren, we expect that you would read and use this book. Please pray for us also. We find in the first chapter the details regarding the blessings of observing the feast, use of holy water, conducting procession, membership to *sabhai* (society), novena details and the seven days in a week and other details. The rest of the chapters deal with the season of advent, feast of the Immaculate Conception of Mary, the four seasons, birth of Jesus, the feast of Christmas, visit of the magi, followed by the lent season, feast of St Joseph on 19 March, the feast of annunciation on the 25 March, the Holy Week, the Easter and goes on with various other feasts till the beginning of advent. Thus for a whole year all the feasts are given and the book ends (p. 105).

Printing the Book of Liturgy: Pusai Udhavi Mandiram Authored by Louis Marie Mousset, 1859

Pusai udhavi mandiram (*maniere de server la messe*) was the book authored Louis Marie Mousset the MEP missionary in Pondicherry. This book is also commonly known as *Pusai Aayatham* or *Pusai Ketkira Vagai*.[75] L.S. Dupuis had printed this book in 1859.

Printing Karunaakara Kadal in 1868

Louis Saint-Cyr the Jesuit in Nagapattinam wrote a book of devotion addressed to the divine heart of Jesus and to the spotless heart of divine mother. This book titled *Karunaakara Kadal* was printed by L.S. Dupuis in Pondicherry in 1868.[76]

Printing Beschi's Gnaana Unarthuthal in 1842 and reprinting in 1846

Dupuis was keen to print books for spiritual reading for the use of the Catholic Christians after assuming charge of the printing press as manager in 1841. As he came across *Gnaana Unarthuthal* the work composed by Beschi he immediately decided to print the book and successfully completed it in 1842. The same book was reprinted again in 1846. The title page mentions that *Gnanna Unarthuthal* was printed after obtaining an order from Rome along with the permission of Bishop Clement Bonnand at *senmavirakkkini maatha* church press.[77]

L.S. Dupuis, the publisher mentions that the author Beschi had given spiritual milk like the mother who cares for her children and it helps to lead a good life. Hence it is suggested to read this book and also to lead a virtuous life. The book has been prepared and published to make the readers understand easily and so *senthamizh* and *kodunthamizh* had been well mixed and composed. When the preface ends (at p. 80) the printed text continues and ends (at p. 99) followed by the contents of the book (p. 100). The total printed pages are 100. L.S. Dupuis in his letter dated 18 April 1842 from Pondicherry to Jean Tesson in Paris mentioned that *Gnaana Unarthuthal* of Beschi had been printed.[78]

Printing Charles Michele Bertoldi's Gnaana Muyarchi, 1843

Gnaana Muyarchi composed by Charles Michele Bertoldi (1662–1740) the Jesuit was very popular among the Christians. The manuscript in paper had found way to France in 1750 and it has 96 folios. It is even now preserved in the National Library, Paris.[79] L.S. Dupuis took efforts to publish *Gnaana Muyarchi* and the book got printed in 1843.[80] Dupuis mentioned that in the seventeenth century there lived a Jesuit by Tamil name Gnaanapragasa swami and he was the author of *Gnaana Muyarchi*. As his book is very useful to the Catholics, permission was given by Bishop Clement Bonnand to print and an order was also obtained from Rome for printing. The book printed has a preface and it ends at page 8. It states that there is nothing very bad like sin and it has been explained in the book (p. 6). One who mediates well will not commit sin. Those who sin would go to eternal hell. The author explains the days of judgment and punishment and he outlines the beauty of reaching the heaven. Therefore 24 spiritual efforts have to be made and each effort had been described. The book deals with the fate of the humans, mortal sin, how the bad came to the world through sinning and other details. The printed text ends at p. 256. The book has a total of 261 pages. The contents had been found at the end (pp.257-61). L.S. Dupuis in his letter to Jean Tesson in Paris dated 23 October 1843 mentioned that this book *Gnaana Muyarchi* had been printed.[81]

Gnaana Oduukangalukku Niyamikkapatta Archishta Ignaciyar Dhyaanagal printed in 1848 Authored by Charles Michael Bertholdi

L.S. Dupuis came across the manuscript of Charles Michele Bertoldi (1662-1740) the Jesuit of the Madurai mission in Tamil called *Gnaanao-dukkangalukku niyamikkapatta archsishta ignaciyar dhyaanangal* which was very interesting since it dealt with doing retreat. Hence he decided to print. The work contained 76 spiritual instructions about the four ends of human life.[82] Dupuis successfully printed the book in 1848. The title page mentions that Bishop Clement Bonnand granted permission and an order was obtained from Rome for printing.[83] Dupuis in his foreword by the publisher (*Ipprabhanthathi pirasithipaduthiyavaraal paayiram*) stated that there is no account of sinners in this world who have read the spiritual meditations composed by St Ignatius inspired by God. Many had turned a new leaf of life following the virtues and benefitted. This book is printed in order to have such things in this Tamil country. Dupuis said that the name of the person who wrote this work in Tamil is unknown but certainly he belonged to the religious order of the Society of Jesus. The person who wrote this book wished to have many good and virtuous persons in this country. Hence Dupuis also wished the same. He said that he had examined the many hand-written manuscripts and explained the ideas of the original author in detail in many places and the book has been published from Pondicherry. Though the book is useful for making retreat, Dupuis said that reading it every day and always using it for meditation would no doubt help. It is believed that that those who read carefully would derive always spiritual benefit. The book printed has a total of 106 pages.

Aathuma Nesam of C. Gnaanapragasa Nathar Printed in 1860

St. Ligouri's meditation on the passion of our Lord Jesus Christ was translated by C. Gnaanapragasa Nathar @ Charles Michele Bertoldi into Tamil titled *Aathuma Nesam*. He was a Jesuit priest in Madurai mission[84] The book was printed on receipt of an order from Rome and permission was granted by the Bishop in Pondicherry.[85] We find the dedication to St. Ligouri by the translator (pp. 1-2) followed by the prayer to Jesus and

Mary. The preface of Ligouri is also found translated in Tamil. The biography of Alphonse Maria de Ligouri is given where it is stated that St. Ligouri was born on 26 September 1696 and Francisco Heronimus had made a prophecy that Ligouri would become a bishop and he would not die before the age of 90. There are 16 chapters translated and given in the book. We find that chapter 6 deals with commencement of Jesus at Mount of Olive sweating of blood and chapter 13 deals with end of the passion and death of Jesus. The last utterances of the sacred words of Jesus had been provided. The book ends with the prayer of Bonaventure. The total printed pages are 308.

Kristhunaathar Anusaaram of C. Gnaanapragaasa Nathar Printed in 1863

The MEP missionaries also felt the importance of Imitation of Christ composed by Thomas A. Kempis and so they desired to print it. The work was executed by C. Gnaanapragaasa Nathar @ Charles Michele Bertoldi. L.S. Dupuis printed the book in 1863.[86] The title page of the book mentions that *De Imitatione Christi, Kristhunaathar Anusaaram*, whose author was Thomas A Kempis and the translator was C. Gnaanapragaasa Nathar and permission was granted by Bishop Godelle for printing. The book contains four sections. The first section has 25 chapters dealing with the theme of the useful admonitions to spiritual life.[87] The second section has 12 chapters and deals with the admonitions concerning interior things.[88] The third section has 59 chapters and it deals with special features of the interior consolation.[89] The fourth chapter has 18 chapters and it deals with the Blessed Sacrament.[90] The prayers are provided at the end. The book contains a total of 390 pages.

Archsishta Ignaciyar Gnaana Dhyaanagal Printed in 1864 Authored by James Thomas Rossi

L.S. Dupuis came across the manuscript of James Thomas Rossi *Archsishta Ignaciyar Gnaana dhyaanagal* (*meditations spirituelles de saint Ignace* as mentioned by Dupuis in French) and he decided to print. An order from Rome was obtained for printing this book and Isidore Godelle the Bishop of Pondicherry granted permission.[91] The *vivekam* (to the knowledge of the readers, pp. 1-4) of Rossi mentions that Jesus through Blessed Virgin Mary the Mother of God directed to help the sinners easily to come back to the fold. It was necessary to lead a virtuous life so as to become holy and more saintly. Hence Mother of God is called the refuge of the sinners. Therefore the Society of Carmel, the Society of 150 hours and the Society of Dolours were established in the world. When St Ignatius was doing penance at the cave of Manresa, Mary the queen of angels showed to him certain spiritual meditations on the topics such as why man was created, the entry of the origin of the evil, the entry of death, judgment, and the hell. She also made Ignatius to understand the divine model of Jesus, his death on the holy cross and all other related matters. As a result, Ignatius became conscious and he wrote his reflections and preached them to do in course of meditations and so it was called spiritual meditations of St. Ignatius.

Rossi stated that food is important for the physique so as also meditations help the soul. It gives the spiritual strength needed for the health. Therefore retreat should be made for eight days and during that time no routine work should be carried out and everyone should be unemployed at that time. No one should talk and absolute silence should be observed. One should also abstain from having the earthly pleasures. During the retreat one should pray and reflect, meditate and think and should make good confession and receive the Holy Communion. The printed text of the book contains meditations for every day in the morning and evening. A page of contents had been given (pp 143-4). The book has a total of 144 pages.

Printing Pierre Mauduit's Divya Maathrigai in 1866

L.S. Dupuis found *Divya Maathirigai* a manuscript in Tamil and he desired to print the book for it contained good spiritual reading. It was printed at the Catholic press in 1866. An order from Rome was obtained and Bishop Godelle had granted the permission for printing as found mention in the title page.[92] There is a preface (p. 6) which states that Jesus became a man to teach the virtues and to show the way to heaven through his divine model. There is no doubt that those who follow his footsteps would reach heaven. It can be said that a good amount of benefit would come to the souls through reading this book. One of the ancient priests in the past had composed this work. Over a period of time copies of the manuscript text contained mistakes which had crept in because of the carelessness of the scribes. Hence Dupuis said that he had corrected the errors and printed. He said that the book would help all souls to obtain the salvation and he asked the readers to pray for the author and the publisher. According to Jesuit records Pierre Mauduit known as Periya Sanjivi Nathar was the author of the work of *Divya Mathirigai* (Divine model) who built the church of Vadugarpatti. We find that he had also written two more books titled *Gnaana Sanjivi* (vide chapter 3 of *Divya Maathrigai*) and *Nallamaranathu Aaytham* (vide chapter 18). The book contains details on happy death and explains the greatness of Jesus the redeemer, the reasons for devotion to him, his fine teachings concerning the virtues and finally his way of example to a virtuous life.

There is *vivekam* in the book (to the knowledge of the readers, p.10) by Pierre Mauduit and it states that in *Akkiyaana Nivaaranam* a *prabandam* in which he had explained the glory of God and described eternal joy. After this spiritual book this new book *Divya Maathirigai* is written and describes on the redeemer's greatness and the virtues, the divine model shown by him. It aims to present the divine model as gleaned from the Word of God and the Acts of the Apostles. It elucidates how it is important to lead a virtuous life and how it is very easy to follow the footsteps of Jesus. It also explains the good character of Jesus, the divine leader and devotion towards him to be developed. The book has eight points important for the devotion towards Jesus, four ways to follow Jesus and the careful steps to follow Jesus and the virtues to be followed in life. It emphasizes on the three main virtues such as love for neighbour, meekness and patience and then presents 15 lessons given about the various virtues. The book includes the model shown, the words of Jesus and the lessons for good death. The author mentions to seek the blessings of the Virgin Mary before reading this book. He adds the prayers to seek the divine model with the expression of *Amen Sesu*. The book contains 326 pages in total.

The book when got printed again by the Jesuits of the New Madurai Mission in 1891 at Tiruchirapalli we find the name of the author had been mistakenly mentioned as Roberto Nobili. The same error continued to appear in 1966 and it came to be mentioned by S. Rajamanickam.[93]

Lives of saints prepared by the Roman Catholic missionaries in Tamil were available on paper in 1731 and it was observed by the Protestant missionaries of Tranquebar. They have noted the works and mentioned that these dealt with *Archsishtavargaludaya puthumaigal* (the Miracles of the Saints).[94] The list includes the lives of St. Agnes (feast celebrated on 20 April), St. Athanasius (2 May), St. Anthony (13 June), St. Ignatius of Loyola (31 July) St. Francis of Assisi (4 October), St. Polycarp (26 January), St. Maccari (2 January) St. Martin (30 January) St. Lawrence (10 August), John the evangelist, St. Roche, St. Agatha, St. Clare, St. Francis Xavier, St. John of the Cross, St. Cecily, St. Sebastian, St. Tecle, St. Paul the Hermit and St. Therese. Thus we find the devotion to saints had been encouraged by the Jesuits and lives of new saints had also been added from to time by the Catholic missionaries.

L.S. Dupuis came to know of the lives of some saints in Tamil which had been prepared by missionaries in the past. Therefore he wished to have these palm-leaves and paper manuscripts that were available so as print them into books. He collected and consulted the *Arulaanandar Sarithiram* (Life of John de Britto) composed by Bouchet, *Ignaciyar Sarithiram* (Life of St. Ignatius of Loyola) by Angelo de Franceschei, *Dharma Uththiyaanam*

(Life of Thirty Saints) by Jacome Gonçalves and *Varushathin Pradhi Dina Sugirtha Pirasangangalaagiya Archshistavargalin Sarithiram* (Everyday Sermon for the Whole Year on the Lives of Saints) by James Thomas Rossi. He successfully got them from various persons and places.

Printing the Life of the Blessed John de Britto in 1853 and Reprinting in 1857 and 1858

John de Britto was martyred in 1693 and he was beatified by Pope Pius IX on 21 August 1853. Hence Dupuis desired to have the biography printed. We find that in 1853 *Arulanandar Sarithiram* was successfully printed by him. He also mentioned it to Jean Tesson vide his letter dated 7 September 1853.[95] The book of biography in Tamil stated that John de Britto was the son of a viceroy of Brazil, born in Lisbon on 1 March 1647. His parents were Salvador de Britto and Beatrice Pereira. At the age of nine he was chosen to be a companion in studies of a prince, afterwards King Peter II of Portugal. Britto joined the Society of Jesus and after receiving priesthood he volunteered to work in the Madurai mission. He arrived in Goa in 1676 and came with Fr. Andre Freyre to Madurai. His ministry was fruitful and he converted a large number of Hindus. He went to Lisbon in 1688 and returned and worked in the Marava country and died as a martyr at Oriyur on 4 February 1693. Further letters of the MEP missionaries mention that the life of *Arulanandar Sarithiram* was widely read and used by Tamil Catholics.[96] All the printed copies of the book had been sold very well within four years and so L.S. Dupuis had to reprint and at that time he gave a different title *Muthiperupetra Arulaanandar Sarithiram* in 1857. Again the book had been sold like hot cake and within one year and L.S. Dupuis reprinted it in 1858 under the a different title *Vethasatchi-yaana Muthiperupetra Arulaanandar Sarithiram* and it was a reprint of 1857. The title page runs thus: *Vetha saatchiyaana muthiperupettra aru-lanandar sarithiram: Iguthu Iesu sabhai guruswamiyaargalil oruvaraal seyappattu romapurinniru vantha uththaarathin padiye 1858 varusham puthuvai senmavirakkini maatha kovilai serntha achchukoodathil pathipikka pattathu.*[97] This book has a total of 308 pages. We find the essays put under 11 sections. The Novena prayers and the *mandirams* (prayers) are printed at the end of the book. Dupuis was unaware of the original author Jean Venant Bouchet. Hence he had mentioned that the book was composed by one Jesuit. He obtained an order from Rome for printing and the Bishop had accorded also permission for printing.

Dupuis had written the *paayiram* for the book separately (pp. 1-3) in which he stated that martyrs are known for their boldness, courage, faith and the spirit of conquering the devil. The name of mudiyappar (Stephen) and seyyapar and other martyrs are well known and their feasts are celebrated. John de Britto had come to this Tamil country suffered for the cause of faith and did all good works and finally accepted death as a martyr. Hence he stated that he was printing the biography and more specifically on his holy death. Dupuis stated that the book is dedicated to St. Francis Xavier the apostle of India. The text of the book ends (at p. 282) and finally we find the prayers to John de Britto. In this book the letter 'IM' has no dot over it in the printed text. Again the letter 'RA' has no line-stroke below in print.

Devasagayam Pillai Sarithiram Printed in 1858 Authored by Louis Saint-Cyr

Louis Saint-Cyr the Jesuit in Nagapattinam in 1842 heard about Devasagayam Pillai the martyr in Tamil country and so he collected data and successfully wrote a book which interested L.S. Dupuis to publish. The book was successfully printed at the Catholic press in Pondicherry in 1858. The title page of the book is *Vethasaattiyaana Devasagayam Pillai Sarithiram* and the year 1858 is mentioned in Tamil numeral.[98] The book contains ten chapters. Each chapter has a heading for example *Devasagayam pillai anupaviththa avamaanangalum upaathigalum*. The book including preface has 72 printed pages. The text is printed without separating the *sandhi* in Tamil.

Printing Archsishta Gnaanapragaasiyaar Sarithiramum Archsishta Sthanislausudaya Sarithira Pirasangangalummaavana in 1862 Authored by Louis Saint-Cyr

L.S. Dupuis desired to print the life of Gnaanapragaasiyaar (Louis) and St. Stanislaus authored by Louis Saint-Cyr and he successfully printed the book in 1862. The Tamil title is *Archsishta Gnaanapragaasiyaarudya Sarithiramum Archsishta Sthanislasudaya Sarithira Pirasangangalum-maavana.*[99] The book contains ten lessons. The novena prayers and sermons for the novena are also printed. The author name of Louis Saint-Cyre is not mentioned but the title page records that the book was composed by a Jesuit. Bishop Godelle had permitted and the book had been printed. The preface of the book mentions that earlier Jesuits in Tamil country had composed many works on the saints. The two saints Gnaanapragaasiyaar and Stanislaus aspired for eternal things and therefore those who live on this earth could also follow their models and live. Hence it had been decided and the publisher had the idea to print the book.

L.S. Dupuis in his preface states that pope Benedict XIII had declared St. Louis as the patron of school children. Though born in an affluent family he set aside all riches and wealth and gave up the worldly pleasure. Similarly St. Stanislaus loved God and lived like an angel. He joined the Society of Jesus and died at the young age of 18. He thought that he was born for the heaven and not for this earth. Therefore it is meaningful to put the biography of the two saints in a single book and print it. The preface ends at page six but the text continues. The book is divided into two sections while the first contains 10 chapters dealing with the biography and virtues of Gnaanapr-agaasiyaar. The second section deals with the miracles that happened followed by the biography and virtues of Stanislaus.

In this book Louis Saint-Cyr the author presents the details of celebrating the feast for ten days. Hence he had prepared and given the prayers of Louis for the days. The spiritual advices have been given at the end of the book. The text of the book ends at p. 362. Six prayers to St. Louis had been furnished followed by the contents of the book had been provided at the end. It is interesting to find that the copies of the printed books were sold and so the same book got reprinted again in 1863 (within a year). It is clear that there had been wide readership amongst the Catholics.

Printing the Lives of St. Antony, St. Martin, St. Sebastian and St. Lawrence

Dupuis published several lives of saints as separate books from the printing press in Pondicherry by encouraging the devotion to individual saints. We have no idea as to who was the author of these books as it is unclear from records. Dupuis had printed *Archsishta Anthoniyaar Sarithiram* (Life of St. Antony). It is mentioned that Saint Anthony was born in Lisbon, Portugal in AD 1195. His baptismal name was Ferdinand. In the age of 15 he joined the Augustinian order and spent his time in study and prayer. At the age of 25 he urged to die as a martyr for Christ when he heard some Franciscans were martyred by the Muslims in Morocco. Hence he joined the Franciscan order in 1221 and changed his name as Antony. He was an illustrious preacher with the fame of holiness. His died in AD 1231 and his relics are kept in Padua. His feast was celebrated on 13 June by the Church.

Dupuis Printed *Archsishta Marthinaar Sarithiram* (Life of St. Martin). He mentioned that Saint Martin was recruited to the army at Amiens in France at a young age of fifteen. One day as he was going along, he met a beggar, half naked shivering in cold. His heart was moved. He was worried that he found no way to help him. But quickly he arrived at a decision and he tore his own cloak and covered the stranger with one piece, keeping the other piece for him. That night Christ appeared to Martin in his dream and a voice said 'Martin here is the cloak, you covered me with', Later Martin straight away went and met a priest and got baptized. Later he met Saint

Hilary, the Bishop of Poitiers and became his disciple. Martin began leading a life of a hermit. He returned to Poitiers and he was soon in the company of several monks. This eventually became Benedictine Abbey of Liguge. Bishop Hilary gave him a piece of land for the monastery and this was the first monastic community in France. Martin had to tackle Priscillian and Arian heretics. He lived in a rural residence and this became the monastery of Marmoutier. Martin died (in AD 397) and the feast of Saint Martin was celebrated on 11 November.

Dupuis published *Archsishta Sebasthiyar Sarithiram* (Life of St. Sebastian). He mentioned that Saint Sebastian was born in Milan. As there was persecution of the Christians in Milan he left the place and moved over to Rome the scene of bitter persecution. There he gained the crown of martyrdom. Diocletian tried by every means to make Sebastian renounce his belief in Christ. After all efforts had proved fruitless, he ordered him to tie to a post and pierced with arrows. When everyone thought him dead, a devout woman named Irene arranged for his funeral at night. Finding him still alive, she cared for him in her own house. After his recovery, he appeared again before Diocletian and boldly rebuked him for his cruelty. Enraged by the saint's sharp words, he ordered him to be scourged until he expired. His body was thrown into a sewer. In the middle ages, Sebastian was widely venerated as a protector against plague and pox. The feast of Saint Sebastian was celebrated by the Catholic Church on 20 January as per the calendar.

Dupuis published *Archsishta Laurenciyaar Sarithiram* (Life of St. Lawrence). He mentioned that Saint Lawrence had his diaconate ministry under Pope Sixtus II. Lawrence was arrested and placed under the custody of Hippolytus. There in prison Lawrence cured the blind Lucillus. During the persecution of the emperor Valerian (AD 253-260) he was martyred. The feast of Saint Lawrence was celebrated by the Church on 10 August.

We have come to know from the press list of books printed by L.S. Dupuis that he had also continued to publish several other lives of saints. The list includes *Archsishta Agnesammal Sarithiram* (St. Agnes), *Archsishta Athanusiyaar Sarithiram* (St. Athanasius), *Archshista Deva Arulappar Sarithiram* (John of God), *Archsishta Makkaariyaar Sarithiram* (St. Maccarii), *Archsishta Mudiyappar Sarithiram* (St. Stephen), *Archsishta Polycarpiyaar Sarithiram* (St. Polycarp), *Archsishta Saveriyaar Sarithiram* (St. Francis Xavier) and *Archsishta Vanaththu Chinnappar Sarithiram* (St. Paul the Hermit). Louis Marie Mousset the MEP missionary in Pondicherry had mentioned in his letter of 24 March 1859 to Jean Tesson in Paris that many lives of saints had been printed by L.S. Dupuis from the printing press in Pondicherry.[100]

Maasillammal Urpavitha Archsishta Devamaathavin Thiru Irudhaya Sabhai Anusaaram Printed in 1847 and Reprinted in 1856

Catholic missionaries had encouraged formation of societies, sodalities and fellowship to its members so as to help leading good spiritual life by the Tamil Christian men and women. They also wrote down the rules and regulations besides how such units should function. L.S. Dupuis had printed a book on the rules of the Society of the Immaculate and Sacred Heart of the Holy Mother of God in 1847 at the Catholic press in Pondicherry. Its Tamil title is *Maasillammal Urpavitha Archsishta Devamaathavin Thiru Irudhaya Sabhai Anusaaram*. It is mentioned that a Jesuit had composed this work.[101] We come to know that the name of the Louis Saint-Cyr who was at Nagapattinam.

As the copies of the book printed had exhausted, the same book was reprinted in 1856. The Tamil title of the book runs thus: *Ich sabhai sthaabikkapatta vagaiyum ithinudaya kattalaigalum ithin mulama nadanatha arputhangalum ithir seyathaguntha sepangkalum ippusthahathir kaanapadum Igthu sesu sabhai guru swamiyargalil oruvarar seyappatu puthuvail yezhuntharuli irruukum mahaa ganam porunthiya aandavaragiya clemesu bonnand drusipar yennum naamatheyang konduirukira mettraniyarravargal anumathiyil romapurin ninru vandha uthaarathin padiye 1856 varusham puthuvai senmavirakkini maatha koyilai serntha achchu koodathil irandaavathu pathipikka pattathu*. We find the logo IHS (*Iesus Humanis Salvador*).

L.S. Dupuis in the preface of this book (mentioned in French *Manuel des associes de l'archiconfrerie de notre dames des victoires*) had explained how devotion to Blessed Virgin Mary is important. There are four chapters. The first deals with the establishment and founding of the society of the Sacred Heart of Mary. The second chapter deals with the orders and commandments of the society. The third deals with the miracles that had happened through the society. The fourth chapter contains prayers to be said by the members of the society. The book also contains morning prayers, Litany of the holy name of Jesus, St. Bernard's prayer, litany of Our Lady of dolours, meditation and holy mass, examination of conscience, prayers to Our Lady, prayers to the Sacred Heart of Mary, litany of the Sacred Heart of Mary and everyday prayers from Sunday to Saturday on Blessed Virgin Mary. The total printed pages are 342.[102]

Kanniyar Anusaaram Printed in 1865

Etienne Louis Charbonnaux (1806-1873) entered the MEP seminary and was ordained a priest on 5 June 1831. He left France for India on 16 August 1831 and reached Karaikal and was there till 1837. He was consecrated bishop on 29 June 1845 and became the Vicar Apostolic of Mysore in 1850. He went to Europe in 1853 and obtained some religious nuns from the Good Pastor of Angers for the Mysore mission. Etienne Louis Charbonnaux wrote the rules and prayers for nuns in the province of Mysore and the book titled *Kanniyar Anusaaram* was printed in Pondicherry by L.S. Dupuis in 1865. It has 80 pages.[103]

Printing Nanmarana Aayatham in 1860

L.S. Dupuis mentions that *Nanmarana Aayatham* the book was prepared by a Jesuit and it was printed in 1860 at Pondicherry on receipt of an order issued from Rome along with the permission of Bishop Clement Bonnand.[104] The book states that the Society for Good Death was established by Fr. Caraffa the Superior-General of the Jesuits in the church of Il Gesu in Rome in 1638. The *paayiram* (preface) of the book states that man who is born on this earth has to die and this is the judgment of God. It is a truth that all people irrespective of any status have to die. If he is well prepared for facing the death it is sure that he will go to heaven. Hence it is the duty of everyone to get prepared for good death. In some places in this Tamil country the Society of Good Death has been established. But many are not familiar with the rules and regulations and its functioning. Hence the book is printed and it deals with the formation of the society and we have given the prayers to be recited by the members of the society. To be found useful we have taken many prayers from different books and translated them into Tamil and they are given here. The prayer to the Sacred Heart of Jesus and Sacred Heart of Mary had been given at the beginning of the text of the book.

We find printed the morning prayer (p. 10), litany of the name of Jesus (p. 21), night prayer (p. 30), the litany of Our Lady (p. 37), *puasi kaanum vagai* or the way of participation in the Holy Mass (p. 43), and the Dolours of Mary (p. 46). Then the book explains *Nanmarana Aayatham* in the first chapter (pp.1-56) and goes on till the end. We find details of how to start the society in the third chapter (p. 58) and the fifth chapter notes how to assemble the members of the society and pray (p.76). The book has a total of 234 pages.[105]

Printing Beschi's Vethiyar Ozhukkam (1858) and Pierre Mauduit's Gnaana Kannaadi (1858)

L.S. Dupuis printed the catechist's guide *Vethiyar Ozhukkam* in Tamil composed by Beschi. The title page of the printed book states that *Veeramaamunivar rajarishi Dhairiyanaatha swami* composed this book and an order was issued from Rome and necessary permission was granted by the Bishop in Pondicherry for printing in 1858. L.S. Dupuis in his *mugavurai* (preface) as the publisher of *Vethiyar Ozhukkam* states that even the Protestants have published this manual for catechists (in 1844 and 1849 from Madras) adapted to the use of Protestant missions and their false teachings, many mistakes have crept into their writings and so it had become very bad and poisonous to the souls. Hence all those poisonous elements have been deleted and removed while printing this present book. Dupuis states that he had incorporated many items which had been earlier found missing after having a glance thorough the various available manuscript copies of Beschi both in palm-leaves and paper. The preface of Dupuis ends at page 8 with an asterisk mark. Dupuis had mentioned here that as the two treatises of *Vethiyar Ozhuakkam* and *Gnaana Kannaadi* had been highly useful to catechists he had put them together and printed separately but bound as a single book. Dupuis noted that these two books are also very useful to the general public for they contain vital instructions to all Christian families. The preparation of the catechists for receiving the sacraments mentioned had been very useful to families. Dupuis said that the catechists must read often and meditate and get spiritual consolation. The contents of the book had been given towards the end (pp. 198-9) and the book has a total of 199 pages.[106]

L.S. Dupuis printed the book titled *Gnaana Kannaadi* containing devotional readings for Catholics in 1858. It has 126 pages. The name of the original author was unknown to Dupuis, but we have come know that it was the work of Fr. Pierre Mauduit, the Jesuit. The title page mentions that the book was printed on receipt of an order issued from Rome, and permission granted by Clement Bonnand the Bishop in Pondicherry. It is stated that the book is printed for the second time in 1858. The year of the first printing of the book is unknown. I have not been successful in locating the first printed book. Dupuis in his preface had mentioned that to derive spiritual benefits and utility to the catechists, meditation that has been titled *Gaanna Kannaadi* is published. The author of *Gnaana Kannaadi* had expressed the good feelings and good teachings in the book. Dupuis wrote that he had found mistakes in the available copies of the manuscript of *Gnaana Kannaadi* and so he had rectified them and printed this book.

The book explains the various types of catechists and their performances. Eight meditations are composed so as to help the catechists while rendering valuable service to the people and the church. Therefore the author mentioned the readers to use the book without any distraction. He had given the points and ideas related to meditation. He told the catechists to store them in their mind and practice often. As the dust and other defective things in the face could be seen after having a glance through the help of a mirror, so also the mistakes found in the catechists could be observed and the eight meditations presented here for practical use. Hence the author of the said that book is so titled as *Gnnana Kannaadi*.[107]

Printing Vetha Vizhlakkam of Beschi in 1842 and Reprinted in 1855 and 1868

Polemical writing was a new development in Tamil literature defending Catholicism and Protestantism. It must be mentioned that the three works of Beschi are significant which attracted the attention of the MEP missionaries since it dealt against the missionary activities of the Lutherans. Clement Bonnand Drusipare the Bishop of Pondicherry in his letter to Jean Tesson dated 22 October 1841 made mention of *Vetha Vizhlakkam* to be printed which would be around 100 pages.[108] The Catholic missionaries regarded the Protestants as a menace and ecumenical sentiments were then totally absent from the Christian scene. L.S. Dupuis wished to print *Vetha Vizhalakkam* i.e., a genuine Catholic doctrine in refutation of Lutheranism and he successfully executed the work in 1842. The book had 324 pages. L.S. Dupuis the manager of the press in Pondicherry mentioned in his letter dated 18 April 1842 to Jean Tesson in Paris that *Vetha Vizhlakkam* was printed.[109] The same book was reprinted by Dupuis again in 1855. This was the second edition.[110] The title page mentions that this book *Vetha Vizhlakkam* was composed by *Veermamunivar alias Rajarishi Dhairiyanatha Swami*. It states that the book was printed on receipt of an order issued from Rome with the permission of Bonnand the Bishop of Pondicherry. The printed text of the book ends at p. 300 and the contents had followed. Further we find that *Vetha Vizhlakkam* was once again reprinted in 1868 and this is the third edition.[111]

The *mugavurai* (preface) by L.S. Dupuis states that darkness had only been spread by the Protestant missionaries and it had been dispelled by the light of true religion. Many a time *Vetha Vizhlakkam* work was copied in palm-leaf and in paper and as a result so many mistakes had crept in by the scribes. Whatever was available in palm-leaf and paper had been carefully examined and corrected and a research was also conducted. Finally a fair copy (*suththa prathi*) was made and based on it Dupuis had printed the book. He said that he was sure that it should be spiritually useful. The *mugavurai* in the book ends at page five with an asterisk mark to show that the publisher's introduction would follow.

Then we find the *paayiram* which starts with page number one without asterisk mark and it states that bangle and diamond when kept together could be easily identified so also the Protestantism and the Roman Catholicism. St. Thomas, St. Francis Xavier had come to this land and they preached the true religion. Priests like Thathuva Pothagar (Roberto Nobili) had come around 122 years ago (in AD 1620) and explained the doubts raised by people on the *vetham*. The chapters as composed by Beschi printed in the book had been divided into 140 sections for the convenience of the readers. Dupuis said that he had only presented the details and given contents of this book.

The printed book ends as found in common style sheet of the palm-leaf manuscript and the paper manuscript, according to the Tamil tradition, with the mention that this work was completed by *Rajarishi Guru* Beschi who was born in 1728 (in Tamil numerals) *Kila* year in Tamil, *Vaikasi* month dated 25th and had composed it at Yelakurichi Tirukaavalur and it had been completed in the year 1742 (in Tamil numeral). The book printed contains a total of 379 pages.

Printing Lutherinithiyalbu of Beschi in 1842 and Reprinted in 1847 and 1868

L.S. Dupuis thought that Beschi's book on apologetic in Tamil titled Lutherinithiyalabu was worth printing so that Catholic Christians would read and understand the heretical writings of the Protestant missionaries. Therefore he published it in 1842 and it has 38 pages. It was reprinted in 1847. The title page mentions that *Veeramamunivar the raja rishi* known as *Dhairiyanatha Swami* had composed this work of Lutherinithiyalabu. It is mentioned that the book was printed on receipt of an order issued from Rome and the permission was granted for publishing by Clement Bonnand the Bishop of Pondicherry.[112]

In the printed book we find details on the *Pathithar Puththaga Thaguthi* (The qualification of the pagans on Books). It stated that a fellow who had became local and he had come to the East from Europe had written and gave high opinion of the heaven. He has written a book in Tamil and if you happen to start reading a line in that book the eyes will burn, the tongue will become dry and bitter and the *senthamizh* (pure Tamil) had been found spoiled. The ears would blast when you hear the word when read from the book and people would think that it is written in another language. It is commonly known to all that the sweet honey should not be mixed with bitter neem plant paste but this is what had been done by the author. Therefore Beschi said that he had planned to write this book titled Lutherinithiyalabu in refutation of the earlier work of the Protestants of Tranquebar. The character of the Lutherans had been well exposed in this book. Lutherinithiyalabu was reprinted in 1868 for the third time. Adrien Launay is wrong in mentioning that Dupuis as the author of Lutherinithiyalabu and also the year of printing as 1850.[113]

Printing Pethaga Maruththal of Beschi in 1842 and Reprinted in 1855 and 1868

Dupuis printed *Pethaga Maruththal* another work of Beschi refuting the Protestant religion in 1842. It is the denial of alleged aberrations in the Catholic Church. The book has 139 pages. The same book was reprinted in 1855. The title page mentions Veeramamunivar alias *rajarishi Dhairiyanatha Swami* had composed it. It also recorded that on receipt of an order issued from Rome Clement Bonnand the Bishop of Pondicherry permitted for printing at Pondicherry. The book has a total of 324 pages. *Pedhaga maruththal* was reprinted for the third time in 1868 and the book had 121 pages.[114]

Dushana Maruthalaagiya Tharkka Kummi of Anthoni Nathar Printed in 1865

Anthoni Nathar a native priest of the Pondicherry mission composed a controversial song for native women in which Roman Catholic doctrines are stated and defended. It was printed in Pondicherry in 1865 under the title '*Pathimaththesu Dushana Maruthalaagiya Tharkka kummi*'. The book has 60 pages.[115]

Printing the Books of Roberto Nobili on Religion: Sathiya Vetha Paritchai Printed in 1842, Reprinted in 1846 and Deyva Paritchai Printed in 1843, Reprinted in 1863

L.S. Dupuis in his letter dated 18 April 1842 to Jean Tesson in Paris mentioned that the book titled *Sathiya Vetha Paritchai* (True Religion Examined) dealt with explanation of true religion had been successfully printed and the print order was 2000 copies. He stated that he had also reprinted the two first chapters of this earlier book *Sathiya Vetha Lakshanam* (of Roberto Nobili) and an additional chapter prepared by him. Dupuis had given therefore a new title *Sathiya Vetha Paritchai*. The three chapters are put together in a volume that represents a historical picture of Catholic religion from the origin of the world. He said that this could be very well used by the gentiles, Christians and everyone.[116]

Sathiya Vetha Paritchai was reprinted in 1846 because copies of the printed books were unavailable.[117] The title page of the book mentions that *Sathiya Vetha Paritchai* was reprinted in 1846 as per an order issued from Rome and with the permission of Bonnand the Bishop of Pondicherry. There is a preface (ends at p.12) and then there is *paayiram*. The author of the book states that this life in the universe is a temporary one and not permanent. Man is born, and he lives and dies. People are after pleasure to enjoy and so they go astray. Therefore they are subjected and condemned to go to hell after death. They should try to know what is the true faith and religion. Hence the first *kaandam* of the book explains who is the true God and continues to explain the Holy Trinity and the mystery. The second *kaandam* mentions the creation of the world and the man. The third *kaandam* explains how people in the past worshipped false Gods and led the evil way. God became man and he redeemed the mankind. The Catholic Church was thereafter established. The fourth *kaandam* deals with the end of the world and the days of judgment. Thus the book focuses upon one God, the identity of God, trinity and its mystery, creation of the first man, how man became bad, how god became man to save mankind, the birth of Jesus, mystery, miracle and the wonder, how he redeemed, his resurrection, ascension, decent of the Holy Spirit, glory of Blessed Virgin Mary, end of the world, judgment, heaven and hell. There is a *mudivurai* (conclusion at p. 425). The contents of the book had been given at.p.426. The errata had been put up at p. 427. The total printed pages are 427.

L.S. Dupuis in his letter wrote on 9 February 1847 to Jean Tesson in Paris said that he took the opportunity of departure of the ship 'St. Josephine' to send him five copies of *Sathiya Vetha Paritchai*. In the beginning, Christianity had faced many trials due to dogmas and mistakes of the gentiles who were against Christ. Later on, Christianity faced the obstacle from Hinduism, with idol worship and abomination. Therefore he said that this book *Sathiya Vetha Paritchai* composed earlier by a Jesuit had been modified by him in Pondicherry. He had added all those new passages which did not appear in the earlier work.[118] Dupuis in his letter of 9 February 1847 to Jean Tesson in Paris had requested him to forward a copy of *Sathiya Vetha Paritchai* to the Sacred Congregation for the Propagation of Faith in Rome.

L.S. Dupuis vide his letter dated 18 April 1842 to Jean Tesson in Paris mentioned that *Deyva Paritchai* (Test of God) the book was under printing. He wrote that this book dealt with vanity of Hinduism and truth of Christianity.[119] It dealt with a criticism of the cults and histories of Hindu divinities by Roman Catholic missionaries. We find the book successfully printed in 1843 at the Catholic press in Pondicherry. The title page mentions that on receipt of an order issued from Rome Bonnand the Bishop of Pondicherry granted permission for printing the book.[120] It is interesting to note that the book begins with a Sanskrit verse: The one God who is present in all the elements, who I omniscient, who is the spirit in all the elements, who is the cause of all activity in souls, the first cause and the witness of all activity is he who is one and without any quality. It must be stated that this is also exactly found in the work of *Pethaga Paritchai* of Roberto Nobili. Dupuis had printed it under the title *Deyva Partichai* and the book in detail explained one God, the falsehood of atheism and polytheism, worship of idols, myths and no reasoning in Hinduism, the history of trinity, Brahma, Vishnu and Siva, the ten *avatars* (incarnations) of Vishnu, like *matsya, kurma, varaha, narasimha, vaamana, parasurama, srirama, balarama, krishna* and *kalki*. The book also dealt with god devendran, vigneswaran, the worship at kamatchi temple and the manners, the worship at Mannarkovil and the manners, the worship at Uththara Kadappai in Veerabhadran temple and the manners, besides the worship at Tirupati temple and the manners. It may be mentioned that Roberto Nobili in his another work titled *Nithiya Jeevana Sallapam* had mentioned the worship at Chokkanatha temple at Madurai and Ramanatha temple and worship at Rameswaram. We find also the mention of *sakthi puja, naamdharis*, false priest, *sathya vetha lakshnam* and true priests. The contents of the printed book had been given (at p. 98) and the errata (found at p. 99). The book has a total of 99 pages. The same book *Deyva Paritchai* was again reprinted in 1863 when printed copies were unavailable.

Reprinting in Pondicherry Sathiya Vetha Bhodhaga Surukkam Earlier Printed in Colombo, 1846

L.S. Dupuis had printed the book *Sathiya Vetha Bhodhaga Surukkam* in 1846. The title page of the book runs thus: *Sathiya vetha bhodhaga surukkam: Iguthu christhu vedha visuvasikalukku piraiyosanamaaga vetha virpannargalal inglishu bhashayir pirayogikka patta vannath tamzhilil mozhipeyarthu ilangapuriil maha maatchimai poruthiya don Caetano anthoni mettrani aandavargal anumathiyil kolumbil vyagula maria naayaggiyin dharma sampradhya achchu kudathil achchil pathikka patta pragaarame, romapurin ninru vantha utharaththin padiye 1846 varusham puthuvaiyri sanmavirakkini maatha koilai serntha achchu kudathir pathikka pattathu.*

It is gleaned that *Sathiya Vetha Bhodaga Surukkam* was translated from English into Tamil for the use of the Christians and it was printed by the permission of Dom Caetano Joseph the Bishop of Sri Lanka and it was printed at *vyagula mariya nayagi* press in Colombo. An order was issued from Rome and so it was reprinted in Pondicherry in 1846.[121]

Printing Poorviga Marai Vizhlakkam in 1856

L.S. Dupuis printed a book titled *Poorviga Marai Vizhlakkam* that dealt with exposition of Hindu religion. It contained Hindu explanations of ancient *vethas*. The title page of the book mentions that it was composed by *Sathiya vetha gurukkal* (Catholic priests-names unknown) and now printed through the permission of the superiors.[122] The preface of the book states that many people aimed to seek true pleasure and gifts and this desire is common to all. But many do not know in the world the ways to obtain and so they face many difficulties. Some are after seeking wealth while others are driven towards seeking material pleasure. Many are subjected to these diseases yet do not get cure in spite of taking medicine. Whatever may be the highest amount of wealth and pleasure they seek still they are not satisfied. They would not know how to get joy and eternal happiness. Only those who know God and followed his ways had understood it. There is no doubt that this is greater than the worldly pleasures. One should follow the teachings and commandments of God and should serve him sincerely and help others. Hence we have desired to explain the details in this book. There are 37 chapters as follows:

1. The oldness of the true religion
2. The truth that there is God.
3. The truth that there is only one God
4. The divine characteristics of the true God
5. The divine characteristics are applicable to the God of the Christians
6. The divine characteristics are not applicable to the Hindu Gods.
7. The truth that God is trinity
8. The three *murthis*
9. The creation of the world
10. The truth on the existence of the angels and the devil.
11. The truth that there is original sin
12. The ghost *ratshadar*
13. The details of the great deluge
14. God became man
15. Vishnu incarnation (*avatars*)
16. The essence (*saaranam*) of the true religion
17. The singularity of true religion
18. End of the world
19. Hell
20. Heaven
21. *Sathya vethaagammangal* (Holy Scripture)
22. Scripture of the Hindu religion
23. The *puranas* and other myths
24. The origin of the many false gods.
25. The churches divine worship and holy images

26. The offering of the Mass
27. Sin, *paava parigaaram, gnaana ditchai*
28. Priests
29. Penance
30. *Munis*, *Sanyasi*, etc.,
31. Nuns
32. Prayer
33. Dharma
34. Praying for the dead
35. Fate and freedom of conscience
36. Compilation in summary form of the book
37. Conclusion.

There is also a dialogue between Lakshmi and Paarvathi.

It is stated in the book that people try to say that Christianity is new and it is of foreign origin and they try to simply set aside. Hence this idea is refuted in the book. Christian religion is explained as an ancient one and has the true teachings. Hence the book is so titled as *Poorviga Marai Vizhlakkam*. The author had differentiated the Roman Catholicism from other religions. Hence try to read and learn more. The contents of the book had been given at the end. The printed book has a total of 276 pages.

Printing Sathiya Vetha Sarithira Surukkam of C. Gnaanapragaasa Nathar in 1865

L.S. Dupuis had printed the book titled *Sathiya Vetha Sarithira Surukkam*. The title page of the printed book mentions that C. Gnaanapragasa Nathar @ Charles Michele Bertoldin had translated the book and Bishop Isidore Godelle had granted permission for printing. There are two sections in the book.[123] The first is called *Vari Vetham* deals with the Old Testament beginning with the creation of the world, Adam and Eve and the text goes on and ends at page 170. The second section is titled *Arul Vetham* and it deals with the New Testament, commencing from the birth of Jesus to his ascension to heaven and the text ends at p. 338. The contents had been given at the end (pp.339-44). The book has a total of 344 pages.

Meymarai Uththiyaanam Printed in 1873

L.S. Dupuis printed a book titled *Meymarai Uththiyanam* (Guide to True Religion) in 1873. It contains three *kaandams* and in the first *kaandam* what is *vetham* is explained. Dupuis the author explains God is one and the proof of his existence. God only teaches the *vetham* and to know the *vetham* and the steps to know are given in the book. In the second kaandan questions the *chatur vethams* and seeks to explain whether they are true vedhams and also questions whether Hindu religion is a true religion. In the third kaandam the author explains the Christian Bible and he has given ideas on 45 topics. He also gives the list in the end.

L.S. Dupuis, the author mentions that before writing this book he had heard about several religions, known the tenets of the religions. The preface contains all the details that he had known from various religions. He says that as a child he had mainly learnt and knew only the true Christian religion. He had enquired and learnt the teachings of the various religions in the world. Having stayed and lived 41 years in India he continuously came to eagerly know the various teachings and rituals and practices of the religions. He said that there is no doubt that he had come to know about the various Gods and goddesses in Hindu religion. He had related all these details more than the Hindus would know. The printed book contains a total of 382 pages.[124]

Dupuis in his letter of 22 January 1874 to Jean Tesson in Paris mentioned that for more than six months, he had been very ill and suffered. This has left him weak and very feeble. He was also getting a kind of dizziness, feeling always like fainting and nausea. His health was improving but he was still ailing. However, the work in the printing press was not affected and it was going on. In spite of his illness, he had completed writing the big volume of Meymarai Uththiyaanam to prove the truth of Christianity and the obscurantism of Hinduism. This book also contained details against idolatry, superstition, black-magic, sooth-saying and signs which had been largely followed by the Hindus.[125]

Printing the New Testament in Tamil in 1857

L.S. Dupuis had printed the first Catholic New Testament in Tamil which was translated by Fr. Louis Marie Mousset and Fr. Arul in 1857 at the printing press in Pondicherry.[126] Bible was seen as an essential ingredient that would cure the natives of all the alleged ills of Tamil society. It was introduced as a textbook of scripture in the seminary to receive directly the morals for those Tamils who aspired for priesthood.

The amount of labour put up in printing and the hours spent in the printing press is touchy as gleaned from the missionary letters. Dupuis was always helped by Fr. Mousset and he wrote in his letter dated 10 March 1846 to Jean Tesson in Paris that he and Fr. Dupuis worked in the printing press up to 9 pm with the help of oil lamps and candles.[127] Composing Tamil texts and correcting the proofs had been their daily food. Again in his letter dated 3 September 1860 Mousset wrote that he and Fr. Dupuis is very busy in compiling the second volume of the Tamil-French dictionary and they would like to see the book printed before they take eternal rest in the grave.[128]

Printing the Calendar of Church Festivals, 1844-1849

Dupuis had printed a perpetual calendar of Roman Catholic Church festivals in Tamil under the title *Nedunaat Panchangam* in 1844. [129] It has 64 pages. Dupuis had annually printed this for the use of the laity. We find a calendar of festivals again printed in 1849.[130]

Printing Vethapurattalai Maruththalaagiya Sathiya Thirusabaiyin Surkkamaana Vizhlakkam, 1840

Louis Savinien Dupuis (1806-74) the MEP missionary sailed from France and arrived at Pondicherry on 9 February 1832. He stayed for six months at Pondicherry and began to learn Tamil in the mean while. He was deputed for apostolic work in Bangalore on 21 August 1832 by Clement Bonnand Drusipare the Bishop of Pondicherry and so he travelled to Bangalore and began his missionary work.[131] L.S. Dupuis saw the Protestant missionaries were very active in Bangalore and they were doing havoc against Catholicism. Hence he had desired to write a treatise in Tamil. It is mentioned by him while looking after the Christians of Bangalore in 1837 that he felt the urgent need to compose books to fight against the Protestant doctrines and to support the Catholic faith. Dupuis stated that he saw many Christians entrusted to his care were terribly harassed by the heretics. He placed in their hands the books written by Constanzo Giuseppe Beschi (1680-1747) the Jesuit whose powerful and excellent works had been highly appreciated. Moreover as the book was a large volume and it was not printed, he had to make arrangements to copy it by the scribes. Therefore, Dupuis also decided to write a short and simple booklet explaining the controversies brought in by heretics. He stated that he had started writing it but his priority had been to look after the Christians, around six to seven thousand souls belonging to different nations and speaking different tongues. Hence his writing had been slowed down and at the same time he was also learning languages like English and Telugu. Dupuis said that he took many points from several controversial books to write his first book in Tamil.[132]

L. S. Dupuis had stated that after finishing the writing of the book he planned to send it to the MEP superior in Pondicherry to study it. In 1837, he had got the required permission to print it, but he was afraid because it was not sufficiently revised. Therefore he continuously worked on the manuscript for printing. It took two more years when he could free himself from his apostolic ministry. He said that he had added new and rich material and finally finished it, and when he was about to give the finishing touch in 1839 a terrible illness pushed him to the threshold of death. He thought that he almost reached eternity, and at that time he showed it to Fr. Jean Jacques Aulagne (1796-1866), who was helping him when he was in real pain. Dupuis showed the finished version of his book, requesting Aulagne to get it printed. But Fr. Aulagne in a solemn tone struck him with a reply that this would not be the only book, that Dupuis would write but many more and this great consolation had comforted him. However, the Catholic missionaries had no idea of setting up a printing press in Tamil country and Dupuis wanted to get it printed at the earliest. But the Lord God had his own designs and he sustained Dupuis away from his illness. Therefore Dupuis received enough strength to start his work again. He then took advantage of the time to revise and complete his work. He submitted his proposed book to the MEP Superior in Pondicherry in which he had added many more.[133]

Dupuis was highly successful in finishing the writing of the book in 1839. It was titled *Vethapurattalai maruththalaagiya sathiya thirusabaiyin surkkamaana vizhlakkam* (Refutation of Heresy @ An Explanation in Brief of the True Church). It was composed in reply to refute heresy circulated among the people. The Protestants were doing work to the ruin of Catholicism when Dupuis was very ill. As he could not pay visit to the substations of his parish he asked a brother to help him. At that time he sent the writings of Beschi through the brother so that it could read out to the people including the new book of Dupuis the one which he had composed. He thought this book *Vetha purattalai maruththal* would be of great use. It is mentioned by Dupuis that he read the book time and again, corrected personally and sent it finally to His Grace Bonnand the Apostolic-Vicar, to be read, approved and to get it printed if found worthy. Dupuis also stated that he had read earlier some books on the topic published in English supplied by the Bishop of Bombay which helped him a lot to understand the main differences between each sect of the Protestants like the London Missionary Society (LMS) and the Wesleyan Church and why they had been fighting against each other over religion. Dupuis was in search of some more books in English and in French that would explain the differences and the nature of these Protestant sects. He felt that it would be additionally useful to be able to demonstrate their differences and prove that the Protestants are not united by faith, neither with Catholics nor with the religion and the Protestant religion too. He opined that they had great differences and their pastors did not want to listen to Catholic explanations.[134]

Dupuis in his letter dated 18 November 1839 from Chinna Ballapuram stated that he had just finished writing a concise reply of protest defending

Fr. Jacques Henry Gailhot (1810-1890) to prove the knowledge that he had newly acquired in a place, where Protestants had managed to corrupt the Catholics. He mentioned that he hoped the abridged version of his book would be of some use to win back the Christians and the public. As the main book had already been already received the needed authorization for printing, Dupuis believed that in due course of time, the abridged version along with the main book would also be printed. He wrote that in the then prevalent situation, there was a pressing need to find such books which would be helpful to the Catholics. Dupuis admitted that he had made a very small effort in writing the book. But he wrote that God had touched the soul and made him talk. He said that God made a donkey, like him, to pull down the structure of the numerous enemies. He affirmed that he was a humble instrument in God's hands to build great things when it pleased him for his glory.[135]

Clement Bonnand the Bishop of Pondicherry in his letter to Jean Tesson in Paris dated 8 April 1840 had mentioned that the first Tamil book of Dupuis titled *Vethapurattalai maruththalaagiya sathiya thirusabaiyin surkkamaana vizhlakkam* was to be printed by the French government press in Pondicherry without any payment of money.[136] It happened so because the Catholic missionaries did not have a printing press. The book got printed in Pondicherry in 1840 was in octave by Toutin at the Government press. It had 77 pages in total. It is mentioned that the author of this small book *Vethapurattalai maruththalaagiya sathiya thirusabaiyin surkkamaana vizhlakkam* printed was living far away from Pondicherry when the book was under print. Hence some mistakes have crept in. Therefore the publisher had to issue an errata page in the printed book by pointing out the printing errors and mistakes so as to make and the necessary corrections.

The book of Dupuis contained Roman Catholic catechism in question-answer format. It may be pointed out that it was only the penny catechism and not the larger catechism which was also used by the people. Some examples could be cited here for the sake of information and knowledge. Question: How many churches did Jesus Christ establish? The Answer: One Church. There are also other questions, such as Who is the Holy father?, Who are twelve Apostles of Jesus Christ?, How did Jesus Make Peter as the head of the church?[137] The answers were furnished based on the New Testament from the Gospel of St. Matthew chapter XVI: verses 13-20; Gospel of St. Mark chapter VIII: verses 27-30 and Gospel of St. Luke chapter IX: verses 18-21.

L.S. Dupuis extensively quoted the biblical references from the New Testament.[138] We find quotations from the Gospel of St. Matthew chapter VII: 28; Gospel of Mark chapter XVI, Gospel of St. John chapter X besides from the Acts of the Apostles that include Galatians I, the Romans chapter VI, Timothy I, Peter chapter II and Ephesians chapters IV and V. Again we find L.S. Dupuis quoting from the Old Testament from the book of Genesis, Exodus, Leviticus, Numbers and Deuteronomy.[139]

There is an epilogue wherein L.S. Dupuis made refutation on the teachings of the Protestants. He stated that there is no ground to believe the teachings of the Protestants are true. He added that there is a strong foundation for the establishment of the Roman Catholic Church as being founded by Lord Jesus Christ. Hence he recorded that those who followed the teachings with piety and devotion and lead good life would definitely reach the heaven. The book ends with the expression Amen Sesu. It may be mentioned that the book is printed in large size letter founts in Tamil.

Printing Vethapurattalai Neekum Sanjiviyaagiya Meyyaana Thirusabaiyin Vizhlakkam in 1841

The first book *Vethapurattalai maruththalaagiya sathiya thirusabaiyin surkkamaana vizhlakkam* (The Medicine for the Refutation of Heresy @ An Explanation of the True Church) got expanded by Dupuis and it got printed in 1841. It was the second book authored by Dupuis. It is titled *Vethapurattalai neekum sanjiviaagiya meyyaana thirusabaiyin vizhlakkam* but got printed at the Catholic printing press for the first time after its establishment in 1841 in Pondicherry. One can see the different types of Tamil fonts used in printing both in the first and the second book in 1840 and 1841. This second book of Dupuis printed at the Catholic press was in octave and it had 388 pages.

It is stated this second book composed by L.S. Dupuis was printed at the *Periyakovilai serntha Achchukoodam* (printing press belonging to the big church) which was newly established in 1841. The title page of the book in Tamil records thus: *Vethapurttalai neekum sanjiviyaagiya meyyaana thirusabaiyin vizhlakkam* (The medicine for the Refutation of Heresy @ An Explanation of the True Church): *Allathu Roman katholikku thirusbaiyenbathu parama kartharaagiya Yesu Kristhunaathar sthabiththa sathiyaththin thoon aagavum asthivaaramaay irukkirathenthrum protestendu mathangal manithargallal undaakkapatta abaththa markkangalaay irukkintrana yenru kaanpikkira dishthaanthangal.* The book was printed with the permission of Clement Bonnand Drusipare the Bishop of Pondicherry.

It is mentioned in a letter of Bishop dated 15 October 1840 that Dupuis in the long run had collected more material and the book became thicker than what he had earlier thought of.[140] The main argument of Dupuis was to say that the Catholic church was established by Lord Jesus Christ with strong foundation and the Protestant religion was created by men and it contained evils. L.S. Dupuis in his letter of 18 August 1841 from Pondicherry to the authorities in Paris had mentioned that the Catholic printing press newly set up in Pondicherry was doing well. He stated that his book on refuting the heresy was earlier printed in the Government press. He has new plans to publish a book for the junior catechists and the senior catechists, some prayer books, a book on the Way of the Cross, and notices for the propagation of the faith, and a circular of His Grace Drusipare. If all these completed it would be of great help in this pagan country. He sadly noted that many a time he had to be interrupted in his work and only a few pages he could write.[141]

The second book Dupuis printed opens up with the caption and expression: Praise the name of the Holy Trinity. The foreword states what the true religion is. It records that in the beginning Apostle St Thomas came and then St Xavier came and thus spread the true religion. Dupuis stated that the readers should carefully read this book and benefit so that they may receive salvation and reach heaven. We find interesting details made known through this book. Use of the words Iesu and Jesu had been explained. Dupuis requested not to read the Gospel books translated and printed by the Protestant missionaries and he said that he would provide the details later in this book. He stated that he uses the plural form to respect God. Dupuis neatly mentioned that the Pope had granted permission vide an order dated 11 March 1841 for starting Catholic printing press in Pondicherry.[142] He stated that as an author the book he wrote in high and low Tamil mixed up language. The singular and plural forms had been explained well so that all people could easily understand.

The printed book contains three parts while part one of the book has 12 chapters, part two 13 chapters and part three 12 chapters. The views of the Protestants and the objection against it by the Catholic Church regarding devotion to the various saints had been furnished.[143] The fitting reply of the Catholic Church and the views had been well elucidated.[144]

The first chapter explains the differences between the Catholic Church and the Protestant Church. In the second chapter L.S. Dupuis explains the devotion to martyrs and other saints and the theme had been justified based on the scriptural passages by quoting from the Letters of St. Paul to the Romans, XV:30, First Corinthians IV:9 and Gospel of St. Luke XV:10. Dupuis also furnishes the explanation offered by the Catholic Church in this connection.[145] Further he explains the sacraments and the sacred tradition of the church and the various councils held.[146]

Dupuis explains why the Latin language is used in the Catholic Church rituals. As the Church around the world has been one and single, the rituals followed had also been one and the same. As a result, one language formula is followed. He states that Latin is preferred in worship and ritual because it does not change like French, English and other languages of the world. Further he mentions that as the prophet Malachi has said Holy Mass should be celebrated from East to West the Latin language has been the best one. Since people speaking so many languages assemble for the Holy Mass it has been felt ideal to have one language without any partition and division among the people to have a common and single language which had been Latin.[147]

The contents of the book had been interesting to note and Dupuis had emphasized the one Holy Catholic and Apostolic church. He explained how the church was born, protected and developed. He explained the following in this manner:

How Jesus established the church (p. 15)

How Peter was appointed as the head of the church (p. 32)

The Holy Father is the head of the church (p. 42)

The seven sacraments of baptism, confirmation, Holy Eucharist, confession, extreme-unction, priesthood and marriage (pp. 51-69)

The priestly ordination (p. 57)

How the church had spread out in the world (p. 87)

The details of the saints (p. 96)

The signs of the true Church (p. 103)

How the Protestantism came into existence (p. 120)

Explaining the new religious sects (p. 136)

Martin Luther and his details (p. 146)

Refuting the beliefs of the Protestants (p. 176)

Regarding the Holy Scripture and the holy books (p. 356)

The difference between the Catholic Church and the Protestants (pp. 431-59)

The book has an epilogue and it ends at p. 459. The contents of the book had been given (pp. 460-4) along with the errata (pp. 465-6) for 47 words mentioned with lines and pages.

Reprinting Books of L.S. Dupuis in 1843 and 1865

As the copies of the small book on apologetic printed in 1840 were unavailable Dupuis had reprinted the *Vetha purattalai maruththalaagiya sathiya thirusabaiyin surkkamaana vizhlakkam* at the Catholic press in Pondicherry in 1843. After many years also *Vetha purattalai neekum sanji-*

viaagiya meyyaana thirusabaiyin vizhlakkam was reedited by Dupuis and it got again printed for the second time at the Catholic press in 1865. This new edition has 388 pages.

Catholic Devotional Literature in Tamil: Printing Nanraai Ninai: Maatha Anudhina Dhyaanam in 1844

Dupuis collected the prayers and litanies of saints prepared earlier by the missionaries in Tamil country and included also the way of participating in the holy sacrifice of the mass besides Christian beliefs and doctrine. He assembled all of them neatly in a book titled *Nanraai Ninai: Maatha Anudhina Dhyaanam* (Think Well on it: Daily Meditations for a month). He got it published it at the Catholic press in Pondicherry in 1844 with the permission of the Bishop Clement Bonnard Drusipare, by an order that was issued from Rome.[148] This book contains 404 pages in total. It begins with a cross and the word anaathi nama.

The prayers are printed at first and it begins with the prayer after opening the eyes after sleep and the morning prayer.[149] Then we find the night prayer and thanksgiving. There are details in this book on the participation in the holy mass which was held in Latin and so the Tamils could understand and participate well.[150] Dupuis felt the need to explain it in the book. The details are listed as follows:

Prayer before the commencement of the holy mass

Prayer while reading the epistle by the priest

Prayer while reading the gospel by the priest standing at the right side of the altar

Prayer while saying credo while the priest standing in the middle of the altar

Prayer while offering the Holy Eucharist

Prayer while saying prayer for the dead

Prayer before offering the Eucharist

Prayer while holding the Eucharist high

Prayer while holding the chalice

Prayer while saying the Pater Noster

Prayer while breaking the Holy Eucharist

Prayer after receiving the Holy Communion

Prayer before meditation

The book has *paayiram* (preface by the author). Dupuis, the author chooses to provide details on various subjects and topics for everyday meditation. I found that pages 26 and 27 had been found missing in the printed book which I had consulted at the Library of the Foreign Mission Society in Paris. However another copy I consulted is preserved at the Archives of the Archdiocese of Pondicherry-Cuddalore and it contains pages 26 and 27 but the book is not in good condition.

1st day – Fate of the people

2nd day – Towards redemption

3rd day – Hating the world

4th day – The evil effects of sin.[151] Dupuis also outlines the desire for acquisition of the land and property, money, pleasure and women.[152]

5th day – Details of death

6th day – The judgment of the individual

7th day – The phase of the last day of the judgment

8th day – The suffering in the hell

9th day – The hell

10th day – The joy of heaven

11th day – Faithful behavior

12th day – The presence of God everywhere

13th day – The importance of penance

14th day – The evil effect in delaying for the change of heart

15th day – The evil effect of showing partiality

16th day – Not believing in one self

17th day – Firm belief in divine hope

18th day – Urgency for obtaining divine grace and faithfulness

19th day – The evil effect for wasting the time

20th day – Details for obtaining the holy sacraments

21st day – The glory of the holy mass

22nd day – The explanation on charity

23rd day – The evil of the bad conduct

24th day – The urgency and importance of submitting to God's will during suffering

25th day – The duty of the love of God

26th day – Explaining the friendship of Jesus

27th day – Following Jesus and its importance

28th day – The duty of the love of neighbour

29th day – The duty of loving the enemies

30th day – Veneration to God's Mother, Our Lady

31st day – The piety towards guardian angel, other angels and all saints

Thereafter we find the printed book with the litany of the guardian angel (p. 316), litany of St. Joseph (p. 322) Prayer and hymn to St. Joseph translated from Latin (p. 330), litany of St. Antony (p. 333), Litany of St. Francis Xavier (p. 343), the novena prayer to St Xavier, the litany of St. Sebastian (p. 390). Towards the end the contents of the book had been printed.[153] We find also the errata of 36 words with lines and pages given.[154] There are many pictures of the saints, Sacred Heart of Jesus and Sacred Heart of Mary. It is important to note the novelty of printing with two types of Tamil fonts used while one being the small for the text and other the big font to differentiate the thought and action needed while doing the meditation.

Printing Ainthukaaya Varampetra Archsishta Franciskuvin Sarithira Surukkam in 1859

L.S. Dupuis wrote the life of St. Francis of Assisi. He completed the work and the title page of the printed book in 1859 runs: *Ainthukaaya varampetra archsishta franciskuvin sarithira surukkam* (A short biography of Saint Francis of the Five Wounds). Dupuis in this book gave the short biography of St Francis and he desired to make known the great virtues of the saint.[155]

Printing Archsishtavargalin Sarithiram in Four Volumes in 1866-7

L.S. Dupuis wanted the Catholics in Pondicherry to lead an exemplary Christian life. Therefore he realized the need to have a book useful on the lives of all saints for the whole year to be printed and circulated. He came across the work of James Thomas Rossi the Jesuit. After glancing through his work Dupuis planned to revise, and expand the contents and he successfully carried out the work in four volumes. Thereafter he printed it at the Catholic press in Pondicherry in 1866. The title page of the first volume is *Varushathin pradhi dina sugirtha pirasangangalaagiya archsishtavargalin sarithiram: Muthal Kaandam* (Everyday Sermons on the Lives of Saints for the Year, Volume One). It is stated in the printed title page that James Thomas Rossi composed the lives of saints and the work has been expanded, corrected and revised by Louis Savinien Dupuis and Printed at the Catholic press in Pondicherry in 1866.[156] The book had been printed and published with the permission of Bishop Godelle and an order was issued in this connection from Rome. There is a *mugavurai* (preface) by Dupuis and it states that there is no doubt that among all the books, the lives of saints has been the most useful and the desired book. The reason is that it shows the true way for the good model of conduct and living on this earth and to reach the next world. It explains the divine mercy of God showered upon those who serve him, the wonderful graces that he had been showered upon them, and the miracles that happen through them on this earth. When we read all this in the biographies of the saints the happiness and the joy gained by the soul could not be adequately expressed.

Dupuis printed the second volume on the lives of saints in 1866. The title page of the second volume is *Varushathin pradhi dina sugirtha pirasangangalaagiya archsishtavargalin sarithiram: Rendaam kaandam* (Everyday Sermons on the Lives of Saints for the Year, Volume Two). The preface also states that the first volume was well received by one and all. The activities of the saints and what benefits the world had derived from and the wonders and the miracles that happened were explained in detail. Reading the lives of saints would certainly help the soul. Prayers, meditation and penance have been done by people after reading the book. They could get divine inspiration and obtain other virtues to gain spiritually. Hence Dupuis had requested the people to read and benefit. The second volume contained the lives of saints and the sermons for the period from 1 April to 30 June of the year.[157]

The preface to the third volume of the lives of saints mentions that the earlier two volumes of the lives of saints had been gladly received by people. Hence there is no doubt that the third volume would also help the soul and do all good. Through the grace of God alone the good deeds had happened on this earth. Everything that is going to happen would also follow the same and through the intercession of the saints. Hence devotion to saints would be natural. He said reading their lives brings a lot of utility to the soul. Many would leave evil ways and turn to good life. Many persons did prayers and meditation and so acquired the virtues and left the worldly pleasures and thought of God and his presence always and they all became saints. Therefore they are in paradise. Hence the people should try to follow the footsteps of the saints and so the book is composed with hope that the readers would benefit immensely and receive the good and the blessings abundantly. The third volume is titled *Varushathin pradhi dina sugirtha pirasangangalaagiya archsishtavargalin sarithiram: Moonraam kaandam* (Everyday Sermons on the Lives of Saints for the Year, Volume three) and it was printed at the Catholic press in Pondicherry in 1867. It contains the lives of saints and sermons for the period from 1 July (Tamil calendar aadi month 15th day) with the feast of theopaalthappar (St. Thibault) to 30 September on the feast of Yeronimar (St. Jerome).[158]

The fourth volume of the book is titled *Varushathin pradhi dina sugirtha pirasangangalaagiya archsishtavargalin sarithiram: Naalaam kaandam*

(Everyday Sermons on the Lives of Saints for the Year, Volume four) and it was printed in 1867. The preface of the book states that by following the model and life of the saints has been the only way to heaven. We would become their relatives if we follow and reach the heaven. As all efforts on this made bring forth the fruits so also we should take efforts to reach the heaven. Dupuis wrote that saints have come from all countries. The Catholic Church encourages the devotion to saints. Such a practice is not followed in any other religion. Hence this is a true religion. Hence all should believe the church in its teachings and should try to follow the same so as to reach the heaven. The fourth volume contains the lives of saints and sermons for the period from 1 October (*Aypassi* month, 16th day of Tamil calendar) commencing with feast of Remijiyar (St. Remi) to 31 December ending with the feast of St. Sylvestre.[159]

Books for the Catholic Laity: Printing Ainthu Thirukaaya Varam Petra Archsishta Franciskuvin Thavathukkuriya Moonram Sabhai Ozhukkam in 1859 and Illara Uththiyanam in 1867

L.S. Dupuis wrote a book on the rules and regulations of the Third order of St Francis of Assisi of five wounds and he published it in 1859 with the permission of Bishop Clement Bonnand Drusipare and as per an order issued from Rome.[160] The printed book starts with the prayer: 'Our Lady of Immaculate Conception, Protect and Save Us', and we find a picture of Our Lady. The book contains 278 pages in total. There are 7 chapters and the book contains the rules of the society of St. Francis of Assisi and the profession of vows (p. 32). The prayers to be said daily had been noted (pp. 39-40). Participation in the holy mass had been mentioned (pp. 43-4). The prayers in Latin had been printed (vide chapter 7, section 5). The various feasts to be celebrated (pp. 119-23) and the benefits to be derived out of it (pp. 123-43) had been noted. The joyful events of Mother Mary are remembered as mysteries in saying the holy rosary beginning with the announcement of angel Gabriel, visit of Elizabeth, birth of Jesus, visit of the magi, finding the Jesus in the temple, participation in resurrection and ascension of Jesus Christ. (pp. 164-266). Thereafter Dupuis provides the litany of St. Francis (p. 205) Litany of Elizabeth (p. 209), prayers in Latin with Tamil transliteration (pp. 266-72). The contents of the book had been given at the end of the book.

L.S. Dupuis composed a work titled *Illara Uththiyanam* (Guide for Married People) for the betterment of the Catholic Christian families. The book was printed with the permission of the superiors at the Senmaviraakkini maatha church printing press in Pondicherry in 1867.[161] He had tried to explain the duty of the Christians that have to be fulfilled at every stage of life. While placed in good position, Christians should follow virtues and avoid the vices. Castes and superstitions, different marriage ceremonies, the marriage of widows have been dealt in detail. The printed book has 540 pages and contains 26 chapters. The duties of a good Christian had been recorded (pp. 1-180). Dupuis furnishes the separate duties and responsibilities for the husbands (pp. 263-79) and the wives in family life (pp. 267-92). Dupuis was very familiar with Tamil poetical works such as Naaladiyar and so he quotes song no. 133 and song no. 195. He mentioned that these have much relevance in the context of virtues to be adopted and to be followed in married life (p. 75). He had also referred to widows and their status. He laid emphasis on giving respect to widows and they should not be ill treated or disrespected in the society (p. 412). There is *anupandham* (annexure) and it gives 7 advices to the husband and wife in the family. We find interesting details on the superstition and information against such beliefs the Christians should follow and he explains what and how it should be done. Thus L.S. Dupuis had laid stress on the morals to be followed by the laity in his fascinating work. It may be mentioned that even after his death the book was reprinted (after twenty years) and it went through the second edition in print in 1894.

Books for the Use of the Religious Nuns of the Immaculate Heart of Mary: Printing Thuravara Uththiyanam Volume One in 1869 and Volume Two in 1872

L.S. Dupuis founded the first women religious Congregation in India/ Asia. The nuns of the Immaculate Heart of Mary Convent in Pondicherry were trained spiritually by him. He composed a work in Tamil titled *Thuravara uththiyaanam* (Guide to Religious People) in two volumes. The first volume was printed in 1869. It was printed at the Senmaviraakkini maatha church printing press with the permission of Bishop Xavier Laouënan Flaviopolis as per an order issued from Rome. The book has a total of 468 pages.[162] In the *mugavurai* (preface) of the book Dupuis stated that religious life is a higher standard of life as said by *vetha sastris* which had been correct. However by only following the nobler and higher virtues alone one could attain a true religious life and nothing else. Dupuis says that he had printed the first volume so that the virtues to be attained and followed by the religious could be made known and the special efforts to gain the grace of God should be done towards that direction. He also mentioned that it is necessary to remain faithful and stand firm in the religious life and to receive the necessary help and assistance from the Holy Spirit. (pp. 82-3). The rituals to be followed while becoming a nun, taking a new name (pp. 76-9, 83), the three vows of profession, such as poverty, chastity and obedience had been well explained in the book (pp.

126-41). The book thus contains 13 chapters and is printed with 468 pages. The second volume of *Thuravara Uththiyaanam* appeared in print in 1872. The book contains 552 pages in total with 25 chapters. A page of contents is given at the end.[163] The author had said that his belief and intention in writing the book was to help women so that many may find their way to vocation to religious life.

L.S. Dupuis had made excellent contribution to prose writings in Tamil on apologetics by writing two books titled Refutation of Heresy @ An Explanation of the True Church in Brief and The medicine for the Refutation of Heresy @ An Explanation of the True Church. These books executed were in continuation of Beschi's popular writings such as *Vetha Vizhlakkam* (genuine Catholic doctrine in refutation of Lutheranism) *Pethaga maruththal* (denial of alleged aberrations in the Catholic Church) and Lutheraninattiy-albhu (on the character of Lutherans). Dupuis was very eager to see that the Catholic laity may improve in spiritual matters and so he had written two books titled the rules and regulations of the third order of St. Francis of the Five Wounds and guide for married people. Dupuis being the founder of the Congregation of the Immaculate Heart of Mary in Pondicherry he composed two volumes of guide to religious people.

To conclude it may be said that the spiritual books printed by Dupuis captured the attention between the picture's subject and the beholder because many images and pictures had been printed in the book. These are very important elements and the religious art had become one of the central concerns of the printed books. The various catechism books printed and published by L.S. Dupuis had presented an organic synthesis of the essential and fundamental contents of Catholic doctrine, as regards both faith and morals. Its principal sources are the Sacred Scriptures, and the liturgy. The catechisms contained the baptismal profession of faith (the Creed), the sacraments of faith, the life of faith (the Commandments), and the prayer of the believer (the Lord's Prayer). The printed catechisms explained how God's salvation, accomplished once for all through Christ Jesus and the Holy Spirit, is made present in the sacred actions of the Church's liturgy especially in the seven sacraments. The catechism books printed by Dupuis included prayers too dealt with the meaning and importance of prayer in the life of believers. They concluded with a brief commentary on the seven petitions of the Lord's Prayer. It may be mentioned that Pala *Archsishtavar-galin Sarithiram* (Lives of Many Saints) a book had been though printed by L.S. Dupuis, he also chosen to print the individual saints and their lives as separate books. He had also done a great job of including in the series the life of John de Britto who was canonized in 1947 and Martyr Devasagayam Pillai now declared Blessed by Pope on 28 June 2012. Dupuis as a printer and publisher thus had practised a wider social practice and his printing works included larger historical and missionary role performed by publishing these books of catechism, prayers, litany, devotion to saints and spiritual reading.

Notes

1. E.W. Grinfield, *Sketches of the Danish Mission on the Coast of Coromandel*, London, 1831, pp. 89-90; see also, Gerald Duverdier, 'Les debuts de l'imprimerie Tamoule a Madras et la finde celle de Halle, 1761–1772', *Gutenberg–Jahrbuch*, 1977, pp. 184–94.
2. Gnanou Diagou, *Arrets du Conseil Superieur de Pondichéry*, 4 vols., Pondichéry, 1937, vol. III, pp. 458–9. Gerald Duverdier,' L'apparition de L'Imprimerie a Madras et disparititon a Pondichéry', *Guternberg–Jahrbuch*, 1976, pp. 355–63.
3. Guillame Leonard de Bellecombe, *Capitulation Pour Pondichéry*, Jean Fischer, Imprimeur, 17 October 1778. pp 1–9.; The Tamil version of the treaty from article 12 to 26 had been found in the diary of Veera Nayakkar, see, Gobalakichenane, M., *Irandaam Veera Nayakkar Naatkurippu, 1778-1792*, Madras, 1992, pp. 43–50; see also, Gnanou Diagou, *Arrets du Conseil*, vol. 4, p. 83.
4. Bibliothèque Nationale de France (hereafter BNF), V.31015; *Manuel de Cipaye, Contentant quelques reflexions sur ler parti que l'on pourrait tirer du militaire Indien; avec un précis de l'ordonnance de l'infanterie, tant pour l'exercise que pour tout ce qui peut mener a l'instruction d'une troupe. Le tout adapte a la formation particuliere des corps des cipayes*, par M. Aubineau–Duplessis, Pondichéry, 1784, pp. 1–271.
5. Adrien Launay, *Histoire de la Mission de Siam, 1662–1811, Documents Historiques*, 2 vols., Paris, 1920, see the letter of Janvier 1788 in vol. II, p. 338,. See also, Gerald Duverdier, 'La Transmission de L'Imprimerie en Thailande: Du Catechismo de 1796 aux Impressions Buddhiques sur feuilles de Latanier', *Bulletin d'L'Ecole française d'Extreme–Orient*, vol. 68, no.1, 1980, pp. 209–260.
6. BNF, LK 10.24; Daniel Baron Lescallier, *Discours pronounce aux troupes de Pondichery, a l'occasion de la publication de l'amnistie par M.lescallier, Commissaire civil, delegue aux etablissemens francais au–de la du Cap de Bonne–Esperance*, Le 4 Octobre 1792, A Pondichery; see also, BNF, LK 10.25, *Proclamation des Commissaires Civils, sur la loi du 17 Octobe (sic) 1792, pour la prochaine convocation. Au nom de la nation, de la loi, et du Roi, les commissaries civils delegues par le Roi, en vertu des decrets de l'Assemblee Nationale, aux etablissemens français au–de la du cap de Bonne –espernace*, A Pondichéry, 1792.
7. BNF, LK 19.18, *Assemblee Coloniale representative des establissmens français del'Inde*, Seances des 11, 13, 14, et 15 Octobre 1792, A Pondichéry.
8. BNF, LK 19.19, *Assemblee Coloniale representative des establissmens français del'Inde*, Seances des 11, 14, 15, et 17 Octobre 1792, A Pondichéry.
9. BNF, LK 19.20, *Assemblee Coloniale de Pondichery: Précis de la premiere séance de l'Assemblee Coloniale du lundi 17 Decembre 1792*, A Pondichéry.

10. BNF, LK 19.21, *Extrait des regisres du consiel superior de Pondichéry*, De neuf Janvier, mil sept cent quatre vingt–treize, A Pondichéry.
11. BL, 7293.bb.25, *The practice of farriery, calculated for the East Indies, collected from the best authors, and founded upon experiments made during a residence of ten years in this country, by Antoine de Letang, captain of cavalry*, Pondichery, printed for the author, 1795. See also, *The Practice of Farriery Calculated for the East Indies*, Madras, 1839.
12. *Archives Administratives des Etablissments Français de L 'Inde, Contentant de Lois, Ordonnances, Reglements et Toute Autres Publication Faites Par Orde du Gouverneur*, Pondichéry, 1823-7; *Bulletin des Actes administratifs des Etablissments Français dans l'Inde,* Pondichéry, 1828.
13. *Impartial de Pondichéry*, Pondichéry, 1838.
14. '*Soleil Indien*'. Pondichéry, 1838.
15. Archives de la Société des Missions Etrangères de Paris (hereafter AMEP), MSS *Correspondance Pondichéry-Paris, Lettres*, vol. 998, pp. 951-7, see the letter of Jarrige written from Bangalore dated 26 July 1828 to Langlois in Paris.
16. AMEP, MSS *Correspondance Pondichéry-Paris, Lettres*, vol. 998, p. 995, see the letter of Bishop Bonnand from Pondicherry dated 12 June 1830 to Jean Tesson in Paris.
17. AMEP, MSS *Correspondance Pondichéry-Paris, Lettres*, vol. 999, p. 436, see the letter of Bishop Bonnand from Pondicherry dated 4 June 1837 to Jean Tesson in Paris.
18. AMEP, MSS *Correspondance Pondichéry-Paris, Lettres*, vol. 999, p. 1187, see the letter of Bishop Bonnand from Pondicherry dated 20 December 1840 to Cardinal Fransoni in Rome.
19. AMEP, MSS *Correspondance Pondichéry-Paris, Lettres*, vol. 999, p. 40, see the letter of Bishop Bonnand from Venkatagiri dated 9 February 1841 to Langlois in Paris.
20. *Collectanea S. Congragationis de Propaganda Fide seu Decreta Instructiones Rescripta Pro Apostolicis Missionibus*, Romae, 1893, see no. 1879, p. 768.
21. British Library, London, *Vethapurattalai Neekum Sanjivi*, Pondicherry, 1841, pp. 14-15.
22. Collectanea S. Congragationis de Propaganda Fide seu Decreta Instructiones Rescripta Pro Apostolicis Missionibus, Ibid., see no. 1880.
23. Archivium Congregationis de Propaganda Fide, Roma (hereafter ACPF), MSS lettere e decreti della Sacra Congregatizione e Biglietti di Monsignor Segretario (hereafter LDB), vol. 326 (1841/II) fls. 1201-1201v, see the letter of Cardinal Fransoni from Rome dated 20 November 1841 to Bishop Bonnand in Pondicherry.
24. Adrien Launay, *Histoire des Missions de L'Inde: Pondichéry, Maissour, Coimbatour*, 5 vols., Paris, 1898, vol. II, p. 137.
25. AMEP, MSS *Correspondance Pondichéry-Paris, Lettres*, vol. 999, p. 995, see the letter of Bishop Bonnand from Pondicherry dated 12 June 1841 to Jean Tesson in Paris.

26. AMEP, MSS *Correspondance Pondichéry-Paris, Lettres*, vol. 999, see the letter of L.S. Dupuis from Pondicherry dated 18 August 1841 to Jean Tesson in Paris.
27. AMEP, MSS *Correspondance Pondichéry-Paris, Lettres*, vol. 999, see the letter of L.S. Dupuis from Pondicherry dated 21 October 1841 to Jean Tesson in Paris.
28. AMEP, MSS *Correspondance Pondichéry-Paris, Lettres*, vol. 1000, see the letter of Marion Bressiliac dated 2 October 1842 to Jean Tesson in Paris.
29. AMEP, MSS *Correspondance Pondichéry-Paris, Lettres*, vol. 999, see the letter of L.S. Dupuis from Pondicherry dated 9 December 1839 to Jean Tesson in Paris.
30. AMEP, MSS *Correspondance Pondichéry-Paris, Lettres*, vol. 1000, pp. 1009-11, see the letter of L.S. Dupuis from Pondicherry dated 21 March 1845 to Jean Tesson in Paris.
31. AMEP, MSS *Correspondance Pondichéry-Paris, Lettres*, vol. 1000, see the letter of L.S. Dupuis from Pondicherry dated 11 October 1845 to Jean Tesson in Paris.
32. AMEP, MSS *Correspondance Pondichéry-Paris, Lettres*, vol. 1000, see the letter of L.S. Dupuis dated 12 October 1845 to Jean Tesson in Paris.
33. AMEP, MSS *Correspondance Pondichéry-Paris, Lettres*, vol. 1000, see the letter of L.S. Dupuis from Pondicherry dated 11 October 1845 to Jean Tesson in Paris.
34. Ibid.
35. AMEP, MSS *Correspondance Pondichéry-Paris, Lettres*, vol. 1000, see the letter of L.S. Dupuis from Pondicherry dated 11 January 1847 to Jean Tesson in Paris.
36. AMEP, MSS *Correspondance Pondichéry-Paris, Lettres*, vol. 1000, see the letter of L.S. Dupuis dated 11 August 1848 to Jean Tesson in Paris.
37. AMEP, MSS *Correspondance Pondichéry-Paris, Lettres*, vol. 1001, see the letter of L.S. Dupuis dated 9 April 1850 to the MEP Superior in Paris.
38. AMEP, MSS *Correspondance Pondichéry-Paris, Lettres*, vol. 1002, see the letter of L.S. Dupuis from Pondicherry dated 10 November 1858 to Jean Tesson in Paris.
39. AMEP, MSS *Correspondance Pondichéry-Paris, Lettres,* vol. 1003, see the letter of L.S. Dupuis dated 10 April 1861 to Jean Tesson in Paris.
40. AMEP, MSS *Correspondance Pondichéry-Paris, Lettres*, vol. 1003 see the letter of L.S. Dupuis from Pondicherry dated 20 March 1864 to Jean Tesson.
41. AMEP, MSS *Correspondance Pondichéry-Paris, Lettres*, vol. 1003, see the letter of L.S. Dupuis from Pondicherry dated 9 December 1869 to the MEP superior in Paris.
42. Fernando de Mello Vargas, *Evolution of Tamil Type Design*, MA Dissertation, University of Reading, United Kingdom, 2007, p. 35; D. Udaya Kumar, *Transformation of Tamil Letter-forms from Palm Leaf Manuscripts to Early Letter-press Printing*, Ph. D Thesis, Indian Institute of Technology Bombay, 2010, pp. 138-9.
43. AMEP, MSS *Correspondance Pondichéry-Paris, Lettres*, vol. 1000, pp.1009-11, see the letter of L.S. Dupuis from Pondicherry dated 21 March 1845 to Jean Tesson in Paris.
44. Centre des Archives d'Outre–Mer (hereafter CAOM), Aix–en–Provence, Inde 1855, *Specimen de typographie et de fonderie envoye a l'exposition universelle*

de Paris annee 1855, par l'Imprimerie des missionaires apostoliques de Pondichery Indes orientales, see also, *Circulaire addresse aux colonies et relatives a une subscription a des ouvrages en langue tamoule edites par l'Imprimerie de la mission Catholique en Inde 1863-1865.*

45. AMEP, MSS 0627.2, Caractere Tamouls/graves par M. Bertrand Loeulliet; sous la dir. De M. l'abbe Ch. Dallet, Missionaire Apostolique de la Congregation des Missions Etrangères, Paris, Impr. Imperiale de France, 1863, 1 table, 53 X 70 cm.
46. AMEP, MSS *Correspondance Pondichéry-Paris, Lettres*, vol. 999, pp. 448, see the letter of Clement Bonnand dated 13 June 1837.
47. Adrien Launay, Histoire des Missions, vol. II, pp. 130-32.
48. Bibliothèque Asiatique des Missions Etrangères de Paris (hereafter BAMEP), *Saathaaranam*, Pondicherry, 1841.
49. Thomas Anchukandam, *Catholic Revival in India in the 19th Century: Role of Mgr. Clement Bonnand (1796-1861)*, Bangalore, vol. I, 1996, p. 342.
50. Madurai Province Jesuit Archives (hereafter MPJA), Shenbaganur, no. 221/313, *Gnaanamirdham*, Pondicherry, 1841.
51. A. Louis, *Panmaiyil Orumai and Orumaiyil Panmai*, Pondicherry, 2016, p. 66.
52. BAMEP, TA 154, *Gnaamirtha Thadaagam*, Pondicherry, 1847.
53. AMEP, *MSS Correspondance Pondichéry-Paris, Lettres*, vol. 1000, see the letter of L.S. Dupuis dated 9 February 1847 to Jean Tesson in Paris.
54. MPJA, 221/315, *Gnaanmirdha Thadaagam*, Pondicherry, 1858.
55. A. Louis, Panmaiyil Orumai, P. 66.
56. MPJA, 221/134, *Sarithirathuuku aduththa gnaanopadesa surukkam*, Pondicherry, 1858; BL, 14172.h.9, *Sarithiraththukkuaduththa Gnaanopadea-ththin Vinaa Vidai: Questions et reponses du petit catechisme Historique de Fleury, avec quelques lecons supplementaires par un member des la congregation des mission-etrageres,* Pondicherry, 1858.
57. BL, 14170.b.34 (1), *Padangalaal Vizhalakkapatta Gnaanopadesam,* Pondicherry, 1863; BL, 14170.a.34 (5), *Sugirtha Mandirangalum Gnaaopadesa Kurippidamum*, Pondicherry, 1865.
58. MPJA 221/277.
59. BAMEP, *Vaalar Pokkisham*, Pondicherry, 1844.
60. BL, 14170.8.32, *Vaalar Pokkisham*, Pondicherry, 1861. We find the book reprinted again in 1897.
61. A. Louis, Panmaiyil Orumai, p. 72.
62. AMEP, *Correspondance Pondichéry–Paris, Lettres,* vol. 1000, see the letter of L.S. Dupuis dated 3 December 1844 to Jean Tesson.
63. BAMEP, *Vaalar Thunai*, Pondicherry, 1844.
64. A. Louis, Panmaiyil Orumai, pp. 67, 72.
65. AMEP, *Correspondance Pondichéry–Paris, Lettres,* vol. 1000, see the letter of L.S. Dupuis dated 3 December 1844 to Jean Tesson.
66. AMEP, *Correspondance Pondichéry–Paris, Lettres,* vol. 1003, see the circular of L.S. Dupuis, the Pro–Vicar Apostolic to all the native priests and MEP

missionaries in the vicariate of Pondicherry dated 31 December 1867; AAPC, *Collection Louis Faucheux: Copies d' lettres et circulaire du L. S. Dupuis en française et tamoule, XIXe siècle,* no. 16.

67. BAMEP, *Devamaathavin Vanakka Maatham*, Pondicherry, 1850; MPJA, 221/464, Accesssion no. 006634; see also *Devamaathavin Vanakka Maatham*, Pondicherry, second edition, 1897.
68. François Andre, *Vie du Pere Louis Saint-Cyr*, Paris, 1889; S. Jeyaseela Stephen, *Louis Savinien Dupuis and His Circulars in French to the Priests and in Tamil to the Religious Nuns in Pondicherry Mission, 1860-1874*, Pondicherry, 2017, p. 40.
69. BAMEP, TA 133, *Archsishta Susaiyappar Vanakka Maatham*, Pondicherry, 1867.
70. MPJA, 221/141, *Utharikkira Aathumaakalin Vanakka Maatham*, Pondicherry, 1870.
71. AMEP, MSS *Correspondance Pondichéry-Paris, Lettres*, vol. 1000, see the letter of L.S. Dupuis dated 18 April 1842 to Jean Tesson in Paris.
72. BAMEP, *Siluvai Paathai*, Pondicherry, 1842, MPJA, 221/244, *Siluvai Paathai*, Pondicherry, 1842; BL, 14170.a.19, *Siluvai Paathai*, Pondicherry, 1856.
73. AMEP, *Correspondance Pondichéry–Paris, Lettres,* vol. 1000, see the letter of L.S. Dupuis dated 3 December 1844 to Jean Tesson in Paris.
74. MPJA, 221/422, *Thirunaatkalin vizhlakka surukkam*, Pondicherry, 1859.
75. MPJA, 222/304 Accession no.007144, MSS *Pusai Ayatham*. We find not dots over the consonants. See, Pusai Aayatham Kezhagira Vagai, pp. 77-95 (15 pages).
76. BL, 14170.a.18, *Karunaakara Kadal*, Pondicherry, 1868.
77. MPJA, 221/650, *Gnaana Unarthuthal*, Pondicherry, 1846; BAMEP, *Gnaana Unarthuthal*, Pondicherry, 1842, pp vi+99; *Gnaana Unarthuthal: Veeramaa-munivar aruliseythathu: Manithanyudaya anthiyangalaikuruithu uthamamaana pirasangganggal*, seventh edition, Pondicherry, 1913.
78. AMEP, MSS *Correspondance Pondichéry-Paris, Lettres*, vol. 1000, see the letter of L.S. Dupuis dated 18 April 1842 to Jean Tesson in Paris.
79. Bibliothèque Nationale, Paris (hereafter BNP), Rue Richelieu, MSS Indien, no. 463.
80. MPJA, 221/304, *Gnaana Muyarchi,* Pondicherry, 1843.
81. AMEP, MSS *Correspondance Pondichéry-Paris, Lettres*, vol. 1000, see the letter of L.S. Dupuis dated 23October 1843 to Jean Tesson in Paris.
82. E.R. Hambye, *History of Christianity in India: Eighteenth Century, Vol. III*, Bangalore, 1997, p. 194.
83. MPJA, 221/30, *Gnaana Odukkangalukku Niyamikkapatta Archsishta Ignaciyar Dhyaanangal*, Pondicherry, 1848.
84. Henriette Bugge, *Mission and Tamil Society*, London, 1994, p. 83. There was a native priest called Gnaanapragaasa Nather who was ordained in 1862 and he died in 1891. We should not get confused with this priest to Fr. Bertoldi.
85. MPJA, 221/58, *Aathuma Nesam*, Pondicherry, 1860.
86. MPJA, 221/191, Accession no. 141000, *Kristhunaathar Anusaaram*, Pondicherry, 1863.

87. Ibid., pp. 1-80.
88. Ibid., pp. 81-125.
89. Ibid., pp. 126-173.
90. Ibid., pp. 174-374.
91. MPJA 221/33, *Archsishta Iganciyar Gnaana Dhyaanagal*, Pondicherry, 1864.
92. BAMEP, *Divviya Maathirikai*, Pondicherry, 1866; MPJA, 221/350, *Divviya Maathirikai*, Pondicherry, 1866.
93. S. Rajamanickam, ed., *Divviya Maathirikai*, Tamil Literary Society, Tuticorin, 1966.
94. Det Kongelige Bibliotek (hereafter KB), Kobenhavn, NY KGl.Saml.589C; Albertine Gaur, 'Bartholomäus Ziegenbalg's Verzeichnis der Malabarischen Bucher', *Journal of the Royal Asiatic Society of Great Britain and Ireland*, no. 3-4, October, 1967, pp. 63-95, see pp. 91-2.
95. AMEP, MSS *Correspondance Pondichéry-Paris, Lettres*, vol. 1001, see the letter of L.S. Dupuis dated 7 September 1853 to Jean Tesson in Paris.
96. AMEP, MSS *Correspondance Pondichéry-Paris, Lettres*, vol. 992, p. 795.
97. BAMEP, TA 137, *Vetha Saatchiyaana Muthiperupettra Arulanandar Sarithiram*, Pondicherry, 1858.
98. BL, 14170.a.12, *Vethasaatchiyaana Devasagayam Pillai Sarithiram*, Pondicherry, 1858; See also, MPJA, 222/304, *Vethasaatchiyaana Devasagayam Pillai Sarithiram*, (bound in a volume along with Gnaana Maalai) Accession no. 007144, pp. 126-148 (22 pages).
99. MPJA, 221/42, *Archsishta Gnaanapragaasiyar Sarithiramum Archsishta Sthanislausudaya Sarithira Pirasanagangalumaavana*, Pondicherry, 1862.
100. AMEP, MSS *Correspondance Pondichéry-Paris, Lettres*, vol. 1002, see the letter of Louis Marie Mousset dated 24 March 1859 to Jean Tesson in Paris.
101. BL, 14170.a.17, *Maasillaamal Urpavitha Archsishta Devamaathavin Thiru Irudhaya Sabhai Anusaaram*, Pondicherry, 1856.
102. Ibid.
103. BL, 14170.a.34 (4), *Kanniyar Anusaaram*, Pondicherry, 1865.
104. MPJA, 221/480, *Nanmarana Aaytham*, Pondicherry, 1860
105. Ibid.
106. MPJA 221/664, 221/311, 221/662, *Vethiyar Ozhukkam*, Pondicherry, 1842.
107. BL, 14170b.29 (2), *Gnaana Kannaadi*, Pondicherry, 1858; MPJA, 221/291, 221/291a, *Gnnana Kannaadi*, Pondicherry, 1906 and 1929.
108. AMEP, MSS *Correspondance Pondichéry-Paris, Lettres*, vol. 999 see the letter of Clement Bonnand Drusipare the Bishop of Pondicherry dated 22 October 1841 to Jean Tesson in Paris.
109. BL, 14170.b.9.1, *Vetha Vizhlakkam*, Pondicherry, 1842; AMEP, MSS *Correspondance Pondichéry-Paris, Lettres*, vol. 1000, see the letter of L.S. Dupuis dated 18 April 1842 to Jean Tesson.
110. MPJA, 221/654, *Vetha Vizhlakkam*, Pondicherry, 1855, see also, MPJA, 221/652.

111. MPJA, 221/666, *Vetha Vizhlakkam*, Pondicherry, 1868; See also, BL, 14170.b.10 (1), *Vetha Vizhlakkam*, Third edition, Pondicherry, 1868.
112. BL, 14170.b.9. (3), *Lutherithiniyalbu*, Pondicherry, first edition, 1842; BL, 14170.b.12 9. (1). *Lutherithiniyalbu*, second edition, 1847; MPJA, 221/654, *Lutherinithiyalbu*, Pondicherry, 1847.
113. BL, 14170.b.10. (3), *Lutherithiniyalbu*, Third edition, 1868; See, Adrien Launay, Histoire des Missions de L'Inde, vol. IV, p. 582, see the *catalogue des principaux ouvrages publies par les eveques, les missionaries et les pretres indigenes des missions de Pondichéry, du Maissour, et du Coimbatour.*
114. BL, 14170.b.9. (2), *Bedhga Maruthal*, Pondicherry 1842; MPJA, 221/654, *Pethaga Maruththal*, Pondicherry, 1855; BL, 14170.b.10.(2), *Bedhga Maruthal*, Pondicherry, 1868.
115. BL, 14170.a.34 *Pathimaththesu: Dushana Maruthalaagiya Tharkka Kummi*, Pondicherry, 1865.
116. AMEP, MSS *Correspondance Pondichéry-Paris, Lettres*, vol. 1000, see the letter of L.S. Dupuis dated 18 April 1842 to Jean Tesson.
117. MPJA, 221/225, *Sathiya Vetha Paritchai*, Pondicherry, 1846.
118. AMEP, MSS *Correspondance Pondichéry-Paris, Lettres*, vol. 1000, see the letter of L.S. Dupuis dated 9 February, 1847 to Jean Tesson.
119. AMEP, MSS *Correspondance Pondichéry-Paris, Lettres*, vol. 1000, see the letter of L.S. Dupuis dated 18 April 1842 to Jean Tesson.
120. BL, 14170.b.23, *Deyva Paritchai*, Pondicherry, 1846; MPJA, 221/225, *Deyva Paritchai*, Pondicherry, 1846.
121. BAMEP, TA 193, *Sathiya Vetha Bhodhaga Surukkam*, Pondicherry, 1846.
122. MPJA, 221/553, *Poorviga Marai Vizhlakkam*, Pondicherry, 1856.
123. MPJA, 221/209, Accession no. 006366, *Sathiya Vetha Sarithira Surukkam*, Pondicherry, 1865.
124. BAMEP, *Meymarai Uththiyaanam*, Pondicherry, 1873.
125. AMEP, MSS *Correspondance Pondichéry-Paris, Lettres*, vol. 1004, see the letter of L.S. Dupuis dated 22 January 1874 to Jean Tesson.
126. S. Jeyaseela Stephen, *The First Catholic Bible in Tamil and Louis Savinien Dupuis at Pondicherry: A History of Translation and Printing, 1850-7*, Pondicherry, 2017, pp. 123-144.
127. AMEP, MSS *Correspondance Pondichéry-Paris, Lettres*, vol. 1000, see the letter Louis Marie Mousset dated 10 March 1846 to Jean Tesson in Paris.
128. AMEP, MSS *Correspondance Pondichéry-Paris, Lettres*, vol. 1002, see the letter of Louis Marie Mousset dated 3 September 1860.
129. BL, 14170.a.34 (1), *Nedunaat Panchankam*, Pondicherry, 1844.
130. BL, 14170.a.34 (1), Nedunatt Panchankam, Pondicherry, 1849.
131. S. Jeyaseela Stephen, *Louis Savinien Dupuis: A Biography of the MEP Missionary in Pondicherry*, Pondicherry, 2017, p. 25.
132. Archives de la Société des Missions Étrangères de Paris (hereafter AMEP), Paris, MSS Correspondance Pondichéry-Paris, Lettres, vol. 999, see the letter of Clement Bonnand from Bangalore dated 15 October 1840.

133. Adrien Launay, Histoire des Missions de l'Inde, vol. II, p. 134.
134. Ibid., vol. III, pp.134-5.
135. AMEP, MSS Correspondance Pondichéry-Paris, Lettres, vol. 999, see the letter of L.S. Dupuis written from Chinna Ballapuram dated 18 November 1839 to Reverend Superior and Reverend Directors of the Seminary of the missions Etrangères de Paris; See also, S. Jeyaseela Stephen, *The Heartbeat of a Missionary: Letters and Reports of Louis Savinien Dupuis in Pondicherry, 1839-74*, Pondicherry, 2017, see document no. 1.
136. AMEP, MSS Correspondance Pondichéry-Paris, Lettres, vol. 999, see the letter of Clement Bonnand the Bishop of Pondicherry dated 8 April 1840 to Jean Tesson in Paris.
137. Bibliothèque Asiatique des Missions Etrangères de Paris (hereafter BAMEP), TA 231, *Vetha purattalai maruththalaagiya sathiya thirusabaiyin surkkamaana vizhlakkam*, Pondicherry, 1840, pp. 12-13.It is given in Tamil numerals.
138. Ibid., pp 6-9.
139. Ibid., pp. 36, 40-1, 46-9.
140. AMEP, MSS Correspondance Pondichéry-Paris, Lettres, vol. 999, see the letter of Clement Bonnand the Bishop of Pondicherry written from Bangalore dated 15 October 1840.
141. AMEP, MSS Correspondance Pondichéry-Paris, Lettres, vol. 999, see the letter of L.S. Dupuis dated 18 August 1841 to the MEP superior.
142. BL, 14170.aaa.17, *Vetha purattalai neekum sanjiviyaagiya meyyaana thirusabaiyin vizhlakkam*, Pondicherry, 1841, pp. 14-5.
143. Ibid., pp. 237-41.
144. Ibid., pp. 241-54.
145. Ibid., p. 272.
146. Ibid., pp. 282-310.
147. Ibid., pp. 343-48.
148. BAMEP, TA 152, *Nanraai Ninai: Maatha Anudhina Dhyaanam*, Pondicherry, 1844.
149. Ibid., pp. 1-7.
150. Ibid., see Pusai Kaanum Vagai, pp. 7-32.
151. Ibid., p. 56.
152. Ibid., p. 69.
153. Ibid., pp. 400-3.
154. Ibid., pp. 403-4.
155. BAMEP, TA 142, *Aindhukaaya varam petra archsishta franciskuvin sarithira surukkam,* Pondicherry, 1859.
156. Madurai Province Jesuit Archives (hereafter MPJA), Shenbaganur, 221/30, *Varushathin pradhi dina sugirtha pirasangangalaagiya archsishtavargalin Sarithiram, Muthal Kaandam*, Pondicherry, 1866.
157. MPJA, Shenbaganur, 221/30, *Varushathin pradhi dina sugirtha pirasangangalaagiya archsishtavargalin Sarithiram: Rendaam Kaandam*, Pondicherry, 1866.

158. MPJA, *Varushathin pradhi dina sugirtha pirasangangalaagiya archsishtavargalin Sarithiram: Moonraam Kaandam*, Pondicherry, 1867.
159. MPJA, *Varushathin pradhi dina sugirtha pirasangangalaagiya archsishtavargalin Sarithiram: Naalaam Kaandam*, Pondicherry, 1867.
160. MPJA, 221/53, *Ainthu thirukaaya varam petra archsishta franciskuvin thavathukkuriya moonram sabhai ozhukkam*, Pondicherry, 1859.
161. BAMEP, TA 121, *Illara Uththiyaanam*, Pondicherry, 1867.
162. BAMEP, TA 40, *Thuravara Uththiyaanam: Kaandam Onru*, Pondicherry, 1869.
163. BAMEP, TA, 129, *Thuravara Uththiyaanam: Kaandam Rendu*, Pondicherry, 1872.

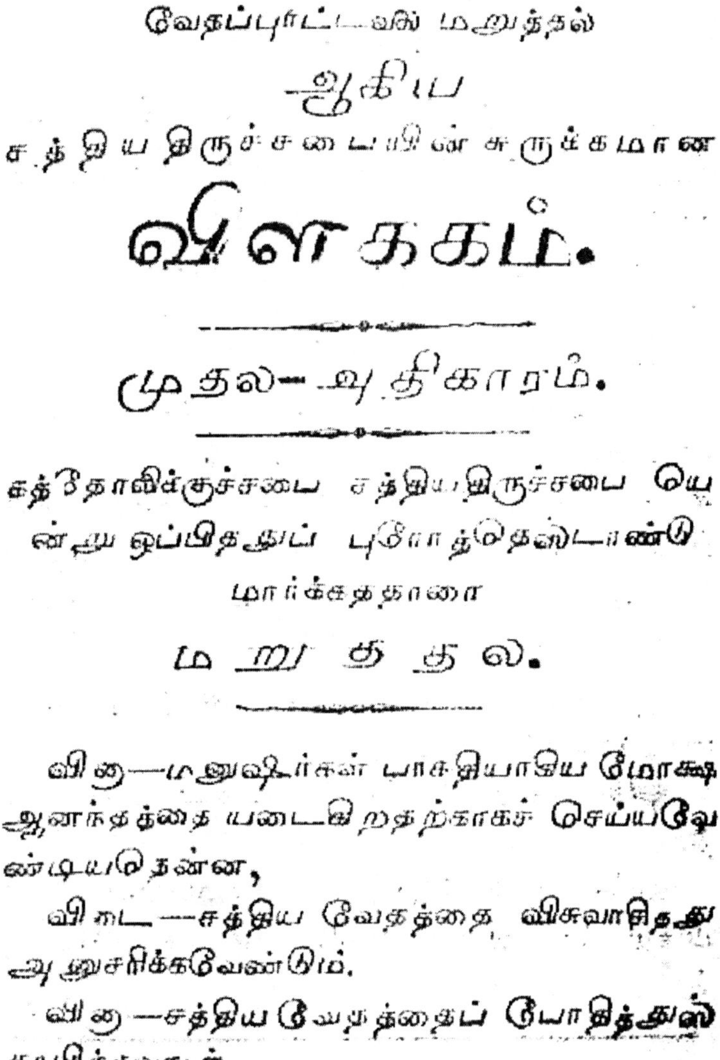

வேதப்புரட்டலை மறுத்தல்

ஆகிய

சத்திய திருச்சபையின் சுருக்கமான

விளக்கம்.

முதல் அதிகாரம்.

கத்தோலிக்குச்சபை சத்தியதிருச்சபை யென்று ஒப்பிதலும் புரோத்தெஸ்டாண்டு மார்க்கத்தாரை

மறுத்தல.

வினா—மனுஷர்கள் பாக்கியமாகிய மோக்ஷ ஆனந்தத்தை யடைகிறதற்காகச் செய்யவேண்டியதென்ன,

விடை—சத்திய வேதத்தை விசுவாசித்து அநுசரிக்கவேண்டும்.

வினா—சத்திய வேதத்தைப் போதித்துஸ் தாபித்தவர்யார்,

6.1. The first page of Vethapurattalai Maruththal Aagiya Sathya Thirusabhaiyin Surukkamaana Vizhlakkam printed by Toutin the manager of the French Government Press in Pondicherry in 1840. (*Courtesy*: Bibliothèque Asiatique des Missions Etrangères de Paris, TAM 231).

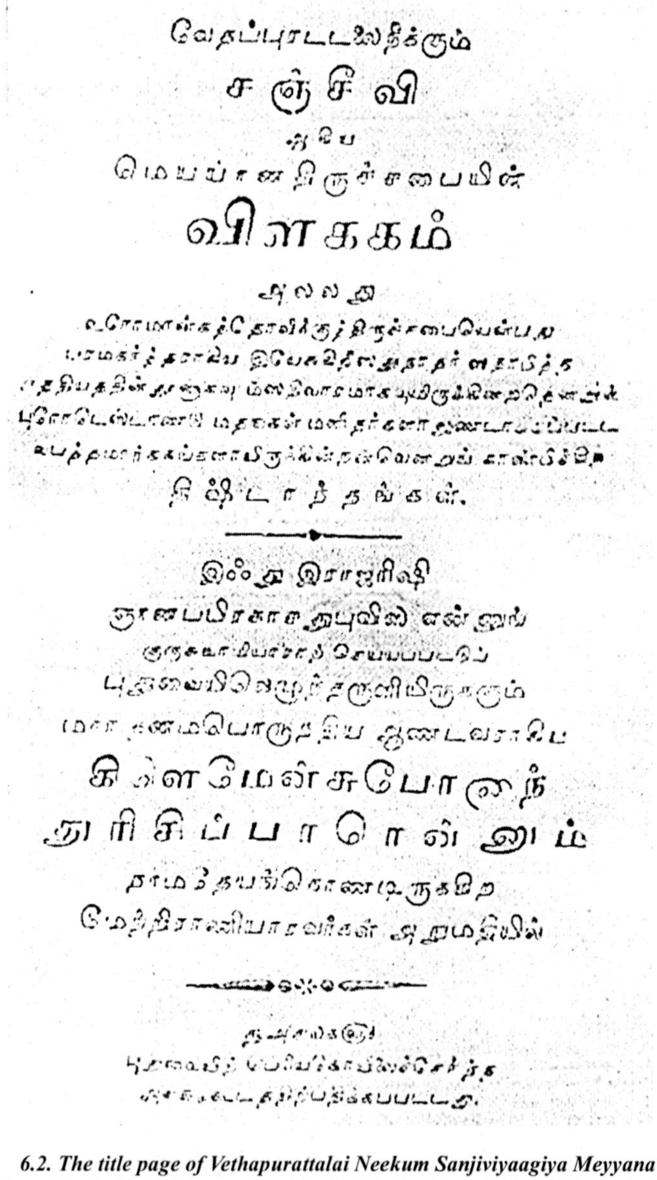

வேதப்புரட்டலைநீக்கும்

சஞ்சீவி

ஆகிய

மெய்யானதிருச்சபையின்

விளக்கம்

அல்லது

6.2. The title page of Vethapurattalai Neekum Sanjiviyaagiya Meyyana Thirusabhayin Vizhlakkam printed at the Mission Press in Pondicherry in 1841.* (Courtesy: *British Library, London, 14170. aaa.17).

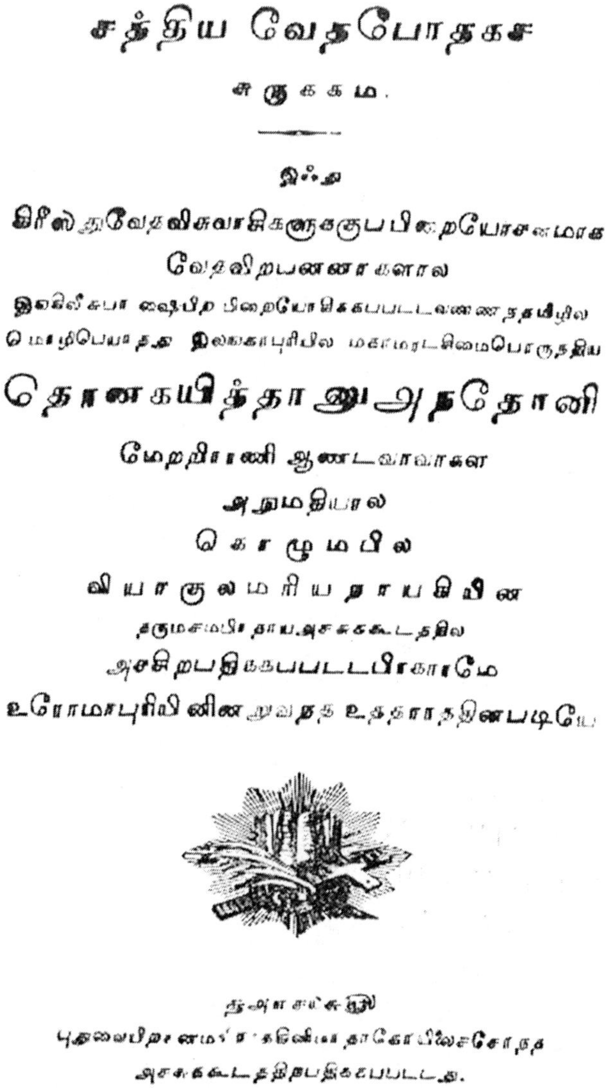

6.3. *The title page of Sathya Vethabhodgaga Surukkam printed at the Mission Press in Pondicherry without dots over the consonants in 1846.* (Courtesy: *Bibliothèque Asiatique des Missions Etrangères de Paris, TAM 193).*

இப்பிரபந்தத்தைப்

பிரசித்தப்படுத்தியவரால்

பாயிரம.

தேவ ஏவுதலால் அர்ச். - இஞ்ஞாசியார் நியமித்
துவழங்கச்செய்தருளின ஞானவொடுக்கங்களினு
னும் அதுக்கு எழுதிஏற்படுத்தின தியானங்களின்
முறையினுலுஞ் சர்வலோகத்திலுந்தேவதோத்திர
மாக விளைந்தஞானநன்மைகளுஞ் சுகிர்தவழியிற்
றிடப்பட்ட புண்ணியாத்துமாக்களும் நன்னெறி
யில்மனந்திரும்பினபாவிகளு மித்தனையென்றுக
ணக்கில்லை. இப்படிப்பட்டபரமநன்மைகள் இத்
தேசத்திலுமுண்டாகும்பொருட்டு அத்தியானமு
றையாக விந்தப்பிரபந்தமுண்டாக்கப்பட்டது. த
மிழிலிதனை யெழுதிவைத்தவருடையபேர் தெரிய
ப்படாதிருந்தாலும் அவர் அர்ச். - இஞ்ஞாசியார்
சபைச்சந்நியாசிகளிலொருவனெனத்தகும். அவர்வி
ரும்பினதன்மைக்கு இப்பிரபந்தத்தினுல்திரளான
புண்ணிய விளைவுண்டாவதைநாடி இதின்கைப்பிர
திகளைப்பரிசோதித்துத்திருத்தி அநேகவிடங்களிற்
கருத்தைவிவரித்துவிளக்கி அச்சிற்பதிப்பித்து வெ
ளிப்படுத்துகிறோம். இதுயாவர்க்குந் தெளிவாகிச்
சம்பூரண ஞானபிரயோசனமாகத்தக்கதாக வெ
ளிச்சமானவிதமா யெழுதப்பட்டது. ஆயினு மத்
தோடியன்றமட்டுந் தக்கவிலக்கணம் பொருந்தின
தாமே.

6.4. The page of paayiram from Gnaana Oddukkangalukku Niyami-kapatta Archsishta Ignaciyar Dhyaanangal printed at the Mission Press in Pondicherry in 1848.* (Courtesy: *Madurai Province Jesuit Archives, Shenbaganur, 221/30).

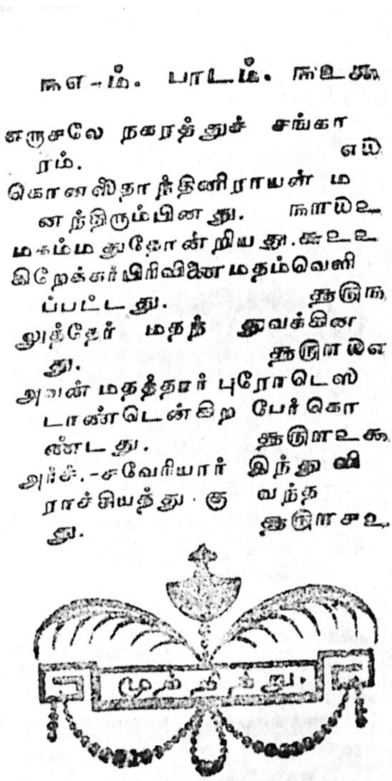

௧௭-ம். பாடம். ௱௨௬

எருசலேம் நகரத்துச் சங்காரம். ௭௰

கொன்ஸ்தாந்தீனிராயன் மனந்திரும்பினது. ௩௱௰௨

மகம்மது தோன்றியது. ௬௱௨௨

கிரேக்கர் பிரிவினைமதம் வெளிப்பட்டது. [illegible]

லுத்தேர் மதந் துவக்கினது. [illegible]

அங்ளிக்கன் மதத்தார் புரோடெஸ்டான்டென்கிற பேர் கொண்டது. [illegible]

அர்ச். சவேரியார் இந்து விராச்சியத்துக்கு வந்தது. [illegible]

முற்றிற்று.

6.5. The last page of *Sarithirathukku Aduththa Gnaanopadesa Surukkam* printed at the Mission Press in Pondicherry in 1858. (Courtesy: *Madurai Province Jesuit Archives, Shenbaganur, 221/134*).

LIVRES SORTIS

DE CETTE IMPRIMERIE

[illegible] *Gnânânandam*, ou l'ambroisie spirituelle, livre de poésies, rédigé par l'abbé Dupuis et imprimé en 1841, puis réimprimé en 1845 et 1852; in-18 relié 1 fr. 20

[illegible] *Véda pourattoukiraga*, ou traité contre l'hérésie, et surtout contre le Protestantisme, composé en 1828 par l'abbé Dupuis et imprimé en 1841, puis réimprimé en 1848; in-12 relié 2 fr. 40

[illegible] *Satta rédi paritchei*, l'examen ou la recherche de la vraie eglise, composé par le même, et imprimé en 1841, puis réimprimé en 1845; in-12 broché 15 c.

[illegible] *Védaviallecam*, ou explication de la religion et réfutation du Luthéranisme; ouvrage du P. Beschi Jésuite, composé en 1728, imprimé en 1842 et réimprimé en 1851; in-12 relié 3 fr.

[illegible] *Gnâna vamertoudal*, ou instructions spirituelles; ouvrage ancien et anonyme, retouché par l'abbé Dupuis et imprimé en 1842, puis réimprimé en 1846; in-12 cartonné 52 c.

[illegible] *Sattiavédapoudanjoulai soucoucam*, ou abrégé des merveilles de la vraie religion, par l'abbé Dupuis, imprimé en 1842 et réimprimé en 1848; in-12 broché 15 c.

[illegible] *Loutherinattiellou*, ou caractère des Luthériens, par le P. Beschi, imprimé en 1842 et réimprimé en 1850; in-12 broché 15 c.

[illegible] *Gnâna mouvritchi*, ou exercices spirituels, composés au 17e siècle par le P. Louis d'Avour et imprimé en 1843; in-12 cart. 1 fr. 5

[illegible] *Gnânâmirdatatâhâgam*, ou lac d'ambroisie spirituelle, livre de prières, méditations, cantiques etc.... rédigé par l'abbé Dupuis et imprimé en 1843, puis réimprimé en 1847; gros in-18 relié 2 fr. 70

[illegible] *Nendâi ninei*, ou pensez-y-bien, méditations pour chaque jour du mois, suivies de prières et de litanies, composées par l'abbé Dupuis et imprimées en 1844, puis réimprimées en 1853; in-18 cartonné 20 c.

[illegible] *Silouvei pâdei*, chemin de la croix, suivi des prières et de litanies en l'honneur de la passion de Notre Seigneur, du Sacré Cœur de Jésus, du St. cœur de Marie, du scapulaire etc., par le même, imprimé en 1844 et réimprimé en 1851; in-18 relié 1 fr. 20

[illegible] *Vâler pokicham*, ou trésor de la jeunesse, petit livre de prières avec catéchismes, rédigé par le même et imprimé en 1844, puis réimprimé en 1853; in-32 cartonné 52 c.

[illegible] *Vâler toumbei*, ou compagnon de la jeunesse, petit livre de prières avec un petit catéchisme, rédigé par le même et imprimé en 1844; in-32 cartonné 37 c.

[illegible] *Sôddirouhom*, ou livret contenant les principales prières et le petit catéchisme, rédigé par le même et imprimé en 1844, puis réimprimé en 1848 et 1854; in-18 broché 15 c.

[illegible] *Nedounath pagnangam*, espèce d'almanach perpétuel, avec une concordance des mois européens et des mois tamouls, l'indication jusqu'à la fin de ce siècle des éclipses de soleil et de lune visibles à Pondichéry, ainsi [illegible]

[illegible] *Atitchouvadi*, alphabet tamoul [illegible] 22 c.

[illegible] *Paramârtagourouvin cadei*, le même alphabet avec la fable de Paramartagourou et quelques poésies, imprimé en 1844; in-12 broché 45 c.

[illegible] *Prânyailacanka noul soutouram*, ou abrégé de la grammaire française, par l'abbé Dupuis, imprimé en 1845; in-12 cartonné 1 fr. 30

[illegible] *Ilacanka soutoucam*, ou abrégé de la grammaire tamoule, composé par M. Savérimouttoupoullé, et imprimé en 1845; in-12 cartonné 1 fr. 5

[illegible] *Paramârtagourouvin cadei*, ou fable de Paramârtagourou, par le P. Beschi, imprimé en 1845; in-12 broché 22 c.

[illegible] *Ilattinitamoulamoudalipadhi cadei*, la même fable avec la traduction latine en regard, par le même, imprimée en 1845; in-12 broché 45 c.

[illegible] *Prânçasa nedounc ravancee*, alphabet pour apprendre le français, par l'abbé Dupuis, imprimé en 1845; in-12 broché 30 c.

[illegible] *Pâler souvadhi*, ou alphabet pour les petits enfants, imprimé en 1845 et réimprimé en 1851; in-8 broché 15 c.

[illegible] *Ilattinilacca-nka noul soutour*, ou abrégé de la grammaire latine, par l'abbé Dupuis, imprimé en 1845; in-12 cartonné 1 fr. 80

Grammatica-Latino-Tamulica, Grammaire Tamoule-Latine par le P. Beschi, avec des notes et un abrégé de la grammaire du Haut-Tamoul par l'abbé Dupuis, imprimée en 1843; in-8 relié 3 fr. 60

[illegible] *Sattiavédaparitchei*, ou examen de la vraie religion; ouvrage qui renferme l'exposition et les preuves des principaux dogmes du Christianisme, avec une réfutation sommaire du paganisme indien; ébauché par un ancien Père, il a été refait par l'abbé Dupuis, et imprimé en 1846; in-12 relié 2 fr. 40

[illegible] *Ilattin prânçasa tamoulagaradi*, ou Dictionnaire Latin-Français-Tamoul, composé par les abbés Dupuis et Mousset, et imprimé en 1846; gros in-8 relié 12 fr.

[illegible] *Teiva paritchei*, ou examen de la divinité; réfutation abrégée de la mythologie indoue, ancien ouvrage anonyme retouché par l'abbé Dupuis, et imprimé en 1846; in-12 cartonné 32 c.

[illegible] *Véda pourattoukiraga*, ou réfutation de l'hérésie du Protestantisme, par l'abbé Dupuis, imprimée en 1846; in-18 cartonné 30 c.

[illegible] *Anouairam*, ou manuel de l'archiconfrérie du saint et immaculé Cœur de Marie, par le P. St. Cyr, Jésuite, imprimé en 1847; in-18 relié 1 fr. 20

[illegible] *Védieroupadecam gnânacannâdi*, ou règles de conduite des catéchistes, par le P. Beschi, suivies du miroir spirituel aussi destiné à leur direction, ouvrage ancien et anonyme retouché par l'abbé Dupuis, et imprimé en 1847; in-12 cartonné 1 fr. 50

[illegible] *Artsiantcha Ignâciar tiânam*, ou méditations de Saint Ignace,

6.6. The catalogue of books printed in 1863. (Courtesy: Centre des Archives d' Outre-Mer, Aix-en-Provence, Inde 1863).

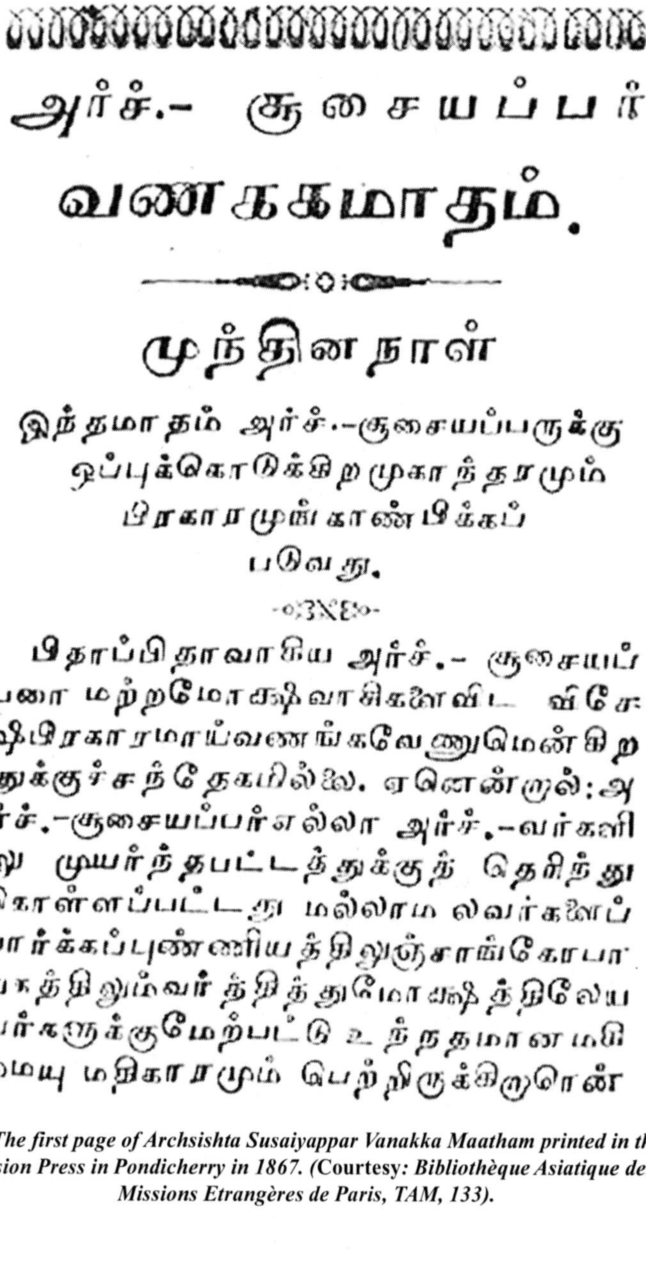
அர்ச்.- சூசையப்பர்
வணக்கமாதம்.
முந்தின நாள்
இந்தமாதம் அர்ச்.-சூசையப்பருக்கு
ஒப்புக்கொடுக்கிற முகாந்தரமும்
பிரகாரமுங் காண்பிக்கப்
படுவது.
பிதாப்பிதாவாகிய அர்ச்.- சூசையப்
பரை மற்றமோக்ஷவாசிகளைவிட விசே
ஷப்பிரகாரமாய்வணங்கவேணுமென்கிற
துக்குச்சந்தேகமில்லை. ஏனென்றால்: அ
ர்ச்.-சூசையப்பர்எல்லா அர்ச்.-வர்களி
லும் உயர்ந்தபட்டத்துக்குத் தெரிந்து
கொள்ளப்பட்டதுமல்லாமலவர்களைப்
பார்க்கப்புண்ணியத்திலுஞ்சாங்கோபா
ங்கத்திலும்வர்த்தித்துமோக்ஷத்திலேய
வர்களுக்குமேற்பட்டு உந்நதமானமகி
மையுமதிகாரமும் பெற்றிருக்கிறான்

6.7. The first page of Archsishta Susaiyappar Vanakka Maatham printed in the Mission Press in Pondicherry in 1867. (Courtesy: Bibliothèque Asiatique des Missions Etrangères de Paris, TAM, 133).

7

Printing Tamil Grammar, Dictionary, Poetry and Textbooks in the Mission Press, Government Press and in the College Printing Press in Pondicherry, 1838-73

Tamil books came to be printed in Pondicherry through the efforts of scholars and certain individuals who were patrons of printing. Beschi's *Thonnul Vizhlakkam* edited by Vethagiri Mudaliar was subsidized for printing by Maria Saveriya Pillai in Pondicherry and so the book got printed in 1838. This grammar book in Tamil was used for teaching in the school. Appavu Muthusami Pillai had mentioned in 1840 that he was sorry to state that the book printed was quite incorrectly done because the proof sheets were examined by an illiterate Hindu who without understanding the plans of Beschi made several omissions and useless additions.[1]

Louis Savinien Dupuis the MEP missionary in Pondicherry noticed that there was hardly any textbook used in the Tamil schools which was influenced by modern western educational ideas. Some of the palm leaf manuscripts used in the centres of learning had been traditional literary texts and classics such as *Kural* of Thiruvalluvar, *Aaththichoodi* of Avvaiyar, *Raamaayanam* of Kamban, *Chinthamani*, *Nannul*, *Nikandu* and *Panchathanthra Kathai*. These *Thinnai* (verandah) schools inculcated a set of moral instructions of exemplary conduct in personal and social life, but lacked ordered syllabus, orderly timings and prescribed textbooks in Tamil country.

L.S. Dupuis established a school for the Tamil girls in the French colony of Pondicherry and also caused for the opening up of many such schools in the British India of Tamil region. The nuns of the congregation of the Immaculate Heart of Mary which he founded opened schools. Dupuis evinced interest in the development of the curriculum of the schools and so he composed textbooks in Tamil and got them printed at the Catholic printing press in Pondicherry. He distributed the books and the children benefitted and it also helped the nuns in their educational activities.

Printing Textbooks for Learning Tamil Language: Aathi Chuvadi and Paramaartha Guru Kathai Muthaliyavai, 1844

A book titled *Aathi Chuvadi* (the alphabets) was printed in 1844. It had 44 pages. It is reported by Dupuis to Jean Tesson vide his letter dated 3 December 1844 that six copies of *Aathi Chuvadi* the book printed had been sent to Paris. He said that he was sure that Tesson would send the copies to the Sacred Congregation for the Propagation of Faith in Rome.[2] It is reported that Fr. Charles Dallet (1829-78) had rendered necessary help in preparing the annotations found in the book.[3]

Aaathi Chuvadi is prepared so as to help to the practice of Tamil reading easy for the children. It contains *nedungkanakku* (alphabets) in Tamil and also one *asai* to four *asai* words and the proverbs. The title page mentions that it was printed by the permission and order of the superiors in Pondicherry at Senmavirakkini Maatha church printing press in 1844.

The book begins with the expression *kadavul thunai* (May God Assist). It points out then the Tamil vowels, consonants, other Tamil letters, three grantha letters (ksha, ssha and sa), single-word list, two-words list and three-words list. There are two stories mentioned for the use of the children. The good manners that the children should follow and obey are listed and they are 16 in number. *Ozhuka Maalai* the poetry of Avvaiyar composed on morals had been printed. We find 101 Tamil proverbs listed followed by *Nalluranrickuriya sarithirangal* (history of good morals). The book goes on to teach Tamil mathematics to the children what they are expected to know–with the fractions and numerals and number names. *Paramaaratha Guru Kathai* as given by Beschi had been furnished and the publisher had made elegant stories from 1 to 8. *Thembaavani* poetry of Beschi had been included and we find the selected stanzas such as, 16, 96, 100, 102, 143, 146, 20, 24, 66, 67 and 72. Thiruvalluvar's *Kural* numbers 109, 208, 274, 298, and 396 had been printed. Three poems from *Naaladi Naanuru* had been given and the themes come from the chapters not-being angry, generosity, and examining friendship

Dupuis though printed *Aathi Chuvadi* and he also added *Paramaartha Guru Kathai Muthaliyavai* in a separate book and got it printed in 1844. This book has 91 pages. It contains *nedungkanakku*, proverbs, and the *Paramaartha Guru Kathai.*[4] It was helpful to children also for developing the reading skill since the fables of Paramaartha had been printed. *Paramaartha Guru Kathai* was reprinted in 1859 and 1862.

Printing Textbooks for Learning European Languages: Paramaartha Guru Kathai Lathinilum Thamzhilillum in 1863 and Sambaashanai Anusaaram in 1865

It is known that *Paramaartha Guru Kathai* of Beschi was translated into English by Benjamin Guy Babington in 1822. It was printed in London and popular among the British as a book of comics.[5] Dupuis printed in 1863 *Paramaartha Guru Kathai* in Latin and Tamil. It was chiefly meant for the use of the students in the seminary in Pondicherry. It was helpful for making translation and also reading and learning the language of Latin by Tamil students.[6] Thus Dupuis had printed textbooks for learning Tamil and Latin languages.

Louis Marie Mousset in his letter to Jean Tesson in Paris dated 10 November 1850 had recorded the importance and need for a French-Tamil book of conversation for the use of the French missionaries.[7] Therefore L.S. Dupuis had taken steps to print a book titled *Sambaashanai Anusaaram* to learn French and Tamil. This book is written in bilingual and it was printed in 1865. It is a book on face to face conversation and dialogue.[8] The author was Benjamin Hyppolyte Goust (1796-1863) born at Invendee in 1796 in France, entered the MEP society on 26 October 1829, left for India on 21 January 1830 and reached Pondicherry. He stayed for a few months in the French colony in 1830 and later did missionary work at Salem in 1832 and at Coimbatore in 1836, and he was at Dharmapuri in 1837, at Thanjavur in 1840-43, at Vadugarpatti 1845-46, at Paalyam in 1857-58 and died at Viragalur on 13 September 1863 and buried at Purathakudi. L.S. Dupuis revised his work and expanded it. Hence the title page of the book mentions that it was done by MEP priests (in plural). Dupuis in his preface wrote the related details.

He said that some fifteen years ago this work first drafted by Fr. Goust and it had seen the light of printing in 1865. He mentioned that the writings in the notebooks were scattered during a storm. It was so badly soaked that it was almost impossible to read.[9] Hence Dupuis took the work and later at the request of some individuals he planned and designed to make it expand. Hence it is made use for the school children and the new book had been printed. This conversation manual or collection of ordinary words and sentences to facilitate the study of French language and Tamil was though available Dupuis forgot about it while preparing and working on the other large books. Finally at the request of a number of influential individuals, Dupuis took it up again the notebooks of Fr. Goust and he planned to make it a substantive one for the use in schools. This necessitated some modifications, which had been done and the whole book has the new appearance.[10] The manual of conversation printed contains 94 pages of

French-Tamil thematic glossary and 91 pages of parallel dialogue. Words of Christian origin in Tamil are found along with equivalent French terms in Tamil.

The first part of the book is like a dictionary giving meanings for French words in Tamil.[11] The subject matter deals with God, religion, the church, divine worship, virtues, good-men, paradise, vices, bad-men, hell, religion, the world, the sky, the atmosphere, the earth, 8 directions, 5 elements, metals, precious stones, the mankind, the soul, the qualities of the soul, the human body, the 5 senses, the defects in the body, maladies medicine and remedy, human relations, dignity, art, army, caste, dress and habits, house hold articles, kitchen, instruments, death, animals, reptiles, birds, insects, fish, tree, plants, grain, time , calculation, numbers, accounts money, measurements and dimensions, adjectives, pronouns, verb, participle, adverbs, prepositions, conjunctions and interjections.

The second part of the book contains sentences in French and the meanings are given in Tamil for easy conversation.[12] It deals with conversations in sentences on education and studies, domestic servant, bazaar-news, washer-men, barber, horsemen, manner indicating time, voyages, hunting, feasts, maladies, rain, agriculture, trade and commerce and duties of the man. An index is found at the end.[13] It is interesting to note in the book that at first under various headings the meanings of the words appear in French. Then the Tamil meanings have been given. It helps to remember the words and the meanings. There are additional words which have been also included for easy conversation. We find sentences used in conversation for the use of the students. It enables for learning French, and those who already knew French to learn Tamil. Thus the book helps for learning both the French and Tamil languages.

Printing Grammar Books for Learning Tamil, French and Latin, 1845-1863

Dupuis printed *Kodunthamizh*: *Grammatica Latino Tamulica* of Beschi in 1843. He printed a book titled *Piranchu Ilakkana Noolsurukkam* (elements of French grammar in Tamil) in 1845, *Lathin Ilakkana Noorsurukkam* (elements of Latin grammar) in 1845, *Ilakkana Surukkam* (elements of Tamil grammar in Tamil, 1845 and 1860), *Ilakkana Noolaathaaram* (the basics of Tamil grammar in Tamil, 1849 and 1865) for the use of schools/seminary in Pondicherry.[14]

Printing Dictionaries for Easy Learning of Tamil, French and Latin, 1846-1870

Louis Savinien Dupuis and Louis Marie Mousset compiled Latin-French-Tamil dictionary for the use of the students of the seminary and printed it in 1846. They prepared a French-Tamil vocabulary and printed it in 1850. They compiled Tamil-French dictionary of the first volume and printed it in 1855. They prepared the Tamil-French dictionary of the second volume and got it printed in 1862. They compiled French-Tamil dictionary and printed it in 1866. Dupuis reprinted French-Tamil dictionary in 1870. *Chaturgaraathi* of Beschi was printed in 1872 and it is found mention in the press list publications by L.S. Dupuis. Thus great service to the students and the public helping to learn languages had been rendered.[15]

There are other books printed that had been found mention in the press list of publications by Dupuis. It includes *Piranchu Thamizh Yezhithaana Paadangal* (Easy Lessons in French and Tamil) in 1863 and *Piranchu Thamizh Vinaa Vidai* (Question and Answer in French and Tamil) mentioned in 1869.

Printing C.J. Beschi's Epic Thembaavani in 1851, 1852 and 1853

Dupuis wanted to publish the best Christian Tamil literary works. As he was searching for, he felt that the works of Beschi would be highly useful to the people and society. He also realized that Christian knowledge of Tamil literature should be imparted to the natives in order to reach out to the Hindus so that the Catholic faith would spread. Thembaavani he chose for publication among the works. As it contained 3615 tetrastichs in 36 *padalams* (cantos) he decided to print and publish it into three *kaandams* (volumes). He successfully executed the work. At first he obtained the palm-leaf and paper manuscripts of Thembaavani. He took the assistance of *Pulavar* (poet) Arokia Samy Pillai the son of Dhairiyam Pillai, a Catholic for preparing the *pathavurai* (meaning in prose for poem) for easy understanding for those who do not know poetry. Dupuis said that the *Kural* of Thiruvalluvar had various prose texts for the poetry and so he thought it would be useful to have the prose text for this epic and so it is not a wonder. On receipt of the *pathavurai* of the first four *padalams* of Thembaavani the first volume was printed by Dupuis in 1851.[16] The title page mentions that on receipt of the order issued from Rome, Clement Bonnand the bishop of Pondicherry permitted the printing of the *kaapiyam* (epic).

Dupuis in his preface mentioned that there are many cooked-up stories in the various epics. But Thembaavani in fact contains evidences from the Holy Scripture. He said that Beschi in his Thembaavani had praised the true God who gave his only begotten son for the salvation of mankind. Beschi had mentioned that he chose the theme (in the seventh *padalam* and *viruththam* no. 20) of Marie de Agreda (1602-1665) the Spanish Franciscan nun and mystic who had been instructed and explained the virtues through apparition of the Mother of God which is mentioned in the mystical city of God. Beschi wrote this great work in AD 1729 and it had spread out all over the country. There were many mistakes that occurred in copies of the manuscripts made out of the original by the scribes. Many were anxious to know when the treatise would be printed. No one came forward to print owing to huge financial expenditure involved. A copy of Beschi's original manuscript was available with Mr. Walter Elliot and so he approached him and received it on loan for printing use.[17] Dupuis noticed that there were many points to prove that it was Beschi's own handwriting and style for the lines scribbled too. There were no dots over the consonants and no difference between *Yagara* and *Ogaara* letter *kombu.* Hence as per the then printing system adopted and followed, Dupuis said that he had introduced these changes and printed the book.

Dupuis said that in Tamil poetry the *muchchiradi* 4 was called *Vanji Viruththam*. The *Naarchchiradi* 4 was called *Kali Viruththam*. The *Aynji-chiradi* 4 was *Nedil Viruththam*. The *Aruchir*, *Yezhuchir* and *Yenchiradi* 4 had been called *Asiriya Viruththam*. The printed book had *mugavurai*, the details of the *viruththams* in the work, the list of *sandhams*, *paavurai pathigam* and *paayiram*. The errata have been found at the end of the book at page 486.

The first *kaandam* of Thembaavani book contained 12 *padalams,* such as *Naatu padalam*, *Nagara padalam*, *Vazhlan saniththa padalam*, *Paalamaatchi padalam*, *Thirumana padalam*, *Yeeraramporuththu padalam*, *Ayyanthottru padalam*, *Ayyamneengu padalam*, *Magilvinai padalam*, *Magavarul padalam*, *Kaatchi padalam* and *Maganerntha padalam*.

Dupuis printed the second *kaandam* of Thembaavani in 1852. It contained the next 12 *padalams* such as *Baithira neengu padalam*, *Izhlavan maatchi padalam*, *Sosuvan vettri padalam*, *Sothaiyon vettri padalam*, *Kaasai ser padalam*, *Seenaayi maamalai padalam*, *Paalai pugu padalam*, *Siththirakuda padalam*, *Neer varamadaintha padalam*, *Yesiththu ser padalam*, *Kunungu mandira padalam* and *Sogu thorvai padalam.*[18]

The third *kaandam* of Thembaavani contained the last 12 *padalams* and it began with *Kuzhavigal vathai padalam*, *Karunaiyan maatchi padalam*, *Gnaapaga padalam*, *Vaaman aatchi padalam*, *Vethakezhumai padalam*, *Meetchi padalam*, *Printha magavai kaan padalam*, *Progheetha padalam*, *Pini thottru padalam*, *Thuthurai padalam*, *Uthaana padalam* and *Mudisoottu padalam*. It was printed by Dupuis in 1853. He in his preface mentioned that he was glad to note that by the grace of God the sweet Thembaavani had been printed as desired by the learned men and the others. The poetry textbook is published as found in the original manuscript of Beschi.[19] He said that he had given the various *sandhams* that are found in the end of the book. The contents would help people with a desire to read again and again. The printed book ends at page 532. Thembaavani was reprinted in Pondicherry in 1866. We find books I and II besides part V with a commentary and the printed book is incomplete breaking at page 160.[20]

Printing Tamil Poetry: Thembaa Maalai (1851), Thiruppaavani (1856), Tiruvalluvar Seytha Kurat Sanghiragam (1860) and Vedhapuri Andhaathi (1863)

Dupuis also wrote an essay in French on Tembaavani, the epic of Beschi and made it known to the westerners. It was published in 1851.[21] He explained in detail on Tamil poetry, the contribution of Fr. Beschi and all the 36 cantos of Thembaavani outlining the significance of each canto. Dupuis published a book titled *Thembaa Maalai* containing the poems of Beschi in 1851. Beschi's Thembaavnai contained songs and so Dupuis selected them and compiled under the headings God is with us, God was born as a man, in praise of the Blessed Virgin Mary and printed the book *Thembaa Maalai*. These titles are printed and given as contents at the printed book.[22]

Thiruppaavani a book was published by Dupuis in 1856 and it had 46 pages.[23] He included hymns to the Virgin Mary forming the last section of Thembaavani and Beschi's poems *Adaikala Maalai*, *Karunagara Kadal*, *Annai Azhungal Andhaathi* and *Thirukaavalur Kalambagam*. Dupuis also printed the *Karunaagara Kadal* a poetic work of Beschi separately. He also printed separately Beschi's *Thirukaavalur Adaikala Naayagimel Venkalippaa* as found in the press list of publications.

Kural of Thiruvalluvar was popular among the Tamils. Since it was taught through palm-leaf manuscript, Dupuis decided to print the poem of Tiruvalluvar and successfully executed under the title *Thiruvalluvar Seytha Kurat Sanghiragam*. The title page runs thus: *Tiruvalluvar seytha kural sangragham, Moolamum Uraiyum: Iguthu viseshamaay pallikudangalukku upayogamaha sila vidwangalaal niyameither paduthi athi sreshatarudaya uththarathin padiye 1860 varusham Puthuvai senmavirakkini maatha koilai serntha achchu koodathil pathipaikkapattahu.*[24] We find the expression *Anaathi nama* in the book. This book was printed by Dupuis to explain on morals and giving moral instruction to the children. *Kurat sangiraham* is an abridgement of *Arathupaal* of the *Kural* with commentary for the use of Catholic schools and the book had 50 pages.

Vedhapuri Andhaathi a Catholic devotional poem was composed by Thirukudanthai S. Duraisamy Mudaliar. Arumugam Pillai and B. Vethnaagayam Pillai and Arokkiyam Pillai had met the cost of printing in Pondicherry. L.S. Dupuis had printed it at the Catholic printing press in

Pondicherry in 1863. It had 13 pages. We find that *Vedhapuri Andhaathi* is also mentioned in the press list of publication by Dupuis. It was reprinted in 1868.[25]

Printing Books on Mathematics in Tamil: Vaalar Kanidham (1853), Siruvar Yen Chuvadi (1863), Vaalar Kanidha Noolaathaaram (1870)

Vaalar Kanidham was an elementary arithmetic book printed in 1853 and it had 196 pages. It was *(L'arithmetique tamoul* as mentioned in French) authored by Louis Marie Mousset. L.S. Dupuis mentions vide his letter dated 7 September 1853 to Tesson in Paris that *Vaalar Kanidham* was printed by him at the printing press. He had printed this textbook for the use of the Tamil children and it was on mathematics that explains addition, subtraction, multiplication and division along with the multiplication tables.[26]

Sirvar Yen Chuvadi (*table de multiplication* as mentioned in French) was an arithmetic book for the children printed in 1863 and it had 36 pages. It is found in the press list of publications of Dupuis in 1864.[27] The *Yen Chuvadi* was a book of reckoning used in Hindu schools and it contained various kinds of information viz., the revolving of the 60 years, the movement of the days of the month, the 27 particular ways of denoting the moon's age or passing, the 12 signs of the zodiac, the 9 planets and 59 countries. *Vaalar Kanidha Noolaathaaram* (*elements d' arithmetique* as mentioned in French) is also found mention in the press list of publications by Dupuis in 1870.[28] These books printed by L.S. Dupuis was contrary to the *thinnai* school pedagogy where mathematics was taught with privileged calculations, riddles and palindromes abound in early arithmetic works and in lexicons, suggesting that computational techniques laid at the heart of its goal.

Printing Books on Geography in Tamil: Bhumi Saasthira Padangal (1861), Bhumi Saasthira Surukkam (1862), Anda Vizhlakka Saathirathin Sangsebangkoodiya Bhumi Sathira Noolaatharam (1864)

The study of geography in Tamil was promoted through books printed by the English in Madras. Rhenius the Protestant missionary published his book *Bhumi Saasthiram* in Madras in 1832. Again a book titled *Bhumi Saasthira Surukkam* was published from Nagercoil in 1849 and in Madras in 1856.[29] L.S. Dupuis therefore desired to encourage the study of geography at Pondicherry in French India. There is a mention of the *Bhumi Saasthira Padangal* the geographical atlas (in the printed book of *Bhumi Saasthira Surukkam* in 1862) which had been helpful to locate the places in the world prepared and printed in Pondicherry in 1861. Dupuis states that there are many atlases in French language. We have also printed an atlas in Tamil in lithography press in Pondicherry. There were also many copies of the book still available unsold at the Catholic press. Thus an atlas had been printed for the use of students.[30] This atlas containing geographical maps prepared and printed in Pondicherry was sent to Paris and it had attracted the attention of Jean Tesson in Paris. He mentioned to L.S. Dupuis in October 1863 about the geographical maps where the names of countries have been substituted by numbers in France. Hence Dupuis asked Tesson if possible, please arrange to send the same so that it would be of great help and use to him in the near future.[31]

Bhumi Saasthira Surukkam (*elements de geographie en tamoule*) was authored and printed by L.S. Dupuis in 1862. The title page of *Bhumi Sasthira Surukkam* mentions that it was composed by one of the apostolic priests of the foreign mission and printed with the permission of the superiors in 1863 at the *senamaviraakini maatha* church printing press. The book contains main tenets from three sastras in Tamil like Anda *vizhlakka sarithiram*, (the cosmography) *vedha matha vizhlakkam*, (the precise of religious sects) *kaala vizhlakkam* (the chronology). While tracing the authors of three books we find Louis-Noel de Bourzés the Jesuit worked in the Madurai mission from 1710 to 1721 became the Jesuit superior of mission in Madurai and served for three years, had come to Pondicherry in 1714, had written these books in Tamil such as *Ulaga Pramaana Sasthiram* a tract on the dimensions of the world in 1718 (geography)[32] and *Anda Pinda Viyakkiyanam* (macrocosm and microcosm) on physical science.[33] There are cross-references to each of these works completed in Tamil by him and the information had also been corroborated by other Jesuit letters and correspondence referring to Louis-Noel de Bourzés.[34] Dupuis had used them and he wrote in detail the book of *Bhumi Saasthira Surukkam*.

The preface mentions that the wonders in many countries and many cities have seen and observed after visits through travel of long distance by people by spending a lot of money without being afraid of danger and suffering. It may not be possible for any single individual to go around and see the whole world. Hence the geographers began to collect the details and compiled the data and wrote on the books of geography. It is stated that the publisher thought that such a book would be also useful for the people in this Tamil country and so examined the books of the experts. Hence in this book the author had aimed to touch upon five main topics such as cosmography, geography, history, the precise ideas of the religions and sects and the chronology.

At first the book deals with the sun and the stars. Next the author deals with continents, countries, islands, rivers and the landscape. Third he deals with the character and the living conditions of the people. Fourth the role of religion played in all these countries may be an important factor for the reason of development and so it is touched upon. Fifthly the chronology adopted by people in various lands had been important and so an event happened around the globe has to be made known through a common system of chronology and so the author had aimed to cover the topic.

The author states that it is a fact that people in this Tamil land did not know about these five aspects. There are also many stories being used by the Hindus. These stories are well decorated and old too. Those mentioned in the present book are not such stories. These are given by the authorities who dealt with the subject. If you see the book of *Kanthapuranam* you would find seven seas and four *yugams* which are cooked-up stories. The great years as told by the people of the Tamil land are not clearly known. These years and accounts are not precise and exact. Hence what happened in the earlier periods had been unknown. Hence calculations so far made have been mere speculations with mention of 200 or 330 years old 2000 or 3000 years. The *Salivahana* years have been adopted to calculate the years. This system and method is not followed anywhere in the other parts of the world. The author had also examined the system of calendars followed by people all over the globe. Since the creation of the world till the advent of Jesus Christ has been made into one system and after the coming of Jesus and till now has been the second way of calculating the years. As this calendar system is universally followed the author had tried to follow and introduce the same in this book. Hence the author earnestly believed that this book would help and interesting to acquire the truth and knowledge. The book has a total of 576 pages. It has six chapters. 1. Europe 2. Asia 3. Africa 4. America 5. South America 6. Oceania. There is a chapter of conclusion and a page of contents. The errata of five words with pages and mistakes and the corrections to be made had also been given.[35]

Anda Vizhlakka Sathirathin Sangsebangkoodiya Bhumi Sasthira Noolaatharm, a bilingual book on geography was printed by L.S. Dupuis in 1864. It was authored by Louis Marie Mousset and it is mentioned in missionary records as '*Elements de la geographie en francias et en tamoul, avec un précis de cosmographe*'. The title page of the book runs thus: *Iguthu anniya desathu bhodhagar sabhaiyilulla apostolica gurukalil oruva-raar seythu puthuvaiyil yeluntharuli irrukkum mahaa ganam porundhiya aandavaraagiya susai isidore Godelle yennum naamatheyankondu irukkira thermopiles mettraniyaaravargal anumathiyil romapuriinninru vantha uththarathin padiye 1864 varusham puthuvaiyir senmavirakkini maatha koilai serntha achchu koodathir pathipikka patathu.*[36]

The preface in bilingual states that there is no doubt that among all sciences, the earth science/geography is one of the useful sciences. Explaining the cosmos is therefore natural. The Hindus who did not know were therefore subjected to false beliefs. This led them to inferior status. As the publisher wished to make popular this earth science they had published previously in 1863 a book completely written in Tamil. The book had dealt with the related subjects like *Anda Vizhlakkam* explaining the cosmos, *sarithiram* the history and *vetha nool* the religious texts *and kaala vilakakam* with the explanation of time. Thus the book had contained all these aspects. In this book of *sankshebam* the author had presented the history of the nations and their religious texts. The publisher had suggested also that those who were interested to know more they may consult the earlier book published titled *Bhumi Saasthira Surukkam*.

Printing Books on Tamil Language: Siruvar Chuvadi (1863), Siruvar Kalvi Puthaiyal (1864)

Siruvar Chuvadi a Tamil spelling book with easy reading lesson from poetess Avvaiyar and others was printed in 1863. It had 48 pages.[37] It is found mention in the press list of 1863. *Siruvar Kalvi Puthaiyal* is a collection of verses from standard Tamil poets for use in elementary schools. It was printed in 1864 and had 169 pages.[38] It is found mention in the press list of 1864. These books are useful to children for the study of Tamil language.

Sending Printed Books to France

L.S. Dupuis was sending printed books to France in order to make publicity. In his letter dated 9 August 1862 Dupuis mentioned that he was sending copies of the dictionaries and other printed books to Jean Tesson in Paris and further added that the preface in the second book should be retained, while the rest could be published in 'Le Monde' the newspaper. He also stated Fr. Denis Jean Alphonse Deleage (1823-1866) the procurator of Pondicherry vicariate had sent a parcel and amidst the books, he had kept a letter addressed to the President of the Royal Asiatic Society in Paris so that he may do the needful for the spread of the knowledge of the printed books in France among the scholars interested in oriental studies.[39]

The Marketing Strategy and the Sale of Printed Books in the Overseas and Local

Dupuis in his letter of 18 October 1844 to Jean Tesson in Paris mentioned that during that year the printing press had brought in enough money, and the books were sold and appreciated and people purchased with eagerness had made him feel happy. He noted that it was a fact that these books were moderately priced. However, he would not be able to meet all the cost and expenditure. He said to please tell Fr. Jean Felix Onesime Luquet (1810-1858) that he had found people at last to bind thick prayer books and other books and their work was very satisfying, which in fact was very beautifully done in this part of the country and thus he got many books bound in leather.[40] The sale of the printed books had been mentioned by Dupuis in 1858 wherein he stated that in spite of the great drought of the year and the instability of the government, books printed at the Catholic press were being sold well. Dupuis said that it was true that when good seeds were being sowed in tears and pain, it would be harvested in great joy.[41]

Some of the printed books like French-Tamil dictionaries and Tamil-French dictionaries had attracted the sales in the overseas. The French government had taken much interest in the diffusion.[42] Dupuis printed a catalogue of the books printed which reveals a comprehensive list with titles, authors and prices and brief description of the books to target audience.[43] Enclosing such a catalogue of recent works published by the Catholic press Dupuis in his letter to the Minister of Marine in Paris wrote in 1863 and he suggested that the books printed in Pondicherry would be equally useful for European officers living in India and France. The books would be also useful for the immigrants and indentured labourers living in French overseas plantations and colonies where the promotion of the knowledge of Catholicism was an undeniable good.[44] In order to let the Government in France to decide if the products of the printing press, of which he was enclosing a catalogue, could be of use in learning Tamil in the various French colonies around the world where a large population that spoke Tamil language could render it useful to government officials; whether these could also for Tamil classes offered in Paris and paid for by the government, and most of all, whether these could be greatly useful in teaching and inculcating morals to the large number of immigrants who work in the French colonies, nevertheless if the French Minister for Marine judged that the good this printing press produced derives some encouragement, it would be welcome with gratitude and could contribute even more to the general good.

The French governor of Guiana ordered a shipment of bilingual Tamil-French books to be possibly given as end–of–year prizes to the children of the Tamil speaking indentured labourers attending plantation schools there in 1863. Later in 1865 a single shipment reached French Guiana to become among the first collections of bilingual books to be traded across far-flung peripheries of the French empire. Heeding Dupuis request that the book catalogue be forwarded to the French Governor of Reunion, Martinique, Guadeloupe and Cayenne overseeing Tamil indentured labourers the governor of French India wrote to the Minister of the Navy and Colonies in Paris about the Catholic printing press on Dupuis' behalf. The Governor of Pondicherry wrote at that time that his attention focused especially on the Tamil-French dictionary and grammar that was published. Important works long in the making were due to the science and the irrepressible zeal of Fr. Dupuis and Fr. Mousset of the MEP mission. After examining these works, he asked the superior of the Pondicherry mission if the colonies with Tamil-speaking immigrants have been informed of the resources that were being offered by such an institution, as much as for easing relations between owners and workers as much as to guarantee the functioning of courts and tribunals. Since no positive response was given to me concerning this request, he had asked to be given an update about this situation and the works of the printing press, as well as the book catalogue that could be given either to other colonies of Reunion, Martinique, Guadeloupe, Cayenne or to scientific institutions of France.[45] Of all the governors contacted, only French Guiana's governor responded affirmatively and ordered 76 volumes of books, including dictionaries, grammars, workbooks, catechism, bible and copies of fables written or translated into Tamil from French or Latin.[46]

There are individuals like Karl Graul the Protestant missionary who had visited Tamil country and purchased the books printed in Pondicherry and taken them to Leipzig in Germany in 1856. The list includes five books mentioned by him.[47]

1. *Vetha Vizhlakkam*, Pondicherry, 1842.
2. *Pethaga Maruthal*, Pondicherry, 1842.
3. *Aathi Chuvadi*, *Paramartha Guru Kathai Muthaliyavai*, Pondicherry, 1844.
3. *Lathin Thamizh Piranchu Agaraathi: Dictionarium-Latino-Gallico-Tamulicum*, Pondicherry, 1846.
4. *Lutherinathiyalbu* (the Quality of the Lutherans). Pondicherry 1847.

Works of C. J. Beschi published by Louis Savinien Dupuis in Pondicherry in 1842, 1844 and 1847 had been later reprinted and it is very important to note.[48]

The Regulations Issued for Printing by the French Government in Pondicherry, 1852-1872

As early as in 1810 Pondicherry began to witness a new intellectual culture through the birth of a public library. On 5 February 1810 a decree was passed concerning printing by the Government and also maintaining a library and the observance of rules for reading the books in the library.[49] On 22 March 1852 the French Governor passed a decree regarding the exercise of the profession of printing in Pondicherry and possession of printing equipments used in small scale and the sale of printing machines and its utensils.[50] On 30 September 1869 he fixed the tariffs of local service and the press works executed by authorized agencies.[51] On 10 September 1870 a decree was passed regarding the profession of printing books and the supply of books to the library in Pondicherry.[52] On 18 November 1872 the President of the Republic of France had issued a decree for the organization of the printing services in Pondicherry and other French colonies.[53] Thus the French government had regulated the activities of printing and the missionaries had to also follow the instructions and rules.

Fr. Dupuis wanted someone else to take charge of the printing press as early as in April 1855 since he alone was struggling to do all the works related in printing. Bishop Bonnand found his regret to Paris and he wrote that Fr. Dupuis had charged him the other day that he was hardly able to find time since he was alone employed in printing works. Hence the bishop said that it was high time and necessary to have another missionary who would be specialized in printing.[54] We find that Dupuis was composing new books and looking after the printing press for fifteen years and he had ruined his health. Bonnand considered the printing press to be a very important work. Hence the Bishop requested in June 1855 for a suitable missionary to take the place of Fr. Dupuis and wrote to the MEP authorities in Paris.[55] After a long time, Jules François Bergez (1835-1891) the missionary returned from Kumbakonam in 1871 and he was appointed to help Dupuis at the printing press. However, Dupuis had mentioned in his letter dated 16 April 1873 that he was still busily engaged in printing works at the press.[56] Bergez had succeeded Fr Dupuis at the press after his death on 4 June 1874.

The College Printing Press in Pondicherry and Printing Stories and Morals: Kathaa Manjari Neethisaara Vaakiyam Theriyala-anavaiyum (1864), Panchathanthira Kathai (1865)

Kathaa Manjari of Villipakkam Thandavaraya Mudaliar was printed in Madras in 1820 and reprinted in 1826. The French government in Pondicherry established the colonial college and the college printing press in Pondicherry. It desired to publish textbooks in Tamil for the use of children. Therefore it printed the book titled *Kathaa Manjari* (Anthology of Stories) of Thandavaraya Mudaliar with certain revisions in 1864.

Neethisaara Vaakiyam Theriyalaanavaiyum of Kottamangalam Ramasami Pillai was printed in Madras in 1844. The French Government also desired to publish it and so printed the book with certain revisions in 1864. The book had 176 pages.[57] Records make mention of *Kathaa Manjari* (*recueil de fables*) and *Neethisaara Vakkaiyam* (*livre de sentences ou proverbs en poesie*) printed were chiefly for the use of children in the school. The preface of the book mentions that children like the fables and stories. Intelligence and tactics have been taught to them through this method. It could be events that happened once in the past, others could be speech or spoken language by animals and yet others could be fabricated stories, cooked-up ones that could be detected by the intelligent persons only. *Kathaa Manjari* the book printed had 82 short stories.

The second part of the book contains *Needhi Saaram* (the spirit of morality). This popular Hindu work in Tamil contained hundred verses and hundred precepts. Dupuis in his printed book explained ideas from Thirukural under the titles such as *deva vandhanam, kalvi, kezhvi, arivudamai, pagai, kopam, vanjani, soothu, theevinaiachcham, ubhagaaram, igai, iniyavaikooral, purangkooraamai, payanilasollamai, ukkamudamai, sombal, kilmai, kudipirappu, menmakkal, adakkmudamai, naduvunilamai, ozhukkam, poraiudamai, seynanari arithal, vaaymai* and *karppu*.

The French Government desired to publish the *Panchathanthira Kathai* printed earlier in Madras in 1826, and reprinted in 1847 and also again in 1852. *Panchathanthira Kathai* got printed at the college printing press (*Kalvi Saalai Achchukkudam*) in Pondicherry in 1865. The book has 143 pages and it was meant for the use of the children.[58] The Tamil poems of Savarrayalu Nayagar (1829-1911) in Pondicherry had been compiled by Solai Appaa Samy Mudaliar and the book was printed by A. Saligny, the manager of the Government press in Pondicherry in 1869.[59]

To conclude it may be said that L.S. Dupuis composed works for the use of school children on geography and science. He also wrote books for the use of the seminarians and printed. These books meant for the use of Tamil students added to the world of secular literature and his contribution in this direction is praiseworthy. Along with the efforts of education, the Catholic press also developed under his dynamic and sincere efforts. There were ten printing presses functioning in Pondicherry in 1874. They printed largely in Tamil and they brought out also printing in French, English, Telugu and Sanskrit languages. However, the Catholic press under Dupuis had mainly printed books in Tamil, besides some works in French and Latin.[60] The reprinting of the Jesuit Tamil literature of the seventeenth and eighteenth centuries had well begun and the printing press was very active.

The history of printing and publishing in Pondicherry like that of all human progress had been a record of the interplay between technological innovation and social change. Whilst each of these two streams of human activity promoted the other, with each in turn playing the leading role, the really crucial leaps ahead had always been made when the two converged to become an irresistible tide. Thus, the development of printing in the French colony had equally responded to the spread of literacy and to the social climate. Dupuis in the beginning had collected Catholic Tamil palm-leaf manuscripts and he simply printed the books. In the next stage we find that he did his best for editing and pruning the matter from the palm-leaf to printing in paper and binding the book. Further he reprinted the books again when went out of stock and required but in many books he had added his own new material such as introduction, keeping the preface of the original author separately besides having the publisher's note differently which earned a name and fame in the world of Tamil printing. Tamil epics like Chinthaamani, Silapathikaaram, Kambaraamaayanam and Bhaaratham had born many centuries ago before Thembaavani but did not see the light of printing. Hence the credit goes to L.S. Dupuis singularly for printing Thembaavani the epic. He was a man of many talents because he not only did the design and made arrangements to cast his own typefaces, but also fulfilled the functions of a publisher, an editor, the printer and bookseller.

Notes

1. Rojah Muthaiah Library, Chennai, *Veeramaamunivar Thiruvaaymalaruthu Aruliseytha Ayinthilakkana Thonnul Vizhlakkam, Moolamum Uraiyum*, edited by Vethagiri Mudaliar and subsidized by Maria Saveriya Pillai, Puthucherry, 1838; See also, Muttusami Pillai, *Brief Sketch of the Life and Writings of Father C. J. Beschi or Vira-Mamuni, Translated from the Original Tamil*, J.B..Pharoah, Madras, 1840, p. 21.
2. Archives de la Société des Missions Etrangères de Paris (hereafter AMEP), MSS *Correspondance Pondichéry-Paris, Lettres*, vol. 1000, see the letter of L.S. Dupuis dated 3 December 1844 to Jean Tesson in Paris.
3. Bibliothèque Asiatique des Missions Etrangères de Paris (hereafter BAMEP), TAM 4, *Aathi Chuvadi*, Pondicherry, 1844; See also, *Aathichuvadi, premieres lectures en tamoul, annotataions par le p. Ch. Dallet*, AMEP, 0627.6; British Library, London (hereafter BL), BL, 14172h.10, *Aathi Chuvadi* (A first Tamil reader for the use of Catholic schools), Pondicherry, 1844.
4. BAMEP, *Aathi Chuvadi and Paramaartha Guru Kathai Muthaliyavai*, Pondicherry, 1844, BL, 14172.h.58, *Aathi chuvadium paramaaartha Guru Kathaiyum*, Pondicherry, 1862; BL,14171.a.39, *Paramartha Guruvin kathai*, pp. 34, Pondicheryy, 1859. It has 34 pages. BL, 14172.h.58.3, Paramartha Guru Kathai in *Aathi Chuvadi*, 1862, pp. 45-89.
5. Benjamin Guy Babington, *Paramarta Gooroo Cadei* (translated into English), London, 1822.

6. BAMEP, *Paramaartha Guru Kathai Lathinilum Thamzhilillum*, Pondicherry, 1863.
7. AMEP, MSS *Correspondance Pondichéry-Paris, Lettres*, vol. 1001, see the letter of Louis Marie Mousset dated 10 November 1850 to Jean Tesson in Paris.
8. BAMEP, C 3172, *Sambashanai Anusaaram: Manuel de la Conversation ou Recueil de mots usuels et de phrases propres a faciliter l'etude du français et du tamoul*, Pondicherry, 1865. See also, BL, 14172h.15, *Sambashanai Anusaaram*, Pondicherry, 1865.
9. Ibid., p. 8.
10. Ibid., p. 1.
11. Ibid., pp. 1-94.
12. Ibid., pp. 95-181.
13. Ibid., pp. 182-4.
14. S. Jeyaseela Stephen, *From Anrique Anriquez to Louis Savinien Dupuis: The Tamil Grammar and Dictionary Quest*, Pondicherry, 2017, pp. 121-42. BL, 14172.h.6, *Ilakkana Surukkam* of Myilai Saveri Muthu Pillai was printed first in 1845. It got reprinted in 1860 and had 180 pages. *Ilakkana Noolaathaaram* was first printed in1849 was reprinted as second edition in 1865 and it had 79 pages.
15. Ibid., pp. 213-42. The Piranchu Thamizh Agaraathi of Dupuis and Mousset printed in Pondicherry is available at the Public Library in Toronto, Canada.
16. Madurai Province Jesuit Archives (hereafter MPJA), Shenbaganur, 221/624 *Thembaavani: Muthar Kaandam*, Pondicherry, 1851.
17. Ibid., pp. 5-7.
18. MPJA, 221/623, *Thembaavani: Rendaam Kaandam*, Pondicherry, 1852.
19. MPJA, 221/623, *Thembaavani: Moonraam Kaandam*, Pondicherry, 1853, pp 5-6.
20. BL, 14170.c.4, *Thembaavani*, Pondicherry, 1866.
21. BAMEP, H/DUPU1, *Notice sur la poesie tamoule le rev Beschi et le tembavani, par un member de la congregation des missions etrangères*, Pondicherry, 1851.
22. BAMEP, TA 88, *Thembaa Maalai*, Pondicherry, 1851, BL, 14170.6.24, Thembaa-malai, Pondicherry, 1865. It has (1) devotional poems from the Thembaavani with commentary (2) other hymns by Beschi separately published in the Thirupaavani. The book contains 244 pages.
23. BL, 141170.b.11, *Thiruppavani*, Pondicherry, 1856.
24. BAMEP, TA 219, *Thiruvalluvar Seytha Kurat Sanghiragam*, Pondicherry, 1860; BL, 14172.a.21, *Thiruvalluvar Seytha Kurat Sanghiragam*, Pondicherry, 1860.
25. MPJA, 221/ 701, *Vethapuri Andhaathi*, Pondicherry, 1863; BL, 14170.C.32, Thirukudandhai S. Duraisamy Mudaliar, *Vethapuri Andhaathi*, edited by Arogyam Pillai & M. Vedanayaka Pillai, Pondicherry, 1868.
26. BL, 14172.h.13, *Vaalar Kanitham*, Pondicherry, 1853. See also, AMEP, MSS *Correspondance Pondichéry-Paris, Lettres*, vol.1001, Letter of L.S. Dupuis dated 7 September 1853 to Tesson.
27. BAMEP, *Siruvar Yen Chuvadi*, Pondicherry, 1863.

28. BAMEP, *Vaalar Kanidha Noolaathaaram*, Pondicherry, 1870.
29. S. Jeyaseela Stephen, *A Meeting of the Minds: European and Tamil Encounters in Modern Sciences, 1507-1857*, Delhi, 2016, pp. 803-4.
30. BAMEP, *Bhumi Sasthira Surukkam*, Pondicherry, 1862, p. 6; BL, 14172.h.8, *Bhumi Sasthira Surukkam*, Pondicherry, 1863. It was a compendium of geography with information on history, theology and Christianity, for use in Catholic missionary schools. The book had 575 pages. See, BL.14172h.16, Elemens de geographie avec un précis de cosmographie (Tamil and French) *Bhumi Sasthira Noolaathaaram*, Pondicherry, 1864. It has 216 pages. See, BL, 14172.h.43, *Bhumi Sasthira Noolaathaaram*, Pondicherry, 1864. It contains the Tamil text of the book and has 368 pages. See, BL, 14172.h.43, *Bhumi Sasthira Shank-sebham*, Pondicherry, 1869. It is a compendium of Geography and has 64 pages.
31. AMEP, MSS *Correspondance Pondichéry-Paris, Lettres*, vol. 1003, see the letter of L. S. Dupuis dated 20 March 1864 to Jean Tesson.
32. British Library (hereafter BL), London, no. 14170 i.11, Gnanapragasanatha Swami, ed., *Ulaga Pramana Sasthiram*, Chennapatanam, 1874.
33. BL, London, no. 14170 i.11, Gnanapragasanatha Swami, ed., *Anda Pinda Viyakki-yaanam*, Chennapatanam, 1874.
34. *Lettres édifiantes et curieuses, écrites des missions étrangères par quelques missionaires de la Compagnie de Jésus* (hereafter *Lettres édifiantes et curieuses*), 34 vols., Paris, 1702-1777, (hereafter *Lettres édifiantes et curieuses*), vol. XIII, pp. 90-140; Archives Françaises de la Compagnie de Jésus (hereafter AFCJ), Vanves, Hauts-de-Seine, Fonds Brotier, vol. 83, fls.119-55v.
35. BAMEP, *Bhumi Saasthira Surukkam*, Pondicherry, 1862.
36. BAMEP, *Anda Vizhlakka Sathirathin Sangsebangkoodiya Bhumi Sathira Noolaatharam*, Pondicherry, 1864.
37. BAMEP, *Siruvar Chuvadi*, Pondicherry, 1863.
38. BL, 14172.h.19, *Siruvar Kalvi Puthayal*, Pondicherry, 1864.
39. AMEP, MSS *Correspondance Pondichéry-Paris, Lettres*, vol. 1003, see the letter of L.S. Dupuis dated 9 August 1862 to Jean Tesson in Paris.
40. AMEP, MSS *Correspondance Pondichéry-Paris, Lettres*, vol. 1000, see the letter of L.S. Dupuis dated 18 October 1844 to Jean Tesson.
41. AMEP, MSS *Correspondance Pondichéry-Paris, Lettres*, vol. 1002, see the letter of L.S. Dupuis dated 22 June 1858 to Jean Tesson.
42. Centre des Archives d'Outre-Mer (hereafter CAOM), Aix-en-Provence, France, see Inde 1831, *Rapport du Ministere de la Marine et des Colonies 26 Avril 1831*, Proposition de Souscrire a Exemplaires d'un Dictionnaire Francais-Malabar.
43. CAOM, Inde n.d, *Catalogue des livres de l'Imprimerie de la Maison des missions etrangeres a Pondichery, Circulaire addresse aux colonies et relative a une souscription a des ouvrages en langue tamoule edites par l'imprimerie de la mission Catholique en Inde, 1863-1865*.
44. CAOM, Inde 1863, Envoie du catalogue des ouvrages en langue tamoule edites par l'Imprimerie de la mission, see the letter from the Governor of Pondicherry dated 18 February 1863 to the Minister of the Marine and Colonies in Paris.

45. Ibid.
46. Sonia N. Das, *Linguistic Rivalries: Tamil Migrants and Anglo-French Conflicts*, Oxford, 2016, p. 106; see also, Sonia N. Das, 'Failed Legacies of Colonial Linguistics: Lessons from Tamil Books in French India and French Guiana', *Comparative Studies in Society and History*, vol. 59, Issue 4, October 2017, pp. 846-883.
47. Karl Graul, 'Notizen, Correspondenzen und Vermischtes. Die tamulische Bibliothek der evan. luth. Missionsanstalt zu Leipzig', *Zeitschrift der Deutschen Morgenländischen Gesellschaft*, H.VII, Leipzig, 1853, pp. 558-568.
48. BL, 14170.b.9.1, *Vetha Vizhlakkam*, Pondicherry, 1842; BL, 14170.b.9.(3), *Lutherithiniyalbu*, Pondicherry, first edition, 1842; BL, 14170.b.12 9(1). *Lutherithiniyalbu*, second edition, 1847; BL, 14170.b.9.(2), *Bedhga Maruthal*, Pondicherry 1842.
49. *Table Generale du Bulletin des Actes Administratifs des Etablissments Français de L'inde de 1867-1877*, Paris, 1881, (volume followed by page numbers) 80-354.
50. Ibid., 80-356.
51. Ibid., 69- 323-329.
52. Ibid., 80-356.
53. Ibid., 73-83.
54. AMEP, MSS *Correspondance Pondichéry-Paris, Lettres*, vol. 1001, p. 1782, see the letter of Bishop Bonnand written from Pondicherry dated 23 April 1855 to Jean Tesson in Paris.
55. AMEP, MSS *Correspondance Pondichéry-Paris, Lettres*, vol. 1001, pp. 1820-21, see the letter of Bishop Bonnand written from Kovilur dated 27 June 1855 to Jean Tesson in Paris.
56. S. Jeyaseela Stephen, *Louis Savinien Dupuis and His Circulars in French to the Priests and in Tamil to the Religious Nuns in Pondicherry Mission, 1860-1874*, Translated from Original French and Tamil with Notes, Pondicherry, 2017, pp. 74-75.
57. BAMEP, *Kathaa Manjari*, Pondicherry, 1864, MPJA, 221/176, *Kathaa Manjari Neethi saara Vakkiyam*, Pondicherry, 1864; see also, 221/177, *Kathaa Manjari Neethisaara Vakkiyam*, Accession no. 006331, Third edition, Pondicherry, 1888.
58. BL, 14170.k.9, *Panchathanthira Kathai*, Pondicherry, 1865.
59. Sole Appasamy Moudeliar, *Recueil de Chants Tamouls par Mr. Z. Savarayalou nayagar: Poete Laureat de L'Inde*, A. Saligny, Imprimieur du Gouvernement, Pondichery, 1869; See also, BL, 14172.cc.21, *Paadartirattu: Recueil de Chants Tamouls par Mr. Z. Savarayalou nayagar: Poete Laureat de L'Inde*, Reprint, Pondicherry, 1904-1906.
60. *Synode de Pondichéry et instruction de la S.C. de la Propagande sur la formation du Clerge Indigene*, Imprimerie des Missionaires Apostoliques de la Congregation des Missions-Etrangeres, Pondichéry 1845; *Constitutiones secundae synodi vicariatus orae Coromandelicae, Pudicherii habitae mense Januario Anni 1848*, Typographis Missionarium Apostolicorum Congregationis ad Exteros, Pudicherii, 1849; *Statuts du Vicariate Apostolique de Pondichéry concernant L'administration des Sacrements*, Imprimerie des Missionaires Apostoliques de la Congregation des Missions-Etrangeres, Pondichéry 1874.

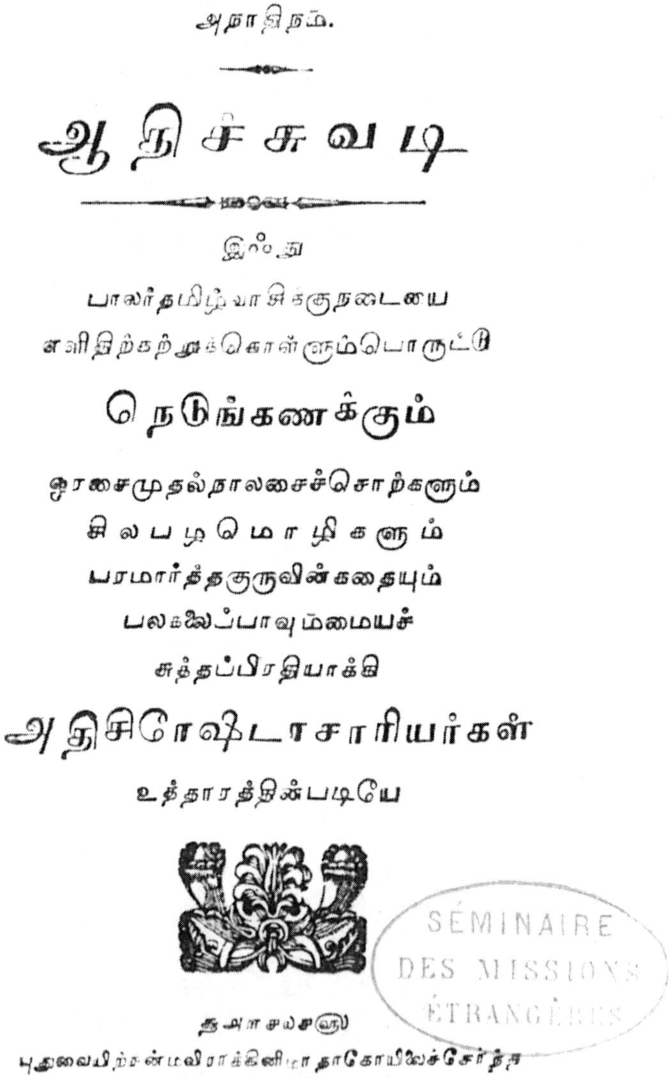

அநாதிநம்.

ஆதிச்சுவடி

இஃது

பாலர்தமிழ்வாசிக்குநடையை

எளிதிற்கற்றுக்கொள்ளும்பொருட்டு

நெடுங்கணக்கும்

ஓரசைமுதல்நாலசைச்சொற்களும்

சிலபழமொழிகளும்

பரமார்த்தகுருவின்கதையும்

பலகலைப்பாவும்மையச்

சுத்தப்பிரதியாக்கி

அதிசிரேஷ்டாசாரியர்கள்

உத்தாரத்தின்படியே

௲௮௱௪௰௪

புதுவையிற்சன்மவிராக்கினிமாதாகோயிலைச்சேர்ந்த

அச்சுக்கூடத்திற்பதிப்பிக்கப்பட்டது.

7.1. Aathi Chuvadi printed at the Mission Press in Pondicherry in 1844. (*Courtesy*: Bibliothèque Asiatique des Missions Etrangères de Paris, TAM 5).

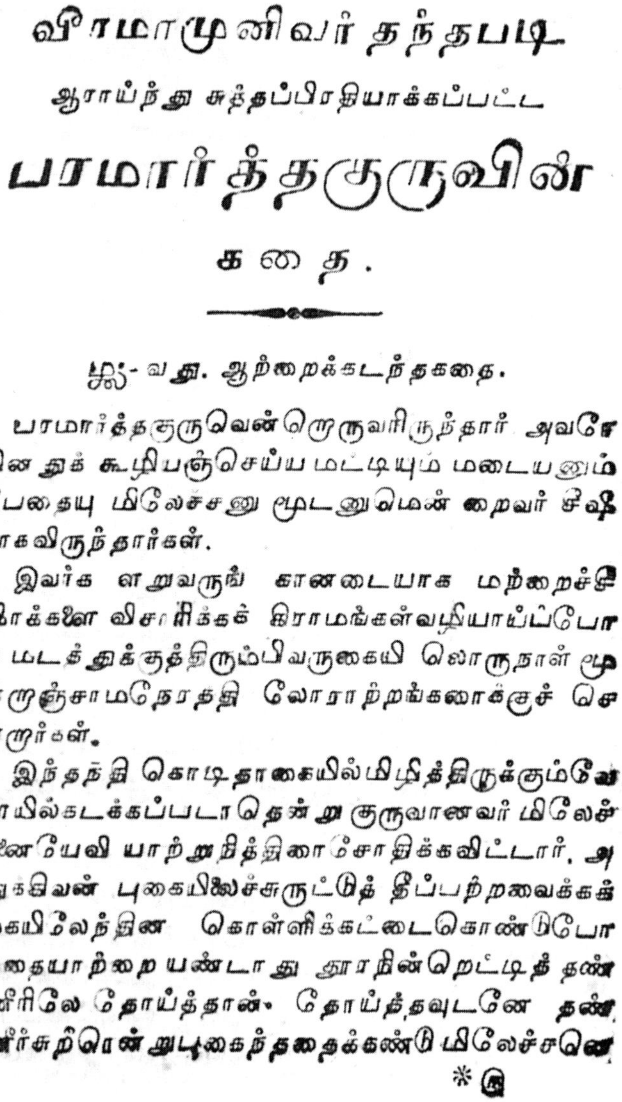

வீரமாமுனிவர் தந்தபடி
ஆராய்ந்து சுத்தப்பிரதியாக்கப்பட்ட
பரமார்த்தகுருவின்
கதை.

௧-வது. ஆற்றைக்கடந்தகதை.

பரமார்த்தகுருவென்றொருவரிருந்தார் அவரே
வினைத்துக் கூழிபஞ்செய்ய மட்டியும் மடையனும்
பேதையு மிலேச்சனு மூடனுமென் றைவர் சீஷ
ராகவிருந்தார்கள்.

இவர்க ளறுவருங் கானடையாக மற்றைச்சீ
ஷர்களை விசாரிக்கக் கிராமங்கள்வழியாய்ப்போ
ய் மடத்துக்குத்திரும்பிவருகையி லொருநாள் மூ
ன்றுஞ்சாமநேரத்தி லோராற்றங்கரைக்குச் செ
ன்றார்கள்.

இந்தத்தி கொடிதாகையில் மிழுந்திருக்கும்வே
ளையில்கடக்கப்படாதென் று குருவானவர் மிலேச்
சனையேவி யாற்றுநித்திரைமோசாதிக்கவிட்டார். அ
துக்கிவன் புகையிலைச்சுருட்டுத் தீப்பற்றவைக்கக்
கையிலேலந்தின கொள்ளிக்கட்டைகொண்டுபோ
யதையாற்றை யண்டாது தூரநின்றெட்டித் தண்
ணீரிலே தோய்த்தான். தோய்த்தவுடனே தண்
ணீர்சுறிறென் றுபுகைத்ததைக்கண்டு மிலேச்சனே
*கு

7.2. Paramaartha Guruvin Kathai Printed at the Mission Press in Pondicherry in 1844. (Courtesy*: Bibliothèque Asiatique des Missions Etrangères de Paris, TAM 4).*

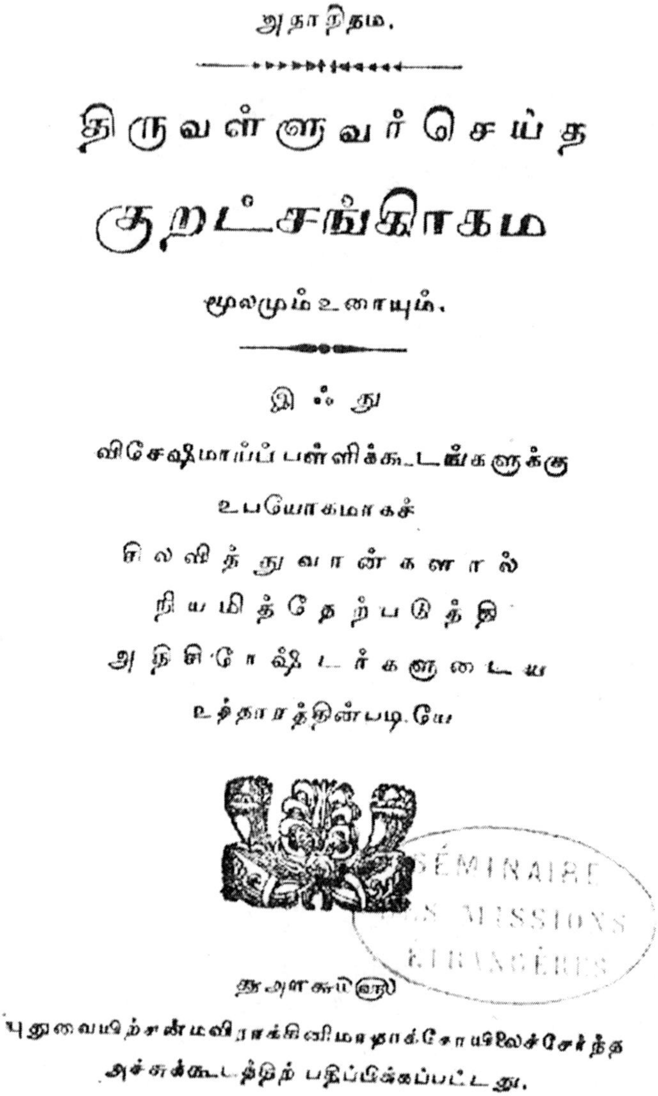

அதாநிதம.

திருவள்ளுவர் செய்த

குறட்சங்கிரகம

மூலமும் உரையும்.

இஃது

விசேஷமாய்ப் பள்ளிக்கூடங்களுக்கு

உபயோகமாகச்

சில வித்துவான்களால்

நியமித்தேற்படுத்தி

அதிசிரேஷ்டர்களுடைய

உத்தாரத்தின்படியே

௲அ௱௬௰

புதுவையிற்சென்மவிராக்கினிமாதாக்கோயிலைச்சேர்ந்த

அச்சுக்கூடத்திற் பதிப்பிக்கப்பட்டது.

7.3. Thiruvalluvar Seytha Kurat Sangiraham printed at the Mission Press in Pondicherry in 1860. (*Courtesy*: Bibliothèque Asiatique des Missions Etrangères de Paris, TAM 219).

பூமிசாஸ்திரச்

சுருக்கம்.

இதிலே

அண்டவிளக்கச் சரித்திரம், வேதபதவிளக்கம்,

காலவிளக்கம் என்னுஞ்சாஸ்திரங்களின்

பிரதானவுணர்ச்சிகளுங்கூட

அடங்கியிருக்கின்றன.

இஃது

அந்நியதேசத்துப்போதகர்சபையிலுள்ள

அப்போஸ்தொலிக்குக் குருக்களில்

ஒருவரால்செய்யப்பட்டு

அதிசிரேஷ்டர்களுடைய

உத்தாரத்தின்படியே

௲௮௱௬௰௩ம்-௵

புதுவையிற் சன்மவிராக்கினிமாதாக் கோயிலைச்சேர்ந்த

அச்சுக்கூடத்திற்பதிப்பிக்கப்பட்டது.

7.4. Bhumi Saasthira Surukkam printed at the Mission Press in Pondicherry in 1863 (*Courtesy*: Bibliothèque Asiatique des Missions Etrangères de Paris, TAM 3).

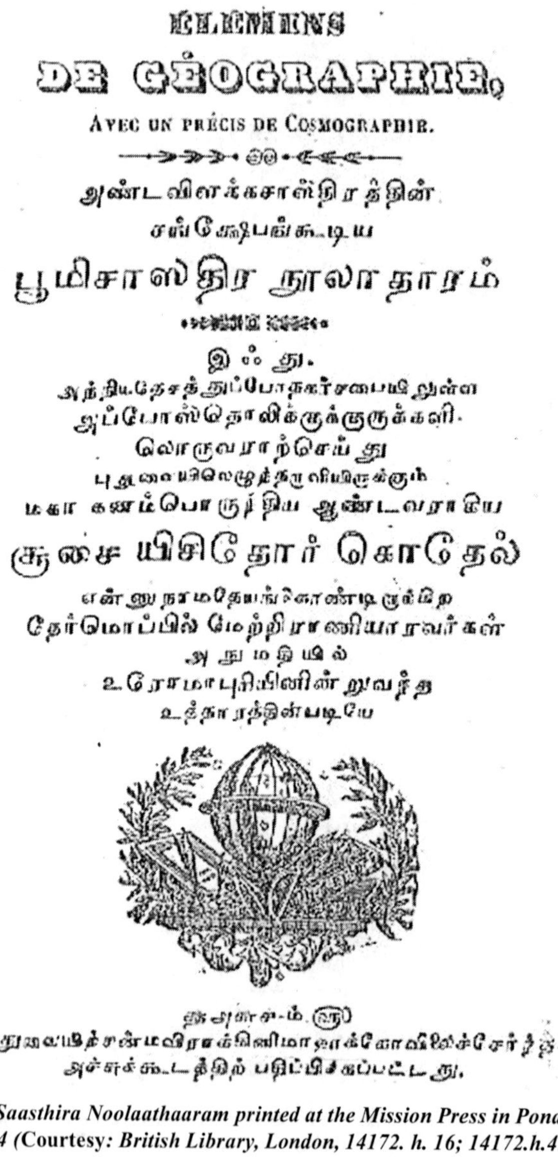

ELÉMENS
DE GÉOGRAPHIE,
AVEC UN PRÉCIS DE COSMOGRAPHIE.

அண்டவிளக்கசாஸ்திரத்தின்
சங்க்ஷேபங்கூடிய
பூமிசாஸ்திர நூலாதாரம்

இஃது.
அந்நியதேசத்துப்போதகர்சபையிலுள்ள
அப்போஸ்தொலிக்குருக்களி-
லொருவரார்செய்து
புதுவையிலெழுந்தருளியிருக்கும்
மகா கனம்பொருந்திய ஆண்டவராகிய
குலைசு யிசிதோர் கொதேல்
என்னு நாமதேயங்கொண்டிருக்கிற
தேர்மொப்பில் மேற்றிராணியாரவர்கள்
அநுமதியில்
உரோமாபுரியினின்றுவந்த
உத்தாரத்தின்படியே

௲அ௱௬௰ச-ம் ௵
புதுவையிற்சன்மவிரதக்கிளிமாதாக்கோவிலைச்சேர்ந்த
அச்சுக்கூடத்தில் பதிப்பிக்கப்பட்டது.

7.5 Bhumi Saasthira Noolaathaaram printed at the Mission Press in Pondicherry in 1864* (Courtesy*: British Library, London, 14172. h. 16; 14172.h.43).

கடவுள் துணை.

கதாமஞ்சரியும்

நீதிசாரவாக்கியங்களில்

தெரியலானவையுமாவன.

இஃது

விசேஷமாய்ப்பள்ளிக்கூடங்களின்

உபயோகமாகச்

சுத்தப் பிரதி யாக்கிப்

பெரியோருத்தாரத்தின்படியே

௲அ௬௪ ௵

புதுவையிற்கல்விசாலையச்சுக்கூடத்திற்

பதிப்பிக்கப்பட்டது.

7.6. *Kathaa Manjariyum Neethisaaravakkiyangalil Theriyalaavayumaavana printed at the College Printing Press in Pondicherry in 1864.* (Courtesy*: Madurai Province Jesuit Archives, Shenbaganur, 221/126).*

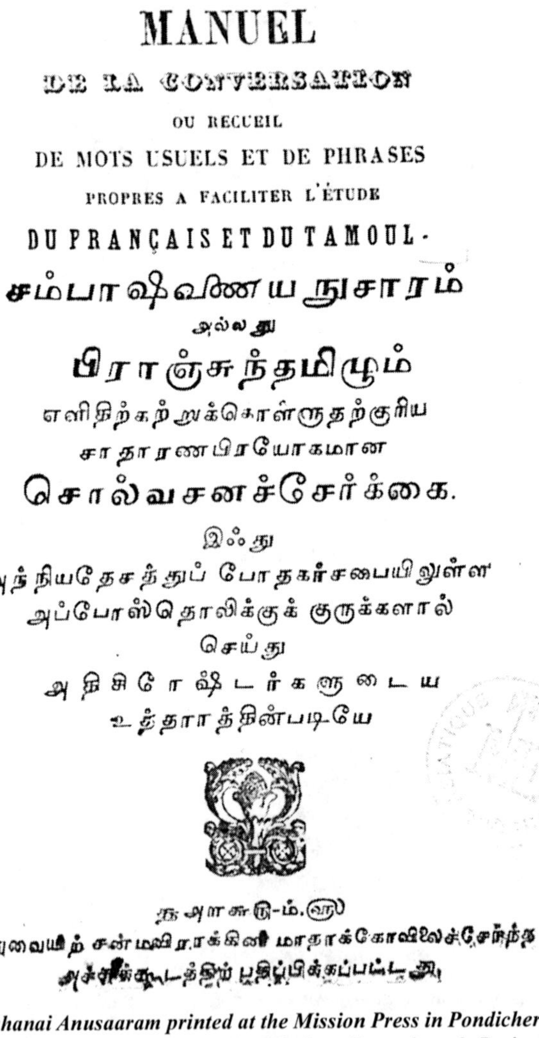

MANUEL
DE LA CONVERSATION
OU RECUEIL
DE MOTS USUELS ET DE PHRASES
PROPRES A FACILITER L'ÉTUDE
DU FRANÇAIS ET DU TAMOUL.
சம்பாஷணையநுசாரம்
அல்லது
பிராஞ்சுந்தமிழும்
எளிதிற்கற்றுக்கொள்ளுதற்குரிய
சாதாரணபிரயோகமான
சொல்வசனச்சேர்க்கை.
இஃது
அந்நியதேசத்துப் போதகர்சபையிலுள்ள
அப்போஸ்தொலிக்குக் குருக்களால்
செய்து
அதிசிரேஷ்டர்களுடைய
உத்தாரத்தின்படியே
௲௮௱௬௰௫-ம்.௵
புதுவையிற் சன்மரிமாக்கினி மாதாக்கோவிலைச்சேர்ந்த
அச்சுக்கூடத்திற் பதிப்பிக்கப்பட்டது.

7.7. Sambaashanai Anusaaram printed at the Mission Press in Pondicherry in 1865. (Courtesy: Bibliothèque Asiatique des Missions Etrangères de Paris, C3172).

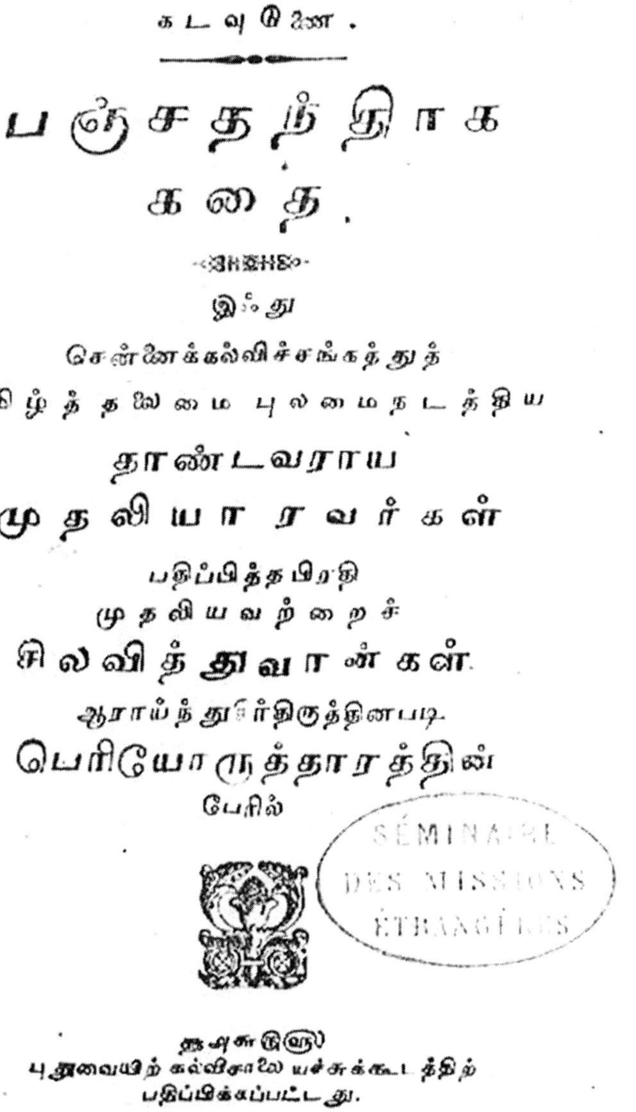

கடவுடுணை.

பஞ்சதந்திரக்
கதை.

இஃது
சென்னைக்கல்விச்சங்கத்துத்
தமிழ்த்தலைமைப்புலமைநடத்திய
தாண்டவராய
முதலியாரவர்கள்
பதிப்பித்தபிரதி
முதலியவற்றைச்
சிலவித்துவான்கள்
ஆராய்ந்துதிருத்தினபடி
பெரியோருத்தாரத்தின்
பேரில்

௲௮௱௬௰௫
புதுவையிற் கல்விசாலை யச்சுக்கூடத்திற்
பதிப்பிக்கப்பட்டது.

***7.8. Panchathanthira Kathai printed at the College Printing Press in Pondicherry in 1865* (Courtesy*: Bibliothèque Asiatique des Missions Etrangères de Paris*).**

8

The Litho Press in Pondicherry and Madras: An Expanding Horizon of Printing Tamil Books, 1859-69

The lithographic technique was discovered by chance in 1796 when the Munich dramatist Aloys Senefelder, searching for a economical method of printing his own work, tried writing on a finely-ground stone surface and discovered the water-repellent properties of his greasy, oil-based ink. The images initially to be reproduced were hand-drawn on a litho stone and printed on a manual press. In India Mr. Rind introduced lithography as early as in 1822 and it was first used for map-making. But its special applicability to Tamil scripts was later recognized by the Europeans. The litho press came into working in Tamil country when the English East India Company established it Madras in 1825.[1] The design was applied to the fine limestone stone block in the process with dry greasy substance such as a coloured wax fixed in the stone through a variety of different techniques. The stone was then damped with water and greasy ink was applied. This was repelled by the water and altered only to the design, leaving a reverse image on any paper pressed on the stone for printing. The only limitation on the litho press was finding someone capable of writing neatly and clearly what was wanted in Tamil script required.

Introducing Lithography in Pondicherry, 1859

Louis Savininen Dupuis the manager of the Catholic printing press found skilled persons who could write and so established a litho printing press at Pondicherry in 1859.[2] It would not be surprising to know that Dupuis discovered lithographic writers in Pondicherry and they were drawn from the Tamil traditional scribal castes and communities. The technique of lithograph was though found to be new to Tamils yet it was a link with the past, combining the cultural authority of the Tamil manuscript with the intellectual advantage of rapid duplication of books. Lithography thus made the printed Tamil book no longer an alien artifact but something visually more familiar and therefore culturally more acceptable. In short lithography the mass produced manuscript was a paradox realized and it began to assume an important position within publishing in Pondicherry mainly introduced by L.S. Dupuis. The new technique quickly passed and got spread into the main stream of book production of Catholic literature. In France during the early years of book production lithography had remained on the fringes of publishing, and it resorted to only when letter press failed either on economic grounds or through problems of text-configuration.

Lithography's development and popularity in Pondicherry was also mainly due to reasons of practicality, its enduring appeal among the Tamil population. It was chiefly due to the profound cultural questions of textual acceptability and the aesthetics of the Tamil printed book. Taking at first the practicality, the use of lithography came to emerge in Pondicherry when the local source of stones suitable for the technique had been found in the Telugu speaking areas where the MEP missionaries were doing missionary work. Dupuis also at that time felt that it would be time consuming to import the art of lithography from France. He could easily overcome the problem of required stones when the right type of porous limestone was discovered at Kurnool. These Kurnool stones were also found far superior in quality being both much denser and finger-grained than to the stones that could be imported from France.

Dupuis next found skilled persons and began to employ them in the publication of Tamil books lithographed. He was keen to employ them at any cost by understanding the skill and importance of these good writers. Knowing lithography avoided many of the practical difficulties associated with letter press, not least the tendency of the rather large early Tamil type-faces to devour too much printing paper, Dupuis began to work on these lines. With lithography the size or style of handwriting was instantly adjustable, whereas with type there was the bother of selecting sorts from different cases according to fount size. Maxing different scripts such as French, Tamil and Latin within a single page of text was again made simple with lithography but a complex operation was found in type-setting. Though Tamil tradition of typography had been well established by earlier missionaries, Dupuis realized that lithography did not prevent the obvious advantages. He understood that local availability of types was the determining factor for lithography. For the letter press, printing the script produce was not simply confirmed to the unavailability or limited supply of the requisite types. It was also a question of how effective the printed type faces were in terms of acceptability to the reader's eye. The standardized orthography which type-design imposed tended to distance the script for the reader especially when that standardization was imposed by missionaries working from a European perspective in book printing.

L.S. Dupuis had keenly observed the circulation of Catholic Christian texts incised on palm-leaves using native scribes to copy them out a traditional stylus. Lithography was though used for printing tracts at that time Dupuis felt that he could do it for book production. It was obvious that a lithographed book lacked the visual authority of the letter press printed page. It was still the manuscript which was vested with visual and cultural authority and this was the key to lithography's rapid acceptance and lasting appeal among the Tamils. Lithography laid emphasis on the handwritten work in its highest artistic expression—calligraphy. It may be mentioned here that Tamil manuscript culture did not immediately die out with the advent of printing. Therefore Dupuis adopted this technique. He felt that it was the arrival of lithography, more than typography, which introduced the concept of printing as an alternative method of book production to the traditional patrons of the manuscript scribes, the rulers and their courtiers and religious institutions in Tamil country.

The Catholic Tamil writings composed by the missionaries during the seventeenth and eighteenth centuries were largely circulated in palm-leaves. Though paper was in high demand Catholic missionaries took efforts to copy them in paper and they sent these manuscripts to Lisbon and Paris. Since a large number of writings continued to remain both in palm-leaf manuscripts and in paper in the absence of the Catholic press, L.S. Dupuis took sincere efforts to print them in the nineteenth century. In the past owing to paucity of funds, required volume of paper for printing and the permission or clearance needed to be obtained from the Catholic Church authorities for printing were also other hurdles present at that time. L.S. Dupuis wanted the books to be printed and circulated among the Tamil Christians those which were not earlier printed. He felt that no doubt they need to be served for the express purpose for guiding the laity to lay a strong foundation for the spiritual life of Christians.

Earlier missionaries before L.S. Dupuis through their works had spread the light of Christian knowledge among the natives. Many poor Christians did not have the means to buy the palm-leaves but heard the writings of the missionaries when read in the church by the catechist and others. Those who had spent money for that purpose have stored a copy as a treasure of knowledge. Therefore L.S. Dupuis collected such precious writings and began his work of litho printing. Further he found that there were persons who had read and used the missionary writings. He did not bother about the marketing of these books if printed. He did not wish to continue the practice of circulating the missionary writings in palm-leaves in the absence of the Jesuit printing press as per the then local customs prevalent. L.S. Dupuis wished that the physical labour of composing the works by missionaries should not go waste. In fine, L.S. Dupuis printed the books on spirituality linking serially with one and the other topics. Therefore he had been highly successful in printing lithographed books in Tamil for the Christians.

Printing Catholic Tamil Literature: Gnaana Aarudhal in 1859 and Archshista Ignaciyar Dhyaanagal in 1860

Gnaana Aaruthal (Spiritual Consolation) was composed by Jean Venant Bouchet the Jesuit at Ariyankuppam near Pondicherry in the eighteenth century. L.S. Dupuis found this manuscript to be very useful to Christians and so he decided to print it. The book was printed at the *kallachchu* (Litho-press in Tamil) in Pondicherry in 1859.[3] The printed book of L.S. Dupuis has *vivekam* (to the knowledge of the readers).[4] It states that suffering is common to all. All kings, lords and nobles also suffer. Suffering has to be borne patiently according to the will of god. Disease, poverty and defamation bring sufferings. In this connection the worst should not happen and that the words of consolation therefore need to be given. St. Christostão said that Christians have spiritual consolation and not the pagans because they do not follow the true religion and go to hell immediately after death. Christians should follow good morals and they should go to heaven and the details are explained in this lithographed book. It contains eight consolations and the details are given. However, the manuscript mentions the twelve types of consolation wherein Fr. Bouchet had outlined how to console the various types of people such as the poor, the sick, those who have no children and those on death bed.[5] This shows that L.S. Dupuis had selected only the first eight consolations and got printed in 1859. The total printed pages are 147. This book *Gnaana Aaruthal* is mentioned in the printed press list found in another book called *Thingalkilamai puthumai* in 1861. The selling price was 4 *annas*.

James Thomas Rossi wrote a book on the spiritual exercises of Ignatius of Loyola in Tamil.[6] This palm-leaf manuscript was widely circulated among the Christians and so L.S. Dupuis decided to print it at the litho press. The book was printed in the year 1860. The book printed is mentioned in press list found in another book called *Aathuma nesam* printed in 1860. The book is also again mentioned in another book titled *Thingalkilamai Puthumai* printed in 1860. The selling price of Ignaciyar Dhyaanagal in 1861 was 8 *annas*.

Vellikilamai Puthumai and Sanikilamai Puthumai Printed in 1860

James Thomas Rossi had composed a work called *Yezhu kizhamaikku dhyaanam* laying emphasis on meditation of Christian ideas for all the seven days in a week. L.S. Dupuis printed successfully the portions of Friday and titled it as *Vellikilamai puthumai*. He printed the book at the litho press in Pondicherry in 1860. It contains 52 Friday sermons and explained the passion of Lord Jesus Christ for 52 Fridays in a year.[7] The book printed is mentioned in the press list found in the book called *Thingalkilamai puthumai* in 1861. The selling price of *Vellikilami puthumai* was 14 *annas*.

L.S. Dupuis who found the manuscript of *Yezhu kilamaikku dhyaanam* highly useful chose again to print the Saturday Miracles alone which dealt with devotion to Blessed Virgin Mary. He selected the text and printed a book titled *Sanikilamai Puthumai* from the litho press in Pondicherry in 1860.[8] The book contained 52 Saturday miracles of Mary the Mother of God since 52 Saturdays are there in a year. The book printed is mentioned in the press list of *Thingalkilamai puthumai*. The selling price of *Sanikilamai puthumai* was 14 *annas* in 1861.

Printing Karumpaambin Vishakadikku Marunthu in 1860 authored by Benoit Brisard

Benoit Brisard born on 26 October 1816 at Saint Hilaire de Cahleons entered the MEP seminary on 26 February 1846, ordained a priest on 29 May 1847 left France and reached Pondicherry on 1 August 1847. He was posted at Aththipakkam and at Tiruvathigai where he learnt Tamil and worked as a missionary in 1848-9. Later he served at Vadugarpatti during 1856 and 1863 and at that time he composed a book in Tamil called *Karumpaambin Vishakkadikku Marunthu*. There is no medical prescription of any sort for the bite of cobra in the printed Tamil book titled 'Medicine for the bite of black cobra' printed in 1860 in Podicherry. Contrary to one's expectation, we find Catholic criticism and heresy against Martin Luther and his teachings. Such a criticism and heresy by the Catholic missionaries was not unexpected. This book was printed at the *Sanmavirakini Maatha kalachchukudam* (Our Lady of Immaculate Conception litho press) owned by the Foreign Missionary Society of Paris in Pondicherry. What the Catholic missionary in this book meant was that the Lutheran Protestant mission was dreadful and a poisonous one that of the black cobra. The Catholic Christianity had been the medicine to cure people from poison.[9] The printing of the book is mentioned in the press list of *Thingalkilamai Puthumai* book printed in 1860. Thus polemical writings in Tamil had continued to appear in print.

Printing the book Aayatham in 1860

L.S. Dupuis wished to get the books printed on the preparation to the holy sacraments for the use of the Catholics. He printed the book *Aayatham*. It contained the matter related to the preparation of the holy sacraments mentioned in Tamil such as *gnaanasgnaanam* (baptism), *uruthipusuthal* (Confirmation), *narkarunai* (Holy Communion) *paavasangirthanam* (Confession), *avasthaipusuthal* (Extreme-unction) and *koil kaliyaanam*. (Marriage in the Church).[10] The printing of this book is mentioned in *Thingalkilamai Puthumai* printed in 1861. The selling price of *Aayatham* was 4 *annas*.

Nine Books on Devotion to Mary the Mother of God Printed at Litho Press in 1860

L.S. Dupuis desired to encourage the devotion to Mary the Mother of God. Hence he printed a book titled *Devamaathavin navanaat pirasangam* (Sermons on the novenas of the feasts of the Blessed Virgin Mary) at the litho press in 1860. This book printed is mentioned in the press list books mentioned in *Thingalkilamai Puthumai* in 1861. The selling price of *Devamaathavin navanaat pirasangam* was 14 annas. The same book got reprinted in 1871. He printed also another book titled *Devamaathaa senmapaavanmillamal urpavitha thirunaal pirasangam* at the litho press in 1860 and it is mentioned in the press list of books mentioned in *Thingalkilamai Puthumai* in 1861. The selling price of *Devamaathaa senmapaavanmillamal urpavitha thirunaal pirasangam* was 1 anna and 6 paise. He printed also another book titled *Devamaatha pirantha thirunaal pirasangam* in 1860 at the litho press and it was sold at 1 *anna* and 6 paise.

L.S. Dupuis printed a book titled *Devamaatha kannikaiyaana thirunaal pirasangam* at the litho press in 1860. This book printed is mentioned in the press list of *Thingalkilamai Puthumai* in 1861. The selling price of *Devamaatha kannikaiyaana thirunal pirasangam* was 1 anna and 6 paise. He printed another book titled *Devamaathaa mangala vaarthai sonna thirunaal pirasangam* at litho press in Pondicherry in 1860. He printed also a book titled *Devamaathaavin suththigara thirunaal pirasangam* at the litho press in Pondicherry in 1860.

L.S. Dupuis printed a book titled *Devamaathaavin viyagula thirunal pirasangam* at litho press in 1860. He printed also a book titled *Devamaatha motchathukuu yezhuntharuliya thirunaal pirasangam* at the litho press in 1860. Further he printed another book titled *Devamaathaa yelisaba-thammalai minavina thirunaal pirasangam* at the litho press in Pondicherry in 1860. This book printed has been mentioned in the press list of

Thingalkilamai Puthumai in 1861 and the selling price of *Devamaathaa yelisabathammalai minavina thirunal pirasangam* was I *anna* and 6 paise.

Thingalkilamai Puthumai, Sevvaykilami Puthumai and Puthankilamai Pirasangam Printed in 1861

L.S. Dupuis carefully selected the portions of the Monday Miracles from the work of *Yezhu kizhamaikku dhyaanam* by James Thomas Rossi. He thereafter printed the book titled *Thingalkilamai Puthumai* at the litho press in Pondicherry in 1861.[11] The title page reads: *Puthuvai maanagaram sanmavirakkini maatha kovilai serntha kalachhu kudathair pathipikka pattathu*. There is a *vivekam* (to the knowledge of the readers).[12] It states that rich men do not have mercy on the beggars. If there is no help from the rich and the wealthy certainly the beggars would suffer, so also the souls in purgatory. Monday is assigned for praying for the souls in purgatory. Since 52 Mondays are there in a year the book printed contains 52 Monday miracles that happened in various places of the world. Hence avoid going to purgatory and do prayer and penance on this earth. The handwriting in the book is by a single individual. The book has a total of 306 pages. It ends saying that recite one *Pater Noste*r, *Ave Maria* and praise to the Holy Trinity for the one who wrote the book. Please pray for the author of the book as many as times as you read or hear the reading by others. The selling price of the book was 10 annas.

L.S. Dupuis selected the portions related to Tuesday Miracles from the work of *Yezhu kizhamaikku dhyaanam* by James Thomas Rossi. Thereafter he printed the book titled *Sevvaikilamai Puthumai* at the litho press in Pondicherry in 1861. The title page runs: *Puthuvai maanagaram sanmavirakkini maatha kovilai serntha kalachhu koodathir pathipikka pattathu*. The printed book by L.S. Dupuis contains *vivekam* (to the knowledge of the readers) and it mentions the importance of angles and guardian angels and the archangels, Michael (feast 8th of *vaikasi* month), Gabriel (15th of *panguni* month) and Raphael (24th of *aypasi* month). Hence 52 Tuesday miracles that happened in various places have been given. Since people do not know and understand the help received through the angels the author of the book had recorded the miracles happened. The printed book has a total of 264 pages.[13]

L.S. Dupuis printed the relevant portions on Wednesday Miracles from the work of *Yezhu kizhamaikku dhyaanam* by James Thomas Rossi titled *Puthankilamai Pirasangam* at the litho press in Pondicherry in 1861. The title page runs: *Puthuvai maanagaram sanmavirakkini maatha kovilai serntha kalachhu koodathir pathipikka pattathu*. The *vivekam* (to the knowledge of the readers) mentions that many Christians believe that St Joseph is just like any other saint. They do not know about St Joseph and so the author mentioned that he had written the wonders of St Joseph. Since Wednesday is assigned for devotion 52 sermons have been given for 52 Wednesdays highlighting the sanctity and holiness of Saint Joseph. We find finally sermon on St. Anne and Joachim which has been also added towards the end. The book has a total of 263 pages.[14]

Viyaalakilamai Puthumai and Gnaayittrukilamai Puthumai Printed in 1865

L.S. Dupuis printed the portions of Thursday Miracles from the work of *Yezhu kizhamaikku dhyaanam* by James Thomas Rossi titled *Viyaalakilamai Puthumai* at the litho press in Pondicherry in 1865. The author had given 52 sermons on the Blessed Sacrament and explained the glory of the Holy Eucharist for 52 Thursdays.[15]

L.S. Dupuis printed successfully the portions of Sunday Miracles from the work of *Yezhu kizhamaikku dhyaanam* by James Thomas Rossi titled *Gnnayittrukilamai Puthumai* at the litho press in Pondicherry in 1865. The *vivekam* of the book mentions that though the book is called Sunday Miracles do not please think that all happened on Sundays. The Sunday is assigned for divine worship and rest. Hence all religious truth and all other scriptures should be read and meditated. Hence in this book he had given them and explained the glory of the holy trinity for 52 Sundays.[16] *Gaannyittrukilamai Puthumai* was reprinted in letter-press in 1882. There is a note which reads thus: Savari Naayagam, the son of Kulathur Innasiya Pillai, the resident of Aananda Puram belonging to St. Xavier's church at Varahaneri assisted and helped for the publication of the book in 1882 so as to easily understand the Catholic Christian doctrine and to increase devotion among the people through the miracles found in the book.

Paavasangirthana Pirasangam Printed in 1865

Ippolito Desideri (1684-1733) a Jesuit on Tibet mission between 1715 and 1721 came to Delhi and served as a missionary and finally moved over to Pondicherry. He learnt Tamil and spent some years and was back in Rome in 1726. During his stay in Tamil country he had prepared in 1724 a manual of confession. He wrote movingly of the deprivations endured by his conferers in the Carnatic mission. His work of *confessionairo* in Tamil titled *Aaytham Sollugira Vagai* is now preserved at the Archivum Romanum Societatis Iesu, Roma.[17] Rajamanickam had wrongly attributed this work to Roberto Nobili.[18]

Louis Savinien Dupuis found this manuscript of Confession Manual useful for printing because it was followed by the Tamil Christians since 1725. The book was printed at the litho press in Pondicherry in 1865.[19]

Later the same was reprinted again at the letter press in 1871. The title page of the Confession Manual printed mentions that this title *Paavasangeerthana Pirasangam* was composed by one of the former missionaries (*purva gurukkal*). With the permission of François Jean-Marie Laouënan the bishop of Pondicherry it was printed according to an order issued from Rome. It was printed at the *Senmaviraakini maatha achchukudam* at Pondicherry in 1871.[20] The book contains a total of 105 pages. There is a *vivekam* for three pages in the beginning. It states confession is the fourth sacrament. A sinner should make confession to obtain salvation. It will help him to go to heaven. Many people make confession without proper preparation. Making good confession is important otherwise it is a great sin. There are eight sermons presented in the book teaching how to make good confession (pp. 5-89). The prayers before and after making confession are also given (pp. 100-4). The contents of the book had also been given in the book (p. 105). It has been said that *puththimathi* (advice) has been given in the eight sermons commencing from the *paavasangeerthanthin muthalam pirasangam*. The preparation to the sacrament of confession has been given thereafter and the prayers to be said before and after the administering the sacrament had been furnished.

Printing Karumpaambin Vishakadikku Thailam in 1868 authored by Benoit Brisard

Benoit Brisard (1816-1878) was posted as the parish priest at Purathakudi in 1865 and he remained there till August 1869. He wrote at that time a book against the Protestants. One cannot lose the thread of this ongoing religious controversy between the Roman Catholics and the Protestants. A counter or a protest or a book of denial titled *'Remedy for the humiliation/sarcastic criticism of the Pope's religion-Catholic faith'* was published by the Protestants in 1866. This book was in the form of conversations between two brothers. The title page of the book of the Protestants runs thus: Conversations, to deny the earlier book of Benoit Brisard titled *Karum Paambin Vishakkadikku Marundhu* (Medicine for the bite of black cobra) and to prove that Martin Luther was the true and faithful follower of *Parabaran* (Jesus Christ).[21] In retaliation to this Brisard prepared another book titled *Karumpaambin vishakadikku thailam* (An oil medicine for black snake's poisonous biting) and L.S. Dupuis printed the book at litho press in Pondicherry in 1868.

Printing Kaanaa Vishakkaddikku Marundhu in 1869 authored by Benoit Brisard

Benoit Brisard the MEP missionary also wrote another book attacking the Protestants severely. L.S. Dupuis had printed it in 1869 and it was titled

Kaanaa vishakkaddikku marundhu (medicine for the poisonous bite unnoticed).[22]

It may be mentioned that *Aaytham, Karumbambin vishakkadikku marundhu, Devamaathavin navanaat pirasangam, Paavasangeerthan pirasangam* the four books which had been printed at the litho press in the beginning (as found in the press list of publications in 1865-6 vide *Sathiya vetha sarithira surukkam* and *Dhivya Maathirigai*) were also found printed in the letter press (as found in the press list vide *Paavasanggerthana pirasangam* and *Gnaanopadesa surukkam* in 1871-2) later. The reason was that the copies of the earlier lithographed books had exhausted and so Dupuis got printed them again in the letter press when needed for use by the Catholics.

Tamil Book Lithographed in Madras in 1865

The administration of the English East India Company came to an end in India after the suppression of the revolt of sepoy mutiny in 1857. The Crown rule was introduced thereafter in Madras in 1858. Petitions in Tamil filed by the natives before the courts of justice were lithographed and the book got printed in Madras. We find this book published in 1868 containing a collection of 100 official documents in Tamil consisting of *urzees* and other papers of South Arcot, Chingleput Tiruchirapalli and Salem districts for the year 1865. It was meant for the use of candidates for the Indian civil service. The lithographed book has two different handwritings while one had used dots over the Tamil consonants and the other had not used by following the Tamil manuscript writing style. The book has 211 pages in total. It was lithographed at the Foster press which functioned at 23 Rundall's Road, Vepery near Madras in 1868.[23]

It may be relevant to note that a manuscript journal '*Puthinaathipathi*' had appeared in 1870 in the island of Sri Lanka. It mentions that the printed letter (alphabet) in Tamil had been called *Varaiyaa Yezhuththu*.[24] Tamil pundits like Purasai Yenkavanar Sabaapathi in the mainland of India called the Tamil printed letter *Yezhuthaa Yezththu*. Samuel Pillai of Thanjavur had it mention in the Tholkaapiyam and Nannul edited by him in 1858.[25] Thus the print in Tamil had been differentiated between the manuscripts by various names by the Tamil scholars in this expanding age of book production.

To conclude, lithography in Pondicherry had thus undoubtedly stimulated the production of books of Catholic religious literature and an atlas under Dupuis since 1859. It is quite clear from the above lithographed works of Dupuis that copying was done from actual manuscript to produce in effect a facsimile. Over and above this, there was very frequently a conscious attempt to imitate the layout of the manuscript page with rubricating the text. L.S. Dupuis had stated explicitly in the books printed the aim of printing. He wrote that in order that the people of the Tamil country to know, and love and serve with devotion and also to obtain the divine grace and blessings from God and receive favours, he had prepared prayer books and other books and published them. He prepared books in Tamil so as to be read by the Catholics and so printed them in the press.[24] It may be mentioned here that European printing, European wood-cuts and engravings were unobjectionable to Tamils and even desirable particularly for their edifying qualities in the letter press. Dupuis had followed the European style of binding the books that were also acceptable by the Tamil readers. In lithography the works published possessed itself both a conservative and a progress with the Tamil cultural consortium. Progress in that respect may be said that it accelerated the process by which printing was taken by Dupuis to the needs of the Tamil Catholic population. Lithography was also far simpler and quicker to master than typography. Further it was less cumbersome and more portable involving less equipment. Additionally we find lithographed book was cheaper, and much appealing to people and so Dupuis became the operator in Pondicherry. However, it may be said that Dupuis had successfully combined the twin modern invention of printing, both the letter press and the litho press in Pondicherry. Thus devotional books were printed on a large scale from the litho press. These include meditations, retreats, miracles, sermons and devotion to Mary the mother of God. We find 24 titles in total printed in Pondicherry from the litho press. However, lithography had also developed in Madras and the records of the courts of justice in Tamil had been printed by the English company.

Notes

1. Herman Losty, 'Sir Charles Royly's Lithographic press' *India a Pageant of Prints*, Bombay, 1989, pp. 137-9.
2. Archives de la Société des Missions Étrangères de Paris (hereafter AMEP), Paris, MSS Correspondance Pondichéry-Paris, Lettres, vol. 1002, pp. 1563-4, see the annual report of the Pondicherry vicariate by L.S. Dupuis sent to the Superior and Directors of the MEP seminary in Paris dated 22 December 1860.
3. Madurai Province Jesuit Archives (hereafter MPJA), Shenbaganur, no. 221/275. *Gnaana Aaruthal*, Pondicherry, 1859.
4. Ibid., p. 8.
5. S. Rajamanickam, ed., *Gnaana Aaruthal*, Tuticorin, 1965, pp. 65–92.
6. E.R. Hambye, *History of Christianity in India: Eighteenth Century*, Bangalore, 1982, p. 194. MPJA, *Ignaciyar Dhyanangal*, Pondicherry, 1860.
7. Bibliothèque Asiatique des Missions Etrangères de Paris (hereafter BAMEP), *Vellikilamai Puthumai*, Pondicherry, 1860, Rossi, *Vellikilamai Puthumai,*

Sesunaatharudaya thirupaadugalin peril puthumai, Third edition, Pondicherry, 1910; S. Ponnad, 'Fr Thomas de Rossi: The Sinna Saveriar of the Marava (1701-1704)', *Caritas*, LVIII, 1979, pp. 73-8.

8. BAMEP, *Sanikilamai Puthumai*, Pondicherry, 1859; Rossi, *Sanikilamai Puthumai: Archishta Devamaatha seytharuliya pala puthumaigal*, Fourth edition, Pondicherry, 1908.
9. BAMEP, Paris, *Karumpaambin Vishakadikku Marunthu*, Pondicherry, 1860, pp. 1-102.
10. MPJA, 222/304, Accession no. 007144; Devanarkaurani Aayatham, pp. 1-27; Avasthaipusuthal Vaangurathatku Aayatham, pp. 28-60; Paavasangeerthana Aayatham, pp.101-112. It is bound in a volume along with manuscript titled Gnnana Maalai and it contains others works such as Devanarkarunai Aaytham, pp. 1-27; Avasthaipusuthal Vangirathukku Aaytham, 28-60.
11. MPJA, 221/361, *Thingalkilamai Puthumai*, Pondicherry, 1861, see also, Rossi, *Thingalkilamai Puthumai: Utharikkira sthathu aathumakkalai pattriya puthumaigal*, Third edition, Pondicherry, 1910.
12. Ibid., pp. 5-6.
13. MPJA, 221/365, *Sevvaikilami Puthumai*, Pondicherry, 1861, see also, Rossi *Sevvaikilamai Puthumai: Sammnasukkazhlaal nadantheriya puthumaigal*, Second edition, Pondicherry, 1903.
14. MPJA, 221/366, *Puthankilami Pirasangam*, Pondicherry 1861. There is another copy of the same book see MPJA, no. 221/367. See also, *Puthankilamai Puthumai: Archista Susaiapparaipattri*, Second edition, Pondicherry, 1905.
15. BAMEP, *Viyaalakilamai Puthumai*, Pondicherry, 1865, See also, Rossi, *Viyaazhlakilamai Puthumai: Devanarkarunaiyaal undaana arumaiyaana puthumaigal*, Second edition, Pondicherry, 1902.
16. BAMEP, *Gnaayittru Kilamai Puthumai*, Pondicherry, 1865;See also, Rossi, *Gnaaittrukilamai Puthumai: Pazhaya yerpattilum puthiya yerpaatilum yeduttha adhisayamaana varthamaanangal*, Third edition, Mission Press, Pondicherry, 1910.
17. Archivum Romanum Societatis Iesu (hereafter ARSI), MS Goa 76b, fls.1-19, Ippolito Desideri, Aayatham Sollugira Vagai; See also, Dialogus inter confessorem et penitentem, fls.20-35. The folios from 29 to 35 are not numbered. On Ippolito Desideri's mission to Tibet see, Michael J. Sweet and Leonard Zwilling, *Mission To Tibet, The Extraordinary Eighteenth Century Account of Father Ippolito Desideri, S. J*, Boston, 2010.
18. S. Rajamanickam, *Paavasangeerthana Kurippidam*, Palayamkottai, 1966, pp. 1-50; S. Rajamanickam, *The First Oriental Scholar*, Palayamkottai, 1972. It is not found in the list given by him vide pp. 112-113. It is a surprise how attributes to Nobili at p. 280.
19. Litho press book is found at Pavvasnagerrthan aayatham is given from pp 100-104. The same is found is also Paava sangeerthana Aaytham Mss . It is bound in a volume along with manuscript titled Gnnana Maalai MPJA, 222/304, Accession no. 007144., pp. 101-112 (13 pages). BAMEP, *Aayatham*, Pondicherry, 1865.
20. MPJA, no. 221/529, *Paavasangeerthana Prasangam*, Pondicherry, 1871.

21. Bibliothek der Franckeschen Stiftungen (hereafter BFSt), Halle, MSS C: 38 / 54; *Karumpaambin Vishakadikku Thailam*, Pondicherry, 1868; See also, M. Pakkiam, *Paappu Maarga Dhushana Parigaaram*, Lutheran Mission Press, Tranquebar, 1866, pp. 1-126. See also BFSt, C: 38/43. This book was signed and submitted to Rev. William Sthalin by the author M. Pakkiam with his small note in Tamil dated 6 September, 1867.
22. BAMEP, *Kaanaa Vishakaddikku Marundhu*, Pondicherry, 1869.
23. *A Collection of Official Documents in the Tamil Language Consisting of Urzees and Other Papers Filed in the Courts of Justice for the Use of Candidates for the Indian Civil Service*, by Lieut W.F. Wright, Madras Staff Corps, Tamil Translator to the Government of Madras, Printed for the Government of Madras by Caleb Foster, at the Foster Press, 23 Rundall's Road, Vepery, 1868.
24. The text runs thus: *Ith desaththaar sarvesuranai arinthu snegiththu seviththu bhakthiyode vendi kozhlvathinaal deva kirubai aaseervaththinode vendiya nanmai varangalai adaiyumpadikku sepapuththagam muthaliya puthagangalai vezhipaduthinom. Thamizh bhashaiyile padikkiraththukku udhavikka thakka anega puthagangalaiyum undu panni acchil pathipiththom.*
25. Aa, Ma.Samy, *Pathonpatham Nuttrandu Thamizh Ithalgal*, Madras, 1993, p. 96.
26. Ibid., pp. 283-84. The text runs thus: '*Innul iyattri yezhuththaa Yezhuththil, Pannul neriyil pathithu nalginaan*'.

சர்வேஸ்வராய்நம்

ஞான

ஆறுதல்.

௧௲௫௯

புதுவையாமென்ட விசாக்கி
னிமாதாக்கோயிலைச்சேர்ந்த
கல்அச்சுக்கூடத்திற்பதிப்பிக்க
ப்பட்டது.

8.1. Gnnana Aarudhal lithographed in Pondicherry in 1859.
(Courtesy*: Madurai Province Jesuit Archives, Shenbaganur, 221/275*).

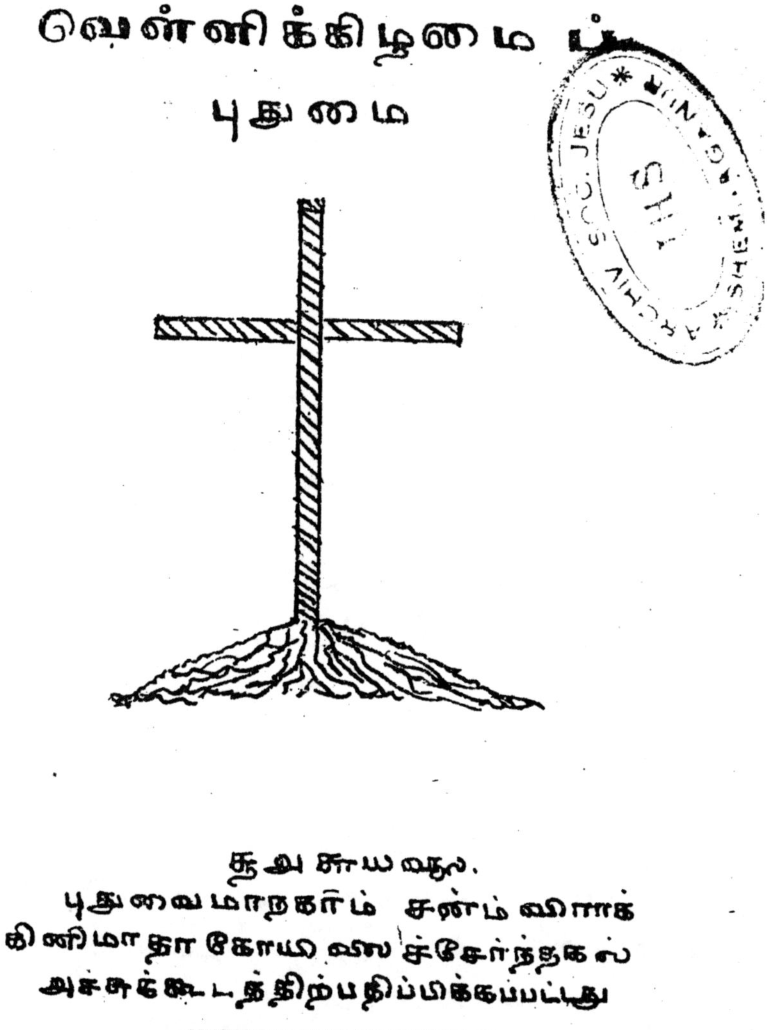

வெள்ளிக்கிழமைப்
புதுமை

புதுவை மாநகரில் சன்மார்க்
கினிமாதா கோயிலைச் சேர்ந்த கல்
அச்சுக்கூடத்திற் பதிப்பிக்கப்பட்டது

8.2. Vellikilami Pudumai lithographed in Pondicherry in 1860.
(Courtesy*: Madurai Province Jesuit Archives, Shenbaganur, 221/371).*

செவ்வாய்க் கிழமைப் புதுமை.

22/36

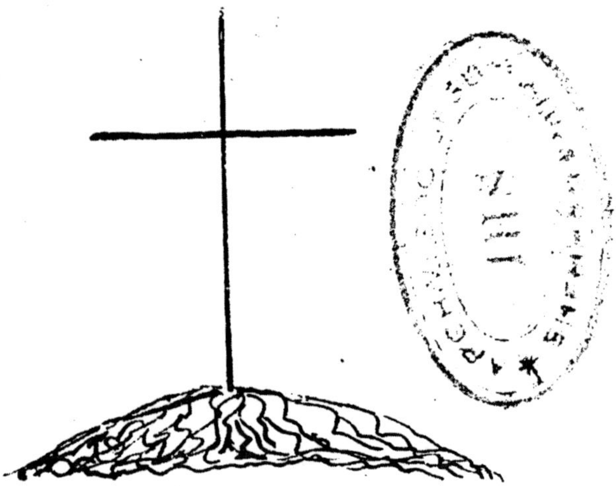

௲௮௱௬௰௧

புதுவை மாநகரிற் சென்மவிரா
க்கினிமாதாக்கோயிலைச்சேர்ந்
தகல் அச்சுக்கூடத்திற் பதிப்பிக்கப்
பட்டது

8.3. *Sevvaikilami Pudumai lithographed in Pondicherry in 1861.*
(Courtesy*: Madurai Province Jesuit Archives, Shenbaganur, 221/365).*

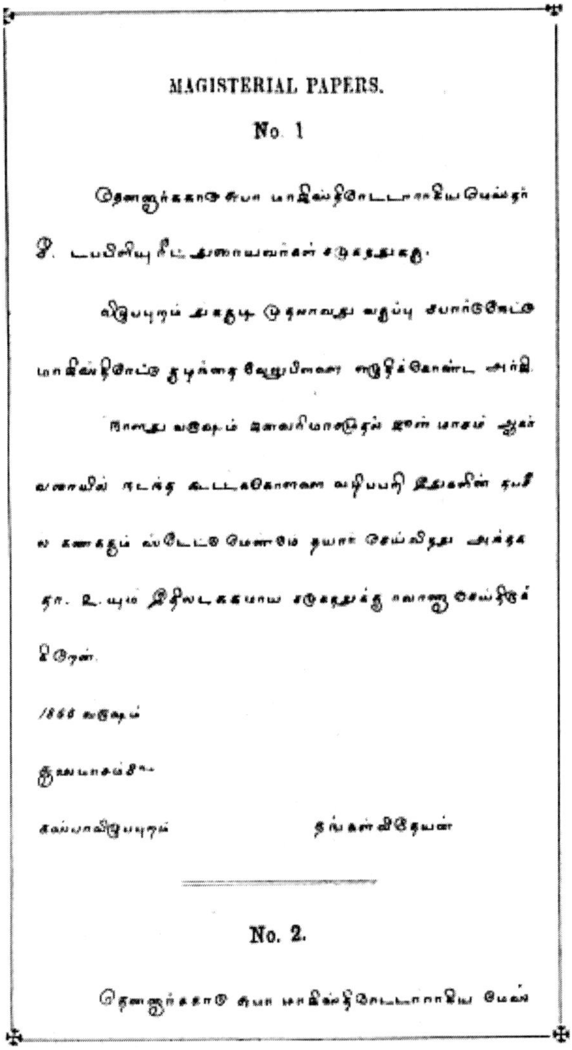

MAGISTERIAL PAPERS.

No. 1

[illegible]

No. 2.

[illegible]

8.4. The Magisterial Papers lithographed in Madras in 1868.
(Courtesy*: Bodleian Library, Oxford*).

9

The Diffusion of Tamil Printing in Halle, Hamburg, Dresden, Erlangen, London, Colombo and Jaffna, 1671-1873

Philippus Baldaeus the missionary in Sri Lanka had referred to a Bible printed in Rotterdam in Tamil as early as in 1671. In his travelogue vide chapter 46 of the Ceylon portion he made it very clear that Francisco de Fonseca a native from Jaffna had translated the Gospel of St. Mathew from Portuguese into Tamil. [1] He also mentioned which portions of translations had been intended for the use in the churches. Francisco de Fonseca had revised the translation of the Bible from Portuguese into Tamil. Baldaeus had mentioned about the translation of the Psalms also at various stages of work in progress.[2]

Printing in Tamil fonts appeared in Europe and the first work to display the Tamil characters was the work of Philippus Baldaeus (two editions of it one in the original Dutch and one in German both published in Amsterdam in 1672). This book contains three pages of what is called *Malabarischet letter-Konst* (a set of Tamil characters with very peculiar transliteration). We find transliteration by 'nha', 'L' by 'ra',' 1/2' by 'hna, and ',' is supposed to stand for 'ca','k', 'ka', 'qua'. A character written as '9' and transliterated by 'rra' obviously stands for the present 'E'. To this is added a Tamil version of *Pater Noster* and *Credo* (the declaration of faith) with original text in Latin written under each line.[3]

Tamil script continued to appear in the books printed in Europe and it was introduced by travellers. The travelogue of Thevenot published in 1686 we find the plate of the characters for Tamil. John Fryer's New Account of the East India and Persia being Nine years, 1672-81 published in London in 1698 had given two plates of showing samples of Tamil and Telugu. In 1715 '*Celsissimo Principi Georgio*' was printed at Amsterdam and it contains 'The Malabaricum' which is Tamil of which two versions are given while one is titled '*Malabaric*' and the other is titled '*Tranquebarensi dialecto Malabric*'. The latter is called a dialect being more Sanskritized Tamil. Thus we notice fascinating evolution and spread of Tamil script which also explains the biologic and phonetic bases of vowels and consonants. Next we find appearance of Tamil characters in the next year (1716) when a printing press began functioning at Halle in Germany to print books in Tamil. As early as 1716 in Halle *Grammatica Damulica* (Tamil grammar in Latin) by Bartholomäus Ziegenbalg was printed. The characters are large and square quite different from the one used in Tranquebar, India. They resemble Tamil inscriptions of the period but on the whole, they are rather pleasing in design.[4]

Printing the Tamil Book Gnaana Mandira Selva Pungaavanam in Halle in 1749-50

Benjamin Schultze the Protestant missionary in Tranquebar felt the need to translate Johann Arndt's *Paradies-Gärtlein, Voller Christlichen Tugenden, Wie solche Durch geistreiche Gebete in die Seele zu pflantzen; Worzu ietzo kommen, 1. Dreyzehn Wunder-Geschichte, welche sich mit diesem Büchlein, und dieses Mannes andern Schriften begeben. 2. Bernhardi völlig verteutschtes Jubel- und Jesus- Lied und 3. Ein dreyfaches Register, so den Nutz und Gebrauch dieses Gebet-Büchleins weiset, Magdeburg, Druckts Christian Leberecht Faber* published in Germany in 1727. He began the work and also took the assistance of Rayanayakkan the Tamil catechist stationed in Thanjavur. He had made a reference to this in his letter. The work was completed by Schultze in 1747.[5] The translation of the book completed was sent to Halle and the book got printed in 1749 at Halle in Germany.[6] It has the Tamil title, '*Gnaana Mandira Selva Pungaavanam: Athinudaya muthalam vaguppiley paththu karpanaigaludaya varisayin padiey kristhavargalukkotha punniyangaliley vathikka thakkathaaga seyya veyndina 48 sevangal adangi irukkuthu*' (The rich flower garden of spiritual prayers: Its first part contains 48 prayers ordered according to the ten commandments which would help further the increase of Christian qualities). The book also had a title in Latin '*Libellus Precum Religiosissimarum, Dictus Hortulus Paradisiacus, et eius quidem Pars Prima, Ex Germanico in Tamulicum convertit Beniamin Schulzius, Missionarius Evangelicus, Halae Magdeburgicae, 1749*'.

The second part of the book was also printed in 1749 at Halle in Germany with the Tamil title, '*Gnaana Mandira Selva Pungaavanam: Athinudaya rendaam vaguppiley thiruthivamaagira yega sarvesuranaagira pithaa suthan parisuthammana arubiyaaanavar aruliseytha nanmaigaluk-*

kaagavum, ubagarangalukkagavum seyya vendia 29 thothirangal adangi irukkuthu' (The rich flower garden of spiritual prayers: Its second part contains 29 thanksgiving prayers for the benefits and help wrought by the Triune god, father, son and the holy spirit).[7]

The third part of the book also was printed in 1750 at Halle in Germany with the Tamil title, '*Gnaana Mandira Selva Pungaavanam: Athinudaya munaam vaguppiley ubathdiriyathai anupavikkira kaalathiley aarudhal peratthakkathaga seyya vendina 31 sepangal adanagi irukkuthu*' (The rich flower garden of spiritual prayers: Its third part contains 31 prayers to be said in the period of suffering and to get consolation).[8]

The fourth part of the work also got printed at Halle in 1750. It has no individual title but it is brought out along with part three. This fourth part contained 12 prayers used from the 26th Sunday after Trinity and contained order of the readings for prayers and prayers for each day in the year and on festival days (*Gnaana Mandira Selva Pungaavanam: Athinudaya naalam vaguppiley sarvesuranyudaya thirunaamathukku sangaiundagavum, thuthiundaagavum seyya vendina gnaana santhosham uzhla 12 isthothirangal adangi irukkuthu*'. It dealt with liturgy and religious worship.[9]

The press in Halle has thus brought out in 1749-50 the translation of Johann Arndt's devotional classic the Garden of Paradise from German to Tamil. The book printed has 532 pages. Part I and II of *Gnaana Mandira Selva Pungaavanam* have distinct title pages and pagination. Part III and IV have a common title page and a continuous pagination. The book after printing in Germany had been sent to Tranquebar for the use of the laity and the missionaries.

Catechism Book Printed in Tamil in Halle, 1750

A Tamil catechism book titled '*Oru Kristhavanaa Motchaththai adairathukku vetha pramaanathin padiye ariya vendina vilakkangaliyum mandirangalaiyum padichu seyya vendina nayayangalaiyum pothichivikkira gnaana upadesam*' was printed in Halle in 1750. The imprint in Tamil at the title page mentions 'Kiristhu pirantha aayiraththi yezhlunuthi ampatham varushamaagira pothu sasonniley irukkum aalai engira pattanathiley ithu achchile pathikaapattathaathu'.[10] This book after printing in Germany had also been sent to Tranquebar for the use of the laity and the missionaries.

Printing the Book Gnaana Kannaadi in Halle in 1751

Benjamin Schultze felt the need of translating Johann Arndt's *Fünff Geistreiche Bücher vom wahren Christenthum*, published from Leipzig in 1696.[11] He therefore began the translation on 1 June 1736.[12] He translated 42 chapters into Tamil. It described how the old man Adam accepted Jesus

Christ and transformed into his image. The book was printed at Halle in 1751. There is a Latin title followed by the Tamil title of the book which runs: '*Unmaiulla Kirisithiyaniyudaya Magimaiyai Thezhlivaaga Kaanpikkira Gnaana Kannaadi: Athinuadaya muthalaam posthangathilay adangiirukkira 42 athigaarangal, kristhu piranthu 1751 varushamaagirapoothu saasoniley irukkum aalley pattanathiley ithu achiley pathikapattathu*' (The spiritual mirror which clearly shows the glory of True Christianity: Part One containing 42 chapters).[13]

According to missionary records Schultze who continued the translation had completed the next portion of the book successfully on 27 December 1736. The translated 58 chapters formed part two of the book and it described how love, humility, suffering, hope and prayer are important in Christian life. The book was printed at Halle in 1751. The Tamil title of the book is '*Unmaiulla Krisithiyaniyudaya Magimaiyai Thezhlivaaga Kaanpikkira Gnaana Kannaadi: Athinuadaya Rendaam Postham: Ithiley adangiirukkira 58 athigaarangal, kiristhu piranthu 1751 varushamaagirapoothu saasoniley irukkum aalley pattanathiley ithu achiley pathikapattathu*' (The spiritual mirror which clearly shows the glory of True Christianity: Part Two containing 58 chapters).[14] It has 48 pages. Graham Shaw had wrongly attributed this book printed at Tranquebar in 1750. In fact the book was printed at Halle in Germany in 1751.[15]

Schultze continued the third part of the translation and he had begun the work on 2 January 1737. He completed it successfully on 27 December 1737.[16] The translated 23 chapters formed part three of the work. The book was printed at Halle in 1751. The Tamil title of the book is '*Unmaiulla Kirisitiiyaniyudaya Magimaiyai Thezhlivaaga Kaanpikkira Gnaana Kannaadi: Athinuadaya munraam posthangathilay adangiirukkira 23 athigaarangal. kiristhu piranthu 1751 varushamaagirapoothu saasoniley irukkum aalley pattanathiley ithu achiley pathikapattathu*' (The spiritual mirror which clearly shows the glory of True Christianity: Part Three containing 23 chapters).[17]

Schultze began the final part of the translation on 4 March 1738 and completed it successfully on 1 October 1738.[18] It deals with creation and it contained 46 chapters in total and it formed part four of the work. The book was printed at Halle in 1751. The Tamil title of the book is '*Unmaiulla Kirisithiyaniyudaya Magimaiyai Thezhlivaaga Kaanpikkira Gnaana Kannaadi: Athinuadaya naalam posthangathin muthalam vagupille aaru athigaarangalum rendaam vagupilley 40 athigaarangalum adangiirukkuthu*' (The spiritual mirror which clearly shows the glory of True Christianity: Its fourth book contains 6 chapters in its first part and 40 chapters in its second part).[19] Thus Johann Arndt's Vier Buecher vort Wahren

Christentum (True Christianity) was translated by Benjamin Schultze from German to Tamil titled *Gnaana Kannaadi* (Mirror of Wisdom) and the book got printed at Halle in 1751.

All these Tamil books printed at Halle in Germany were sent in ships for circulation and the books were received at Tranquebar. What circumstances prompted the Danish-Halle missionaries to print the books in Germany and distribute it from there are really unknown. It was not that easy perhaps to do printing in Tamil in Germany. Labour, paper, ink and other supplies for binding must have been costly in Europe. They could have reduced the outward-bound loads and greatly reduced the cost of actual production. However, it is made perfectly clear that the press in Halle was organized for printing the German translations of the books into Tamil. However through printing Tamil books, the missionaries caused the spread of Protestant Christianity in Tamil country.

Printing the Book Kalvi Ozhukkam in Halle in 1791

Some Tamil literary works had also evinced the interest of the Protestant missionaries who sent the palm-leaf manuscript composed in paper. We find *Kalvi Ozhukkam* known also as *Ozhukka Maalai* of Avvaiyar got translated and it was printed at the printing press in Halle in 1791.[20] The book has 28 pages.

Printing Tamil Books in Hamburg, Dresden and Erlangen in 1855, 1856 and 1865

Naalu Mandiri Kathai the old Hindu romance composed by Rama Ayyan got translated and printed in Hamburg in 1855. The book has 94 pages.[21] *Paramartha Guru Kathai* of Beschi also got translated and narrated into German by Johannn Georg Theodor Grasse (1814-1885) and the book was printed in Dresden in 1856. The book had 81 pages.[22] Tamil poems translated into German appeared in print from Erlangen in 1865. The book had 227 pages.[23]

Printing Tamil Books in London, 1790-1873

A sermon in Tamil preached by Sathyanathan on 26 December 1790 was translated into English by Johann Christian Kohloff. It was printed in London in 1792 and it had viii+14 pages.[24] Nathaniel Edward Kindersley translated Hindu works of morality which included Thirukural from Tamil to English and the book was printed in 1794 and it had 335 pages.[25]

Benjamin Guy Babington brought out the text and translation of Beschi's *Paramaartha Guruvin Kathai* in 1822. It was printed in London and it mentioned that the letter 'na' is never marked as quiescent and the reason is that the font of letters which he purchased did not contain a requisite character. It would have been easy to have had a new matrix cut, but of this circumstance he was not aware until a considerable portion of the work was printed; and then for the sake of consistency it appear to better to make no alterations. Having made his confession he has to add that the larger type used for heading of chapters, does not contain any dotted letters either. The Tamil characters are square and quite attractive in appearance bearing certain resemblance to the Tamil types used in Halle. There are dots over consonants for some words and there are no dots over consonants for many words printed in the book.[26] B.G. Babington's version of *Paramaartha Guru Kathai* was adopted by Grey Goosequill and the book adorned with 50 illustrations drawn on wood by Alfred Croquill was printed in London in 1861. The book had 223 pages.[27]

Arichandra Vilasam of Ranga Pillai was translated into English by Muthu Kumarasamy Mudaliar and the book was printed in London in 1863 and it had 262 pages.[28]

Saiva Samaya Vizhlakka Vinaa Vidai composed by Kanchipuram Sabaapathi Mudaliar and Sadurangapattinam Sadasiva Mudaliar was translated from Tamil to English by Thomas Foulkes and the book was printed in London in 1863.[29] Edward Jewitt Robinson translated traditions concerning Hindu sages and selections from their writings from Tamil into English and the book was printed in London in 1873 and it had 148 pages.[30] An enlarged version of the book appeared in print in London in 1885 and the book had 388 pages.[31]

The Printing Press in Colombo and the Tamil Fonts Prepared, 1732-39

A printing press was introduced by the Dutch in Sri Lanka in 1736. In a request made by Imhoff for the assistance of running the printing press, the son of Peter Michaelsen, the Danish type-founder in Tranquebar was sent to Colombo in 1737. He prepared the first Colombo type Tamil fonts and these were used for the printing of the Lord's Prayer in Tamil on 28 April 1739.[32] The letter types cast at Yazhpaanam (Jaffna) in Sri Lanka were more rounded and slightly sloping type faces.

The Christian Literature Books in Tamil Printed by Dutch, 1739-1789

The Dutch prepared a book in Tamil titled '*Katharyudaya Vanakkam*' and it was printed in 1739. The Dutch title page is '*Het Gebed Onses heeren in de Tamilsche Tale met de tweed sort der Malabaarsche*, Compagnies Drukkery tot Colombo, gedrukt den 28 April 1739'.[33]

The Dutch also prepared a catechism and printed under the title '*Kathekisamu*' in 1739. The Dutch title page is '*Mallebaars Catechismus, en Gebede-boek Gedrukt tot Colombo ten dientse der Scholen Anno* MDCCXXXIX'.[34]

In 1747 the Dutch printed the book '*Pathinaaru Pirasangam*' (Sixteen sermons). The Dutch title page is '*Sestien Praedictien Overgeste In de Tamulsche Taal, Ten dienste van de Christelyke Tamulsche Gemeentens, Door den Praedikant Philippus De vriest, (S.G.) Zynde ook, naar Kerken-ordre, behoorlyk revideert*, Compagnies gewone Druckety, Anno MDCCXLVII'.[35]

The book '*Sathiyathin Jeyam*' was printed in 1753. The Dutch title is '*Triumph der Waarheid Zynde Eene beknopte en kragtige wederlegging van der Voornaamste dwaalingen der Roomsche kerje, Med verdediginge van daar tegen gestelde Catholyke Waarheid, die in de gereformeerde kerke geleers word. Door Last van den Wel-Edelen groot-Agtbaaren here Julius Valenthyn Stein van Gollenesse, Eersten Raad En Directeur Generaal van Nederlnads Jndia Ten tyde van des zelvs Regeeringe op Ceilon gegeven, in de Tamulsche Taale Opgesteld, Ten dienste van de Christelyke Tamuklsche Gemeenten, Door. Philippus De Melho, Beroepen Praedikant te Jaffana-patnam*, Gedrukt te Colombo, s' Compagnies gewoone drukkery door Johann Bernhardt Arnhardt, Anno MDCCLIII'.[36]

The Dutch prepared the Heidelberg Catechism in Tamil and printed in 1754. The Tamil title is '*Kathekisamu: Aththaavathu Thiruthapatta sabaigalilum pallikudangalilum padipikkapadugira Krisithamaana deva araathanaiyin upadesam*'. The Dutch title page is '*Catechismus, Ofte Onderweyzing In de Christelicke Leere Die In de Hervormde Kerken en Schoolen geleerd word, Ten Dienst der Kerken en Schoolen In de Tamulsche Spraak Overgezet, En Op Goed-Keuring van De Hooge Overheid Deezes Eilands, In 't licht gegeven, Door. Sigisbertus Abrahamsz Bronsveld, Bedienaar des H. Evangeliums in Christi Gemeinte Te Columbo*. Gedrukt in's Comps: gewoone Drukkery, Door Johann Bernhardt Arnhardt. Anno MDCCLIV'.[37]

In 1754 the Dutch also printed the book '*Sirupillai kathekisamu*'. The Dutch title page is '*Vraagen en antwoorden voor de eerst beginnende kinderen...in de Tamulsche sprakk overgezet...door Sigisbertus Abrahamsz Bronsveld...Gedrukt te Colombo in s' Comps: gewoonw drukkery door Johann Bernhardt Arnhardt, anno* MDCCLIV'.[38]

Aandavrudaya suthamaana Raaposanathukku sera virumbugiraval ariya vendina Krisithavargaludaya vethaa padippinaiyin surukkamaana thogai was printed by the Dutch in 1754. The Dutch title page is '*Kort*

Begryp Der Christelyke Religie, Voor Die zig willen begaven tot des Heeren heilig Avondmaal; ten dientse der kerken en Schoolen, In de Tamulsche Spraak overgezet, En, op Goed-keuring Van de Hooge Overheid deezes Eilands, In t' Licht gegeven, Door Sigisbertus Abrahamsz Bronsveld Bedienaar des H. Evangeliums in Christi gemeinte Te Colombo, Comps: gewoone Drukkery: Door Johann Bernhardt Arnhardt, MDCCLIV'.[39]

In 1760 the Dutch printed '*Thiruthapattta Thiruchabaigazhin Vazhipaatu Allatha Murai Noolhal*'. The Dutch title page is *Liturgie der Gereformeerde kerken, ofte De Fornulieren by Dezelve in den uiterlyken dienst gebruykelyke: I in't doen van de gemeene gebeden; II. In de bedieninge der H.Sacramenten; III. Ind'inzegeninge des Houwelyks; en Iv.int' vertroosten der zicken. uit de hollandsche in de tamulsche taale overgezet ten dientse van de Christelyke Tamulsche gemeenten, door Philippus de Melho, Bedienaar des Godlyken words, in de Gemeente jesu Christi te Jaffanapatnam, En naar kerk order behoorlyk overzien*, Gedrukt te Colombo, in's comps: gewoone drukkery, door Pieter Bruwaart, Anno MDCCLX'.[40]

'*Thamizh Bhaashayir Sirupillai Kathekisamu*' was published in 1768. The Dutch title page is '*Tamulsch Kinder-catechismus. Inhoudende het Gebed des heeren. e XII. Geloovs Artykelen; de X. Geboden Gods; het Morgen en Avond Gebed; het Gebed voor en na den Eeten, de Instelling van den H. Doop, van 't H. Nagtmaal, en van de Kerkelyke Tugt; nevens den Christen Zegen: Als mede Korte Vraagen en Antwoorden Noopens De Grondstukken der waare Leere, En De Geschiedenissen des Ouden en Nieuwen Testaments; Gelyk ook de Register der H. Schrift. Ten dientse der Schoolen in een evervolg geschikt en uitgegeven Door Sigis: Abrah: Bronsveld, Bedienaar des H. Euangeliums en Rector in't Seminarium Te Colombo. De derde Druk*, Gedrukt in 's Comp: gewoone Drukkey door Johann Fredrik Christoph Dornheim, MDCCLXVIII'.[41]

The Dutch printed the book '*Katekisamu: Aththaavathu Thiruthapatta sabaigalilum pallikudangalilum padipikkapadugira Krisithamaana deva araathanaiyin upadesam*' in 1769. The Dutch title page is '*Catechismus, Ofte Onderweyzing In de Christelicke Leere, Die In de Hervormde Kerken en Schoolen geleerd word, Ten Dienst der Kerken en Schoolen, In de Tamulsche Spraak Overgezet, En Op Goed-Keuring van De Hooge Overheid Deezes Eilands, In het licht gegeven, Door. Sigisbertus Abrahamsz Bronsveld, Bedienaar des H. Evangeliums in Christi Gemeinte Te Columbo de Twede Druk*, Gedrukt in 's Comps: gewoone Drukkery Door Johann Fredrik Christoph Dornheim. Anno MDCCLXIX'.[42]

'*Aandavrudaya Suththamaana Raaposanathin Muraipaavippu*' was published in 1775. It's Dutch title page is '*Het regt gebruik Van des Heeren*

H: Avondmaal Bestaande in Meditatien, gebeden en Dankzeggingen Door G: Drelincourt, P: Du Moulin en andere Godsgeleerde Mannen, in de Nederduitsche Taal opgesteld, En de zelve Ten Dienste van de Tamulsche Gemeente in derzelver Taale, overgezet Door Jan Franciscus proponent in de Hervormde Tamulsche Gemeente. Te Colombo', Gedrukt, door Joh: Fred: Christ: Dornheim, Anno MDCCLXXV'.[43]

In 1788 '*Thamizh bhaashaiyir sirupillai kathekismu*' was published. The Dutch title page is '*Tamulsch Kinder-catechismus. Inhoudende Het Gebed des Heeren. de XII. Geloovs-Artykelen; de X. Geboden Gods; het Morgen en Avond Gebed; het gebed voor en na den Eeten, de Instelling van den H. Doop, van 't H. Nagtmaal, en van de Kerkelyke Tugt; nevens den Christen Zegen: Als mede Korte vraagen en Antwoorden Noopens De Grondstukken der waare Leere, En De Geschiedenissen des ouden en Nieuwen Testaments; Gelyk ook de Register der H. Schrift. Ten dientse der Schoolen in een evervolg geschikt en uitgegeven Door Sigis: Abrah: Bronsveld, Bedienaar des H. Euangeliums en Rector in't seminarium Te Colombo*. MDCCLXXXVIII'.[44]

'*Devapadikku thakathaay irukkira sathiyathinaya padippinnaiyinudya surukkamaana thogai*' was printed in 1789. The Dutch title page is '*Kort Uittrekzel Van De Leere der Waarheid die na de Godsaaligheid is ten dienste der Schoolen Uit de hollandsche in de Tamulsche taale Overgezet Door Mattheus Jurgen Ondaatje, Proponent in de Hervormde gemeente, En Geredivеerd Door den mede Proponent Mattheus Jurgen Ondaatje. In de Tamulsche Gemeente, En door de Taalkundigen Philip Jansz: en Adrian Frans Farnando, Te Colombo*; Joh: Christoph Dornheim, Anno MDCCLXXXIX'.[45]

Printing the Bible in Tamil at the Printing Press in Colombo and Jaffna by the Dutch, 1741-1790

Translation of the Bible began to develop and Adolphus Cramer translated parts of New Testament and he began the work in 1732 under the patronage of Gustavus Whilhem Baron Imhoff the Dutch Governor of Sri Lanka. Ziegenbalg's New Testament printed in Tranquebar was useful to him. Cramer paid attention and he used the pattern adopted in Greek original Bible. In 1741, the Gospel according to St Mathew translation which was completed by Adolphus Cramer was printed in Colombo. The work is based partly on the Tranquebar New Testament. The Tamil title is '*Archasishta Apostalanum Suviseshakanumaagiya Mathevusu enbavar Yezhuthi vaitha Yesukristuudaya suthamaana suvisesham*'. There is a Dutch title page printed and it runs: *Het Heylige Evangelium Onzes Heeren en Zaligmakers Jesu Christi na de Beschryvinge van den Heilingen Apostel en Evangelist*

Mattheus, uyt de Oorspronkelyke Grieske, in de Mallabaarse Tale overgebragt en behoorlyk na Kerken ordre geredíveert. Then we find the Printers' mark, Gedrukt tot Colombo. Then we find in the book a rule, Compagnies Druckeryre, Anno 1741. Both the Dutch title and the Tamil title page had been printed with the help of woodcut made. The Bible has a preface and the Tamil text follows. It may be mentioned that page four of the gospel is blank. The book has 120 pages in total.[46] The New Testament had been printed in 1741 at Colombo under the auspices of Dutch Governor. It was in the Tamil language different from that of the earlier printed version by the missionaries in Tranquebar in 1714. Regarding the format we find the verses number of the gospel had been printed in the beginning of the verse in the Dutch version. In the earlier Tranquebar printed Gospel of St. Mathew the verse number had been found at the end of the sentence. The Tamil word *senipithaar* (meaning born) had been used in Tamil in the Dutch version. The Tranquebar Gospel had the Tamil word *piranthaar* (meaning born). Hence it may be said that the Gospel of St. Mathew printed in Colombo had used sanskritized Tamil words. Thus the second Tranquebar edition was reprinted at Colombo in 1741-3, after having undergone some alterations adapting it to the Tamil spoken in Sri Lanka. This edition was designed for the Tamil Christians in the island.

Beschi the Jesuit missionary in Tamil country introduced changes in Tamil scripts. He spoke of it in his Tamil grammar work *Kodunthamizh* (1728), *Thonnul Vilzhakkam* in his grammar in one *suttiram* (1731) and in the preface of *Chaturagaraathi* (1732) He wrote that to the short letter (e) he added a slanting stroke and wrote the long form as (e/long) and similarly to the short 'O' Beschi added a loop at the bottom to make it the long letter 'O'. In vowel consonants the sound 'ye' is represented by a *kompu*. Beschi wrote that he added a loop at the top to this *kompu* to make it represent the long sound.[47] These changes made by Beschi came to be permanent features of the Tamils script as early as in 1741 and we find it in the Bible edition of 1741 by the Dutch in Sri Lanka. We find the use of a dash above the letter to indicate that the vowel sound is long. The short vowel sound has no special distinguishing marks. This must be said only a flourish and not used to denote any changes in sound.[48] It is interesting to find that the Bible in Tamil printed in Sri Lanka had Beschi's reformed Tamil letters or scripts. This copy of the Bible is preserved in the Colombo Museum.

The four Gospels and the Acts of the Apostles translated by Adolphus Cramer and group in Tamil was printed by the Dutch in 1748. The title in Tamil is '*Saruvesaparanuk kuganthavarkalul Suthamaana Suviseshagarumaana Mathevus, Maarkku, Lukkaas, Yovannes yezhuthina posthagam*'. The title page in Dutch runs: '*Het Heylige Evangelium onzes Heeren ende*

Zaligmakers Jesu Christi, na de Beschryvinge, van de Mannen Gods, en de H: Evangelisten, Mattheus, Marcus, Lucas, ende Johannes. Waar by nog komt het Tweede Boek, door Lucas, beschreeven, ende genaamt, de Handelingen de Apostelen, uit het Oorspronkelyke Grieks, in de Tamulsche Tale'. It is followed by the Printer's mark, Gedrukt tot Colombo, a rule in's Compagnies Druckerye, Anno 1748. The Dutch title was followed by the Tamil title with vignette, and we find Voor-reden (Tamil preface), then begins the Tamil text. It has 212 pages in total. The text is completely set in two columns. It may be mentioned that this edition of 1748 had also used Beschi's reformed letters. We find here the dash is used occasionally, but generally it dispensed with the dash. From the context the reader has to decide whether the vowel sound is short or long.[49]

Steps were undertaken for further translation of the Bible and it was commenced by Philippus de Melho (1723-1790) who was the son of a wealthy Protestant *vellala* serving on the personal staff of the Dutch Governor in Colombo. He had learnt languages such as Hebrew, Greek, Latin, Dutch, Portuguese and Tamil and studied theology in Colombo. But he turned down an offer of further study in Leiden in favour of an appointment and began ministering to Sri Lankans. Six years later he was the first Sri Lankan to receive the ordination in the Church of Holland.[50]

Philippus de Melho translated 13 Psalms in Tamil and also other Bible songs and he completed the work in 1755. Hence the work in Tamil was printed in Jaffna in 1755. As customary in the Colombo printed books, the 1755 Psalter has both a Dutch and a Tamil title page. The Tamil title is *Iraasa Thirkatharisyahiya Thaavidthinudaya sila sangeethangalum veru pugazhlchi paatukalum adang ulla posthagam.* The title page in Dutch runs: *Eenige Psalmen des Koninglyken Prophete Davids en andere Lofzangen. Uyt den Nederduytschen in Tamulschen Digte overgeset door Philippus De Mello Bedienaer des H. Evangeliums in de Gemeente Jesu Christi, Te Jaffanapatnam: En uitgegeven naar gewoone Kerkorder, Anno 1755*. It has 112 pages in total.[51] The date in old-fashioned Tamil numbers: 1,000 plus 700 plus 50 plus 5, really being letters with numerical values. Opposite the Tamil title page (verso of the Dutch) are two musical scales to illustrate the system. No textual explanation is included simply the ascending and descending scales with tonal names. Included are metrical Psalms numbers 1, 22, 23, 47, 51, 68, 69, 90, 100, 103, 110, 117, 118, 121, and 122. The six metrical '*Lofzangen*' are known in Dutch as by a serious error (6) the words Simeon and Solomon have been confused. The Song of Simeon was printed at Colombo and the Song of Solomon was not. There is a note with mention of this first edition of David's psalms set to music by Philippus de Melho.[52] The Psalms he translated were in poetry as in the original and also he translated them as it could be sung in European music.[53] It would be interesting to know what portion of the 1755 Tamil poetry in this Psalter might be attributed to Clement Marat, through Philippus Baldaeus, and then through the revision by *Predikant* Philippus de Melho. The 1755 Psalter in Tamil language and characters is the earliest vernacular book of music to be produced by a printing press anywhere in Asia.

Philippus de Melho became the first Sri Lankan translator of the Tamil New Testament. He began revising it in 1746 so that it would follow more closely the original Koine Greek and worked at it for 13 years. In the mean time, he moved from Colombo to lead the Protestant Christians in Jaffna and, while there his New Testament translation appeared in print in 1759.[54] The title page in Tamil is *Puthiya Yerpaadu* and the Dutch title page runs thus. '*Het Nieuwe Testament, ofte Alle De Boeken Des Nieuwen Verbonds Van Onsen Heer Jesus Christus, Door Last van de Hooge Overheid Deeses Eilands Uit de oirspronglyke Grieksche Taal In de Tamulsche Spraak overgezet, En Naar Kerken-order behoorlyk overzien. It is followed by Vignette, Gedrukt te Colombo, in Dutch Company, gewoone Drukkery door Pieter Bruwaart. Anno MDCCLIX*'.

After the Dutch title Dutch quotation from Openbaar, Voor-reden, Colombo, 24 December 1759 is mentioned and also signed by Sigisb Abraham Bronsveld and J. J. Fybrands. The Tamil title *Puthiya Yerpaadu* is found with vignette, Openbaar. Then we find the Tamil preface, Tamil text, and finally index in Dutch and Tamil index. The book has 256 pages. The preface of the Bible is dated 24 December 1759 and the translators are Philippus de Melho and Simon de Sylva. It also reports on the mission work by Philippus Baldaeus, Philippus de Vriest, Joan Anthony, Jan Philips, Philip Emanuels and Simon de Sylva.[55] It may be mentioned here that the translation was largely the work of J.P. Wetzelius assisted by Philippus de Melho and Simon de Sylva. Philippus de Melho had used Greek original Bible and Adrianus de Meij's translation for this work. De Melho's translation of the Tamil Bible was publicly and solemnly read in the Jaffna Fort Church to a large body of learned Tamils and to other auditors. The assembly had agreed that it was intelligible to the common people and that its language was matchless, elegant and heart cheering.[56] It is the first Dutch translation of the entire New Testament in Tamil to be printed in Sri Lanka in 1759.

The Dutch in Sri Lanka printed the Psalms in 1776. The Tamil title is '*Sangeethangalum veru pugazhlchi paatukalum adang ulla posthagam*'. The Dutch title is *Het Boek der Psalmen, Nevens de Gezangen, By de Hervormde Kerk van Nederland In Gebruik; Door Last van de Hoog Mogende Heeren Staaten Generaal der Vereenigde Nederlanden, Uit drie*

Berijmingen, in den Jaare 1773, gekooren, Met de noodige daar in gemaakte veranderingen tweede Oplage, Te Colombo, Johan Fredrik Cristoph Dornheim MDCCLXXVI. This is a re-edition in Dutch of the 1773 Leiden edition.

The approval by the authorities in Sri Lanka is stated on the verso reads as follows: *Dat deeze Kolombosche Druk naauwkeurig overeenstemt met de Eerste volledige openbaare Uitgaave te leiden gedrukt by C. van Hoogeveen Junior 1773, getuigt, als daar toe door de Regeering van Ceilon geautorizeerd.* Then follows the signature of M.J. Ondaatje VDM, followed by En rector van't Seminarium Te Colombo.[57] It may be said that the eldest grandson of Rector Ondaatje had compiled the 'Tabular list of original works and translations published by the late Dutch Government of Ceylon at their printing press at Colombo' and he had listed this 1773 Dutch Psalter found in 12 mm. Presently the Sri Lanka National Archives has this book. Johann Friedrich Christoph Dornheim was the printer for the Dutch East India Company and he used the Dutch term Maatschappy rather than the more usual form Compagnie.

The Dutch had made arrangements for translating the Old Testament from Hebrew into Tamil and it was printed in 1790. Earlier they had paid attention mainly to translation and printing of the New Testament. It is found that after a long period they realized the need for the Old Testament translation. The Tranquebar version of the Old Testament was completed and published in 1723, 1726, 1727 and 1728 was considered to be imperfect. It was therefore in contemplation to prepare a new version in Sri Lanka and for the service of the Tamil Protestant congregation they did the work. With this view Rev. Ondaatje executed in 1774 a translation of the book of Genesis and presented it to the Governor Falk, who directed its revision according to the prescribed rule, previous to publication. But as it was deemed preferable to revise the Tranquebar version itself, directions to that effect were conveyed to him. But these were countermanded as soon as it was known in Sri Lanka that Johann Philip Fabricius the missionary in Madras had already begun that work and that the Pentateuch and the books of Joshua and Judges had been published. On the receipt of this order, Ondaatje represented to the Dutch Governor that he had read the revised version with great care and attention, and had also found it to be faulty stating at the same time his opinion, that it would be preferable to translate the Old Testament anew. He moreover added that he had received some portions of the Old Testament rendered by De Melho, which appears superior to the first (Ziegenbalg version) as well as the second (Fabricius) version. To this communication, the Governor replied that both he and De Melho had permission to commence a new version. De Melho accordingly in 1779 and 1780 submitted to the Governor the versions of the books of Genesis and Exodus made from the original Hebrew with the aid of the Septuagint, the Latin versions of Tremellius and Junius and the Netherlands State Bible.[58] It was however reported to De Melho that the Dutch Government in Sri Lanka would prefer a revision of the recently corrected Fabricius version; and they accordingly wished him such a revision, exhibiting in a separate paper of errors found thereto with the required corrections. Pursuant to this order, De Melho prepared and transmitted to Governor Falk a revised version of the Pentateuch, accompanied by a report on the subject and an annotation of the errors in the Fabricius version. The translation of the Old Testament was carried out by Philippus de Melho before his death on 10 August 1790. The printed Bible had the Dutch title '*Het eerste deel des Ouden testaments van de Heilige Schrivtuur, vervattende de vye Boeken Mosis genaamd Genesis, Exodus, Leviticus, Numeri, en Deuteronomium gedrukt te Colombo, in's Komp: Boekdrukkery, by Johan Frederik Christoph Dornheim, anno 1790*'.[59] Thus Bible in Tamil had been printed with titles in Dutch in Colombo and Jaffna by the Dutch East India Company in 1741, 1748, 1755, 1759, 1776 and 1790.

Printing Tamil Periodicals in Sri Lanka under the British, 1802-1870

The British took over Sri Lanka in 1796. The London Missionary Society and other missionary groups sent missionaries to Colombo and elsewhere on the island. Printing presses soon sprang up and we find at Colombo, Wesleyan Mission Press in 1815; at Cotta Church Missionary Society Press in 1822; at Jaffna Wesleyan Church Missions Press in 1825 and at Kandy Baptist Mission Press in 1841. Trilingual printing (in English, Singala and Tamil) had begun and it is found that '*Arasaanga Varthamanni*' the newspaper a weekly got printed in Jaffna in 1802 by the British Government. It appeared on all Mondays since 15 March 1802.[60] A quarterly journal of the church had appeared from Jaffna in 1815. It contained religious matter and mainly published for the spread of Christianity.[61]

Udhaya Thaaragai (Morning Star) a bimonthly came to be published from Jaffna in 1841. It came out on 1st and 3rd Thursdays of every month. It contained matter in bilingual (in Tamil and English). *Udhaya Thaaragai* was devoted to education, science and general literature and to the dissemination of articles on agriculture, government and religion with the summary of important news. The price of the paper was two pence a number or one shilling a quarter payable in advance. The agents who subscribe for ten copies and pay in advance the price was one and a half pence a number or nine pence a quarter. Postage was said to be free. Persons who wished to act as agents could apply to the publisher at American mission press, Manipaay, Jaffna. Correspondents could send their communications addressed to the editors of the Morning Star, Batticola, Jaffna. There were two agents from Tamilnadu. Rev. F.D. Ward was the agent from Madurai and Rev. J.J. Lawrence had acted from Dindigul.[62]

Udhayaathithan was published from Colombo in 1841 by Simon Kasi. In 1848 *Ilangai Nesan* was published from Jaffna and the editor was Muthusami.[63] *Gnnana Deepikai* was published from Jaffna by W. Night Winslow in 1854.[64]

Ilangaabimaani was published from Manippay and the editor was C. Vai. Kadirvel in 1863. *Ilangai Paathukaavalan* was printed from Colombo in 1863 and the editor was C. Muthaiah. *Ilangai Kaavalan* was published from Colombo and the editor was Robert Newton in 1864. These periodicals had come into existence for the use of Tamils in Sri Lanka. *Paaliyar Nesan* a monthly was printed from Jaffna in 1864 and the editor was William Chinna Thambi. It was for intended for the children.[65]

While many periodicals had appeared in print in Sri Lanka a hand written journal called *Puthinaathipathi* appeared in 1870. It was the first journal of this kind that appeared weekly on all Saturdays. The editor was Ku. Appadurai. The first issue came out in February 1870. An attempt was made to print the journal after one year but it was unsuccessful. It is gleaned here that some more journals like *Sarvavasana Manoranjini*, *Yazhpaana Puthinam* and *Yazhpaana Varthamaani* had been printed prior to 1870 in Sri Lanka.[66]

The American Mission Press at Manippay: Printing Calendars, Books, Dictionary and Grammar in Tamil, 1835-1851

Panchankam or the Tamil calendar was published by the American mission press at Manippay in 1838. It had 48 pages.[67] *Panchankams* had continued to be printed and we find even for the year 1849.[68] A Tamil first reading book for the use of the children was prepared in two parts and it was printed at Manippay press in 1835.[69] *Peyar Agaraathi*, a manual dictionary of the Tamil language was printed in Jaffna in 1842 and it had 771 pages.[70] Peter Percival composed *Thiruttantha Sangiraham*, a collection of proverbs in Tamil with their translations in English and it was published in Jaffna in 1843. It had 266 pages.[71] *Senthamizh Ilakkiya Sangiraham* (a high-Tamil anthology) the classical reader or selections from standard Tamil authors prepared primarily and chiefly for the use of the Battocotta seminary was printed in Jaffna in 1847. The book had 261 pages.[72] *Ilakkana Noorsurukkam*, an abridgement of Tamil grammar was printed in Jaffna in 1848 and it had 43 pages.[73] *Nannul Mulamum Viruthiuraiyum* with the commentary of Sankara Namasivaayar was revised by Sivagnaana Swami of Tiruvaavaduthurai and it was edited by Nallur Arumuga Naavalar that appeared in print in 1851 in Jaffna. It had 312 pages.[74]

Printing Protestant Christian Literature Books and Booklets in Tamil, 1814- 1861

Philip of Birmingham's book 'Renunciation of Evil Ways' was translated from English to Tamil by Joseph Knight. The third edition had appeared from Jaffna in 1814 which had 16 pages.[75] Peter Percival's 'Incarnate Grace' was translated. The third edition appeared in the press in Jaffna in 1842 and it had 47 pages.[76] *Unmai Naatam* of 12 pages, *Thuyya Nadai* of 12 pages and *Nadana Naatam* the booklets also appeared in print in 1842.[77] John Scudder's Exposition of the second commandment was translated from English to Tamil and it was printed in Jaffna in 1843 which had 16 pages.[78] *Yesunaathar Malayin Merchonna Pransangathin Visthaarippu*, the third edition was printed in Jaffna in 1843.[79] The pearl of great price was translated into Tamil and it got printed in 1843.[80]

Protestant missionaries in Sri Lanka published a manual for catechists in Tamil and the second edition appeared in Jaffna in 1844. The book had 24 pages.[81] *Vetha Mozhi Ariviththal* of 12 pages, *Sama Vaatham*, the dialogue between a Christian and follower of Mohammed of 12 pages, *Veri Vilakkal*, on the evils of drunkenness, and *Nyaaya Theerpu* were also printed in 1844.[82] The proverbs of Solomon was printed in Tamil in 1845 and the book had 148 pages.[83]

A Tamil religious book came to be printed in 1846 titled *Gnaana Geetha Sangiraham*. It contained devotional songs.[84] H.R. Hoisington, had printed in 1848 a book on Tamil astronomy titled '*Sothida Saastiram*' a translation with numerous explanatory notes with an appendix at the American mission press.[85] *Dhina Bhodhagam* the book was edited and printed by Peter Percival in Jaffna in 1837. It was edited again by L. Spaulding and the second edition appeared in print in Jaffna in 1848. The third edition also came out in 1849.[86] Philip Doddridge's 'The rise and progress of religion in the soul' abridged in English and Tamil was printed in 1848 and it had 338 pages.[87]

The Pilgrims' Progress got translated from English to Tamil by L. Spaulding and the book was printed in Jaffna in 1853.[88] *Gnaana Deepikai* a primer of catechism was printed in 1854 and it had 36 pages. It came out as No. 72 of the publication of the Jaffna Religious Tract Society.[89] The book of Hannah More, 'The Porter' was translated from English to Tamil and it was brought out under new series, as serial no.1 of the Jaffna Religious Tract Society in 1856. It had 16 pages.[90] *Sonna Rayanukkum Sarvaloga Raasanukkum Undanna Vyachchiyam* of 36 pages got printed in Jaffna in

1857 and it came out as 2 of the new series of the Jaffna Religious Tract Society.[91] *Sathya Vetha Pozhippu*, a compendium of scripture the fourth edition got printed in Jaffna in 1857.[92] *Samaya Partichai* was printed in 1858 and the book had 463 pages.[93] *Daavidin Sangeethangal*, Psalms the Version of the Union Bible, was printed in 1861 and it had 274 pages.[94]

The Catholic Printing Press in Colombo and the Tamil Books Published, 1846-49

The Catholic missionaries had established a printing press called *Vyagula Mari Naayagiyin Dharuma Sambradhaaya Achchukudam* in Colombo. A Tamil book titled '*Sathya Vedha Bhodhaga Surukkam*' was printed before 1846. It was a translation from English into Tamil. The book was printed with the permission of Dom Caetano Antonio, the Bishop of Colombo. It had no dots over the consonants.[95]

Prasaatha Vetha Puranam (Divine Grace from the True Religious Book) composed by Jacome Goncalves (1676-1742) the Oratorian missionary in 1720 dealt with the demonstration of the Catholic Church. This book was printed in 1849 in Colombo. The book had detailed notes on seven items such as the life of St. John the Baptist and his parents, life of the blessed virgin Mary and her parents, life of Jesus and his miracles, the descent of the holy spirit, the five signs of the Christian religion, protest against the Christian religion, consumption of the world, the last judgment and the glory of the heaven. The book was examined a censor board prior to printing by Gabriel Pachecu and by a *vetha vaathiyar* (catechist). The contents of the book were approved for printing. Dom Caetano Antonio the Bishop had granted permission to print. The book was published on 5th of *Aani* the Tamil month in 1849 by D.B. Anandappa. The printing press was said to be located at Neduntheruvu in Colombo.[96]

Vyagula Pirasangam composed by Jacome Goncalves in 1730 was printed in Colombo in 1848. This contains nine sermons in nine parts. Sermon one deals with Jesus and his blood sweating at the garden of Gethsemane. Similarly the second sermon deals with Jesus who was betrayed by Judas. The third sermon deals with scouring of Jesus tied to the pillar. The fourth sermon deals with crowing of Jesus with thorns. The fifth sermon deals with Jesus brought before Pontius Pilot. The sixth sermon deals with Jesus carrying the cross. The seventh sermon deals with crucifixion of Jesus. The eighth sermon deals with death of Jesus on the cross. The ninth sermon deals with Jesus brought down from the cross and the body is laid down on the floor. All these nine sermons have been followed with the prayer to be said immediately after the sermon which is also been given. Thus this book deals with the way of the cross which was done on each Fridays of the season of Lent observed by the Catholics. It was reprinted in Jaffna in 1886.[97]

Printing Press Owned by Hindus in Sri Lanka and the Tamil Pamphlets and Books Published, 1849-51

The Protestant missionaries in Sri Lanka took the assistance of Tamils in the course of translating the Bible into Tamil. Arumuga Naavalar (1822-1879) assisted Rev. Peter Percival in Bible translation. On completion of the work in 1848 the Bible in Tamil it got printed in 1850. Armuga Naavalar in 1849 had set out for Madras, with his colleague Sadasiva Pillai to purchase a printing press. He returned to Jaffna by way of the monastery at Tiruvannamalai, and he set up the printing press in a building near the monastery where the school functioned, in a building that a wealthy Chettiyar of Vannarpannai had given to him in 1849.[98] He named the press *Vidya anubalana yantra salai* (The Preservation of Knowledge Press). He had hired workmen to operate it who had been trained by the American mission press at Manippay.[99] In order to direct both the press and the school he spent his nights in the monastery, which became his residence.[100] Arumuga Naavalar edited the old Tamil texts and we find printing Mandala Purudar's *Chudaamani Nigandu* in 1849 the sixteenth century lexicon of 1197 verses giving approximately eleven thousand words both in verse and prose forms.

The *Vidya anubalana yantra salai* the new printing press started functioning in 1850 and it brought out Saivite literature and commentaries besides Naavalar's own writings. Arumuga Naavalar published *Saundaryalahari*, a poem in praise of the goddess important for devotion with *urai* (commentary).[101] *Nannul* with commentary was printed in 1851 and other books like *Thirumurugattrupadai* the first song from *Paththu Paattu* based on *Nachinaarkiniyar urai* got printed in 1851.

Periya Puranam in prose appeared from the *Vidya anupalana yendira salai* in 1852.[102] Naavalar had introduced the 'split' system of complex *sandhi* forms to facilitate reading and comprehension. The back cover of the book of Periyapuranam of Naavalar contains the list of books printed till date in 1852. We find also the price of the books in rupee and *anna*.

Title	*Rupee*	*Anna*
Nannul Virudhiurai	3	8
Sathyarubamaahiya Periyapuranam	2	8
Chudaamani Nigandu Paththu Thoguthiurai	1	12
Kolai maruththalusaa	1	12
Thiruchendinirotta kayamahavavandhaathiurai	1	3
Paala paadam- muthar puththagam	1	2
Pushpa vidhi	1	1
Vinaayagakavasam, Sivakavasam, Saththikavasam	1	1

Naavalar's publication of Sekkizhlar's Periyapuranam is the first major literary work that appeared in print. It contained 272 pages of prose version a retelling of the twelfth century hagiography of the Saivite Nayanars. In his introduction to prose rendering Naavalar noted that Sekkizhlar wrote the work in fine poetry that was now useless to anyone except scholars. Therefore he had intended his prose version, for everyone—learned scholars, failing scholars, literates and the illiterates who could listen to it being read. Although it was in prose, the sivapuranam would confer its benefits only on those who read it or listened to it in the proper ritual context and with the appropriate attitude. Thus he developed the medieval poetry to modern prose, a style he largely had to create, but to his mind the prose did not alter the sacred nature of the work.[103]

Polemical Writings in Tamil Printed from Sri Lanka, 1836-1857

H. R. Hoisington, the principal of the American mission seminary in Jaffna, lectured on a list of popular objections to Christianity called *kummi* between 1836 and 1839. This was disliked by the Hindus and so *Gnaana Kummi* was composed by Muthu Kumara Kavirayar (1780-1851) a *vellala* poet in retaliation.[104] A long anti-Christian poem had also appeared in print in Jaffna and it was done by Naavalar along with Vinayaka Murthi Chettiar of Nallur and they got printed it titled *Gnaaana Kummi* (the Kummi Song on Wisdom) of Muthu Kumara Kavirayar in 1852. It led to calls by the local Christians to close down the printing press.[105] *Gnaana Kummi* was severely attacked by a Christian in a poem called *Agnaana Kummi* and it was composed by Silambu Natha Pillai. Further another book titled *Yesu Matha Parikaaram* (Abolition of the Jesus Doctrine) had also been printed.[106]

Arumuga Naavalar had himself begun to openly dispute with the claims of the missionaries and he refuted the abuses of the Christians. Therefore the most dramatic anti-Christian literary prints came out from the *Vidya anubalana yantra salai*. Naavalar along with Senthinatha Iyer published *Bibiliya Kutsita* (Disgusting Things in the Bible) highlighting examples of indecent language from the Bible.

John Scudder wrote and printed a booklet of 28 pages titled *Romai Margaththaar Kodukkira Yethirmozhikku Marumozhi*. The third edition got printed in Jaffna in 1843.[107] Scudder also wrote *Nesa Nirupam* a friendly epistle pointing out some of the chief errors taught by the Roman Catholic Church. The fourth edition appeared in 1843 and it had 20 pages.[108] John Scudder also wrote *Yethirmozhukku Marumozhi*, on the ten commandments contracted with the decalogue of the Roman Catholic Church. The third edition was printed in Jaffna in 1843 which had 4 pages.[109] John Scudder published *Guru Vivaha Vizhlakkam* a tract against the celibacy of the

Catholic clergy. The second edition was printed in Jaffna in 1844 and it had 20 pages.[110] Scudder also published *Narkarunai Kuraipaadu* on withholding the cup from the laity a tract against Roman Catholic Church in Jaffna in 1844 and it had 16 pages.[111]

A booklet for effectively countering Christian propaganda titled 'Abolition of the Abuse of Saivism' was published from *Vidya anubalana yantra salai* in 1854. Carrol Vishvanathan Pillai in the same year published his rejoinder to Arumuga Naavalar's Abolition of the Abuse of Saivism vide *Suppira Deepam* (Brilliant Lamp) from Jaffna in 1857. The book had 60 pages.[112] The *Vidya anubalana yantra salai* printed a lot of pamphlets and books which Arumuga Naavalar wrote and a notable text published was 'The Prohibition of killing: Manual of worship of Shiva temple and the essence of the Saiva religion'.

To conclude it may be said that the spread of Tamil in Europe and its printing in various important towns and cities is astonishing. It was chiefly through the efforts of certain interested individuals. In Sri Lanka after the birth of Tamil periodicals we find the language of the Tamils in the island had been born anew. Earlier only the poetic Tamil was found. However through the British contacts a lot of English words had come to be used in spoken and written Tamil widely. The Tamil periodicals continued to appear with some regularity but most did not last more than a few years. The missionaries themselves were to be said responsible for the production of literary periodicals. However periodicals were also printed by the civilians, merchants and native gentlemen.

Notes

1. Philippus Baldaeus, *Nauwkeurige beschryvinge van Malabar en Choromandel, derhalver aangrenzende ryken, en het machtige eyland Ceylon. Nevens een omstandige en grondigh doorzochte ontdekking en wederlegginge van de afgoderye der Oost-Indische heydenen*, 3 vols, Amsterdam, Janssonius van Waasberge en van Someren, 1672, chapter 46.
2. Philippus Baldaeus, *Bahrhaftige Ausfuhr- liche Beschreibung,* Amsterdam, 1672; Philippus Baldaeus, *A True and Exact Description of the Celebrated East-India Coasts of Malabar and Coromandel as also of the island of Ceylon*, translated from the High Dutch London: Printed for Awnsham & John Churchill, 1703.
3. S. Jeyaseela Stephen, *From Anrique Anriquez to Louis Savinien Dupuis: The Tamil Grammar and the Dictionary Quest*, Pondicherry, 2017, p. 26.
4. Ibid., p. 98.
5. Archiv der Franckesche Stiftungen, Halle (hereafter AFSt), M2 B72:13; *Notices of Madras and Cuddalore in the Last Century from the Journals and Letters of the Earlier Missionaries of the Society for the Propagation of Christian Knowledge*, London, 1858, p. 194; Heike Liebau, 'German Missionaries as Research Workers in India: Their Diaries as Historical Sources (Benjamin

Schultze, 1689-1760, Exception or Norm?)', *Studies in History,* new series, vol. 11, no. 1, 1995, pp.101-18.

6. Bibliothek der Franckesche Stiftungen, Halle (hereafter BFSt), C:5B. *Gnaana Mandira Selva Pungaavanam*, part I, Halle, 1749.
7. Ibid, Part II, Halle, 1749.
8. BFSt, C:5B; *Gnaana Mandira Selva Pungaavanam*, part III, Halle, 1750; British Library, London (hereafter BL), no. 14170.bbb.7.
9. Ibid, Part IV, Halle, 1750.
10. BFSt, C:38:89.
11. *Der Königl. Dänischen Missionarien aus Ost-Indien eingesandter ausführlichen Berichten, Von dem Werck ihrs Ams unter den Heyden, angerichteten Schulen und Gemeinen, ereigneten Hindernissen und schweren Umstanden; Beschaffenheit des Malabarischen Heydenthums, gepflogenen brieflicher Correspondentz und mundlchen Unterredungen mit selbigen heyden*, Teil 1–9, (Continuationen 1–108) Waiserihaus, Halle, 1710–1772 (hereafter HB), vol. IV, continuation 42, p. 834.
12. The Latin title of the book is *Joannis Arndtii...de Vero Christianismo Liber Primus...Ex Germanico in Tamulicum Convertit Benjamin Schulzius*, Halle, 1751; BL, no.G.19737. The book has v+399 pages. There is a book with the same title *Gnaana Kannaadi*, authored by Pierre Mauduit the Jesuit and it should not be confused with the printed book of the Protestants. The Roman Catholic missionaries in Pondicherry printed the book in 1858 and the next edition got printed at Pondicherry in 1906. See, S. Jeyaseela Stephen, *Missioner Tamil Written and Printed in Pondicherry: Literature and Louis Savinien Dupuis, 1841-73*, Pondicherry, 2017, pp. 69, 229. 272.
13. BFSt, C: 70; AFSt, 32 M 12.
14. HB, vol. IV, continuation 48, p. 1632.
15. BFSt, C: 70; AFSt, 32 M 12.
16. BFSt, C:38:97; C:38:98; C:38:99; Graham Shaw, *The South Asia and Burma Retrospective Bibliography, Stage1: 1556-1800*, London, 1987, p. 98.
17. HB, vol. IV, continuation 48, p. 1633.
18. BFSt, C: 70; AFSt, 32:M 12.
19. HB, vol. IV, continuation 48, pp. 1635, 1649.
20. BL, no. 14172a. (4), *Aweiar's Kalwiorhuckam: Oder Sittenspruche aus Tamulischen Palamblattern Ubersetzt, mit Bemerkungen uber Indische Gelehrsamkeit, von. J.C.C. Rudiger*, Halle, 1791.
21. BL, 14171.a.32, *Vier Geheimrath-minister Eine Indische Geschite in Gleichnissen aus Tamulischer sprache ubertregen von dem fruheren Braminien Christian Rama Ayen*, Hamburg, 1855.
22. BL, 14170.k,72, *Fahrten und Abenteuer Gimpels und Compagnie Ein tamulischen Reise-und Scherzmarchen, Nacherzahlt von Dr. Johannn Georg Theodor Grasse*, mit 6 color irten Bildern , Dresden, 1856.
23. BL, 14172.a.39, *Indische Sinnpflanzen und Blumen, zur Kennezeichnung Indischen Vornehmlich tamulischen Geistes*, Erlangen, 1865.

24. BL, 115.h.9, J.C. Kohloff, *A sermon on Ezekiel XXIII, 11 in Tamil language composed and preached by Sattianaden, on the 26th day of December 1790*, London, 1792.
25. Nathaniel Edward Kindersley, *Specimen of Hindoo culture: Consisting of translations from the Tamulian language, of some Hindoo works of morality & imagination with explanatory notes, to which are prefixed introductory remarks on the myth of literature & C of the Hindus*, London, 1794.
26. BL.14170.k.70, *Paramaartha Guruvin Kathai: The Adventures of the Gooroo Paramartan: A Tale in the Tamil Language, Accompanied by a Translation & Vocabulary Together with an Analysis of the First Story*, by Benjamin Babington of the Madras Civil Service, London, MDCCCXXII.
27. BL, 14170.k.64, *Strange, Surprising Adventures of the Venerable Gooroo Simple and his Five Disciples, Noodle. Doodle, Wiseacre, Zany and Foozle*, London, 1861.
28. BL, 14170.1.33, *Arichandra the Martyr of Truth, a Tamil drama translation into English by Mutu Coomara Swamy Mudeliar*, London, 1863.
29. BL, 14170.e.36 (6), *A Catechism of the Shaiva Religion Translated from the Tamil by the Rev. Thomas Foulkes*, London, 1863.
30. BL, 14170.k.62, Edward Jewitt Robinson, *Tamil wisdom, Traditions concerning Hindu sages & Selections from their writings with an introduction by the late Rev. Elijah Hook*, London, 1873.
31. BL, 14170.k.63, Edward Jewitt Robinson, *Tales and Poems of South India comprehended and enlarged edition of Tamil wisdom from the Tamil*, London, 1885.
32. S. Jeyaseela Stephen, *The First Catholic Bible in Tamil and Louis Savininen Dupuis at Pondicherry: A History of Translation and Printing*, 1850-7, Pondicherry, 2017, pp. 95-98.
33. Koninklijke Bibliotheek, Den Haag (hereafter KBDH), Handscriften, Oude Drukken, 82 H 9, see plate no. XIV; AFSt, M2 B6:54a.
34. Hendrik Kramer Instituut, Oegstgeest (HKI), K-116; Universiteits Bibliotheek, Leiden (hereafter UBL), 1497 C 43.
35. HKI, K-174; KBDH, 516F.14.
36. HKI, K145, Universiteits Bibliotheek, Amsterdam (hereafter UBA), 1071 C6; UBL, 497 C 37; 1497 C38 and 800 D 17; BL, no. 14170.b.61.
37. HKI, K-142; KBDH, 474 H13, Universiteits Bibliotheek, Utrecht (hereafter UBU), AD: E qu 533; BL, 14170.b.62.
38. KBDH, 1117 E8.
39. HKI, K-134; KBDH, 1117 D 59; UBL 877 G6 and 1144 B 45; BL, no. 14170. b.15.
40. KBDH, 1117E 51; UBL, 877 G 7; BL, no. 1410.a.25.
41. UBL, 877 G5; Det Kongelige Bibliotek, Kobenhavn (hereafter KB), 1117 E58.
42. HKI, K-133; UBL 877 D 27; UBU, AB:E.qu 533a; BL, 141170.b.63.
43. KBDH, 1117 H 45.
44. HKI, K-143; UBL, 1497 C 46; BL, no. 14170.a.36.

45. HKI, K-73.
46. HKI, K-154; HKI, G-9-14; BL, London, 14170.cc.15; Colombo Museum, 1/EF 37.
47. S. Jeyaseela Stephen, From Anrique Anriquez to Louis Savinien Dupuis, pp. 83-86, 103, 106-7, 110, 202-03.
48. C. Balasingham, 'Some Unusual Characters Used in Tamil Printing in Ceylon during Dutch Times', *Proceedings of the International Conference-Seminar of Tamil Studies*, Madras, 1971, vol., II, pp. 528-30, see p. 529.
49. KBDH, 662 B 23; HKI, K-155.
50. Simon Casie Chitty, *The Tamil Plutarch: Containing a Summary Account of the Lives of the Poets and Poetesses of South India and Ceylon from the Earliest to the Present Times with Select Specimens of their Compositions*, Jaffna, 1859, pp. 69-76.
51. HKI, K-10; KBDH, 4 F 20; KBDH, 488 H 3.
52. UBA, 492 E27; 877 G 12; UBL, 1144 F 23.
53. Sabapathy Kulendran, *Kristhava Thamizh Vethaagamathin Varalaru*, Bangalore, 1967, p. 78.
54. Bibliothèque Asiatique Missions Etrangères de Paris (hereafter BAMEP), Call no.27/21; Simon Casie Chitty, The Tamil Plutarch, pp. 69-76.
55. HKI, K-155; KBDH, 662 B 21; 622 B 22; UBA, 220 B11; BL, or.71.d.8.
56. Simon Casie Chitty, The Tamil Plutarch, p. 75.
57. M. P. J. Ondaatje, 'A Tabular List of Original Works and Translations Published by the Late Dutch Government of Ceylon at their Printing Press at Colombo', *Journal of the Royal Asiatic Society of Great Britain and Ireland*, new series, 1, 1865, pp. 141-4.
58. The Old Testament contains in Hebrew 39 books (from Genesis to Leviticus, five books; Joshua to Esther, twelve books; Job to Song of Songs, five books; Isaiah to Daniel, five books and Hosea to Malachi, twelve books). The Old Testament in Septuagint (Greek) contains 46 books.
59. British and Foreign Bible Society's Library (hereafter BFBSL), Cambridge University, Cambridge, *Het eerste deel des Ouden testaments van de Heilige Schrivtuur, vervattende de vye Boeken Mosis genaamd Genesis, Exodus, Leviticus, Numeri, en Deuteronomium gedrukt te Colombo, in's Komp: Boek-drukkery, by Johan Frederik Christoph Dornheim, anno 1790*.
60. A. Maa, Sami, *Paththonpatham Nuttrandu Thamizh Ithalgal*, Madras, 1993, p. 56.
61. Ibid., p. 57.
62. Maraimalai Adigal Library, Chennai, *Udhaya Thaaragai*, Issue no. 3, dated 4 February 1841, Thursday.
63. A. Maa, Sami, Paththonpatham Nuttrandu, p. 70.
64. Ibid., p. 73.
65. Ibid., p. 83.
66. Ibid., p. 96.

67. *Panchankam: Salivaahana Sakaartham 1761 sella ninra vilambi varudathakku vattukottaiyir saathira pallikudathil uvathiyaarayirukkira vanaarpannai vellalan mayil vaahanar somasekaram pillai kaniththathu*; *Panchankam or Tamul Calendar AD 1838-39 Calculated by George Dashiell, Teacher of Sanscrit, Hindu Astronomy & C in the American Mission Seminary, Battocotta, Jaffna*, Published by the Jaffna Religious Tract Society, American Mission Press Manopy, 1838.
68. *Thiriyaangam*, Jaffna, 1849.
69. BL 14172 h.1 (1), *Siru Pillaigal Vaasikka Pazhagiraththukku Seytha Puthagam*, Manippoy, 1835.
70. BL, 14172.e.19, *Peyar Agaraathi, A Manual Dictionary of the Tamil Language*, Jaffna, 1842.
71. BL, 14170.k.6, Peter Percival, Thiruttantha Sangiraham, Jaffna, 1843.
72. BL, 14172.h.79, *Ilakkiya Sangiraham* , Jaffna, 1847.
73. BL, 14172.h.38, *Ilakkana Noorsurukkam*, Jaffna, 1848.
74. BL, 14172.f.2, *Nannul Mulamum Viruthiuraiyum*, ed., Nallur Arumuga Naavalar, Jaffna, 1851.
75. BL, 14170b.1. (31), *Dhunneri Vilakku*, Jaffna, 1814.
76. BL, 14170.b.1.58, Peter Percival, *Arulavadhaaram*, Third edition, Jaffna, 1842.
77. BL, 14170.b.1 (32), *Unmai Naatam*, 12 pp. second edition, Jaffna 1842;

    BL, 14170.b.1 (24), *Thuyya Nadai,* a translation by L. Spaulding Sarah's The Walk of Purity, second edition, Jaffna 1842; BL, 14170b.1 (46), *Nadana Nattam*, Evils of Comedies, Second edition, Jaffna, 1842.
78. BL, 14170.b.1 (10), John scudder, *Irandamm Karppani Vizhlakkam*, Second edition, Jaffna, 1843.
79. BL, 14170.b.1 (40), *Yesunaathar Malayin Merchonna Pransangathin Visthaarippu*, Third edition, Jaffna, 1843.
80. BL, 14170b.1 (7), *Aani Muthu*, Second edition, Jaffna, 1843.
81. BL, 14170.b.1 (20), Charles Mault, *Podhagar Ilakkanam*, Second edition, Jaffna, 1844.
82. BL, 14170.b.1 (32), *Vetha Mozhi Ariviththal*, Third edition, Jaffna, 1844; BL, 14170.b.1.23, *Sama Vaatham*, Second edition, Jaffna, 1844; BL, 14170.b.1 (19), *Veri Vilakkal*, Second edition, Jaffna, 1844; BL, 14170b.1 (39), *Nyaaya Theerpu*, Second edition, Jaffna, 1844.
83. BL, 3068.a.39, *Saalamonin Neethi Mozhighal*, American Mission Society, Jaffna, 1845.
84. *Gnaana Geetha Sangiraham: Ithil Devanai Thuthithu Vanangum Porruttu Kiristhavargal Antharangamaayum Vehirangammayum Paada Vendi Paatukkal Adangi Irukkinrana*, Manipaay Achchukudathir Pathikapattathu, 1846. *Tamil Hymns Selected & Original Adapted for Public, Private and Social Worship*, Published by the Jaffna Religious Tract Society, Jaffna, American Mission Press, 1846.
85. H.R. Hoisington, *Coticattiram: The Oriental Astronomer; Being a complete system of Hindu astronomy, accompanied with a translation and numerous explanatory notes; with an appendix*, Jaffna, American Mission Press, 1848.

86. BL, 14170.a.1, *Dhina Bhodhagam*, Jaffna, 1848, Third edition, Jaffna, 1849.
87. BL, 14170b.36, *Meygnnaodhaya Viruththi*, Jaffna, 1848.
88. BL, 14170.b.9, *Pardesai Motcha Payanam*, Jaffna, 1853.
89. BL, 980.k. 19, Gnaana Deepikai, *A Primer of Catechism*, trs., W. Knight & Miron Winslow, Jaffna, 1854.
90. BL, 14170.a. 33 (3), *Kaavalappan Kathai*, Jaffna, 1856.
91. BL, 14170.a.33 (4), *Sonna Rayanukkum Sarvaloga Raasanukkum Undanna Vyachchiyam*, Jaffna, 1857.
92. BL, 14170.a.14, *Sathya Vetha Pozhippu*, Fourth edition, Jaffna, 1857.
93. BL, 14170.b.38, *Samaya Partichai*, Jaffna, 1858.
94. BL, 3089.aa.27, *Daavidin Sangeethangal*, Psalms, The Version of the Union Bible, Jaffna Auxiliary Bible Society, 1861.
95. BAMEP, TAM 193.
96. S. Jeyaseela Stephen, *Missioner Tamil*, p. 77.
97. BL, no. 14170.c.25. Jacome Goncalves, *Pirasangangal*, ed., J. Vanroyn, II vols, Colombo, 1848.
98. Ve. Kanakarattina, *Arumuganaavalar Sariththiram*, Jaffna, 1882, reprint 1968, p. 31.
99. E. J. Robinson, *Hindoo Pastors: A Memorial*, London, 1867, p. 125.
100. Ve. Kanakarattina, Arumuganaavalar Sariththiram, p. 32.
101. John Murdoch, *A Classified Catalogue of Tamil Printed Books with Introductory Notes*, Madras, 1865, n. 15.
102. BL. 14170.e.10, *Periyapuranam Yenru Vazhangukinra Thiruthondar Puranam*, by Arumuga Naavalar, Jaffna, 1852.
103. Nallur Ta. Kailasa Pillai, *Arumuga Navalar Prabantha Thirattu*, Colombo, 1996.
104. *The Fifth Triennial Report of the American Mission Seminary, Jaffna, Ceylon, with an Appendix*, American Mission Press, Jaffna, 1839, p. 12; See also, S. Jebanesan, *America Missionnum Ilankaiyil Thamizh Valarchchiyum*, Thellippalai, 1983.
105. Ve. Kanakarattina, Arumuganaavalar Sariththiram, p. 34.
106. Simon Casie Chitty, The Tamil Plutarch, pp. 55-56.
107. BL, 14170.b.1 (6), John Scudder, *Romai Margaththaar Kodukkira Yethirmozhikku Marumozhi*, Third edition, Jaffna, 1843.
108. BL, 14170.b.1 (5), John Scudder, *Nesa Nirupam*, Fourth edition, Jaffna, 1843.
109. BL, 14170.b.1 (6), John Scudder, *Yethirmozhukku Marumozhi*, third edition, Jaffna, 1843.
110. BL, 14170.b.1 (11), John Scudder, *Guru Vivaha Vizhlakkam*, Second edition, Jaffna, 1844.
111. BL, 14170.b.1 (18), John Scudder, *Narkarunai Kuraipaadu*, Jaffna, 1844.
112. Carrol Vishvanathan Pillai, *Suppira Deepam*, Jaffna, 1857.

Cax. 75

Cartilha que contẽ breuemẽte
ho q̃ todo christão deue aprẽder
pera sua saluaçam. A qual el rey
dom Joham terceiro deste nome
nosso senhor mandou imprimir
ẽ lingoa Tamul e Portugues
cõ ha decraraçam do Tamul por
cima de vermelho.

9.1. The title page of Cartilha printed in Lisbon in Portugal on 2 February 1554.
(Courtesy: *Belem Museum, Lisboã, Portugal)*

Kyrie eleison. Christe eleison Kyrie eleison.

Pater noster qui es in celis sanctificetur nomen tuum. Adveniat regnum tuum. Fiat voluntas tua: sicut in celo et in terra. Panem nostrum quotidianum da nobis hodie. Et dimitte nobis debita nostra sicut et nos dimittimus debitoribus nostris: Et ne nos inducas in tentationem. Sed libera nos a malo. Amẽ.

Padre — nosso — — tu nos ceos estas: — — — Do teu no-
Pidã éngalaré ni agájatil iriquirrãy: Un trinã
Padre nosso que estas — nos — ceos: — Sãctifica-

me — sanctificado seja. — — — Do teu regno venha — —
mam pũniam agauènum. Un ráiiain varauẽnum
do seja — do teu nome. — Venha a nos do — teu

a nos — — — A tua vontade seja feita assi como nos ceos assi na
engálcu/. Un manadũ ãgaue agájatilũm: auua-
regno — — Seja feita tua võtade: Assi na terra co-

— — terra — — — Nosso — — pam — que cada dia — —
nám bumillũm. Engallaré apám naldcorum: curu-
mo nos — ceos — Do nosso — pam — de cada dia nos —

— — assi — nos — — osc — da — — E perdoa — — a nos —
crã apari éngalau/inddu/tta. Porrutucol éngalcu/
da — — osc — — — — — — E perdoa — — nos —

9.2. A page from Cartilha printed in Lisbon in Portugal on 2 February 1554. (Courtesy: Belem Museum, Lisboã, Portugal)

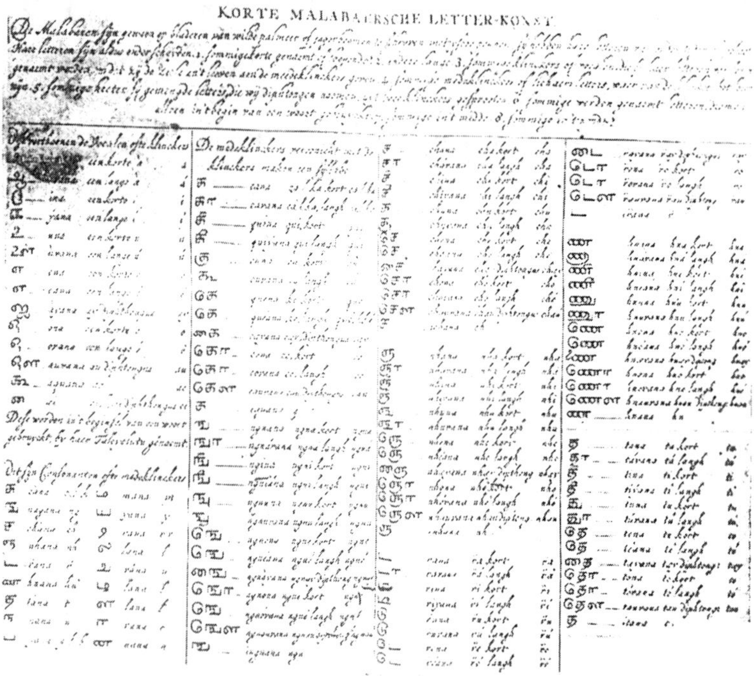
KORTE MALABAARSCHE LETTER-KONST

9.3. The short Tamil orthography by Philippus Baldeaus from his travelogue printed in Amsterdam in 1672. (Courtesy: *Koninklijke Bibliotheek, Den Haag, The Netherlands*)

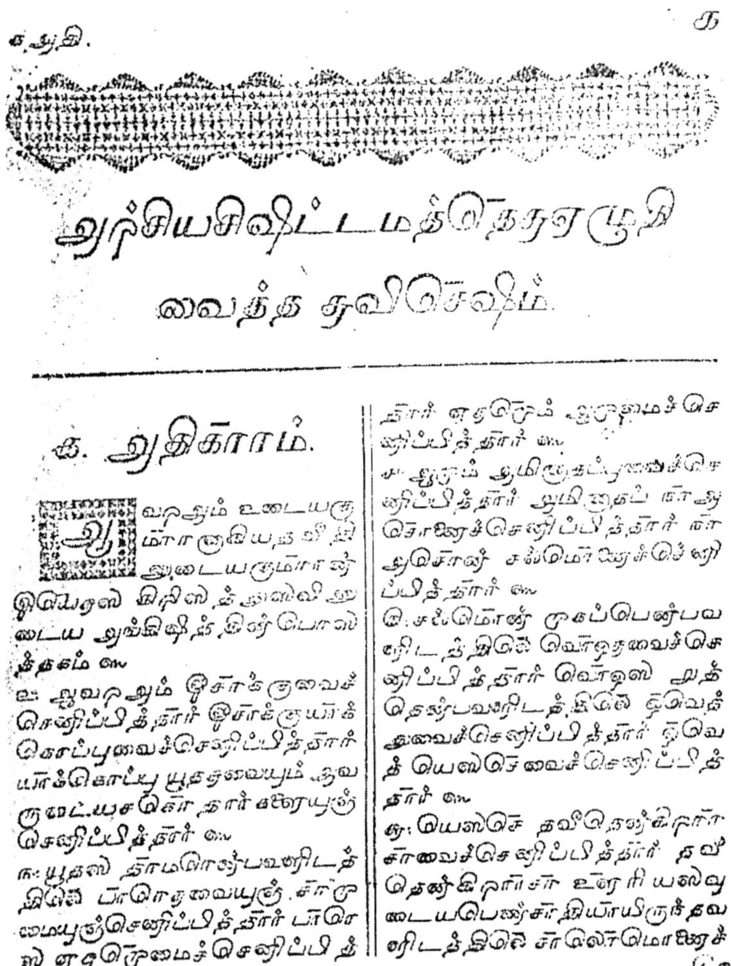

க.அ.இ.

அர்ச்சியசிஷ்ட மத்தேயு எழுதி வைத்த சுவிசேஷம்.

க. அதிகாரம்.

A

9.4. The page of gospel according to St, Mathew printed in Tamil by the Dutch in Colombo in 1741. (*Courtesy*: Bibliothek der Franckesche Stiftungen, Halle, MISS:C 150)

Aweiar's

Kalwiorbuckam

oder

Sittenſprüche

aus

Tamuliſchen Palmblättern überſetzt

mit

Bemerkungen über indiſche Gelehrſamkeit

von

J. C. C. Rüdiger.

Halle,

bey Friedrich Chriſtoph Dreyßig 1791.

9.5. *Kalvi Ozhukkam of Avvaiyar translated from Tamil to German and printed in Halle in 1791.* (Courtesy: *Bayerische Staats-Bibliothek Muenchen*).

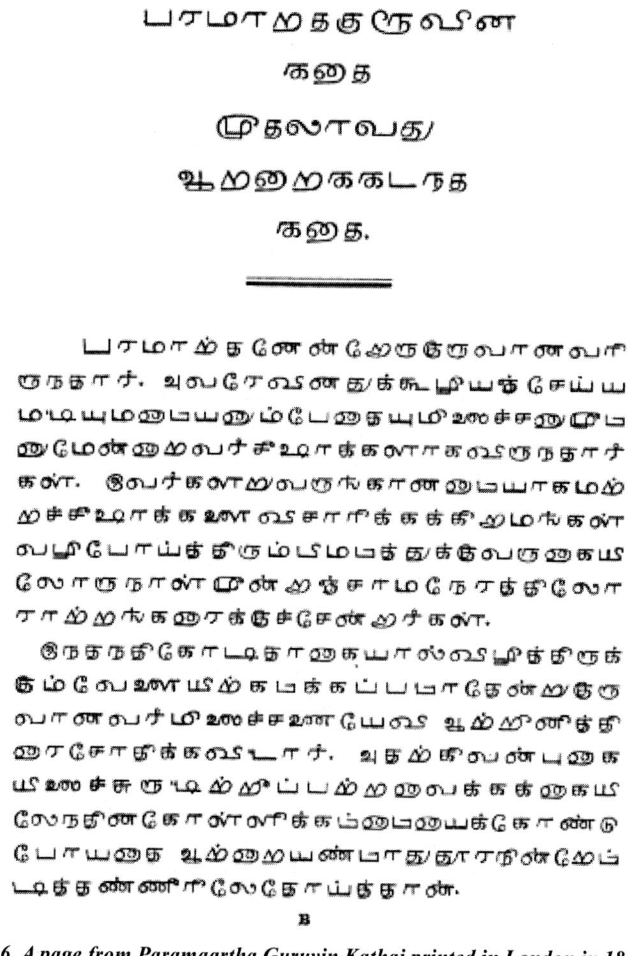

பரமார்த்தகுருவின

கதை

முதலாவது

ஆற்றைக்கடந்த

கதை.

9.6. A page from Paramaartha Guruvin Kathai printed in London in 1822.* (Courtesy*: British Library, London, 14170.k.70).

9.7. The Tamil fonts prepared by Edmund Fry & Son, in London in 1824.* (Courtesy: *British Library, London).

பஞ்சாங்கம்.

௲௮௱௩௰௮ம் ஆண்டு.

சாலிவாகனசகார்த்தம் ௲௭௱௬௰ செல்லாநின்ற விளம்பி வரு
டத்துக்குவட்டுக்கோட்டையிற்சாத்திரப் பள்ளிக்கூடத்தி
ல் உவாத்தியாராகிய வண்ணார்பண்ணை வெள்ளாளன்
மயில்வாகனர் சோமசேகரம்பிள்ளை
கணித்தது.

PANCHANKAM

OR

TAMUL CALENDAR.

A. D. 1838—9.

Calculated by George Dashiell, Teacher of
Sanscrit, Hindoo Astronomy, &c. in the
American Mission Seminary,
Batticotta, Jaffna.

PUBLISHED BY THE JAFFNA RELIGIOUS TRACT SOCIETY.

American Mission Press,—Manepy.
1839.

9.8. Panchangam the Tamil calendar of 1839 printed at the American Mission press at Manippay in Jaffna in 1839. (Courtesy: *British Library, London).*

உதயதாரகை.—MORNING STAR.

Published on the 1st and 3d Thursday of every Month, at one shilling a Quarter, payable in advance.

சஞ்சிகை. க.] Thursday, February 4, 1841. [No. 3.

வாலாறு.

உதயதாரகைப் பத்திரத்தில் கற்கை, சாத்திரம், பொதுவான கல்வி, பயிர்ச்செய்கை, அரசாட்சி மார்க்கம் முதலானவையைப் ...

TERMS.

The MORNING STAR will be devoted to Education, Science, and general Literature, and to the dissemination of articles on Agriculture, Government, and Religion, with a brief summary of important News.

The PRICE of the Paper is *two pence* a number, or *one shilling* a quarter, payable in advance.

To Agents who subscribe for *ten copies* and pay *in advance*, the price is *one and a half pence* a number, or *nine pence* a quarter.

To those who subscribe for *twenty copies* and pay *in advance*, the price is *one penny* a number, or *six pence* a quarter.

N. B. Postage extra.

Persons who wish to act as AGENTS, may apply to the Publisher, at the American Mission Press, Manepy, Jaffna.

CORRESPONDENTS may send their Communications addressed to "The Editors of the Morning Star," Batticotta, Jaffna.

The following persons are authorized to act as *Agents* for the "Morning Star."

JAFFNAPATAM—Mr. C. F. Grenier; POINT PEDRO, A. Holmes; CALPENTYN—John Woodhull; MADURA—Rev. F. D. W. Ward; DINDIGUL—Rev. J. J. Lawrence.

[BRIEF HISTORICAL VIEW OF INDIA.]

[Continued from page 10.]

இந்துதேசச் சரித்திரம்.—*Principal mountains in Hindustan.*

... (Hindu Coosh) ... (Imout or Imaus which is the same with the Indian Caucasus) ...

[பாரதபதிப் படலம்.]

... (Boglipore) ...

9.9. Udhaya Thaaragai, Issue three of the periodical dated 4 February 1841 published from the American Mission Press at Manippay in Jaffna (Courtesy: Maraimalaiadigal Library, Chennai).

Vier

Geheimrath-Minister.

Eine indische Geschichte

in Gleichnissen.

Aus tamulischer Sprache übertragen

von dem früheren Braminen

Christian Rama Ayen.

Hamburg.

Selbstverlag des Verfassers.

1855.

9.10. Naalu Mandiri Kathai translated from Tamil to German and printed in Hamburg in 1855.* (Courtesy: *Bayerische Staats-Bibliothek Muenchen).

Indische

Sinnpflanzen und Blumen

zur Kennzeichnung

des

indischen, vornehmlich tamulischen Geistes.

Von

K. Graul,

der Theologie Doctor zu Erlangen.

Erlangen,

Verlag von Andreas Deichert.

1865.

9.11. The title of page the book containing Thirukural translated by Karl Graul from Tamil to German and printed in Erlangen in 1865. (Courtesy: The New York Public Library, 530307A).

10

Conclusion

The evolution of the Tamil script in type is traced to its origin from inscribed stones to palm-leaf manuscripts. The centuries old systems slowly came to be replaced by the letter-press printing by the Europeans introduced in the early modern age. However, the *pullis* (dots) over the consonants were continued to be avoided in writing on paper and also in printing, though the impression did not affect, unlike the writing on the reverse of the palm-leaf. The letters were fashioned in a slanting position in palm-leaf writing system with a view to avoiding damage to the leaf, which horizontal or vertical writing would possibly cause. The Tamil scribes did not distinguish between the long and short vowels of 'ye' and 'o', and there was no distinction also between the 'ra' and the long vowel marker 'raa' in vowel-consonants. The absence of such distinctions led to much confusion and misreading of the given Tamil text to the foreigners, when they learnt Tamil and prepared the fonts for printing.

With the growth and development of printing, Tamil ushered into modernity as we have observed and discussed in the chapters of the book. The earliest printing introduced by the Portuguese was based on the Tamil inscription and palm-leaf manuscript system. Tamil types and typesetting techniques were developed by the Jesuit missionaries in the sixteenth century. All added vowel components were connected to the consonants, while the disconnected components did not exist in the script with the exception of *pulli*. The punctuation used in early prints was limited to a dot at the end of sentences. Despite modifications and supplements such as the adoption of the grantha letters, the adoption of Latin punctuations and digits had the discontinuation of use of some characters, significant change we find in the proportions of the letters. The Tamil script had continued to be employed in most of its original syllabic.

I

Tamil printing of books having a lot of pages and booklets containing some limited pages under the Jesuits appeared from the printing press at Quilon, Cochin, Goa and Ambalakaadu. In the first press where a small book called *Thambiran Vanakkam* printed in Tamil at Quilon in 1578 we find the fonts used given separately in a page where it showed at the top one title line in Tamil and another in Portuguese saying that the next letters were made in Goa in 1577. The several lines of a Tamil type were then shown. The other titles in both languages attested again that the following letters were made in Quilon in 1578 and eleven lines of another Tamil type followed. After the eleven lines, there was also a line showing the Tamil signs for digits one to ten as well as the numeric signs for one hundred and one thousand. This second type was the one found in use in the previous page of the both. Two types (João Gonçalves in Goa, and João de Faria type cut in Quilon) in the same page were that the letters cut in Goa was displayed to show by comparison the advance in technique of the later work. This proves that Tamil types were first cast at Goa in 1577 by João Gonçalves had been perfected by João de Faria at Quilon in 1578.

In the books printed from the press in Cochin, i.e., *Krisithiyaani Vanakkam* (1579) and *Confessionairo* (1580) we find some more interesting features. The first letter of each chapter is enlarged into bigger points, while the running matter of the text is found in small points. The page numbers have been given at the extreme left side and the numbers are found in Tamil. Pausing is done with marks to be mentioned by the children. In each chapter the explanation is given regarding the contents of the chapter in Tamil and in Portuguese language. There is no *pulli* found over the consonants. Each sixteen pages of the book is put together to make a form and further at the foot of these pages such as, 1,17, 33,45, 65, 81,97 we find A.I.; A.II; A.III; A: IV; A.V; A.VI; A.VII; A.VIII had been given in the book. The Quilon type cuts were used in printing the books.

New Tamil fonts different from the earlier ones of Goa and Cochin had been used in printing the four parts of the *Gnaanopadesam* book of Roberto Nobili at the press in Ambalakaadu in 1677-78. Thus it is learnt that Tamil type-setting and fonts were prepared continuously for future printing. However, the fonts of 'Ai', 'Ou' and 'Ack' the three letters had not been cut and used in any of the books printed including the Tamil-Portuguese dictionary in 1679. Though Tamils used ligatures in manuscript it was not adopted by the Jesuit missionaries while printing. The printing material composed in Tamil by the missionaries had always been carefully scrutinized and a certificate for censorship was issued by the Holy Inquisition and finally the book was destined for publication by taking a good shape.

The Catholic printing press was a blessing and it intended to serve as an aid to effective evangelization.

II

Printing activity in Tamil continued with the coming of the Protestant missionaries to Tranquebar. It further took on added momentum with the Tamil fonts cut in Leipzig and sent to Tranquebar besides making new fonts in the Indo-Danish settlement. Missionaries composed apologetic works in Tamil in 1712 trying to convince the Hindus to join the Christian fold and to counter a negative image of Hindu way of life and culture. The objectives of the European missionaries in developing Tamil literature were meant to serve five purposes. At first it was to present the Christian doctrine in a popular way mainly through accounts of the life and work of Jesus Christ to the non-elite Tamils with whom they came into contact in the beginning. The next thing was to provide manuals to serve as aids to meet out to the needs of the converts to be followed in their daily moral life according to the tenets of the new faith. The third type of literature in Tamil they prepared was to wean away the converts from their old faith of Hinduism. The fourth and the most important factor had been to promote the rapid growth of conversion of the high castes including the Brahmins and the books of Christian philosophy, theology for the elite were composed. The fifth was to avoid reading the printed material freely supplied by the Catholics versus Protestants who came and worked in Tamil country against each other.

According to the investigation 88 Tamil books had been printed between 1712 and 1799 from the press in Tranquebar. Printing books in Portuguese, German, Dutch, Latin and Danish had also continued. Tamil Bibles got printed 19 times. The missionaries revised and reprinted again when the books went out of stock. 14 Tamil textbooks for the missionary school dealing with science, geography, history, grammar and dictionary came to be printed. Thus there was something extraordinary that had gone into printing for promoting the education of natives. We notice 55 spiritual and Christian literature books in Tamil published by the missionaries from the press in Tranquebar. No Tamil books got printed in Tranquebar in 1742-43, 1746, 1749, 1754-55, 1760, 1764, 1768-69, 1771, 1773-74, 1776, 1778, 1780, 1784, 1786, 1789, 1793-95, 1797 and 1798.

The early Tamil printed material by the Portuguese missionaries was used chiefly for devotional purposes. It acted as an agent of social change among the minority Tamil Christians but had little impact on the majority Hindu population. The printing press of the Lutheran missionaries in Tranquebar printed Bible and many Christian texts in Tamil for conversion of Hindus to Christianity and this at large had good impact. It was a fertile period for publication in Tamil despite the difficulties of acquiring paper, ink and other necessary materials from Europe for printing and binding. The Protestant missionaries printed volumes of books, booklets, tracts, pamphlets and calendar in Tamil and fulfilled their objective of the propagation of faith and heavily contributed to the development of Tamil Christian literature. Thus book history and development of Tamil printing targeted and attracted new audience creating a different taste towards reading. In fact publishing included the production and marketing of Christian devotional literature. Tamil prayer books and hymnals printed were repeatedly made as reprints in addition to polemical tracts.

Tamil books printed mostly had a title page in European languages for the convenience of the western readers. Certain books printed had only Tamil titles pages without Latin or Portuguese or German title pages. As the title page of *Grammatica Damulica* printed in Halle in 1716 was in red and black, similarly Tamil book also came to be printed in two different colours. It is noticed that the title of the book *Gnaana Pattukkal* got printed in red colour and black in 1756 in Tranquebar. The indexes of tune titles in this book have also been mentioned both in German and Tamil.

III

The printed word under the English Company and the European missionaries in Vepery near Madras revolutionized the way Tamils and the Europeans were able to share their thoughts and ideas. It may be mentioned that *pulli* came to be used over the consonants in the books got printed in Madras for the first time in 1789. The letter 'ir' (from alphabet R) has a dot and no other consonant letter dotted. This we find in grammar book of Johann Philipp Fabricius. With the coming of the American mission, Tamil printing in Madras had come drastically to change the whole face and state of things. The perfection of Tamil typography by P.R. Hunt, the manager of the American mission press signalled the start of the modern Tamil language. All subsequent printing related to scientific, political, ecclesiastical, sociological, economic and philosophical advances emerged. Tamil books on various subjects like geography, oceanography, astronomy, medicine, history and travel got printed widely.

There was no ban on owning the printing press by the Tamils including the Telugu migrants in Madras to undertake printing and publications in vernacular under the rule of the English East India Company. This brought to the fore a flourishing Tamil printing press from 1812 onwards, and it was well used for promoting Tamil language by creating social and literary awareness of printing Tamil manuscripts. Scholars began to edit literary texts and there was also a strong attempt to foster printing the texts of the palm-leaf manuscripts. In addition, the English Company used Tamil pundits to its full advantage by providing employment to teach civil servants Tamil grammar, both spoken and written language besides helping to learn English and thereafter translations from Tamil to English appeared on large scale besides printing books in bilingual (English-Tamil). The printing presses by the natives flourished without enactment of regulations and this freedom of the press in Madras should be seen as one of the most important factors of order and progress in Tamil publications.

The Copyright Act of 1847 introduced in Madras by the English Company allowed the payment of two rupees after the delivery of books to the Registrar of Books, with an entry of a note and it secured the copyright of the work to the proprietor. It was viewed that this entry in the book of registry had provided for the enforcement of copyright in the whole of British India. Earlier it had to be made with the Home department of the Government of India, being forwarded through the Government in Madras. The registration of copyright was not however made compulsory. The authors or proprietors had formally no copyright unless the copyright was secured. Anyone else could also publish the same work with impunity and deprive him of his interest and no remedy could be had in the court of law. Among the Madras population, the middle class had not fully emerged between 1801 and 1857, and so a literary market for the book had not well developed. However, the peak period of printing Tamil books by the natives in Madras in their various printing presses has been located between 1844 and 1849. The following books had been found mention in the records of the English company.

Title	*Year*
Mahabharata Aathi Parvam	1844
Naidhatha Moola Paadam	1844
Nalan Chakravarthi Kathai	1844
Prabhulinga Leelai Maalai	1844
Tiruporur Sannadhi Murai Moolapaadam	1844
Thirumurugaattrupadai	1845
Panchkarna Vedantha Siddhantham	1845
Manamagan Usal	1845
Bhagavada Puranam first three kaandams	1845
Kambaramayana Vasanam	1845
Krishna Swami Thuthu	1845
Kumari Sathakam	1845
Muthu Thandavar Sarithiram	1845
Panchangam	1845

Sarikai	1845
Sankunta Vilasam	1845
Vairagya Sathakam	1845
Vallalaraasan Saridham	1845
Yembiran Sathakam	1845
Thiruvaasagam	1846
Paka Saastram	1846
Kovitta Sugam	1846
Amirtha Vaasagam	1846
Ananda Lahari	1846
Neethi Venbaa Urai Patham	1847
Pattana Swami Paadal	1847
Agappai Siddhar Paadal	1847
Atchichudi Mulam	1847
Bhattagiriyaar Pulambal	1847
Channipatha Chintamani	1847
Arichandra Vilaasam	1847
Kandapurana Surukkam	1847
Kummi Paadal	1847
Needhi Chintamani	1847
Subramaniyar Viruththam	1847
Soora Chintamani	1847
Thaalaatu	1847
Parathaiyar Maalai	1847
Ponilkam	1847
Sanibhavagaan Sthothiram	1847
Thiru Neeru Pathigam	1847
Vaakundaram Urai	1847
Vaguppoo	1847
Viveka Chintamani	1847
Seyankondar Sathakam	1848
Madana Kamarajan Kathai	1848
Madurai Veeran Kathai	1848
Muvar Amaanai	1848
Uththara Ramayanam	1848
Masthan Sagipu Avargal Paathai	1849
Meygnaana Saaram	1849
Thiruvottiyur Andhathi	1849

The printed books earlier by the Jesuits and the Tranquebar missionaries had not mentioned the price. We find in Madras the books printed by the missionaries had the price neatly being mentioned. The back cover printed

(The Second Brief Report of the American Madras Mission of 1848) had contained the details of the titles and their price in rupee, *anna* and *paise.*

The Press and Registration of Books Act (XXV) introduced in Madras in 1867 only provided for the compulsory submission of three copies of every book, printed or lithographed, to the government along with a statement providing the details such as the title of the book, the language, name of author, translator or editor, the subject, place of printing and of publication, name or firm of printer and of publisher, date of issue from the press, number of pages, the size of the book, the number of the edition, the number of copies printed, the sale-price, and the name and address of copyright-owner. Thereafter the task of policing had developed in the domain of book production. John Murdoch in 1865 produced 'A Classified Catalogue of Tamil Printed Books' and compiled a list of 1755 publications in Tamil that were then available. It provides some sort of a useful account of the nature of book-publishing and printing. He revealed 69 per cent of books as religious works, and 29 per cent of under Hinduism and about 38 per cent of the total had been Christian, and 2 per cent were of Islamic origin. It is sad to note that Murdoch's catalogue does not include either the names of editors or the dates of publication.

The wealthy *vellalars*, *mudaliars*, *pillais* and *chettis* emerged as printers and publishers of Tamil literature among the Hindus in Tamil country. It had to some extent helped to shatter the exclusivity and hegemony of the priestly Brahmins who knew Sanskrit besides Tamil and Telugu. It is also observed simultaneously that recognition of the status of the wealthy natives in publishing industry increased for they had entered into the editing manuscripts, printing books and owning printing press. Gradually the religious leaders of the Saiva mutts were dragged into the scene as patrons. The outpouring of small Tamil books using local paper for printing was done quickly and inexpensively by the native printers. This produced a new group of readers among the lay public in Tamil society which could not be controlled in any way. The opening up of the new readers and audiences included men, women, and school children. They were exposed to aspects of print against a manuscript tradition in Tamil that had been held earlier largely as the exclusive prerogative of a few learned. We notice at that point of time the three concepts of print culture, print commerce, and print capitalism which had come to have a profound impact and meaning in Madras city caused to have the social and mental development of the Tamils.

IV

The mission Press in Pondicherry came to function in 1841 but it had again the origin of the Catholic intellectual dimension and spiritual tradition.

Roberto Nobili's *Sathiya Vetha Paritchai* the work of the seventeenth century got printed in 1842 and it was reprinted again in 1846. His *Deyva Partichai* appeared in print in 1843 through the efforts of L.S. Dupuis the manager of the Mission press and it was reprinted in Pondicherry in 1863. Pierre Mauduit's *Divya Maathirgai* got printed in 1866. James Thomas Rossi's Lives of the Saints of 1751 came to be printed in four volumes in 1866-67. The writings of Rossi on miracles composed in 1745 were printed in the litho press in 1861. Bertoldi's *Gnaana Muyarchi* of 1727 was printed at litho press in 1843. Beschi's *Thembaavani* of 1726 was printed in 1851, 1852 and 1853 in three *kaandams*. His *Lutherinthiyalbu* of 1727 got printed in 1842 and it was reprinted in 1847 and 1868. The press produced more 'old' books of the eighteenth century than 'new' works composed by the missionaries in the nineteenth century.

According to the catalogue of the mission press it had printed only 11 books from 1841 to 1843 (vide *Gnaana Muyarchi*). L.S. Dupuis had printed and added 3 more books newly in 1844 (vide *Nanraii Ninai*). In 1845 he added 12 more books and the number had swelled to 25 books (vide *Ilakkana Surukkam*). In 1865 the list of printed Tamil books increased to 73. The catalogue of the letter press in 1869 shows 108 Tamil books (vide *Thuravara Uththiyannam Kaandam Onru*). Printing from the mission press not only paved way for new literary forms but came to function as an agent of social change. No wonder it had led to innovation rather than revolution. Louis Savinien Dupuis the manager of the press introduced the European–style punctuation, footnotes and editorial techniques. They have been largely accepted in Tamil script publishing. Dupuis also tended to preserve the aesthetic form of Tamil manuscript and he set up a litho-press and employed trained calligraphers. The subject matter of the vast range of material produced is though overwhelmingly evangelical, devotional, spiritual and Catholic religious, the press brought out numerous school textbooks, grammars and dictionaries. Its distribution was not confined to local but extended overseas to Sri Lanka and French Guiana where the migrated Tamils lived.

L.S. Dupuis assigned priority to printing Catholic doctrinal works in Tamil in Pondicherry like catechism, prayer books and the lives of saints. Regarding the contents we find in the books several changes from manuscript to books adopted very suitably. He had enlarged the writings of the earlier missionaries which were available in palm-leaves and paper. He did good service by making efforts to print the books for diffusion of the Catholic literature. A comparison of the manuscript and the printed book undertaken by him reveals changes in the style of words in the language from colloquial to idiomatic.

In manuscript	In the book printed
Athukku	atharku
Apparam	appuram
Athin	athan
Aneyham peyargal	aneyham pergal
Ithinaalay	ithanaal
Ithugal	ivaigal
Pilanaaga	balamaaha
Posthagam	pusthagam
Pisaasu	pasaasu
Bhojanam	posanam
Mihindha	mudintha
Manushar	manithar
Manasu	manathu
Seermai	seemai
Vezhipattuthu	vezhipattathu
Veverey	veveru
Gnaayam	niyaayam

The Sanskrit usages of Tamil words are found like *pirajai, bhojanam* and *yejaman*, as *pirasai*, *posanam* and *yesamaan*. However, certain words continued in Sanskrit alone such as *manushar*, *visham*, *saashatangamaay*, *archasishta*, *avasthai*, *aasthi*, and *kristhuvargal* in the printed books and in palm-leaf manuscripts. The quality of Tamil prose language after the advent of the Europeans had made some scholars to believe that language had deteriorated owing to mixture. Language mixing in Tamil is an age old affair. The British and French colonial powers in Tamil country had contributed to Tamil with Anglo and Franco-Tamil mixtures for they had ruled and administered. The colonial advertisements and tender notices issued in Tamil contained several untranslatable words merely transcribed from English and French. Newspapers, journals and periodicals printed in Tamil contained a lot of foreign words of origin for which equivalent Tamil words could not be coined. Printing came to be spread to many towns like Palayamkottai, Nagercoil and Kanchipuram. The institutions like the religious tract society, the Madras book society, the college of Fort St. George contributed towards the growth of printing in Tamil. Knowledge of Tamil was keenly felt important for it helped missionaries and also to improve governance of the colonial powers. Hence Beschi's grammar of *Kodunthamizh* (colloquial Tamil) in Latin was printed at Tranquebar in 1739. It was further translated into English by Henry Horst and got printed at Vepery in 1806. F.W. Ellis inspired by Beschi's scholarship reprinted *Kodunthamizh* at the Fort St. George College Press in Madras in 1813. Benjamin Guy Babington translated Beschi's *Senthamizh* and it was printed at the College Press in Madras in 1822. These Europeans gradually noticed that spoken Tamil is not written but written Tamil is not spoken. L.S. Dupuis in Pondicherry adopted a new kind of Tamil by judiciously mixing literary and colloquial and he printed the Tamil books and he had very clearly stated this fact. He began to use by combining the Beschi's *Kodunthamizh* and *Senthamizh* together in a book (Tamil grammar book in French printed at Pondicherry in 1863) and he used words that of *Senthamizh* placed within two semicolon (*kaar pulli*) and sentences within parenthesis.

L.S. Dupuis had printed large size books and we find that the Tamil-French Dictionary had 1015 pages, the French-Tamil grammar with 554 pages and the Elements of Geography with 216 pages. Costanzo Giuseppe Beschi had composed the famous Tamil tale *Paramaartha Guruvin Kathai* in the form of a parallel Latin and vulgar Tamil text by assimilating a dictionary format. This tale is included as the second appendix of Beschi's *Vulgaris Tamulicae Linguae Dictionarium Tamulico Latinum* of 1744 (British Library, Additional Manuscripts no. 26110). As the editor and publisher of Beschi's various manuscripts, including *Thembaavani* Dupuis was greatly inspired by Beschi's parallel text model and so he introduced it in printing. We find Dupuis adopting this style in the printed book of *Bhumisaasthira Sangshebham* in 1869 where the texts appear in bilingual with parallel Tamil and French. Thus an innovative format, first introduced into the Tamil manuscript tradition by Beschi was thus transferred on to print by Dupuis after 120 years.

Our investigation shows that 24 books were printed at the litho press in Pondicherry from 1859 to 1869. L.S. Dupuis realized that both in palm-leaves and print there was no room for corrections and a mistake had remained only a mistake. Hence he gave a page of errata in the printed book. This has not been earlier found in the printed books of the Jesuits and the Protestant missionaries. L.S. Dupuis printed books with editorials and he cited the reasons, besides mentioning from where he received the manuscripts and details on the differences between the copies of the same manuscript. Dupuis had thus obtained a unique place in Tamil publishing history. The European style of editing and technique adopted by him added beauty to the books with foot notes.

V

The spread of Tamil printing at the global level had witnessed through publishing books in various European towns like Halle, Hamburg, Dresden and Erlangen besides the city of London. Printing Tamil books, tracts and periodicals flourished in Colombo and Jaffna in Asia. The printed book brought a variety of changes unlike the Tamil manuscript. It led to a more ordinary, systematic approach to the printed word with title pages, regularly numbered pages, punctuation marks, section breaks, running headings and table of contents. Tamil books printed were of three different varieties such as octavo—a book size resulting from folding a sheet of paper of a specified size to form eight leaves, demi—less than full size and duodecimo—with folding a sheet of paper into 12 leaves. The books normally were of 18 cm, 19 cm, 22 cm, 23 cm and 26 cm. Printing had enabled Tamils to easily broadcast their ideas in a form everyone was able to read. Western educational methods and the expansion of school systems introduced by the missionaries in Tamil country enabled printing a significant number of standard textbooks. These became one of the main teaching instruments for most individuals who attended schools. In light of the above, it would be fair to conclude that the more tangible linkages came to exist across the cultural boundaries and local Tamil culture in early modern age. Printing industry and technology radically changed the manner in which the Tamil tradition was transmitted to natives. It expanded the intellectual horizons and made Tamils more aware of the new connections found in the west. It also elevated the study of the classical texts of Tamil around the globe.

Select Bibliography

PRIMARY SOURCES

I. Manuscripts

Denmark

1. *Det Kongelige Bibliotek, Kobenhavn*
NY KGl.Saml.589C

France

2. *Archives de la Société des Missions Etrangères de Paris*

MSS 0627.2. Caractere Tamouls/graves par M. Bertrand Loeulliet; sous la dir. De M. l'abbe Ch. Dallet, Missionaire Apostolique de la Congregation des Missions Etrangères, Paris, 1863

MSS Correspondance Pondichéry-Paris, Lettres Vol. 998

Letter of Jarrige written from Bangalore dated 26 July 1828 to Langlois in Paris

Letter of Bishop Bonnand from Pondicherry dated 12 June 1830 to Jean Tesson in Paris Vol. 999

Letter of Bishop Bonnand from Pondicherry dated 4 June 1837

Letter of Bishop Clement Bonnand dated 13 June 1837

Letter of L.S. Dupuis written from Chinna Ballapuram dated 18 November 1839 to Reverend Superior and Reverend Directors of the Seminary of the missions Etrangères de Paris

Letter of L.S. Dupuis from Pondicherry dated 9 December 1839 to Jean Tesson in Paris

Letter of Clement Bonnand the Bishop of Pondicherry dated 8 April 1840 to Jean Tesson in Paris

Letter of Clement Bonnand the Bishop of Pondicherry written from Bangalore dated 15 October 1840

Letter of Bishop Bonnand from Pondicherry dated 20 December 1840 to Cardinal Fransoni in Rome

Letter of Bishop Bonnand from Venkatagiri dated 9 February 1841 to Langlois in Paris

Letter of Bishop Bonnand from Pondicherry dated 12 June 1841 to Jean Tesson in Paris

Letter of L.S. Dupuis from Pondicherry dated 18 August 1841 to Jean Tesson in Paris

Letter of L.S. Dupuis from Pondicherry dated 21 October 1841 to Jean Tesson in Paris

Letter of Clement Bonnand Drusipare the Bishop of Pondicherry dated 22 October 1841 to Jean Tesson in Paris Vol. 1000

Letter of L.S. Dupuis dated 18 April 1842 to Jean Tesson in Paris

Letter of Marion Bressiliac dated 2 October 1842 to Jean Tesson in Paris

Letter of L.S. Dupuis dated 23 October 1843 to Jean Tesson in Paris

Letter of L.S. Dupuis dated 18 October 1844 to Jean Tesson in Paris

Letter of L.S. Dupuis dated 3 December 1844 to Jean Tesson in Paris

Letter of L.S. Dupuis dated 21 March 1845 to Jean Tesson in Paris

Letter of L.S. Dupuis dated 11 October 1845 to Jean Tesson in Paris

Letter of L.S. Dupuis dated 12 October 1845 to Jean Tesson in Paris

Letter Louis Marie Mousset dated 10 March 1846 to Jean Tesson in Paris

Letter of L.S. Dupuis dated 11 January 1847 to Jean Tesson in Paris

Letter of L.S. Dupuis dated 9 February 1847 to Jean Tesson in Paris

Letter of L.S. Dupuis dated 11 August 1848 to Jean Tesson in Paris Vol. 1001

Letter of L.S. Dupuis dated 9 April 1850 to the MEP Superior in Paris

Letter of Louis Marie Mousset dated 10 November 1850 to Jean Tesson in Paris

Letter of L.S. Dupuis dated 7 September 1853 to Jean Tesson in Paris

Letter of Bishop Bonnand written from Pondicherry dated 23 April 1855 to Jean Tesson in Paris

Letter of Bishop Bonnand written from Kovilur dated 27 June 1855 to Jean Tesson in Paris Vol.1002

Letter of L.S. Dupuis dated 22 June 1858 to Jean Tesson in Paris

Letter of L.S. Dupuis dated 10 November 1858 to Jean Tesson in Paris

Letter of Louis Marie Mousset dated 24 March 1859 to Jean Tesson in Paris

Letter of Louis Marie Mousset dated 3 September 1860 to Jean Tesson in Paris

The annual report of the Pondicherry vicariate by L.S. Dupuis sent to the Superior and Directors of the MEP seminary in Paris dated 22 December 1860 Vol.1003

Letter of L.S. Dupuis dated 10 April 1861 to Jean Tesson in Paris

Letter of L.S. Dupuis dated 9 August 1862 to Jean Tesson in Paris

Letter of L. S. Dupuis dated 20 March 1864 to Jean Tesson in Paris

The circular of L.S. Dupuis, the Pro–Vicar Apostolic to all the native priests and MEP missionaries in the vicariate of Pondicherry dated 31 December 1867

Letter of L.S. Dupuis from Pondicherry dated 9 December 1869 to the MEP superior in Paris Vol. 1004

Letter of L.S. Dupuis dated 22 January 1874 to Jean Tesson in Paris

3. *Archives Françaises de la Compagnie de Jésus, Vanves, Hauts-de-Seine*

Fonds Brotier, vol. 83

4. *Bibliothèque Nationale, Paris, Rue Richelieu*

MSS Indien, no. 463

5. *Centre des Archives d'Outre–Mer, Aix–en–Provence*

Inde 1831, Rapport du Ministere de la Marine et des Colonies 26 Avril 1831, Proposition de Souscrire a Exemplaires d'un Dictionnaire Francais-Malabar

Inde 1855, Specimen de typographie et de fonderie envoye a l'exposition universelle de Paris annee 1855, par l'Imprimerie des missionaires apostoliques de Pondichery Indes orientales

Inde 1863, Envoie du catalogue des ouvrages en langue tamoule edites par l'Imprimerie de la mission

Inde n.d, Circulaire addresse aux colonies et relatives a une subscription a des ouvrages en langue tamoule edites par l'Imprimerie de la mission Catholique en Inde 1863-1865

Inde n.d, Catalogue des livres de l' Imprimerie de la Maison des missions etrangeres a Pondichery, Circulaire addresse aux colonies et relative a une souscription a des ouvrages en langue tamoule edites par l'imprimerie de la mission Catholique en Inde, 1863-1865

Germany

6. *Archiv der Franckesche Stiftungen, Halle*

MSS. M2 B6:1; M2 B6:16; M2 B6:54a

India

7. *Archives of the Arch-diocese of Pondicherry and Cuddalore*

Collection Louis Faucheux: Copies d' lettres et circulaire du L. S. Dupuis en française et tamoule, XIXe siècle, no. 16

8. *State Central Library, Goa*

MS 34. Antão de Proença, *Vocabulario Tamulico Lusitano precedido de uma Arte em Tamul e seguido da termos poeticos*, 1670

MS 38. *Vocabulario Tamulico-Lusitano*

9. *Saraswathi Mahal Library, Thanjavur*

Modi Bundles, 72C/18-4; 160C/45

10. *Tamilnadu State Archives, Chennai*

Foreign Department: Sundries, Correspondence Relative to the Restoration of the Danish Possessions, vol. II, 1815–1816

Tanjore District Records, vol. 3477, 3492, 3503

Italy

11. *Archivium Congregationis de Propaganda Fide, Roma*

MSS lettere e decreti della Sacra Congregatizione e Biglietti di Monsignor Segretario, vol. 326 (1841/II)

12. *Archivum Romanum Societatis Iesu*

MS Goa 76b, Ippolito Desideri, Aayatham Sollugira Vagai, Dialogus inter confessorem et penitentem

Portugal

13. *Biblioteca da Cartuxa, Evora*

E.2098

14. *Biblioteca Municipal, O Porto*

MSS Codice no. 143

The Netherlands

15. *Koninklijke Bibliotheek, Den Haag*

Handscriften, Oude Drukken, 82 H 9

United Kingdom

16. *British Library, London*

Additional Manuscripts no. 26110

C.J. Beschi, *Vulgaris Tamulicae Linguae Dictionarium Tamulico Latinum*, 1744

Oriental and India Office Collection

Government Gazette, Madras, 9 October 1817

Government Gazette, Madras, 7 December 1824

Government order no. 49, Home, 1866

Government order no. 50, Home, 1866

Government order no. 51, Home (Public Branch), 1866

Madras Public Consultations,

11 September 1815

22 December 1815, List of books printed, printing, or preparing for the Fort St. George College Press

4 December 1819, Inventory of books printed, printing, or preparing for the Fort St. George College Press

9 July 1830, 20 April 1836, 17 July 1838

Public Consultations

13 February 1816; 23 February 1836

II. Printed Documents, Contemporary Chronicles, Tracts and Accounts

In English

Murdoch, John., *Papers on Indian Reform – Is India becoming Richer? With the Proposed Remedies for the Existing Poverty*, Vepery, Madras, 1887.

Notices of Madras and Cuddalore in the Last Century from the Journals and Letters of the Earlier Missionaries of the Society for the Propagation of Christian Knowledge, London, 1858.

Second Brief Report of the American Madras Mission, 1843–1847 with an Appendix, American Mission Press, Madras, 1848.

The Fifth Triennial Report of the American Mission Seminary, Jaffna, Ceylon, with an Appendix, American Mission Press, Jaffna, 1839.

The First Report of the Religious Tract Association at Madras, 1819.

The practice of farriery, calculated for the East Indies, collected from the best authors, and founded upon experiments made during a residence of ten years in this country, by Antoine de Letang, captain of cavalry, Pondicherry, printed for the author, 1795.

Twenty Fifth Report of the Madras Tract and Book Society with an Abstract of the Society's Publications for the Year Ending December 1843, Madras: American Mission Press, 1844.

Twenty Sixth Report of the Madras Tract and Book Society with an Abstract of the Society's Publications for the Year Ending December 1844, Madras: American Mission Press, 1845

In French

Archives Administratives des Etablissments Français de L'Inde, Contentant de Lois, Ordonnances, Reglements et Toute Autres Publication Faites Par Orde du Gouverneur, Pondichéry, 1823-1827.

Assemblee Coloniale representative des establissmens français del'Inde, Seances des 11, 13, 14, et 15 Octobre 1792, A Pondichéry.

Assemblee Coloniale representative des establissmens français del' Inde, Seances des 11, 14, 15, et 17 Octobre 1792, A Pondichéry.

Assemblee Coloniale de Pondichery: Précis de la premiere séance de l' Assemblee Coloniale du lundi 17 Decembre 1792, A Pondichéry.

Bulletin des Actes administratifs des Etablissments Français dans l'Inde, Pondichéry, 1828.

Diagou, Gnanou., *Arrets du Conseil Superieur de Pondichéry*, 4 vols., Pondichéry, 1937.

Dupuis, Louis Savinien., *Notice sur la poesie tamoule le rev Beschi et le tembavani, par un member de la congregation des missions etrangères*, Pondichéry, 1851.

Extrait des regisres du consiel superior de Pondichéry, De neuf Janvier, mil sept cent quatre vingt–treize, A Pondichéry.

Lescallier, Daniel Baron., *Discours pronounce aux troupes de Pondichéry, a l'occasion de la publication de l'amnistie par M.lescallier, Commissaire civil, delegue aux etablissemens francais au–de la du Cap de Bonne–Esperance*, Le 4 Octobre 1792, A Pondichéry.

Lettres édifiantes et curieuses, écrites des missions étrangères par quelques missionaires de la Compagnie de Jésus, 34 vols., Paris, 1702-1777.

Manuel de Cipaye, Contentant quelques reflexions sur ler parti que l'on pourrait tirer du militaire Indien; avec un précis de l'ordonnance de l'infanterie, tant pour l'exercise que pour tout ce qui peut mener a l'instruction d'une troupe. Le tout adapte a la formation particuliere des corps des cipayes, par M. Aubineau–Duplessis, Pondichéry, 1784.

Proclamation des Commissaires Civils, sur la loi du 17 Octobe (sic) 1792, pour la prochaine convocation. Au nom de la nation, de la loi, et du Roi, les commissaries civils delegues par le Roi, en vertu des decrets de l'Assemblee Nationale, aux etablissemens français au–de la du cap de Bonne–espernace, A Pondichéry, 1792.

Statuts du Vicariate Apostolique de Pondichéry concernant L'administration des Sacrements, Imprimerie des Missionaires Apostoliques de la Congregation des Missions-Etrangeres, Pondichéry 1874.

Synode de Pondichéry et instruction de la S.C. de la Propagande sur la formation du Clerge Indigene, Imprimerie des Missionaires Apostoliques de la Congregation des Missions-Etrangeres, Pondichéry 1845.

Table Generale du Bulletin des Actes Administratifs des Etablissments Français de L'inde de 1867-1877, Paris, 1881.

In German

Aweiar's Kalwiorhuckam: *Oder Sittenspruche aus Tamulischen Palamblattern Ubersetzt, mit Bemerkungen uber Indische Gelehrsamkeit, von. J.C.C. Rudiger*, Halle, 1791.

Der Königl. Dänischen Missionarien aus Ost-Indien eingesandter ausführlichen Berichten, Von dem Werck ihrs Ams unter den Heyden, angerichteten Schulen und Gemeinen, ereigneten Hindernissen und schweren Umstanden; Beschaffenheit des Malabarischen Heydenthums, gepflogenen brieflicher Correspondentz und mundlchen Unterredungen mit selbigen heyden, Teil 1–9, Waiserihaus, Halle, 1710–1772.

Fahrten und Abenteuer Gimpels und Compagnie Ein tamulischen Reise- und Scherzmarchen, Nacherzahlt von Dr. Johannn Georg Theodor Grasse, mit 6 color irten Bildern, Dresden, 1856.

Indische Sinnpflanzen und Blumen, zur Kennezeichnung Indischen Vornehmlich tamulischen Geistes, Erlangen, 1865.

Vier Geheimrath-minister Eine Indische Geschite in Gleichnissen aus Tamulischer sprache ubertregen von dem fruheren Braminien Christian Rama Ayen, Hamburg, 1855.

Ziegenbalg, Bartholomäus., *Propagation of the Gospel in the East: Being a Collection of Letters from the Protestant Missionaries, and other worthy Persons in the East-Indies, & c. Relating to the Mission; the Means of Promoting it; and the Success it hath pleased God to give to the Endeavours used hitherto, for Propagating True Christianity among the Heathen in those Parts, but chiefly on the coast of Coromandel with a map of the East-Indies. III Parts, Published by the direction of the Society for Promoting Christian Knowledge*, London, Printed and Sold by J. Downing, 1709-1718.

In Latin

Collectanea S. Congragationis de Propaganda Fide seu Decreta Instructiones Rescripta Pro Apostolicis Missionibus, Romae, 1893.

Constitutiones secundae synodi vicariatus orae Coromandelicae, Pudicherii habitae mense Januario Anni 1848, Typographis Missionarium Apostolicorum Congregationis ad Exteros, Pudicherii, 1849.

In Multi-lingual

Dupuis, Louis Savinien, and Mousset, *Piranchu Thamizh Agaraathi: Dictionnaire Français-Tamoul*, Pondichery, 1866.

Fabricius, Johann Philipp., *A Dictionary of English and Malabar*, II vols., Mission Press, Vepery, Madras, MDCCLXXVI.

__________, *Tamilum Inglishumaay Irukkira agaraathi: A Malabar and English Dictionary, Wherein the Words and Phrases of the Tamilian Language, Commonly called by the Europeans the Malabar Language, are Explained in English by the English Missionaries of Madras*, Wepery, near Madras, 1779.

__________, and Johann Christian Breithaupt, *A Dictionary of the English and Malabar Languages, Printed and Completely done at Vepery, near Madras*, 1786.

Thaninayagam, S. Xavier, *Antão de Proença's Tamil-Portuguese Dictionary, AD1679: Vocabulario Tamulico com a significaçam Portugueza composto pello p. Antam de Proença da Companhia de Jesu, Missionario da Missam de Madurey, com todas as licencas necessaries da Santa Inquizicao e dos superiors, na impressa Tamulica do provincia do Malabar, por Ignacio Archamoni impressor della*, Ambalacatta em 30 Julho 1679 annos, Kuala Lumpur, 1966.

In Portuguese

Albuquerque, Affonso de., *Cartas de Affonso de Albuquerque*, eds., Raymundo Antonio de Bulhão Pato and H. Lopes de Mendonça, Academia das Ciências de Lisboã, Lisboã, 7 vols., 1844-1935.

Almeida, Fernando de., ed., *Cartilha em Tamul e Português: Impresa em 1554*, Ministerio da Edução Nacional, Direção-Geral do Superior do Ensino Superior e da Belas-Artes, Lisboã, 1970.

Bertrand, Joseph., *La Mission du Madure d'après de Documents in Edits*, 4 vols, Paris, 1847-1854.

Catalogo dos Livros que se Achao na Biblioteca da Igreja Chamada Jerusalem en Tranquebar, Tranquebar, na Estampa dos Missionarios Reaes de Dennemarck, Anno de 1714.

Conciones per Annum Concannice Compositae a Patre Ignatio Archamone e Societatis Iesu, Goa, 1670.

Purgatorii Commentarium Concannice Compositum, Goa, 1663.

Sousa, Francisco de, *Oriente Conquistado a Jesus Christo pelos Padres da Companhia de Jesus da Provincia de Goa,* III vols., Lisboa, 1710, Porto, 1978.

Stephen, S. Jeyaseela., *Letters of the Portuguese Jesuits from Tamil Countryside, 1666-1688*, Pondicherry, 2001.

Wicki, Jose., and J. Gomes, *Documenta Indica*, 18 vols., Roma, 1948-88.

In Tamil

Aani Muthu, Second edition, Jaffna, 1843.

Aathi Chuvadi, Pondicherry, 1844.

Aathi Chuvadi and Paramaartha Guru Kathai Muthaliyavai, Pondicherry, 1844.

Aathi chuvadium paramaaartha Guru Kathaiyum, Pondicherry, 1862.

Aathikaala Sarithira Sangiraham, A sketch of ancient history with a version of the same in Tamil by Puthuvai Gnanapragasa Moodeliar, Madras, 1828.

Aathuma Nesam, Pondicherry, 1860.

Aayatham, Pondicherry, 1865.

A Collection of Official Documents in the Tamil Language Consisting of Urzees and Other Papers Filed in the Courts of Justice for the Use of Candidates for the Indian Civil Service, by Lieut W.F. Wright, Madras Staff Corps, Tamil Translator to the Government of Madras, Printed for the Government of Madras by Caleb Foster, at the Foster Press, 23 Rundall's Road, Vepery, 1868.

Agappai Siddhar Paadal, Madras, 1847.

Amirtha Vaasagam, Madras, 1846.

Ananda Lahari, Madras, 1846.

Analysis of a Volume in Tamil entitled Practical Expressions of the Parables of Christ, Madras, American Mission Press, 1844.

Anda Vizhlakka Sathirathin Sangsebangkoodiya Bhumi Sathira Noolaa-tharam, Pondicherry, 1864.

Angaathi Paatha Sugarana Vaatha Udarpaalana Nool, Second edition, Madras, 1857.

Aindhukaaya varampetra archsishta franciskuvin sarithira surukkam, Pondicherry, 1859.

Ainthu thirukaaya varampetra archsishta franciskuvin thavathukkuriya moonram sabhai ozhukkam, Pondicherry, 1859.

Archsishta Gnaanapragaasiyar Sarithiramum Archsishta Sthanislausudaya Sarithira Pirasanagangalumaavana, Pondicherry, 1862.

Archsishta Iganciyar Gnaana Dhyaanagal, Pondicherry, 1864.

Archsishta Susaiyappar Vanakka Maatham, Pondicherry, 1867.

Archayasista Narkarunaikku Paathiram Ullavanaka: Solidissima Instituto Sanctae Coenae: Inqua Ostenditu qua Praeparatione Ante: Qua Exteriorum Interiorum que Morum Observationae irca: et qua Novitiate Vitae post Usum Sanctae Coenae Digne Sacramentum Celebraturus se Probare Debeat in Gratiam Christianae Gentis Damulorum Exhibita a Missionaria Danica Benjamin Schultze, Trangambariae, Typis ac Sumptibus Missionis Danicae, MDCCXXII.

Arichandra Vilaasam, Madras, 1847.

Aroolappan, John Christian., *Satta Thittam*, American Madras Mission, Madras, 1845.

__________, *Sathya Vetha Kannaadi*, Madras, 1846.

Atchichudi Mulam, Madras, 1847.

Beschi, Costanzo Giueseppe, *Bedhga Maruthal*, Pondicherry 1842.

__________, *Bedhaga Maruththal*, Pondicherry, 1855.

__________, *Bedhga Maruthal*, Pondicherry, 1868.

__________, *Gnaana Unarthuthal*, Pondicherry, 1842.

__________, *Gnaana Unarthuthal*, Pondicherry, 1846.

__________, *Kitheriammal Ammaanai*, Gnaanodhaya Press, Madras, 1849.

__________, *Dairiyanathaswamigalyennum Veeramaamunivar Aruliseytha Archisista Kitheriammal Ammaanai: Ithu Royapuram Archsista Royappar Aalayathil Mahasangaikuriya The. Mari. Gnaanaparaga-sanatha Swamigal Uthavipetru Merpadikovil Thamizh Kalvisaalai Upaathiyar Pavazhai Vai. The. Ma. Sinnasami Reddiyar Avargazhlaal Paarvai idapattu Mayilai Ponnuswami Muthaliar avargalaal Chennai Lakshmi Vilas Achchukudathil Pathipikkapattathu*, 1876.

__________, *Lutherithiniyalbu*, Pondicherry, 1842.

__________, *Lutherithiniyalbu*, Pondicherry, 1847.

__________, *Lutherithiniyalbu*, Pondicherry, 1868.

__________, *Paramaartha Guruvin Kathai: The Adventures of the Gooroo Paramartan: A Tale in the Tamil Language, Accompanied by a Translation & Vocabulary Together with an Analysis of the First Story*, by Benjamin Babington of the Madras Civil Service, London, MDCCC-XXII.

__________, *Paramartha Guruvin kathai*, Pondicherry, 1859.

__________, *Paramartha Guruvin Kathai* in *Aathi Chuvadi*, Pondicherry, 1862.

__________, *Paramaartha Guru Kathai Lathinilum Thamzhilillum*, Pondicherry, 1863.

__________, *Thembaa Maalai*, Pondicherry, 1851,

__________, *Thembaa Maalai*, Pondicherry, 1865.

__________, *Thembaavani: Muthar Kaandam*, Pondicherry, 1851.

__________, *Thembaavani: Rendaam Kaandam*, Pondicherry, 1852.

__________, *Thembaavani: Moonraam Kaandam*, Pondicherry, 1853.

__________, *Thembaavani*, Pondicherry, 1866.

__________, *Thiruppavani*, Pondicherry, 1856.

__________, *Vetha Vizhlakkam*, Pondicherry, 1842.

__________, *Vetha Vizhlakkam*, Pondicherry, 1855.

__________, *Vetha Vizhlakkam*, Pondicherry, 1868.

__________, *Vethiyar Ozhukkam*, Pondicherry, 1842.

Bhagavada Puranam, Monru kaandam, Madras, 1845.

Bhattagiriyaar Pulambal, Madras, 1847.

Bhoologathinudaiya Mudhalam Pangaagira Europa, Tranquebar, Typis Missionis Danicae, MDCCXXXII.

Bhumi Saasthira Noolaathaaram, Pondicherry, 1864.

Bhumi Saasthira Shanksebham, Pondicherry, 1869.

Bhumi Saasthira Surukkam, Pondicherry, 1862.

Bhumi Saasthira Surukkam, Pondicherry, 1863.

Channipatha Chintamani, Madras, 1847.

Chemistry, Practical and Theoretical, American Ceylon Mission, Nagercoil, 1857.

Chudamani Nigandu, Madras, 1856.

Daavidin Sangeethangal, Psalms: The Version of the Union Bible, Jaffna Auxiliary Bible Society, 1861.

Desikar, Kottaiyur Sivakolundu, ed., *Thiruvaasagam*, Madras, 1857.

Devaaarathaniyiley Paadugira Gnaanapaatum Adangiya Sangeetha Thirattu, Madras, 1848.

Devamaathavin Vanakka Maatham, Pondicherry, 1850.

Deyva Paritchai, Pondicherry, 1846

Dhina Bhodhagam, Jaffna, 1848, Third edition, Jaffna, 1849.

Dhinamari Vizhlakkam: *Reading Lessons, Arranged for every day in the year: Comprising the leading facts connected with theology, astronomy, geography, mineralogy, metallurgy, philosophy, natural history: Selections from Cural, Naladeyar, Mootheri, Nanneri (Historical facts concerning India and England–Anecdotes illustrative of moral, religious duties and vocabulary of English adjectives–Fables and a variety of other miscellaneous matter)*, Madras, Asylum Press, 1844.

Dhunneri Vilakku, Jaffna, 1814.

Divviya Maathirikai, Pondicherry, 1866.

Fabricius, Johann Philipp., *A Grammar for Learning the Principles of the Malabar Language, Properly Called Tamul or the Tamulian Language, by the English Missionaries of Madras*, Printed at Wepery near Madras in the year MDCCLXXVIII.

__________, *Paappu maarkam innathenru kaanpikkira thezhlivaana vilakkam, Irandam Pathithal*, MDCCXCVIII.

First Lessons and Idiomatic Exercises in English and Tamul with Forms of Petitions and C Designed to Assist Tamul Youths in the Study of English Language, Church Mission Press, Nellore, 1830.

Foulkes Thomas., *A Catechism of the Shaiva Religion Translated from the Tamil by the Rev. Thomas Foulkes*, London, 1863.

Gnaana Aaruthal, Pondicherry, 1859.

Gnaana Aaruthal, ed., S. Rajamanickam, Tuticorin, 1965.

Gnaana Deepikai, *A Primer of Catechism*, trs., W. Knight & Miron Winslow, Jaffna, 1854.

Gnaana Desaanthari: Than Paavangalai Nivaaranam Pannum Vagaiyum Motch Gathiyayum Thedik Kandarindhu Paakiyanaarathai Solliya Sarithiram. Ithu Ingilisu Bhashayilirundhu Thamizh Bhashaiyile Thiruppiyathu, Madras, Printed at the American Mission Press for the Madras Tract and Book Society, 1841.

Gnaana Geetha Sangiraham: Ithil Devanai Thuthithu Vanangum Porruttu Kiristhavargal Antharangamaayum Vehirangammayum Paada Vendi Paatukkal Adangi Irukkinrana, Manipaay Achchukudathir Pathikap-attathu, 1846; *Tamil Hymns Selected & Original Adapted for Public, Private and Social Worship*, Published by the Jaffna Religious Tract Society, Jaffna, American Mission Press, 1846.

Gnaana Kannadi: *Joannis Arndtii...de Vero Christianismo Liber Primus ...Ex Germanico in Tamulicum Convertit Benjamin Schulzius*, Halle, 1751.

Gnaana Kannaadi, Pondicherry, 1858.

Gnaana Mandira Selva Pungaavanam, part I, II, Halle, 1749.

Gnaana Mandira Selva Pungaavanam, part III, IV, Halle, 1750.

Gnaanamirdham, Pondicherry, 1841.

Gnaamirtha Thadaagam, Pondicherry, 1847.

Gnaanmirdha Thadaagam, Pondicherry, 1858.

Gnaana Muyarchi, Pondicherry, 1843.

Gnaana Odukkangalukku Niyamikkapatta Archsishta Ignaciyar Dhyaanangal, Pondicherry, 1848.

Gnaana Paatukal, American Madras Mission, Madras, 1853.

Gnnana Paatugalin Posthagam: Hymnologia Sagrada: Isto he, Espirituaes Cantigas Para Excitação da Christaa Devoção, E para Edificação em Fe e Piedade, Com Real Licenca, Tranquebar, Em India Oriental na Costa de Coromandel, em a Estampa da Real Missão de Dennemark, no Anno MDCCXIX.

__________, *Hymnologia Damulica, Sive ex Germanico in Damulorum Idioma, Observatis usque et Melodiis et Rhythmis Odarum, Translatorum Centum et Sexaginta Hymnorum Spiritualium Fasciculus, in Gratiam Juventutis Damulicae Aeque ac Ecclesiae Hujus Gentis, Christo Nomen Dantis, Exhibita a Benjamin Schultze*, Tranquebariae, MDCCXXIII.

Gnaanapaatu Puththagam, Nagercoil, 1848.

Gnnana Upadesam by Manikkam Royappa Swami, Madras, 1839.

Gnaana Upadesathinudaya Kurippidam, Tranquebar, 1718.

Gnaana Vaasittavamala Raamayanam, Thamizh Mulamum Uraiyum, Madras 1851.

Goncalves, Jacome., *Pirasangangal*, ed., J. Vanroyn, II vols, Colombo, 1848.

Good Instruction Called Spiritual Milk and Spiritual Lamp in English and Tamil: Narpothagamaagiya Gnnanapaalum, Gnaana Deepikaiyum Ingilisum Thamizhumaaga Achchadikapattathu, Madras, Printed at the American Mission Press for the American Madras Mission, 1841.

Hoisington, H.R., *Coticattiram: The Oriental Astronomer; Being a complete system of Hindu astronomy, accompanied with a translation and numerous explanatory notes; with an appendix*, Jaffna, American Mission Press, 1848.

Ignaciyar Dhyanangal, Pondicherry, 1860.

Iguthu Veeramaamunivar Seytha Chaturagaraathi, Madras, 1824.

Ilakkana Noolaathaaram Puthucherry, 1849.

Ilakkana Noolaathaaram Puthucherry, 1865.

Ilakkana Noorsurukkam, Jaffna, 1848.

Ilakkana Panchangangalil Nannul Moolamum Agapoorul Moolamum Purapporuatilakiyathodu Venbaamaalai Moolamum, Madras, 1835.

Ilakkana Vinaa Vidai, Madras, 1820.

Ilakkiya Sangiraham, Jaffna, 1847.

Illara Uththiyaanam, Pondicherry, 1867.

INDEX GEOGRAPHICUS exhibens nomina REGIONUM & URBIUM PRAECIPURUM, in tabulis EUROPAE, ASIAE, AFRICAE, AMERICAE, item ITINERARII S.PAULI APOSTOLI & PALASTINAE obvia. Accesserunt aphorismi quidam Cosmographici, TRANGAMBARIAE, Typis Missionis Danicae, MDCCXXXII.

Jeyaraj, Daniel., ed., *Olai Chuvadigalil Thodakakaala Thamizh Kristhava Iraineri Paadalgal: Mulamum Vizhakkamum*, Chennai, 2014.

__________, and Richard Fox Young (translated, introduced and annotated), *Hindu-Christian Epistolary Self-Discourses: 'Malabarian Correspondence' between German Pietist Missionaries and South Indian Hindus (1712-1714)*, Harrassowitz Verlag, Wiesbaden, 2013.

Kaanaan desa Vizhlakkam, Palayamkottai, 1849.

Kaanaa Vishakaddikku Marundhu, Pondicherry, 1869.

Kaavalappan Kathai, Jaffna, 1856.

Kambaramayana Vasanam, Madras, 1845.

Kandapurana Surukkam, Madras, 1847.

Kanniyar Anusaaram, Pondicherry, 1865.

Karaiyerugiradhukku Surukkamaaha Ariya Vendina Gnaana Upadesathinudaya Kurippidam, Tranquebar, MDCCXVII.

Karumpaambin Vishakadikku Marunthu, Pondicherry, 1860.

Karumpaambin Vishakadikku Thailam, Pondicherry, 1868.

Karunaakara Kadal, Pondicherry, 1868.

Kathaa Manjari, Madras, 1826.

Kathaa Manjari, Madras, 1846.

Kathaa Manjari, Pondicherry, 1864.

Kathaa Manjari Neethisaara Vakkiyam, Pondicherry, 1864.

Kathaa Manjari Neethisaara Vakkiyam, Third edition, Pondicherry, 1888.

Kattu Kathaigal: Aesop's fables, containing instructive morals, translated into Tamil by A. Theroovengada Pillay, (together with the English text) and revised by C. Rajah Sooboroya Moodeliar, Madras, 1853.

Kaviraayar, Tharangapuram Shanmuha., *Ithikasamahiya Sri Mahabharatham*, Madras, 1842.

Kindersley, Nathaniel Edward., *Specimen of Hindoo culture: Consisting of translations from the Tamulian language, of some Hindoo works of morality & imagination with explanatory notes, to which are prefixed introductory remarks on the myth of literature & C of the Hindus*, London, 1794.

Kohloff, Johann Christian., *A sermon on Ezekiel XXIII, 11 in Tamil language composed and preached by Sattianaden, on the 26th day of December 1790*, London, 1792.

Kompeciyonaaru: Confessionario, 1580.

Kovitta Sugam, Madras, 1846.

Krishna Swami Thuthu, Madras, 1845.

Krisithiyani Vanakkam: Doctrina Christaa, a maneira de dialogo: feyta em Portugal pello padre Marcos Iorge da Companhia de IESV: Treslada em lingua Malaur Tamul, pello padre Anrique Anriquez da mesma Companhia. Impressa co approuacao do Ordinario, & Inquisidor, & co licenca do Superior, Em Cochim: no Collegio da Madre de Deos, aos quatorze de Nou mbro, do anno de 1579.

Kristhunaathar Anusaaram, Pondicherry, 1863.

Kumari Sathakam, Madras, 1845.

Kummi Paadal, Madras, 1847.

Lund, Thomas., *Alavu Nool, Mudhalam Puthagam*, Madras, 1857.

Maasillaamal Urpavitha Archsishta Devamaathavin Thiru Irudhaya Sabhai Anusaaram, Pondicherry, 1856.

Madhana Kamaraasan Kathai, Madras, 1848.

Madhana Kamaraasan Kathai, Madras, 1855.

Madurai Seemai Viruththaantham, Palayamkottai, 1863.

Madurai Veeran Kathai, Madras, 1848.

Manamagan Usal, Madras, 1845.

Mahabharata Aathi Parvam, Madras, 1844.

Masthan Sagipu Avragal Paathai, Madras, 1849.

Mault, Charles., *Podhagar Ilakkanam*, Second edition, Jaffna, 1844.

Meymarai Uththiyaanam, Pondicherry, 1873.

Meygnaanodhaya Viruththi, Jaffna, 1848.

Meygnaana Saaram, Madras, 1849.

Mokshattukku Pora Vazhiyai Vezhipaduthugira Gnaana Upadesam, Tharanganpadiyil, 1777 (year is mentioned in Tamil characters).

Moudeliar, Sole Appasamy., *Recueil de Chants Tamouls par Mr. Z. Savarayalou nayagar: Poete Laureat de L'Inde*, A. Saligny, Imprimieur du Gouvernement, Pondichery, 1869.

Mudaliar, Thandavaraya., ed., *Senthan Dhivaagaram*, Madras, 1877.

Mudaliar, Vethagiri., ed., *Veeramaamunivar Thiruvaaymalaruthu Aruliseytha Ayinthilakkana Thonnul Vizhlakkam, Moolamum Uraiyum*, Puthucherry, 1838.

__________, *Kaarigai Mualamum Viruthiuraiyum*, Madras, 1851.

__________, *Bhagavatgeethai Moolamum Uraiyum,* Madras, 1852.

Muthu Thandavar Sarithiram, Madras, 1845.

Muvar Amaanai, Madras, 1848.

Naavalar, Nallur Arumuga., ed., *Nannul Mulamum Viruthiuraiyum*, Jaffna, 1851.

__________, *Periyapuranam Yenru Vazhangukinra Thiruthondar Puranam*, Jaffna, 1852.

Nadana Nattam, Evils of Comedies, Second edition, Jaffna, 1842.

Naidhatham Moolamum Uraiyum, by Saravana Perumal Iyer and Kandappa Iyer, Madras, 1842.

Naidhatha Moola Paadam, Madras, 1844.

Nalan Chakravarthi Kathai, Madras, 1844.

Nanmarana Aaytham, Pondicherry, 1860

Nanraai Ninai: Maatha Anudhina Dhyaanam, Pondicherry, 1844.

Nedunaat Panchankam, Pondicherry, 1844.

Nedunatt Panchankam, Pondicherry, 1849.

Nedungakannkennum Yen Chuvadi, ed., T. Kuppan Iyengar, Madras, 1859.

Neethi Chintamani, Madras, 1847.

Neethi Venbaa Urai Patham, Madras, 1847.

Neethisaara Vakkiyam, compiled by Kottamangalam Ramasami Pillai, Librarian of Madras College, Madras, 1844.

Nobili, Roberto., *Gnaanaupadesam: Thathuvapothaga Swamigal Udayathu, Muthal Kaandam*. Ambalakaadu, 1677; *Catechismo Madurense: Escripta em Tamul pelo Padre Robert Nobili S.J. em 1674 e divido em duas partes, Impressoe em Ambalacatta no officina de Ignacio Archamanio em 1677.*

__________, *Gnaanaupadesam, Rendaam Kaandam*: *Catechismo Madurensa em lingoa Tamulica, por Pe. Roberto Nobili da Companhia de Jesus*, e 2a parte, *Impressoe em Ambalacatta no officina de Ignacio Archamanio em 1677.*

__________, *Gnaanaupadesam: Thathuvapothaga Swamigal Udayathu, Munram Kaandam*: *Catechismus P. Roberti Nobili, Tamulico idiomate scriptus ... Pars Tertia*, Ambalacatta: no officinal de Ignacio Archamonio, 1678.

__________, *Gnaanopadesam: Thathuvapothaga Swamigal Udayathu, Naankaam Kaandam*: R.P. Roberti Nobili Romani Societate Iesv, *Catechism Romani Qvarta Pars, Ambalacatta, no officinal de Ignacio Arcchamonio*, 1678.

__________, *Gnaanopadesa Kaandam: Ihuthu R.P. Robert de Nobili yennum Thathuvapodhagaswamingaliyattri, Athisreshtariyargal Parisothithu azhlitha uthaarapadi Madurai missionai saarntha sesu sabhai madathil 1675am Varushathil achchittriundha 1-2 kaandnagalin prathikkinanga rendaam pathippaga melor uthaarapadi Ma. Saa. Iyagappa pillai avargalaal Chennai arch. Susaiyappar achchukodathir pathipikkapattathu*, 1891.

Nyaaya Theerpu, Second edition, Jaffna, 1844.

Oru Paththira Thirattu: A compilation of papers in the Tamil language including general or public business to which is added a glossary in Tamil & English of many words used chiefly in the business of the courts & public cutcherries, edited by Andrew Robertson of the Madras Civil Service, Printed at Vepery Mission Press of the Society for Promoting Christian Knowledge, 1839.

Paadartirattu: Recueil de Chants Tamouls par Mr. Z. Savarayalou nayagar: Poete Laureat de L'Inde, Reprint, Pondicherry, 1904-1906.

Paavasangeerthana Prasangam, Pondicherry, 1871.

Padangalaal Vizhalakkapatta Gnaanopadesam, Pondicherry, 1863.

Paka Saastram, Madras, 1846.

Pakkiam, M., *Paappu Maarga Dhushana Parigaaram*, Lutheran Mission Press, Tranquebar, 1866.

Pala Desa Sarithira Surukkam, Madras, 1857.

Pala Thirattu: Ithiley Tharsamayatchi, Mey Vazhi, Vazhakka Kannaadi, Sathya Vetha Menmai, Gnaanapalum Serkkapattirukirathu: Select Tracts Containing Hinduism's Own Witness, The True Way, Mirror of Custom, Excellency of the Bible and Spiritual Milk, Madras, Printed at the American Mission Press, 1842.

Panchankam, Madras, 1845.

Panchankam: Salivaahana Sakaartham 1761 sella ninra vilambi varudathakku vattukottaiyir saathira pallikudathil uvathiyaarayirukkira vanaarpannai vellalan mayil vaahanar somasekaram pillai kaniththathu; *Panchankam or Tamul Calendar AD 1838-39 Calculated by George Dashiell, Teacher of Sanscrit, Hindu Astronomy & C in the American Mission Seminary, Battocotta, Jaffna*, Published by the Jaffna Religious Tract Society, American Mission Press Manopy, 1838.

Panchkarna Vedantha Siddhantham, Madras, 1845.

Panchathanthira Kathai, ed., E.N. Muthusami Mudaliar, Ezhumur, 1847.

Panchathanthira Kathai, ed., Srinivaspuram Srinivasa Aiyengar, Madras, 1852.

Panchathanthira Kathai, Pondicherry, 1865.

Parathaiyar Maalai, Madras, 1847.

Pardesai Motcha Payanam, Jaffna, 1853.

Patha Manjari, Madras, 1852.

Pathimaththesu: Dushana Maruthalaagiya Tharkka Kummi, Pondicherry, 1865.

Pattana Swami Paadal, Madras, 1847.

Pazhamalaiyandhaathi, ed., Saravana Perumal Iyer, Madras, 1832.

Pazhya Yerpaadu: Het eerste deel des Ouden testaments van de Heilige Schrivtuur, vervattende de vye Boeken Mosis genaamd Genesis, Exodus, Leviticus, Numeri, en Deuteronomium gedrukt te Colombo, in's Komp: Boekdrukkery, by Johan Frederik Christoph Dornheim, anno 1790.

Percival, Peter., *Arulavadhaaram*, Third edition, Jaffna, 1842.

__________, *Thiruttantha Sangiraham*, Jaffna, 1843.

Peyar Agaraathi, A Manual Dictionary of the Tamil Language, Jaffna, 1842.

Pillai, A. Muthusami., *Attrum Uthiyaanam*, Madras, 1817.

Pillai, Carrol Vishvanathan, *Suppira Deepam*, Jaffna, 1857.

Pillai, Daniel., *Paramandalangali Thangal Pokkisham Undenirukkira Paraaparanudaya Pillaigalin Aabarana Petti*, Translated into Tamil by Daniel Pillai, Vepery, 1800.

Pillai, Myilai Saveri Muthu, *Ilakkana Surukkam,* Puthucherry 1845.

__________, *Ilakkana Surukkam*, Puthucherry, 1860.

Pillai, Somasegaram., *Thiri yaangam 1848*, The American Mission Press, Madras, 1848.

Pillay, Vaithiyalinga., *Thiri Yaangam 1852*, Madras Tract and Book Society, Madras, 1852.

Ponilkam, Madras, 1847.

Poorviga Marai Vizhlakkam, Pondicherry, 1856.

Pope, George Uglow., *Thamizh Ilakkana Noor Surukka Vinaa Vidai, Introductory Tamil Grammar*, Second edition, Madras, 1846.

__________, *Tamil Hand Book*, First edition, 1855.

__________, *Thamizh Ilakkana Noor Surukka Vinaa Vidai*, fifth edition, Madras, 1855.

__________, *Ilakkana Nool*, 2 parts, Madras, 1858.

Pothuvaana Sepa Posthagam, Tamil translation by Christian David, Serampore, 1818.

Prabhulinga Leelai Maalai, Madras, 1844.

Rajamanickam, S., ed., *Gnaanopadesam, Kaandam Onru*, Tuticorin, 1966.

__________, *Gnaanopadesam, Kaandam Rendu*, Tuticorin, 1966.

__________, *Divviya Maathirikai*, Tamil Literary Society, Tuticorin, 1966.

__________, *Paavasangeerthana Kurippidam*, Palayamkottai, 1966.

Retchippin Ozhukkam: A Ordem da Salvação, ou Doutrina Christaa Brevemente en Perguntas e Repostas Declarada e Provada com Principaes Testemunhos da Escritura Sagrada, Juntamente com Alhuas Oraçoens e Castigas, Tranquebar en India Oriental na Costa de Coromandel, na Estampa dos Missionarios del Rey de Dennemark, Anno 1712.

Rhenius, Karl Theophilus Ewald., *Bhoomi Sasthiram*, Chennaipatnam, 1832.

__________, *Vetha Sasthira Surukkam*, Neyoor, 1838.

__________, *Vetha Sasthira Surukkam*, Third edition, 1845.

__________, *Vetha Saasthira Surukkam Iraniusaiyaraaley Seyyapattathu: Summary of a Body of Divinity in the Tamil Language by the Late Reverend CTE Rhenius Missionary*, Fourth edition, Madras The Tract and Book Society, The American Mission, Madras, 1852.

Robinson, Edward Jewitt., *Tamil wisdom, Traditions concerning Hindu sages & Selections from their writings with an introduction by the late Rev. Elijah Hook*, London, 1873.

__________, *Tales and Poems of South India comprehended and enlarged edition of Tamil wisdom from the Tamil*, London, 1885.

Rossi, James Thomas., *Gnaayittru Kilamai Puthumai*, Pondicherry, 1865.

__________, *Puthankilami Pirasangam*, Pondicherry 1861.

__________, *Sanikilamai Puthumai*, Pondicherry, 1859.

__________, *Sevvaikilami Puthumai*, Pondicherry, 1861.

__________, *Thingalkilamai Puthumai*, Pondicherry, 1861.

__________, *Vellikilamai Puthumai*, Pondicherry, 1860.

__________, *Viyaalakilamai Puthumai*, Pondicherry, 1865.

Saalamonin Neethi Mozhighal, American Mission Society, Jaffna, 1845.

Saathaaranam, Pondicherry, 1841.

Saathi Viththiyaasa Vizhlakkam, Madras, 1857.

Sagaadevan Sasthiram or Book of Fate Translated by Rev. Joseph Roberts, Madras, 1831.

Sama Vaatham, Second edition, Jaffna, 1844.

Samaya Partichai, Jaffna, 1858.

Sankunta Vilasam , Madras, 1845.

Sarikai, Madras, 1845.

Scudder, John., *Nesa Nirupam*, Fourth edition, Jaffna, 1843.

__________, *Romai Margaththaar Kodukkira Yethirmozhikku Marumozhi*, Third edition, Jaffna, 1843.

__________, *Yethirmozhukku Marumozhi*, third edition, Jaffna, 1843.

__________, *Guru Vivaha Vizhlakkam*, Second edition, Jaffna, 1844.

__________, *Narkarunai Kuraipaadu*, Jaffna, 1844.

Sambashanai Anusaaram: Manuel de la Conversation ou Recueil de mots usuels et de phrases propres a faciliter l'etude du français et du tamoul, Pondicherry, 1865.

Sanibhavagaan Sthothiram, Madras, 1847.

Sargent, Edward., *Pooriviga Sarithiram*, Palayamkottai, 1850.

Sarithirathuukuaduththa gnaanopadesa surukkam, Pondicherry, 1858.

Sarithiraththukkuaduththa Gnaanopadesaththin Vinaa Vidai: *Questions et reponses du petit catechisme Historique de Fleury, avec quelques lecons supplementaires par un member des la congregation des mission-etrageres,* Pondicherry, 1858.

Sathiya Vetha Bhodhaga Surukkam, Pondicherry, 1846.

Sathiya Vetha Paritchai, Pondicherry, 1846.

Sathiya Vetha Pozhippu, Fourth edition, Jaffna, 1857.

Sathiya Vetha Sarithira Surukkam, Pondicherry, 1865.

Scudder, John., *Irandamm Karppani Vizhlakkam*, Second edition, Jaffna, 1843.

Seyankondar Sathakam, Madras, 1848.

Siluvai Paathai, Pondicherry, 1842.

Siluvai Paathai, Pondicherry, 1856.

Sirupillaikalukku Gnaanasnanam Kodukira Varthamaanam, Tranquebar, 1781.

Sirupillaikal Vaasikka Pazhagiraththukku Seytha Puthagam, Manippoy, 1835.

Siruvar Chuvadi, Pondicherry, 1863.

Siruvar Kalvi Puthayal, Pondicherry, 1864.

Siruvar Yen Chuvadi, Pondicherry, 1863.

Soora Chintamani, Madras, 1847.

Sonna Rayanukkum Sarvaloga Raasanukkum Undanna Vyachchiyam, Jaffna, 1857.

Strange, Surprising Adventures of the Venerable Gooroo Simple and his Five Disciples, Noodle. Doodle, Wiseacre, Zany and Foozle, London, 1861.

Subramaniyar Viruththam, Madras, 1847.

Sugirtha Mandirangalum Gnaaopadesa Kurippidamum, Pondicherry, 1865.

Suthanaagiya Sarvesuranaanirukkira yesykristhu naatharaanavar inda bhulogathiley manushanaai pirantha viseshangalaiyum bhoduvicha upadesangaliyum seytha arputhangalaiyum manusharukku vendi paadupattu yellaraiyum moondu raetchithuvitha vaanagalaiyum uyirodey ezhunthiruinthu paralogathiley magaimaiyaga yerinathaiyum avarudaya seshargalagiya apostalarmaargal logam yengum poey ippadikothavichu viseshangalai sagala senangallukkum pirasangam panninathaiyum vezhipaduthugira puthu yerpaadinudaya muthalam vaguppagiya Anju veda posthagam. Kristu piratha Ayirathu yezhunuthu pathonpathaam varushamgairapothu Tharanganpadiyiley irukkira paathrimaargaludaya achiley pathipikka pattathu: *Novum Jesu Christi testamentum ex originali textu in usum gentis Malabaricae in linguam Damulicam.vulgo Malabarica dictam, versum opera & Studio Bartholoamei Ziegenbalg & Joh. Ernesti Grundler, serenissima Daniae Regis Frederici IV ad Indos Orientales missionariorum, Tranquebariae in littore Coromandelino*: Typis Damulicis Missionis Danicae, MDCCXIX.

Suvisesha Sambandha Attavanai, Nagercoil, 1854.

Swami, Gnaanapragasanatha., ed., *Anda Pinda Viyakkiyaanam*, Chennapatanam, 1874.

__________, ed., *Ulaga Pramana Sasthiram*, Chennapatanam, 1874.

Tamil First Book, Tamil Mutharpusthagan, Fifth edition, Madras, Christian Vernacular Education Society, Madras: American Mission Press, 1860.

Tamil Reading Book, Pallikudangalrir Payittruvikka Vendi Tamil Vasaga Puthagam, 1845.

Tamil Reading Book, Pallikudangalrir Payittruvikka Vendi Tamil Vasaga Puthagam, 2nd edition, Madras Christian Knowledge Society Press, Vepery, 1848.

Tamulisk calendar for aaret sathaarana varusham fom begynder den 10 April 1790 og endes den 9 April 1791, Trankenbar, MDCCXC.

Thaalaatu, Madras, 1847.

Thambiran Vanakkam: *Doctrina Christaa tresladad em lingua Tamul pello padre Anrique Anriquez da Companhia de IESV, & pello padre Manoel de Sao Pedro. Com approuacao do Ordinario, & Inquisidor; & co licenca do Superior da mesma Companhia*, Impressa em Coulam: no Collegio do Saluador, aos vinte de Octubro de 1578.

Thamizh pillaigalukkkaha yerpaduthappatta bhumai sasitram muthalam puthagam, South India Christian School Book Society, The London Mission Press, Nagercoil, 1856.

Thamizh Vizhlakkam, Madras, 1811.

Thamizh Vizhlakkam, Second edition, Madras, 1817.

Tharangambadi Thiruchabayil Vazhangum Gnaana Muraimaigazhin Vilakkam: Rituale Trangambaricum, Tharanganpadiyil, 1781.

The Elements of Algebra, Director of Public Instruction, Scottish Press, Madras, 1857.

Thiruneeru Pathigam, Madras, 1847.

Thiriyaangam, Jaffna, 1849.

Thiruchabaiyin Sarithira Posthagam, Trangambariae, 1799.

Thirunaatkalin vizhlakka surukkam, Pondicherry, 1859.

Thiruppaadar Thirattu, Madras, 1851.

Tiruporur Sannadhi Murai Moolapaadam, Madras, 1844.

Thirumurugaattrupadai, Madras, 1845.

Thiruvalluvar Seytha Kurat Sanghiragam, Pondicherry, 1860;

Thiruvilaiyadar Puranam, Madras, 1850.

Thiruvottiyur Andhathi, Madras, 1849.

Tholkaapiyam, ed., Mahalinga Iyer, Madras, 1847.

Thuravara Uththiyaanam: Kaandam Onru, Pondicherry, 1869.

Thuravara Uththiyaanam: Kaandam Rendu, Pondicherry, 1872.

Thuyya Nadai, a translation by L. Spaulding Sarah's The Walk of Purity, second edition, Jaffna 1842.

Thiruvaasagam, Madras, 1846.

Thiruvaasagam, Madras, 1857.

Tulakkar pithitta kaala mutal sollapadum Industhaani sarithira sangiraham: A summary of the history of Hindoostahan from the Muslim invasion in English with a Tamil translation by Gnanapragsa Moodeliar, Vepery, 1830.

Ulagathin retchakaraana kiristhu pirantha aayiraththi thonnoothi rendaam varushaththukku sellum panjangam: Intha panjangam tharangan-padiyil irukkum missiyon achchukudathil pathipikkapattathu, MDCCXCI.

Unmai Naatam, second edition, Jaffna 1842;

Uththara Ramayanam, Madras, 1848.

Utharikkira Aathumaakalin Vanakka Maatham, Pondicherry, 1870.

Uthaya Thaaragai (Morning Star), Issue no. 3, dated 4 February 1841, Thursday.

Vaakundaam, Nal Vazhi, Nanneri, by Saravana Perumal Iyer, Madras, 1841.

Vaakundaram Urai, Madras, 1847.

Vaakundaam, Nal Vazhi, Nanneri, by Saravana Perumal Iyer, Madras, 1859.

Vaalar Kanitham, Pondicherry, 1853.

Vaalar Kanidha Noolaathaaram, Pondicherry, 1870.

Vaalar Pokkisham, Pondicherry, 1844.

Vaalar Pokkisham, Pondicherry, 1861.

Vaalar Thunai, Pondicherry, 1844.

Vaguppoo, Madras, 1847.

Vairagya Sathakam, Madras, 1845.

Vallalaraasan Saridham, Madras, 1845.

Varushathin pradhi dina sugirtha pirasangangalaagiya archsishtavargalin sarithiram, Muthal kaandam, Pondicherry, 1866.

Varushathin pradhi dina sugirtha pirasangangalaagiya archsishtavargalin sarithiram: Rendaam kaandam, Pondicherry, 1866.

Varushathin pradhi dina sugirtha pirasangangalaagiya archsishtavargalin sarithiram: Moonraam kaandam, Pondicherry, 1867.

Varushathin pradhi dina sugirtha pirasangangalaagiya archsishtavargalin sarithiram: Naalaam kaandam, Pondicherry, 1867.

Veri Vilakkal, Second edition, Jaffna, 1844.

Vetha Mozhi Ariviththal, Third edition, Jaffna, 1844.

Vethapurattalai maruththalaagiya sathiya thirusabaiyin surkkamaana vizhlakkam, Pondicherry, 1840.

Vethapurattalai neekum sanjiviyaagiya meyyaana thirusabaiyin vizhlakkam, Pondicherry, 1841.

Vetha Saasthira Surukkam, Neyoor, 1838.

Vethasaatchiyaana Devasagayam Pillai Sarithiram, Pondicherry, 1858.

Vethasaatchiyaana Muthiperupettra Arulanandar Sarithiram, Pondicherry, 1858.

Vethapuri Andhaathi, Pondicherry, 1863.

Vethapuri Andhaathi, by Thirukudandhai S. Duraisamy Mudaliar, edited by Arogyam Pillai & M. Vedanayaka Pillai, Pondicherry, 1868.

Vetha Uthaarana Thirattu, Madras, 1835.

Vetha Uthaarana Thirattu, revised edition, Madras, 1852.

Vethiyar Ozhukkam, Madras, 1844.

Viveka Chintamani, Madras, 1847.

Walther, Christoph Theodosius., *Thiruchabaiyin Sarithira Posthagam: Historia Ecclesiastica Cui adduntur Synchronismi Historiae Exoticae, Praesertim Indicae*, Editio Secunda, Trangambariae, 1799.

Yembiran Sathakam, Madras, 1845.

Yesunaathar Malayin Merchonna Pransangathin Visthaarippu, Third edition, Jaffna, 1843.

III. Travelogues

Baldaeus, Philippus., *Nauwkeurige beschryvinge van Malabar en Choromandel, derhalver aangrenzende ryken, en het machtige eyland Ceylon. Nevens een omstandige en grondigh doorzochte ontdekking en wederlegginge van de afgoderye der Oost-Indische heydenen*, 3 vols, Amsterdam, Janssonius van Waasberge en van Someren, 1672.

__________, *A True and Exact Description of the Celebrated East-India Coasts of Malabar and Coromandel as also of the island of Ceylon*, translated from the High Dutch, London, Printed for Awnsham & John Churchill, 1703.

Johnson, John., *The Oriental Voyager or Sketches and Remarks on a Voyage to India and China in 1803*, London, 1807.

Secondary Works

Articles

Amaladass, Anand., 'Early Jesuit Mission Methods in Asia With Special Reference to the Nanopatecam (the Catechism) of Roberto Nobili', Anand Amaladass and Ines G. Zupanvo, eds., *Intercultural Encounters and the Jesuit Mission in South Asia, 16th-18th Centuries*, Bangalore, 2014, pp. 88-112.

Balasingham, C., 'Some Unusual Characters Used in Tamil Printing in Ceylon during Dutch Times', *Proceedings of the International Conference-Seminar of Tamil Studies*, Madras, 1971, vol., II, pp. 528-30.

Das, N. Sonia., 'Failed Legacies of Colonial Linguistics: Lessons from Tamil Books in French India and French Guiana', *Comparative Studies in Society and History*, vol. 59, Issue 4, October 2017, pp. 846-883.

Duverdier, Gérald., 'Über die Bedeutung Unbedeutender Drucke-Die Ersten Tamilischen Drucke zu Halle (1712-1713)', *Wissenschaftliche Zeitschrift der Martin-Luther-Universität Halle-Wittenberg-Halle*, Jahrgang XXIV, Heft 5, 1975, pp. 103-126.

__________, L'apparition de L'Imprimerie a Madras et disparititon a Pondichéry', *Guternberg–Jahrbuch*, 1976, pp. 355–63.

__________, 'Les debuts de l'imprimerie Tamoule a Madras et la finde celle de Halle, 1761–1772', *Gutenberg–Jahrbuch*, 1977, pp. 184–94.

__________, 'La Transmission de L'Imprimerie en Thailande: Du

Catechismo de 1796 aux Impressions Buddhiques sur feuilles de Latanier', *Bulletin d' L'Ecole française d' Extreme–Orient*, vol. 68, no.1, 1980, pp. 209–260.

Ebeling, Sascha., 'The college of Fort St .George and the transformation of Tamil philology during the nineteenth century', in Thomas R. Trautman, ed., *The Madras School of Orientalism: Producing Knowledge in Colonial South India*, New Delhi, Oxford University Press, 2009, pp. 233-260.

Frykenberg, Robert Eric., 'Modern Education in South India 1784-1854: Its Roots and its Role as a Vehicle of Integration Company Raj', *Journal of Historical Review*, vol. 91, no.1, 1986, pp. 37-65.

Gaur, Albertine., 'Bartholomäus Ziegenbalg's Verzeichnis der Malabarischen Bucher', *Journal of the Royal Asiatic Society of Great Britain and Ireland*, no. 3-4, October, 1967, pp. 63-95.

Gensichen, Hans-Werner., 'Abominable Heathenism: A Rediscovered Tract by Bartholomäus Ziegenbalg', *Indian Church History Review,* vol. I, no. 1, 1967, pp. 29-40.

Graul, Karl.,'Notizen, Correspondenzen und Vermischtes. Die tamulische Bibliothek der evan. luth. Missionsanstalt zu Leipzig', *Zeitschrift der Deutschen Morgenländischen Gesellschaft*, H.VII, Leipzig, 1853, pp. 558-568.

Knowlton, Edgar, C., 'Antão de Proença's Vocabulario Tamulico Lusitano: Indo-Portuguese Elements', *Tamil Culture*, vol. XI, 1964, pp.135-64.

__________, 'Portuguese-Tamil Linguistic Contacts', in *Proceedings of the First International Seminar-Conference of Tamil Studies*, 1966, pp. 607-17.

Liebau, Heike., 'German Missionaries as Research Workers in India: Their Diaries as Historical Sources (Benjamin Schultze, 1689-1760, Exception or Norm?)', *Studies in History,* new series, vol. 11, no. 1, 1995, pp.101-18.

Malten, Thomas., 'Antam de Proença's Tamil-Portuguese Dictionary, Printed in Índia in 1679', in Charles J. Borges and Helmut Feldmann, eds., *Goa and Portugal: Their Cultural Links*, New Delhi, 1997, pp. 271-79.

Muthiah, Subbiah., 'Giving India the Printed Word' in Andreas Gross, Y. Vincent Kumara Doss and Heike Liebau, eds., *Halle and the Beginning of Protestant Christianity in India*, Halle, 2006, vol. III, pp. 1241-8.

Nair, Savithri Preetha., 'Of real use to the people: The Tanjore printing press and the spread of useful knowledge', *The Indian Economic and Social History Review*, vol. 48, no. 4, 2011, pp. 497–529.

Nordstrand, Ove K., 'Some Notes on the Foundation of the Royal Danish Mission Printing Press and Paper Mill at Tranquebar' *Proceedings of the First International Conference-Seminar on Tamil Studies*, 1966, pp. 364-8.

Ondaatje, M.P.J., 'A Tabular List of Original Works and Translations Published by the Late Dutch Government of Ceylon at their Printing Press at Colombo', *Journal of the Royal Asiatic Society of Great Britain and Ireland*, new series, 1, 1865, pp. 141-4.

Pillai, A. Muttusami., 'A Brief Sketch of the Life and Writings of Father C. J. Beschi or Viramamuni Translated from Original Tamil with a Portrait', *The Madras Journal of Literature and Science*, Vol. XI, January-June 1840, pp. 250-300,

Ponnad, S., 'Fr Thomas de Rossi: The Sinna Saveriar of the Marava (1701-1704)', *Caritas*, LVIII, 1979, pp. 73-8.

Rajesh, V., 'Patrons and Networks of Patronage in the Publication of Tamil Classics, c 1800-1920', *Social Scientist*, Vol. 39, No. 3/4 (March-April 2011), pp. 64-91.

Rodeles, C.G., 'Early Printing in India', *Journal of the Royal Asiatic Society of Bengal*, vol. IX, April 1913, pp. 153-155, see p. 155.

Schurhammer Georg., and G.W Cotrell, 'The First Printing in Indic Characters', *Harvard University Library Bulletin*, vol. VI, no.2, Spring 1952, pp. 147-160.

Shaw, Graham., 'The Copenhagen Copy of Henriques' Flos Sanctorum', *Fund og Forskning i Dei Kongelige Biblioteks Samlinger*, vol. 32, 1993, pp. 39-50.

Shulman, David., 'Muslim Popular Literature in Tamil: The Tamimmancari Malai' in *Islam in Asia*, Yohannan Friedman ed., Colo, 1984, vol. I, p. 176-77.

Syed, Safiullah., 'Urdu Journalism in Tamilnadu from 1840 to 1850', *Annals of Oriental Research*, XXVII, Part I & II, pp. 7-9.

Thaninayagam, Xavier, S., 'Tamil Manuscripts in European Libraries', *Tamil Culture,* vol. III, October, 1954, pp. 210-88.

__________, 'The First Printed Books in Tamil', *Tamil Culture*, vol. VII, no. 3, pp. 288-308.

__________, 'Antão de Proença's Tamil-Portuguese Dictionary, 1679, An Introduction', *Tamil Culture*, vol. XI, no.2, April-June 1964, pp, 117-127.

Volmer, Rosenkilde., 'Printing in Tranquebar 1712-1845' *The Library Series* 5, vol. 4, 1949, pp. 179-195.

Wicki, Josef., 'Pedro Luis Brahmane und Erster Indischer Jesuit (ca.1532–1596)', *Neue Zeitschrift für Missionswissenschaft*, 6, 1950, pp. 115-26.

__________, 'O Flos Sanctorum do P. H. Henriques, Impresso na Língua Tamul em 1586', *Boletim do Instituto Vasco da Gama,* vol. 73, 1956, pp. 42-9.

__________, 'The Confraternity of the Charity of Fr. Henriques', *Indian Church History Review,* vol. I, 1967, pp. 3-8.

Županov, Ines G., 'I Am a Great Sinner: Jesuit Missionary Dialogues in Southern India, (Sixteenth Century)', *Journal of the Economic and Social History of the Orient*, vol. 55, 2012, pp. 415-446.

Books

Anchukandam, Thomas., *Catholic Revival in India in the 19th Century: Role of Mgr. Clement Bonnand (1796-1861)*, Bangalore, 1996.

Andre, François., *Vie du Pere Louis Saint-Cyr*, Paris, 1889.

Besse, Leon., *Father Beschi: His Times and his Writings*, Trichnopoly, 1918.

Blackburn, Stuart H., *Print, Folklore and Nationalism in Colonial South India*, New Delhi, 2003.

Bugge, Henriette., *Mission and Tamil Society*, London, 1994.

Caldwell, Robert., *Records of the Early History of the Tinnevelly Mission of the Society for Promoting Christian Knowledge and the Society for the Propagation of the Gospel in Foreign Parts*, Higginbotham & Co., Madras, 1881.

Chitty, Simon Casie., *The Tamil Plutarch: Containing a Summary Account of the Lives of the Poets and Poetesses of South India and Ceylon from the Earliest to the Present Times with Select Specimens of their Compositions*, Jaffna, 1859.

Cutter, Ebenezer., ed., *Life and Letters of Samuel Fisk Green*, London, 1891.

Das, Sonia, N., *Linguistic Rivalries: Tamil Migrants and Anglo-French Conflicts*, Oxford, 2016.

Ebeling Sascha., *Colonizing the Realm of Words: The Transformation of Tamil Literature in Nineteenth Century South India*, Albany, 2010.

Filliozat, Jean., *Un catéchisme tamoul du XVIe siècle en lettres latines*, Pondicherry, 1967.

Gaur, Albertine., *Catalogue of Tamil Books in the British Library*, London, The British Library, 1980.

Grinfield, E.W., *Sketches of the Danish Mission on the Coast of Coromandel*, London, 1831.

Hambye, E.R., *History of Christianity in India: Eighteenth Century, Vol. III*, Bangalore, 1997.

Jebanesan, S., *America Missionnum Ilankaiyil Thamizh Valarchchiyum*, Thellippalai, 1983.

Kanakarattina, Ve., *Arumuganaavalar Sariththiram*, Jaffna, 1882, reprint 1968.

Kulendran, Sabapathy., *Kristhava Thamizh Vethaagamathin Varalaru*, Bangalore, 1967.

Launay, Adrien., *Histoire des Missions de L'Inde: Pondichéry, Maissour, Coimbatour*, 5 vols., Paris, 1898.

__________, *Histoire de la Mission de Siam, 1662–1811, Documents Historiques*, 2 vols., Paris, 1920.

Louis, A., *Panmaiyil Orumai and Orumaiyil Panmai*, Pondicherry, 2016.

Meenakshisundaram, K., *The Contribution of European Scholars to Tamil*, Madras, 1974.

Muller, Roth E., and Roth J. Muller, *Aussereuropaische Druckerein in 16 Jahrundert*, Baden-Baden, 1969.

Murdoch, John., *A Classified Catalogue of Tamil Printed Books with Introductory Notes*, Madras, 1865.

Naadaan, Thamizh., *Thamizh Mozhhiyin Muthal Achchu Puththagam*, Salem, 1995.

Needham, Joseph., *Science and Civilization in China*, Vol. V: Paper and Printing, Cambridge, 1985.

Pillai, Chengalvaraya., *History of the Tamil Prose Literature*, Madras, 1904.

Pillai, Muttusami., *Brief Sketch of the Life and Writings of Father C. J. Beschi or Vira-Mamuni, Translated from the Original Tamil*, J.B..Pharoah, Madras, 1840.

Pillai, Nallur Ta. Kailasa., *Arumuga Navalar Prabantha Thirattu*, Colombo, 1996.

Rajamanickam, S., *The First Oriental Scholar*, Palayamkottai, 1972.

Rajesh, V., *Manuscripts, Memory and History: Classical Tamil Literature in Colonial India*, Delhi, 2014.

Sambandham, Ma. Su., *Achchu Kalai*, Madras. 1959.

__________, *Achchum Pathippum*, Madras, 1980.

__________, *Ezhuththum Achchum*, Madras, 1981.

__________, *Tamil Ithaliyal Varalaru*, Madras, 1987.

__________, *Tamil Ithaliyal Chuvadugal*, Madras. 1990.

Sami, A. Maa., *Paththonpatham Nuttrandu Thamizh Ithalgal*, Madras, 1993.

Schurhammer Georg and Jose Wicki, eds., *Epistolae S. Francisci Xaverii alliaque Eius Scripta*, Roma, II vols., 1944-45.

Shaw, Graham., *The South Asia and Burma Retrospective Bibliography, Stage 1: 1556-1800*, London, 1987.

__________, and John Randall, *From Conversion to Subversion: 250 Years of the Printed Book in India*, Sussex, 2014.

Sri Thaandavaraya Mudaliar Sarithira Surukkam, Rangoon, 1919.

Stephen, S. Jeyaseela., *A Meeting of the Minds: European and Tamil Encounters in Modern Sciences, 1507-1857*, Delhi, 2016.

__________, *Louis Savinien Dupuis: A Biography of the MEP Missionary in Pondicherry*, Pondicherry, 2017.

__________, *Louis Savinien Dupuis and His Circulars in French to the Priests and in Tamil to the Religious Nuns in Pondicherry Mission, 1860-1874*, Translated from Original French and Tamil with Notes, Pondicherry, 2017.

__________, *The Heartbeat of a Missionary: Letters and Reports of Louis Savinien Dupuis in Pondicherry, 1839-74*, Pondicherry, 2017.

__________, *From Anrique Anriquez to Louis Savinien Dupuis: The Tamil Grammar and Dictionary Quest*, Pondicherry, 2017.

__________, *The First Catholic Bible in Tamil and Louis Savininen Dupuis at Pondicherry: A History of Translation and Printing*, 1850-7, Pondicherry, 2017.

__________, *Missioner Tamil Written and Printed in Pondicherry: Literature and Louis Savinien Dupuis, 1841-73*, Pondicherry, 2017.

__________, *Pondicherry under the French, Illuminating the Urban Landscape, 1674-1793*, Primus, New Delhi, 2018.

Subramanian, P., Venkataramaiyaa and Vivekananda Gopal, *Thanjai Maraattiyar Modi Aavana Thamizhaakamum Kurippuraiyum*, 3 vols., Tamil University, Thanjavur, 1989.

Sweet, Michael J. and Leonard Zwilling, *Mission To Tibet, The Extraordinary Eighteenth Century Account of Father Ippolito Desideri, S. J*, Boston, 2010.

Thaninayagam, Xavier, S., *Antão de Proença's Tamil-Portuguese Dictionary, AD 1679*, Kuala Lumpur, 1966.

Venkatachalapathy, A.R., *The Province of the Book: Scholars, Scribes and Scribblers in Colonial Tamilnadu*, Permanent Black, New Delhi, 2012.

Victoria, Mo. Nevis., *Thambiran Vanakkam: Thamizh Mozhiyin Muthal Achchu Puththagam*, Chennai, 2011.

Wicki, Jose., *IV Centenario da Primeira Imprensa de Goa*, Lisboã, 1956.

Županov, Ines G., *Missionary Topics: The Catholic Frontiers in India, 16th-17th Centuries*, Ann Arbor, 2005.

Theses and Dissertations

Kumar, D. Udaya., *Transformation of Tamil Letter-forms from Palm Leaf Manuscripts to Early Letter-press Printing*, Ph. D Thesis, Indian Institute of Technology, Bombay, 2010.

Maheswari, P. Uma., *Advent of Print Culture in Colonial Tamil Region: Technological, Cultural and Social Changes from 1712 to 1947*, Ph.D. Dissertation, Pondicherry University, 2013.

Vargas, Fernando de Mello., *Evolution of Tamil Type Design*, MA Dissertation, University of Reading, United Kingdom, 2007.

Index

T

U

V

W

Y

Z